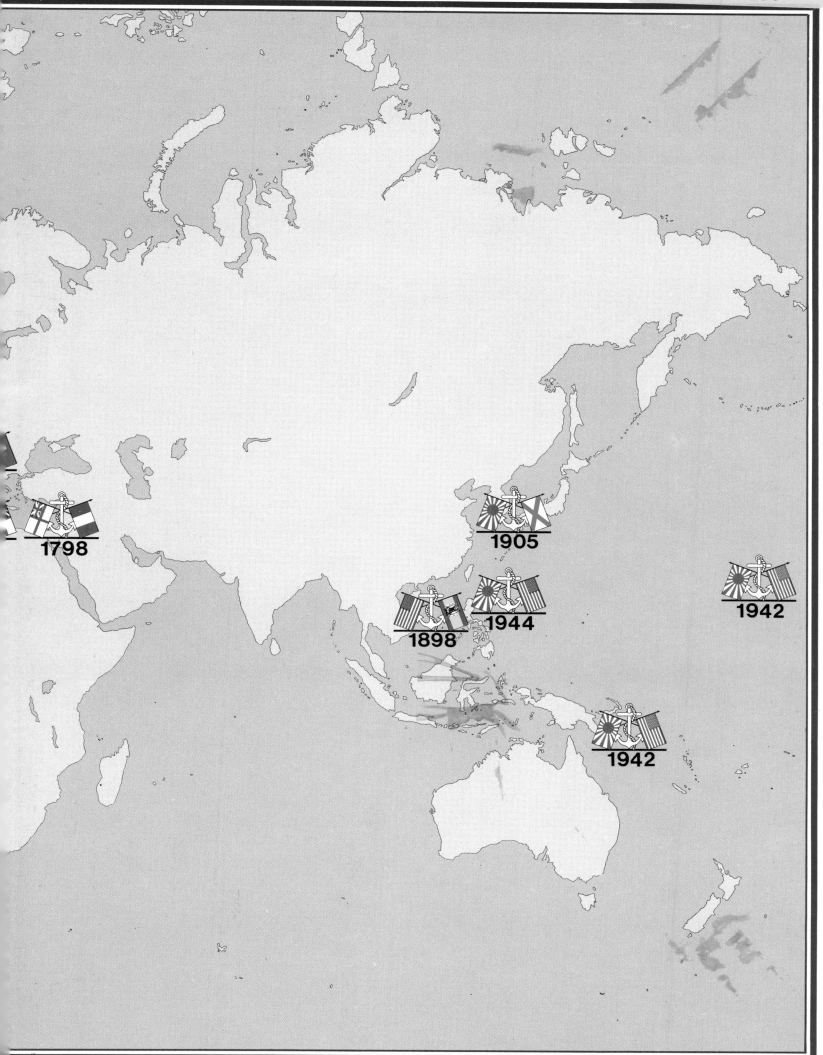

Epic Sea Battles

Epic Sea Battles

William Koenig
Edited by S L Mayer

Designed by David Eldred
Cartography by Arka Cartographics
Picture Research by Robert Hunt

First published 1975 by
Octopus Books Limited
59 Grosvenor Street, London W1

©1975 Octopus Books Limited

ISBN 0 7064 0445 9

Produced by Mandarin Publishers Limited
22A Westlands Road, Quarry Bay, Hong Kong

Printed in Hong Kong

Contents

Introduction

By S L Mayer

Naval historians have suggested that control of the seas implies control of the lands adjacent to them and this theory is known as the 'blue water principle'. It is largely borne out by naval battles of early history. The Greek victory at Salamis in the fifth century B.C. prevented the Persians from continuing their occupation of the Greek peninsula. The defeat of the Spanish Armada by Drake in 1588 prevented the Spanish from occupying the British Isles. In both these instances failure to control the sea frustrated the ambitions of the aggressor. During the 17th and 18th centuries Britain became the foremost naval power in the world; she was able to transport forces and supplies across the seas virtually unopposed. She created her empire throughout the world by occupying strategic ports, leaving the hinterland to the natives while the colonists grew tobacco and sugar cane for export back to Britain. Whenever this empire was challenged by the Dutch, French or Spanish, a short, sharp naval action usually settled the matter and the *status quo* was maintained.

Towards the end of the 18th century, however, this pattern was changed when the inhabitants in the thirteen colonies of North America revolted against the Crown. As long as Britain was able to maintain her naval supremacy supplies to her armies in America were assured. It was a Franco-Spanish challenge in support of the American Revolution that provided the greatest naval engagement of the Revolutionary War, and resulted in the British smashing the French Navy of de Grasse at the Battle of the Saintes in the West Indies in 1782. Yet Britain was to lose this war despite the fact that her sea power was greater than ever. It was her army that was beaten on the battlefield – which taught the British that territories overseas could not be held by sea power and force of arms alone once the colonists of a large area revolted. Shortly after, the British asked for peace negotiations which led to the loss of her thirteen colonies.

The American War of Independence marked the end of an era. The assumption that world hegemony could be achieved by mastery of the world's oceans was called into question. From the French Revolution and the wars of Napoleon onwards, an analysis of the epic sea battles fought in the past two centuries does not really bear out the blue water principle. William Koenig's study of the twelve greatest sea battles contested during this period demonstrates the changing relationship between sea power and military might. One without the other in modern warfare is a formula for failure in war, whilst the combination of both can produce a blueprint for success. Effective control of large land masses can be accomplished only by the occupation of the land itself, but a naval confrontation and subsequent control of the sea can either prevent or pave the way for occupation. Similarly, independent naval warfare which is not related to the movements of the army plays little part in the result of the war. This can be seen clearly in many instances. Wellington's Peninsular campaign was made possible by control of the sea, as indeed was the speedy landing of British forces in Belgium before Waterloo. The crushing defeat of the Turkish Navy by the combined French, Russian and English fleets at Navarino in 1827 both ensured the success of the Greek rebellion and enabled the Russians to occupy much of European Turkey in the subsequent war. Dewey's destruction of the Spanish Fleet at Manila Bay in 1898 facilitated the occupation of Manila itself. The destruction of the Russian fleet by Admiral Togo at Tsushima, in 1905, made a Russian counter thrust in the Far East quite impossible, and soon after the battle a peace conference between the two powers was held in the United States. The Russo-Japanese War was won by Japan after the fall of Port Arthur, (Russia's main port in Asia apart from Vladivostok), and as a result, Korea and Manchuria were more or less in Japanese hands. Prior to Tsushima Japan's armies had won Northeast Asia for the Maiji Emperor, and Japan's Imperial Navy had defended these prizes with distinction. It is therefore apparent that a major naval victory or an amphibious landing is sometimes necessary to make the army's task possible at all.

Episodes in the conduct of the American Civil War illustrate the ineffectiveness of independent naval action. Although the epic struggle between the *Monitor* and the *Merrimack* at

Hampton Roads was the first clash of ironclads in naval history, it had little or no direct effect upon the outcome of the Civil War. If the Confederate States were to be returned to the union they would have to be conquered by the combined efforts of the armies of Grant and Sherman and Farragut's naval forces. Similarly in World War One the clearing of German forces from the high seas by the Royal Navy off the Falklands barely helped Britain's problems of supplies from overseas. Germany's U-boat campaign increased in intensity from 1915 to 1917, and even convoying did not appreciably cut the Allied losses of supply ships during these years. Activity on the seas did not affect Britain's ability to reinforce the BEF in France, nor did the blockade of German coasts break the stalemate on the Western front. Even the greatest sea battle of all time, the Battle of Jutland, left both Britain and Germany exactly where they had been, except that the German dream of cracking the Allied blockade was broken.

World War Two saw the addition of a new factor, aerial warfare, which had only played a peripheral part in previous struggles. Control of the air became more important than control of either land or sea for once air supremacy had been established the control of the land or sea below invariably followed. The epic sea battles of World War Two were basically air battles, aircraft against aircraft and aircraft against ship rather than ships against ships, as had been the case in the epic sea battles of the past. The battle of Matapan in 1941 was to establish British naval supremacy in the Mediterranean. The Afrika Korps continued to advance after Matapan and were only defeated in 1943 as a direct result of the second Battle of Alamein and 'Operation Torch', the Anglo-American landings in North Africa, but these campaigns would not have been possible without Allied control of the sea.

The Pacific War saw its share of naval battles, as most of the war was fought in and around the islands of the Pacific. While these islands were controlled by Japan, she was assured of a constant supply of raw materials, including rice, rubber, tin and petroleum. They also meant control of an ever-widening belt of security for Japan's home islands. The Battle of the Java Sea put an end to European domination of Southeast Asia. The Japanese Fleet had controlled the waters of the Pacific from the International Date Line to Singapore, and the lands of Southeast Asia from Burma to New Guinea, but now the boundaries of the Japanese Empire extended from the Kuriles and Southern Sakhalin in the North Pacific to coastal China, Burma and Thailand. The only way to check this advance toward Hawaii, Australia and the American West Coast was the establishment of aerial supremacy through sea power. The Japanese Navy was checked at the Battle of Coral Sea, when a large number of American planes were launched from ships, against ships, for the first time. Japan's bid to wipe out the balance of the American Pacific Fleet which had not been destroyed at Pearl Harbor collapsed at Midway, one of the most vital naval battles of the entire war. Had Japan won at Midway, not only Hawaii but the whole Allied position in the Pacific would have been jeopardized. When Admiral Yamamoto learned of the loss of all four of his aircraft carriers at Midway he realized that the battle was lost and that the whole war was lost as well.

The Japanese gambled everything they had on preventing the Allied landings in the Philippines from taking place. Hopelessly outclassed, Admiral Ozawa tried to stop the Allied advance and the landings at Leyte Gulf. Admiral Kurita's fleet with only five battleships and no aircraft carriers had little chance, and when Bull Halsey's forces wiped out Ozawa's four remaining aircraft carriers the Japanese, in desperation, resorted to hurling planes against American ships in suicide missions. The *kamikaze* tactics of the Japanese were as futile as they were mad. Japan's final fling of the dice left the Philippines and the home islands of Japan open to attack. Yet the war in the Pacific was far from over. The conquest of the Philippines took the balance of the war and a terrific toll of American lives. The navy could land troops at Iwo Jima and Okinawa but the price was high, as the Japanese fought to the last man. On the assumption that the fight to take the Japanese home islands would cost a million more American lives, President Truman opted to use the atomic bomb at Hiroshima and Nagasaki, not knowing that Japan was already on the brink of capitulation. World War Two ended with the exploding of the atom bomb and the inauguration of a new era in warfare.

Was this to mark the end of epic naval battles in warfare? No great new clashes have taken place since 1944, but no war between major naval powers has been fought since World War Two. There is little doubt that the old ship-to-ship 'slogging matches' of the past are gone forever. Jutland was the last example of these and was to provide a foretaste of the future as the rival navies could hardly see each other and as a result were fighting blind much of the time. The use of aircraft against ships, submarines against surface craft and amphibious invasion supported by naval bombardment is far from over. No one can tell when, and if, there will be any further epic sea battles; but should they occur, and one can only hope that they do not, once the sea battle is at an end it will be the soldiers on land who will have to laboriously occupy enemy territory. Heroic victories can be won at sea but wars are won on land. The majority of the earth's surface may be covered by water, but most of the world's peoples, factories, farms and mineral resources remain on, or under land, and provide the causes for war.

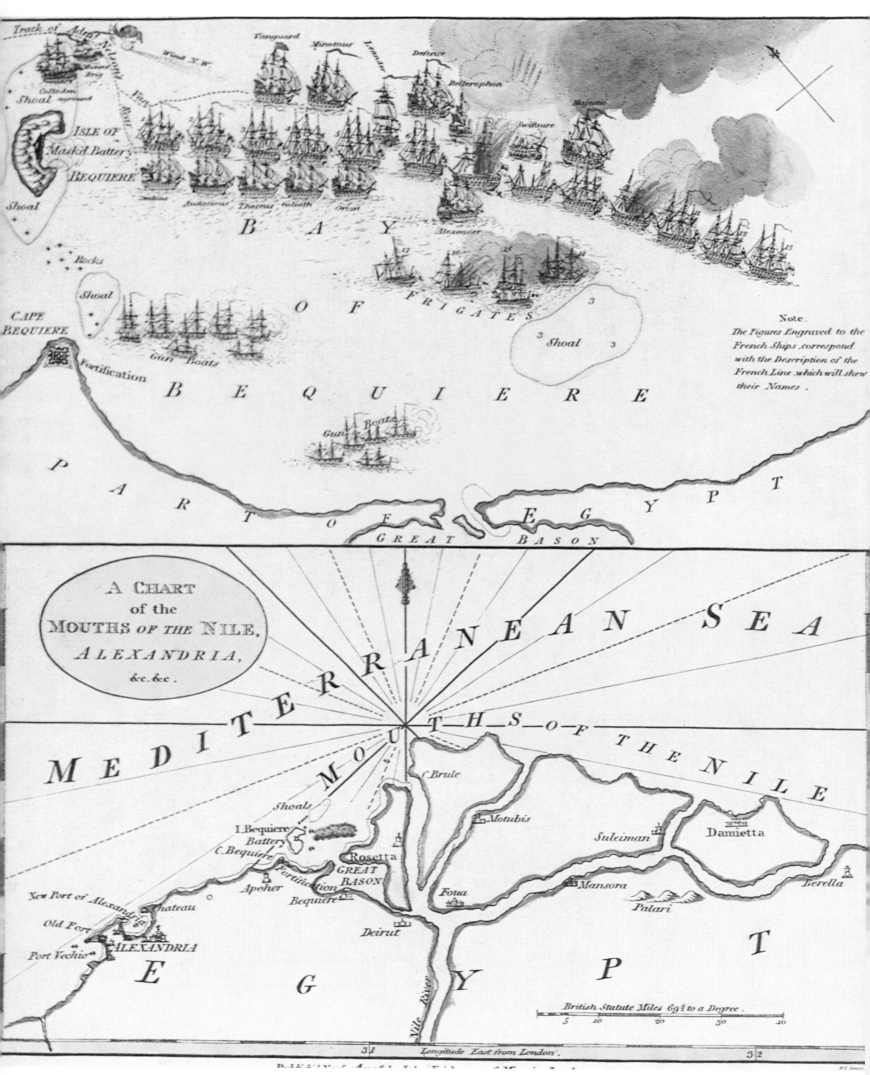

Track of Adm.^l Nelson.   Wind N.W.

Vanguard   Minotaur   Leander   Defence   Bellerophon   Majestic   Swiftsure

Sand Brig

Culloden aground

Shoal

ISLE OF

Mask'd Batter.^y

BEQUIERE

Shoal

Zealous   Audacious   Theseus   Goliath   Orion   Alexander

B   A   Y

Rocks

Shoal

CAPE
BEQUIERE

Gun Boats

Fortification

Shoal

O   F   F   R   I   G   A   T   E   S

Shoal

Note.
The Figures Engraved to the
French Ships, correspond
with the Description of the
French Line which will shew
their Names.

B   E   Q   U   I   E   R   E

Gun Boats

P   A   R   T   O   F   E   G   Y   P   T

GREAT   BASON

A CHART
of the
MOUTHS OF THE NILE,
ALEXANDRIA,
&c. &c.

M E D I T E R R A N E A N   S E A

M O U T H S — O F — T H E — N I L E

C. Brule

Shoals

I. Bequiere

Battery

C. Bequiere

Apoher

Fortification

Bequiere

Rosetta

GREAT
BASON

Motubis

Suleiman

Damietta

New Port of Alexandria

Chateau

Old Port

ALEXANDRIA

Port Vechie

Deirut

Foua

Mansora

Palari

Berella

E   G   Y   P   T

Nile River

British Statute Miles 69¼ to a Degree.
5   10   20   30   40

31   Longitude East from London.   32

The Nile

Britain was almost continuously at war with revolutionary and Napoleonic France from 1793 to 1815. During this period there were a number of sea battles of significance, but two in particular stand out as landmarks in the development of tactics and the handling of fleets. The Battle of the Nile in 1798 was the first and most spectacular of the victories of Horatio Nelson, establishing him at that time as Britain's foremost fighting admiral and a brilliant if unorthodox tactician. Seven years later the Battle of Trafalgar became the most sophisticated expression of Nelson's style of tactics and immortalized him as one of the great naval strategists in western history. Nelson, however, appeared at a time when significant changes in tactics and technology were already having an impact on naval warfare. Thus it is useful to look backwards briefly before examining the Nile and Trafalgar.

In the two centuries preceding the encounter at the Nile, there had been few changes in naval tactics and gunnery. Prior to the reign of Henry VIII, ships had served as floating forts to be attacked and taken by storm by other floating forts. But when Henry VIII built battleships carrying heavy guns capable of firing broadsides, infighting came to be replaced by outfighting. During the Dutch wars of the mid-seventeenth century, an important advance in naval tactics took place: ships were formed into a line bow to stern so that the enemy was presented with the full fire power of the fleet. Fleets also began to be maneuvered skilfully and effectively. These changes were documented by a contemporary French observer of the Four Days Battle of 1665 in the Second Dutch War who noted, 'Nothing equals the beautiful order of the English at sea. Never was a line drawn straighter than that formed by their ships; thus they bring all their fire to bear on those who draw near them . . . They fight like a line of cavalry which is handled according to rule, and applies itself solely to force back those who oppose; whereas the Dutch advance like cavalry whose squadrons leave their ranks and come separately to the charge'. During the First Dutch War the British 'Generals at Sea', predecessors of the Admiralty, issued the first *Fighting Instructions* to the navy. In this document the formation of the 'line ahead' was made the obligatory and official tactic of both defense and attack and remained so until Nelson's time.

The first time the Royal Navy used heavy guns to any extent in a major action was against the Spanish Armada in 1588. This experience proved the guns to be ineffective at long range but good at short range for causing casualties and destroying the ability and will of the enemy to fight. Thus the gunnery doctrine of the British navy came to be to fight at close range, aiming at the enemy's hull with the object of causing maximum casualties, especially from splinters.

This gunnery doctrine was obviously in conflict with the officially prescribed tactic of the 'line ahead', adherence to which made it virtually impossible to close with an enemy ship. Each doctrine had its adherents within the Royal Navy. There were the 'mêléeists' who wanted tactics appropriate to forcing a fight at close range as required by the gunnery doctrine. They were opposed by a formalist school which maintained that in actions between fleets of comparable strength the British fleet was required to fight in a line stretching ship for ship parallel to that of the enemy. Breaking out of the line was forbidden unless the whole of the enemy line fell into disorder, in which case 'general chase' might be signaled. In spite of the contradiction between the gunnery doctrine and the tactic of the line, the formalist view was embodied in the *Permanent Fighting Instructions* issued by the Admiralty. These instructions robbed commanders of initiative and made it impossible to force a mêlée at close range. It was demonstrated over and over again that fleet actions characterized by rigid adherence to the 'line ahead' tended to be tactically indecisive. While this contradiction within British naval doctrine continued, the British fleet did not win a single tactical victory over a fleet of comparable strength. Rare victories occurred only when a British admiral decided that the enemy was flying in disorder, a situation in which the *Permanent Fighting Instructions* allowed him to order a general chase so that his ships could come up at close range.

While British naval tactics were frozen by the *Permanent Fighting Instructions*, the French navy encouraged the study of tactics and worked out an effective counter to the type of fighting imposed on the British. French tactics were based on a gunnery doctrine which had as its object not casualties at close range but material damage at long range. Rather than aiming low for the hull, French gunners fired high, often using chain shot to bring down masts and yards. And it must be remembered that during the eighteenth century the French were foremost among Europeans in gunnery and artillery expertise generally. Their tactics were thus well suited to countering

the rigid British line. In a battle situation a French fleet normally accepted the leeward position so that it could retire downwind refusing a close action but maintaining a duel at long range, a duel in which British gunnery caused few casualties, but French gunnery eventually crippled so many British ships that the fleet could no longer keep formation and had to retire for repairs. The strategic goal of the French was fitted to their tactical doctrine, which was not to destroy the enemy fleet but to gain command of the sea for a limited period to accomplish a specific objective. But the French never switched from defensive to offensive tactics to exploit their limited victories, so in the end their tactics were self-defeating, as they had always to fight the same British ships again once they had been repaired.

A classic example of the impotence of the British fixation on the 'line ahead' and the

French notion of a limited victory was the Battle of Chesapeake Bay on 5 September 1781. With nineteen ships of the line, Admiral Thomas Graves had been sent to relieve General Cornwallis, then besieged at Yorktown by the American General Washington and the French General de Rochambeau. The French Admiral de Grasse was caught in the bay with 24 ships, and on sighting the British fleet immediately tried to stand out against the wind. By the time Graves arrived, only the French van had managed to round Cape Henry and hence the fleet was at his mercy. Instead of reacting in terms of the situation, however, Graves noted that the number of enemy ships was comparable to his own and incredibly ordered 'line ahead' instead of 'general chase'. The French were given time to form their own line, and a typically indecisive 'line' style action followed, in which enough damage was inflicted on Graves' ships that he deemed it necessary to return to New York. Thus the fetish of the 'line' which for so long had exercised a paralyzing effect on British naval initiative lost a heaven-sent opportunity to raise the siege of Yorktown. Although tactically undistinguished, strategically Chesapeake Bay was the battle that helped decide the American Revolution.

Seven months later exactly the reverse situation occurred in the Battle of the Saintes, when a tactically revolutionary encounter turned out to have little strategic significance. The long paralysis imposed by the *Permanent Fighting Instructions* was decisively ended by Admiral George Rodney on 12 April, 1782. The French had been planning an attack on Jamaica and needed one of their temporary victories to clear Rodney's fleet from the path of their expedition. With the French for once holding the windward position, the two lines ran past each other on opposite tacks and another indecisive line action should have resulted. But the wind suddenly veered in Rodney's favor and, in flagrant disobedience of the sacred *Permanent Fighting Instructions*, he took his ship through the enemy line followed by the five ships astern of him. Two other British ships then broke through the French line in two other places. Cut at three points, the French line never reformed, with the result that a number of French ships were assailed by superior concentrations of British ships in a furious mêlée. In the most successful British fleet action for nearly eighty years, Rodney broke the long sequence of inconclusive line actions. Beyond averting the threat to Jamaica, however, the Saintes had no strategic significance, as the outcome of the American Revolution had already been decided.

The Glorious First of June
The next major departure from orthodox tactics occurred in the first great sea action of the French Revolutionary War and was known as the 'Glorious First of June' of 1794. A fleet under Admiral Howe had been waiting in the eastern Atlantic to attack a large grain fleet escorted by a squadron under Admiral Villaret-Joyeuse. Villaret-Joyeuse's sole order was to get the grain convoy through at all costs as it was desperately needed to stave off famine in central France. Indeed, Robespierre himself had told Villaret-Joyeuse that he was destined for the guillotine if he failed. After several days of maneuvering, on 1 June Howe stood down on the enemy in a classic line ahead. Unlike Rodney who had acted instinctively in response to a sudden opportunity, Howe

deliberately threw away the *Permanent Fighting Instructions* and planned to have each of his ships cut through the French line under the stern of her opposite number and engage from leeward. Such a maneuver meant that a heavy raking fire could be poured into the hull of the enemy ship as the opposite British ship passed under her stern and also that the escape of disabled ships would be blocked as they could only retreat to leeward. In the event, the seamanship of most of Howe's fleet was not up to this maneuver and only seven of his 26 ships actually cut the French line. Even so, a desperate mêlée ensued in which a number of French ships were captured. But Villaret-Joyeuse had achieved his object of drawing Howe away from the grain fleet and as he later said, 'I saved my convoy and I saved my head'.

Howe's achievement that day was a significant step toward solving the two main problems faced by British commanders in actions against the French. The first problem was that the proficiency of both British and French in forming and maintaining the close hauled line of battle ahead almost invariably led to a stalemate. The unwillingness of the French to accept a decisive action posed the second problem, which was to 'fix' the enemy fleet. Both problems could be solved by breaking the enemy's line and getting to leeward of it. In fact breaking the line was a virtual necessity to obtain decisive action in the face of the elusive tactics developed by the French. Breaking the line at many points was a tactic first deliberately used at the Glorious First of June and thereafter came to be known as 'Lord Howe's Maneuver'.

It should also be noted that advances in tactics were closely related to advances in signaling. Only a primitive set of signals had been available for use with the few set maneuvers permitted by the *Permanent Fighting Instructions*, but by 1800 efficient signalling was possible and finally enabled admirals to have full tactical control over their fleets. Sir Hugh Popham's *Telegraphic Signals or Marine Vocabulary* was first published in 1800 and enabled commanders to say exactly what they pleased. Nelson's famous message at Trafalgar, 'England expects that every man will do his duty', was made with Popham's code. In fact, the Admiral's original message read 'England *confides* that every man will do his duty'. But to save time the signal lieutenant, John Pasco, recommended the substitution of the word 'expects' since that was in Popham's vocabulary, whereas 'confides' would have to have been spelled out.

In 1798 the ships of the Royal Navy were still classified as they had been during the Seven Years War of 1756–1763. There were lines of battleships whose emphasis was on fire power, cruisers whose emphasis was on speed and seaworthiness, and flotilla craft such as sloops and brigs for inshore work and subsidiary services. Battleships were further classified as first and second rates, which were three deckers of 90 guns or more and as third and fourth rates, which were two deckers usually mounting 74 and 64 guns. At the time of the Battle of the Nile the standard ship of the line in the Royal Navy was the 74.

Throughout the greater part of the eighteenth century British naval construction and design was generally inferior to that of the French and Spanish whose ships were larger in tonnage and correspondingly large in scantling with stout sides not easily pierced by shot. The *Tonnant, Canopus* and *Malta*, all ships of the line captured at the Battle of the Nile, were declared to be the 'finest on two decks ever seen in the British navy; . . . their qualities in sailing and carrying sail have rarely, if ever been surpassed'. The former French ship, *Le Franklin*, taken into British service as HMS *Canopus* after the Nile, was so admirably designed that British dockyards were ordered to build eight more like her. This design superiority, however, was more than balanced by the superior strategy, seamanship and discipline of the British navy, the greatest in the world at this time.

Improving British Gunnery

Toward the end of the eighteenth century, British gunnery was improving through more rapid rates of fire and the introduction of the carronade, so called because it was first cast at the Carron Foundry in Stirlingshire. The carronade was a short piece with a large bore, light and easy to handle in close fighting. Firing a heavy shot, it substantially increased the fire power of the battle fleet. First introduced in 1779, the carronade played a leading role at the Battle of the Saintes where more men were killed in the French flagship than in the entire British fleet. Ideally suited to traditional British gunnery doctrine, the carronade made British battleships even more formidable at a time when the contradiction between gunnery doctrine and tactical doctrine was being resolved by such commanders as Rodney, Howe

Opposite top: The Battle of the Saintes, 12 April, 1782. De Grasse himself was taken prisoner and the French fleet was destroyed to the point from which it would take a generation to recover. The French Revolution broke out well before a fleet formidable enough to effectively challenge the Royal Navy could be reconstructed.
Opposite below: Admiral Howe on board HMS *Queen Charlotte* at the Battle of the First of June, 1794. Captain Neville of the Queen's Regiment was mortally wounded.

Opposite: Admiral Villaret-Joyeuse, defeated French commander in the Glorious First of June. He was promised the guillotine by Robespierre if he lost, but Robespierre himself got the chop before he was able to execute the order and the admiral.

and Nelson. The Saintes, the Glorious First of June, Camperdown, St. Vincent, the Nile, Copenhagen and Trafalgar were all carronade actions fought at close range. With these developments in technology and tactics the stage was set for what has been called the 'golden age of the sailing navy, the prolonged wars against revolutionary and Napoleonic France'.

The *Ancien Régime* in France came to a bloody end with the outbreak of the French Revolution in 1789. The Revolution had supposedly ended with the abolition of absolute monarchy through the Constitution of 1791, but the outbreak of foreign war and the destruction of the throne in 1792 were followed by the execution of Louis XVI early in 1793. The revolutionary ardor in France and the execution of its king, a relative of other crowned heads in Europe, raised the fears of the conservative monarchies, and the new republic quickly found itself assailed by a coalition of Britain, Austria, Prussia, Spain, Piedmont and Holland. Infused with a revolutionary nationalism, however, the raw armies of the republic were able to turn a defensive into an offensive war and carry the revolution beyond the borders of France. By 1795 French arms had overrun the Low Countries and had extracted favorable treaties with Prussia and Spain, Austria was hesitating. In one of the classic instances of great generalship, a young republican officer named Napoleon Bonaparte then conducted a swift and decisive campaign in Italy which forced a peace settlement from Austria in 1797.

Supported by its small ally Portugal, Britain alone still stood against France and Britain had opened negotiations. As the Allies one after the other had deserted the 'First Coalition', the position of the British fleet in the Mediterranean had become increasingly untenable. With the fall of Leghorn in 1796, the Mediterranean squadron had no more bases and faced the real possibility of being overwhelmed by the combined French and Spanish fleets. The Cabinet therefore ordered the Mediterranean to be evacuated and concentrated on the defense of England and Ireland. The Directory, the five-man executive committee of the National Convention which had governed

France since 1795, saw Britain's willingness to negotiate as an indication of weakness and made impossible demands. Correctly perceiving that France had no genuine interest in peace, Britain broke off the negotiations and prepared to defend herself alone.

The Directory believed Britain to be on the verge of revolution and openly proclaimed its intentions. 'It remains, fellow citizens, to punish the perfidy of the Cabinet of England, that has corrupted the courts of Europe. It is in London that the misfortunes of Europe are planned; it is in London that we must end them', announced a French manifesto of 1797. The Directory wanted to accomplish this goal through an invasion of England, a project which had not been successfully attempted since 1066. In October of 1797 command of the 'Army of England' was given to a 29-year old Corsican officer who had already proved his brilliant grasp of military affairs in the Italian campaign, which had resulted in the withdrawal of Austria from the war and the British fleet from the Mediterranean. Napoleon Bonaparte was immensely popular as a result of these exploits and had a genuine flair for politics, which made the Directory anxious to remove him from the seat of power on Paris. On 23 February, 1798, however, a surprised Directory heard Bonaparte report that a landing on the English coast was not feasible: '. . . make what efforts we will, we shall not for many years acquire control of the seas. To make a descent on England, without being master of the sea, is the boldest and most difficult operation ever attempted'. As an alternative Bonaparte proposed an invasion of Egypt. By reviving old dreams of colonizing the Levant and capturing the rich eastern trade, such a project had a ready appeal in France. Talleyrand supported the project strongly for these reasons and also because he wished to avoid a further direct clash with Britain. The remainder of the Directory wanted to continue the war with Britain, but since the invasion was not possible the Egyptian project offered a means of continuing the hostilities and also of removing the over-popular young general even farther from Paris. As a Corsican, Bonaparte himself was more oriented toward the Mediterranean and the

Description of a 24 Pounder Carronade on a Carriage, with an Inclined Plane, agreeable to a plan suggested by Captain Schank, by which it can be seen, Guns of all kinds can be mounted either on board Ship, or on Shore, in Forts &c. &c. &c. — complete Experiments have been made on board the Wolverene Gun Vessel, several Revenue Vessels, Merchant-Ships & Gun Boats, and reports of the experiments made, with the Utility of the Invention, is approved of and lodged in the Admiralty.

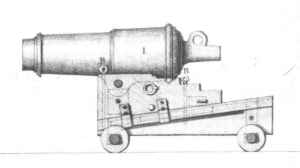

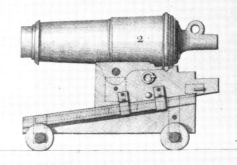

Plan of the lower Carriage.

Scale of Feet.

Section of the Carronade and Carriage.

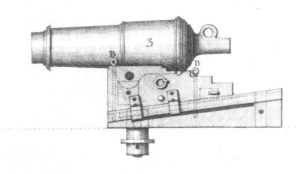

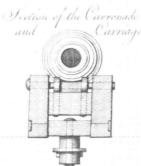

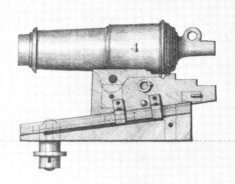

References

1. & 2. The Carronade mounted on a Carriage with Trucks, describing as at 1. the lower and upper Carriages fixed with the bolts B.B. — & at 2. the bolts taken out and the upper Carriage shewn recoiled.

3. & 4. The Carronade mounted on a Carriage fitted with a Spindle to be used on slides, describing the Carriage fixed as at 3. with the bolts B.B. — and at 4. the bolts taken out and the upper Carriage shewn recoiled.

N.B. It is particularly recommended that a middle Breeching should be used; — and it is to be observed that the Inclined Plane is applicable to Gun Carriages of all descriptions, & is not meant to be confined to Carronades only. The Recoil of the Gun in Carriages on this principle is so gentle, that it may be fired athwart-ships in Boats, or in any other Situation without the least danger.

Below: A 32-pounder carronade. Carronades had great penetrating power for their size, and lightness enabled them to be handled by small crews.

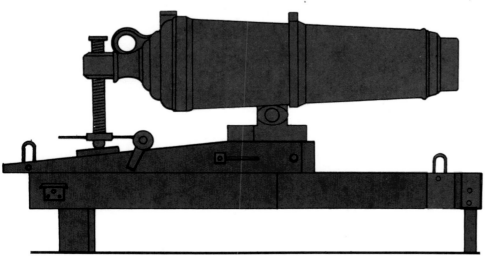

Levant and, tending to ignore Britain, Prussia and the other northern European states, simply was not interested in the invasion of England. As he told his secretary in 1798, 'This little Europe is too small a field. Great renown can only be won in the east'. Thus the Egyptian in expedition was an acceptable compromise, and so from command of the 'Army of England' in October 1797 Bonaparte passed to command the 'Army of the Orient' in March 1798.

The plan approved by the Directory had as its goal the weakening of British power by threaten-ing India and disrupting the rich British trade with the east. Such a move would indeed have touched Britain in a vital spot, as its industry and commerce were now closely bound up with that of Asia. Deprived of India, Britain could not have carried on her extensive commerce with the East Indies and China, a commerce which was almost essential to her survival as a first class power. French contacts were already well de-veloped with Tipoo Sahib, Sultan of Mysore, who was seeking French aid to expel the British from India. (The Sultan was defeated and killed by the future Duke of Wellington at Seringapatam in 1799.) Bonaparte was thus ordered to occupy Egypt and exclude the British 'from all their pos-sessions in the east to which the General can come'. He was further ordered to cut through the Isthmus of Suez to assure French possession of the Red Sea, to better the condition of the people of Egypt and to improve relations with Turkey, one of the few states not at war with France.

Similar plans had appeared a number of times before in French history. Hence the proposal was neither original nor novel, yet was appealing to latent but longstanding French aspirations toward colonizing Egypt and Syria and challenging British power in India and Ceylon. Although advertised as a grandiose blow against British power in the east, the expedition was in fact organized as a practical colonizing venture, including in its complement a corps of engineers, mathematicians, geologists, chemists, artists and others to assist in the foundation of a permanent colony. The international situation was also propitious for such a venture, for Britain's energies were focused on defense of the Channel, Austria was already beaten and Turkey was likely to welcome the expulsion of the Mamelukes from Egypt.

A French Base in Egypt

The future Emperor of France, however, entertained larger aspirations. His idea was to establish a permanent French colony in Egypt as a base from which to menace British interests in India and Ceylon. After conquering the east and founding a great French empire upon the ruins of the British, he wanted to mobilize the Greeks and other Christians, seize Constantinople and smash Turkey, and then 'take Europe in the rear'. And while he could not dream of transporting the 'Army of England' across the Channel for fear of the British Navy, Bonaparte could be quite certain that the passage of the 'Army of the Orient' to Egypt would not be disputed, since British squadrons had been absent from the Mediterranean for over eighteen months.

Speed and secrecy in mounting the expedition were imperative, and both were achieved to a remarkable degree. Speed was needed not because of the British Navy but because in August the Nile River would be in flood, greatly hampering the advance on Cairo and increasing Egyptian opportunities for resistance. The expedition sailed with little more than two month's preparation. The secrecy was so thorough that Bonaparte had defeated the Mameluke armies at the Battle of the Pyramids and occupied Cairo before the British even discovered where the expedition had gone.

Preparations for the expedition were spread between Toulon, Marseilles, Genoa, Corsica and Cività Vecchia. Escorted by thirteen ships of the line, seven frigates and a few gunboats, 300 transports carried 30,000 infantry, 2800 cavalry, 60 field and 40 siege guns, two companies of sappers and miners and a bridging train. The naval forces were commanded by forty-five year old François Paul Brueys d'Aigalliers, who had been a mere lieutenant at the outbreak of the Revolution in 1789. As three-quarters of the officers of the French navy had either been guillotined or driven into exile during the Revolution, Brueys had rapidly been promoted to flag rank. Dismissed during the Reign of Terror in 1793, he had come to the notice of Bonaparte at Ragusa during the Italian campaign. On Bonaparte's strong recommendation, the Directory had appointed Brueys to command the Toulon fleet in 1797, although he was in no way qualified for such a position. Admiral Pierre de Villeneuve, destined for command of the Franco-Spanish forces at Trafalgar seven years later, served as second in naval command, Count Honoré Ganteaume as chief of naval staff, while Rear Admiral Decrès was in charge of the transports.

Brueys' squadron was made up of the remnants of the French Mediterranean fleet, ships that had managed to escape destruction by the British at the evacuation of Toulon in 1793 and which were 'old and rotting, not even able to support the firing of their guns if it became at all heavy'. Some of the guns even had to be unshipped as it was doubtful whether the decks would continue to bear their weight. The crews were in little better condition, for the seamen of the First Republic were badly fed, badly paid and without even a change of clothes. A report to the Directory made a few days before the battle said simply, 'On the whole our ships are very poorly manned, and in my opinion it needs much courage to command such an ill-prepared fleet'.

With Bonaparte and his staff billeted aboard Brueys' huge flagship *L'Orient*, the expedition sailed from Toulon in mid-May. Bonaparte was not a man of the sea and earlier had written to Brueys to request a comfortable berth, 'suitable for a commander-in-chief who expects to be seasick the entire voyage'. After capturing and looting Malta on the way, the expedition arrived at Marabut, a little fishing village four miles west of Alexandria. Here 5000 troops were landed to seize Alexandria so that the rest of the forces could disembark in leisurely safety and the transports shelter in the harbor. With a full month before the beginning of the flood season, Bonaparte marched on Cairo. He occupied that city two days after defeating the Egyptian forces on 21 July at the Battle of the Pyramids, and began to consider how to pacify and administer Egypt, penetrate to Suez and convoy regiments down the Red Sea toward India.

While Bonaparte was organizing his Egyptian expedition, his nemesis-to-be was enjoying a rest and considerable fame at his home in England. At thirty-nine years of age, Horatio Nelson was

Left: Admiral François Brueys, the ill-fated commander of the French Fleet at the Battle of the Nile.

already a rear-admiral of twelve month's seniority. He had gone to sea at twelve, become a lieutenant at nineteen and commanded a ship at twenty. His first action as a commander had been off Toulon in 1795 and although the action in general had been inconclusive, Nelson had distinguished himself and launched a glorious career which was to last just ten years. Already his characteristic qualities of instant decision and brilliant tactical insight, his penchant for swift and audacious action, and his supreme urge to victory were being noted by his colleagues and superiors.

Nelson's role in the Battle of St. Vincent on 14 February, 1797 presaged the brilliance and daring which was to be more fully revealed at the Battle of the Nile the following year. The squadron of Sir John Jervis had sighted a Spanish fleet off Cape St. Vincent, disordered and in two straggling groups. Although outnumbered by nearly two to one, Jervis tried to even the odds by leading his line between the two groups of Spanish ships to force them farther apart. Completing this maneuver successfully, Jervis then tacked to sail back between the enemy but missed his timing so that the Spaniards could reunite before the British fleet could pass through again. Serving as commodore in the third ship from the rear, Nelson saw the situation developing, took his ship out of the line and attacked the Spanish from windward in a desperate attempt to delay the junction of the enemy. Jervis then ordered the rear ships to Nelson's support and a furious mêlée took place with Nelson himself capturing two ships at the head of boarding parties. No officer would have dared attempt such a move twenty years before and even in 1797 it was very bold. Many of his fellow officers thought Nelson should be reprimanded for breaking the line and even he was uncertain if Jervis would approve.

Already minus an eye from shell splinters and having lost an arm leading an unsuccessful expedition against Tenerife in 1797, Nelson was knighted for his part in the Battle of St. Vincent. In the Spring of 1798, his arm now healed, he asked the Admiralty for employment and was sent in the fast 74-gun *Vanguard* to serve under Jervis at the blockade of Cadiz. The British were by this time aware that an expedition was being prepared at Toulon, but British agents had been unable to penetrate French security to discover its purpose and destination. Hence it was deemed necessary for a squadron to re-enter the Mediterranean and keep watch off Toulon. As the Admiralty wrote to Jervis, 'When you are apprized that the appearance of a British squadron in the Mediterranean is a condition on which the fate of Europe may at this moment be said to depend, you will not be surprised that we are disposed to strain every nerve, and incur considerable hazard in effecting it'.

Nelson Enters the Med.

Hence Nelson was ordered by Jervis into the stormy Gulf of Lyons on 2 May 'to endeavour to ascertain the real object of the preparations in the making by the French'. Arriving on 17 May Nelson had at his disposal two other 74's, three frigates and a sloop. Ten more ships of the line

were promised as soon as reinforcements arrived from England. Although both Jervis and the Admiralty were very impressed with Nelson's abilities, the only independent operation conducted by him up to that time had been the ill-fated assault on Tenerife. The Admiralty was gambling with Nelson and both knew it.

A spell of heavy weather on 20 May dismasted the *Vanguard* which was only saved from being wrecked by being taken in tow by one of her sister ships. Assuming that the *Vanguard* would have to put into Gibraltar for dockyard repairs, the frigates returned to base. Weather notwithstanding, Brueys sailed from Toulon that same day, setting a course between Corsica and the Italian mainland. The *Vanguard* was in fact repaired at sea from the resources of her companions. French security was so thorough that it was only on 28 May that Nelson finally learned of the departure of the French expedition from a passing merchantman.

On 7 June ten 74's and a frigate joined Nelson. These were Captains Troubridge in the *Culloden*, Darby in the *Bellerophon*, Louis in the *Minotaur*, Peyton in the *Defence* (the oldest ship in the fleet with thirty-five years of service), Hood in the *Zealous*, Gould in the *Audacious*, Westcott in the *Majestic*, Foley in the *Goliath*, Hallowell in the *Swiftsure*, and Miller in the *Theseus*. The *Leander* under Captain Thompson was a 50-gun frigate then eighteen years old. Already with Nelson were the *Orion* under Captain Saumarez, the *Alexander* under Captain Ball and the eighteen-gun sloop *Mutine*. Jervis had received only eight ships from England but still sent Nelson the ten originally promised. As befitted the importance of his mission, Nelson now had what was prob-

Above: Admiral Sir John Jervis, victor at St. Vincent, who sent Nelson to the Mediterranean prior to the Battle of the Nile.

Opposite: Admiral Horatio Nelson, with the Battle of the Nile in the background.

Above: The launching of HMS *Alexander*, which joined Nelson's squadron on the way to Egypt. It was typical of the British 74s of the period, which formed the backbone of the British Fleet. **Opposite above:** British Fleet about to engage the French at anchor at the start of the Battle of the Nile. The British are sailing in time-honored fashion, in the 'line ahead'. **Opposite below:** The moment when *l'Orient*, the French flagship, blew up. The entire crew was lost. **Below:** A 32-pounder gun, the heaviest weapon normally carried on board British ships. Its long barrel gave it range and and accuracy which the the carronade lacked, but it needed a much larger crew to man it.

ably the finest squadron of 74's ever assembled. And although his original orders had been to gain intelligence, Nelson was now instructed to use 'his utmost endeavours to take, sink, burn or destroy the armament preparing by the enemy at Toulon'.

Once his squadron was assembled, Nelson disappeared into the Mediterranean on his search for the French expedition and was not heard from for almost two months, causing great anxiety to Jervis and the Admiralty. Nelson first followed Brueys' own course down the coast of Italy searching for information. Sicily was considered the most likely goal of the French, but Nelson felt that if the French passed Sicily, the destination was definitely Alexandria. Writing to Lord Spencer, he commented, 'I shall believe they are going on with their scheme of possessing Alexandria and getting troops to India – a plan concerted with Tipoo Sahib, by no means so difficult as might at first view be imagined'. By 22 June he had learned of the fall of Malta and believed that if the French were at Sicily, information would by then be plentiful. With most of his captains concurring, Nelson concluded that Alexandria was the goal and made directly there, only to discover an empty harbor on 26 June.

The search was greatly hampered by the absence of the frigates to extend its range, but the squadron could not be broken up to compensate as its power lay in concentration. 'No frigates to which has been, and may be again, attributed the loss of the French fleet', Nelson wrote despairingly to his friend William Hamilton, British Ambassador at Naples. The search

was renewed and on 19 July Nelson touched in at Syracuse, 'as ignorant of the situation of the enemy as I was twenty-seven days ago'. Next arriving in the Gulf of Koroni in Greece, he learned that the French had been sighted a month before off Crete and sailing southeast. After six weeks of searching had come the first ray of hope and, making direct to Alexandria, morale was lifted still further when the harbor was found to be full of French transports protected by shore batteries. On the following day, 1 August, the frustrating quest came to an end when the *Zealous* reported the French warships peacefully anchored fifteen miles away in Aboukir Bay. Having eaten little for days due to tension, Nelson crowded on sail and ordered dinner.

The irony of the chase is that it was unnecessary. Nelson and his captains had originally guessed too well that Alexandria was the target. As a precaution Bonaparte had steered a course for southern Crete instead of directly for Alexandria. Nelson had actually overtaken the slow moving French convoy, beaten it to Alexandria and sailed off to the north as the French arrived from the northwest. On the night of 22 June the two fleets had even been within one hundred miles of each other but on diverging courses. Had Nelson had his frigates, however, even Bonaparte's precautions would not have saved the French force from detection.

The search was not a complete waste of time. During the weeks at sea, Nelson had carefully drilled his ships and planned tactics to meet any contingency. If the French were caught at sea, he planned to divide his ships into three squadrons, two to attack the escort and the third, the transports. Conversely, an anchored opponent must be allowed no further time in which to prepare. Hence the attack must begin on sighting the enemy. If the strength of the opposing fleet was comparable to his own, Nelson hoped to obtain at least a limited victory by concentrating a superior force on one part of the enemy while containing the rest. His tactic was to pit two of his ships against one of the enemy's and gradually move along the anchored line, blasting it ship by ship. Regular tactical sessions were held with his captains so that, whenever and in whatever

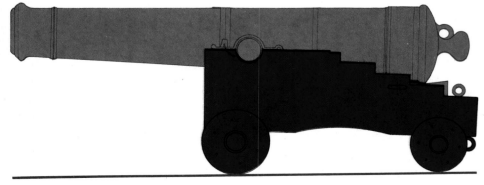

circumstances battle finally came, appropriate action would have been discussed in principle if not in detail. In terms of possible tactics, Nelson wanted his captains to know his mind beyond possibility of misunderstanding.

Bruey's Fleet at Aboukir

When British ships hove into sight off Aboukir Point about two o'clock in the afternoon, Brueys' fleet had been settled in the bay for weeks. After the debarkation of the expedition at Alexandria was complete, Brueys' orders from the Directory had been to go to Corfu both to protect the Ionian Islands and to safeguard his ships. Bonaparte had, however, countermanded these orders and required Brueys to remain at Alexandria, presumably in case the general wished to return to France without delay. The execution of this new order having been left entirely to him, Brueys had moved his ships from the security offered by Alexandria Harbor to Aboukir Bay where he lay awaiting further orders from Bonaparte. Brueys was apparently haunted by a fear of running aground and although his largest ship drew only 22 feet and Alexandria offered a minimum of 27 feet, he decided not to risk it.

Aboukir Bay extends in a semi-circle sixteen miles across from Aboukir Point to the Rosetta Mouth of the Nile River which gave its name to the coming battle. At the site of the ancient city of Canopus lay the then-village of Aboukir. The coast shelves gradually so that the ships had to be moored three miles from shore. The only natural protection was the small island of Aboukir and some rocks and sandbanks. Still, Aboukir could have been made an almost impregnable position had Brueys so chosen. It was already known that the British were again loose in the Mediterranean, for British frigates (actually searching for Nelson at Jervis' orders) had been seen off Crete. Even the knowledge that a British squadron was surely searching for him did not move Brueys to send out guard frigates. Although events were to prove Brueys a most courageous man, he had no orders to seek action and indeed no orders but to remain where he was. He had never commanded a squadron in battle and therefore thought the best course was to wait passively in the bay in a defensive position. Some of his more experienced captains such as Blanquet du Chayla, a veteran of thirteen battles, and Dupetit-Thouars argued that the best chance lay at sea where time and place could be selected with surprise and the wind in their favor. Supported by Ganteaume, the chief of naval staff, who pointed out the poor condition of the ships and how impossible it would be for them to fight on the open sea, Brueys elected to remain at Aboukir.

It was axiomatic in those days that ships could not stand up to shore batteries, a truth which had often been proven, so the proper defense for a fleet in Brueys' position was to anchor in a line which was incapable of being turned and in which the ships were closed up to prevent penetration by the enemy. In effect this arrangement converted the fleet into a long floating battery which should have been able to repulse even repeated assaults by a superior force. During the American Revolution this type of defense had been successfully used by the British admirals Barrington at St. Lucia in 1778 and Hood at St. Kitts in 1782 against heavy French attacks. Attacking a strong anchored position was a risky affair, and although in 1801 Nelson himself boldly attacked a powerful Danish fleet in defensive position in Copenhagen harbor, he would have been the first to admit how close he came to failure.

This pattern of defense was in fact adopted by Brueys, who anchored his battleships in a line extending from Aboukir Island. Five 74-gun ships – *Le Guerrier*, *Le Conquérant*, *Le Spartiate*, *L'Acquilon* and *Le Peuple Souverain* – made up the van. In the center was the 80-gun *Le Franklin*, the massive *L'Orient* which at 120 guns and 1000 men was larger than any ship in the British navy, *Le Tonnant* at 90 guns, and two 74's, *L'Heureuse* and *Le Timoléon*. The rear was composed of *Le Mercure* at 74 guns, the 80-gun *Le Guillaume Tell* which served as Admiral Villeneuve's flagship and the 74-gun *Le Généreux*. Brueys and his four frigates, the 40-gun *La Diane* and *La Justice* and the 36-gun *L'Artémise* and *La Sérieuse*, anchored inside his battle line. He expected any attack to come on the rear and center because of the shoals and had therefore positioned his more powerful units there. Every advantage thus lay with Brueys at Aboukir. He had a heavier weight of metal, an equal number of battleships, frigates, a relatively secure natural position, and above all time to prepare his defenses. In the aggregate, these factors meant that his fleet should have been able to withstand any attack mounted by Admiral Horatio Nelson.

His own mistakes and other circumstances, however, neutralized these advantages for Brueys. From Aboukir Point shoals covered by broken water stretched northeast toward the island and continued in the same direction beyond the island for another two miles. Another irregular shoal lay within the bay itself. To make his line incapable of being turned, Brueys had only to anchor his van as close as possible to the island and his rear close in upon the inner shoal. Then if his ships lay close enough together, his line could neither be turned nor penetrated. But dominated by his obsession of running aground and expecting the British to have as much respect for the shoals as himself, he left a generous margin of safety, anchoring the lead ship of his van too far off the island and his entire line a thousand yards farther out than necessary. With two ship lengths between them, his vessels were also anchored too far apart. Had he also made a strongpoint of Aboukir Island, he could have provided powerful support for his van but as it was, he established only a weak battery of half a dozen six-pounders and a few mortars on the island, not even enough to command the passage between the island and the lead ship of the van. A further problem was that his ships had been stripped of supplies for the troops marching on Cairo. Therefore each day almost half of his manpower was employed ashore either digging wells or searching for food. These work and forage parties were subject to attack by the local population, so Brueys found it necessary to requisition a further 50 men to protect them.

When *L'Heureuse* sighted the *Zealous* early in the afternoon of 1 August, Brueys received the news without alarm. He ordered signals to be made for the work parties ashore to return but more than 4000 men did not reach their ships in time and watched the battle from ashore. Only at this point did Brueys finally order hawsers to be strung between his ships to prevent the enemy breaking through. He believed he had ample time to further his defenses, since standard procedure for a French admiral in Nelson's situation would have been first to make a careful reconnaissance and then test the enemy's reaction to a distant cannonade. This belief was strengthened by the fact that the day was already advanced and that when sighted Nelson's ships were somewhat scattered and obviously not in battle formation.

The British squadron had, however, standing orders that an anchored enemy was to be given no more time to prepare; despite the time and disordered condition of the fleet, the attack began immediately. Although the *Alexander* and the *Swiftsure* were away scouting and the *Culloden* was towing a captured French brig, Nelson signaled an attack on the van and center because this was the weaker part of the French line and could not easily be reinforced due to the wind. A top-gallant breeze, just enough to ensure ease of maneuver, was blowing north-northwest. As Captain Berry of the *Vanguard* later wrote, 'His idea in this disposition of force was, first to secure the victory, and then to make the most of it according to future circumstances'. At 1500

hours the 'prepare for battle' signal appeared. By 1730 the British ships were in line and abreast of Aboukir Island, coming from the north west.

The lead ship in the British line was the *Zealous* under Captain Hood who proceeded slowly, sounding carefully to avoid the reef and shoal. The second ship was the *Goliath* under Captain Foley, one of the most experienced captains in the fleet. As the *Goliath* rounded the island, Foley saw that with luck he could cut between *Le Guerrier* and the island, thus attacking from the side on which the French were unprepared and might not even have their guns run out. They would thus be caught between two fires as other British ships attacked from the outside. Foley also saw that Brueys' position was defective in that he had allowed 500 feet between his ships, a space large enough for the attackers to sail through and take up positions from which the French ships could be raked from bow or stern but at which they could make no effective retaliation without cutting their cables. Foley was more confident about sailing near the island than was Hood because he possessed a French atlas only twenty years old showing the depths of water in the bay.

Foley's decision to cut inside the French line was exactly the kind of spontaneous initiative required by Nelson from his captains and decisively shaped the course of the battle. The *Goliath* was followed by the *Zealous*, *Audacious*, *Orion* and *Theseus* while the *Vanguard* and the rest of the line attacked from the seaward side, thus effectively doubling and overpowering the

25

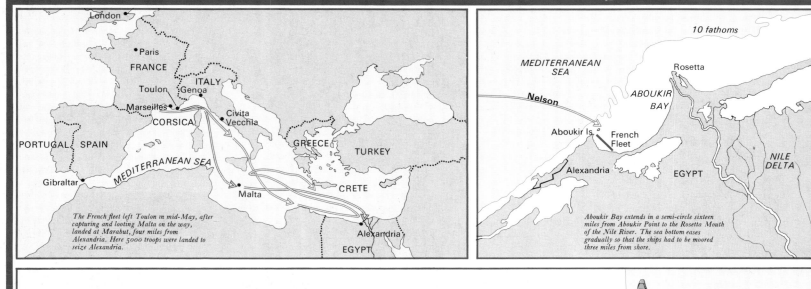

The French fleet left Toulon in mid-May, after capturing and looting Malta on the way, landed at Marabut, four miles from Alexandria. Here 5000 troops were landed to seize Alexandria.

Aboukir Bay extends in a semi-circle sixteen miles from Aboukir Point to the Rosetta Mouth of the Nile River. The sea bottom eases gradually so that the ships had to be moored three miles from shore.

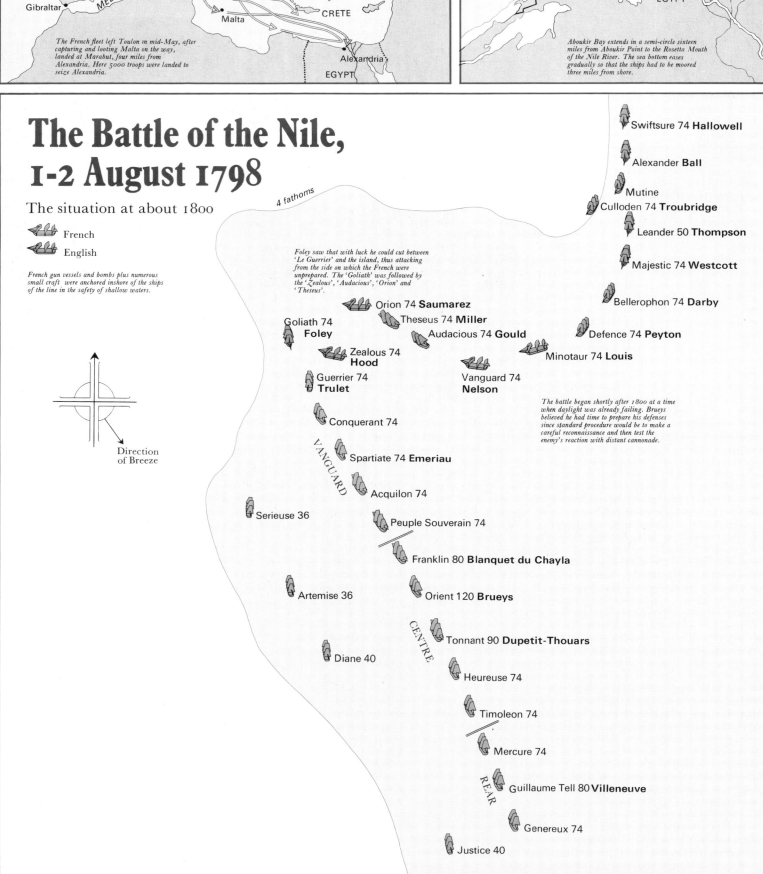

The Battle of the Nile, 1-2 August 1798

The situation at about 1800

French

English

French gun vessels and bombs plus numerous small craft were anchored inshore of the ships of the line in the safety of shallow waters.

Foley saw that with luck he could cut between 'Le Guerrier' and the island, thus attacking from the side on which the French were unprepared. The 'Goliath' was followed by the 'Zealous', 'Audacious', 'Orion' and 'Theseus'.

Direction of Breeze

The battle began shortly after 1800 at a time when daylight was already failing. Brueys believed he had time to prepare his defenses since standard procedure would be to make a careful reconnaissance and then test the enemy's reaction with distant cannonade.

Swiftsure 74 **Hallowell**

Alexander **Ball**

Mutine

Culloden 74 **Troubridge**

Leander 50 **Thompson**

Majestic 74 **Westcott**

Bellerophon 74 **Darby**

Orion 74 **Saumarez**

Theseus 74 **Miller**

Goliath 74 **Foley**

Audacious 74 **Gould**

Defence 74 **Peyton**

Zealous 74 **Hood**

Minotaur 74 **Louis**

Guerrier 74 **Trulet**

Vanguard 74 **Nelson**

Conquerant 74

Spartiate 74 **Emeriau**

Acquilon 74

Serieuse 36

Peuple Souverain 74

Franklin 80 **Blanquet du Chayla**

Artemise 36

Orient 120 **Brueys**

Tonnant 90 **Dupetit-Thouars**

Diane 40

Heureuse 74

Timoleon 74

Mercure 74

Guillaume Tell 80 **Villeneuve**

Genereux 74

Justice 40

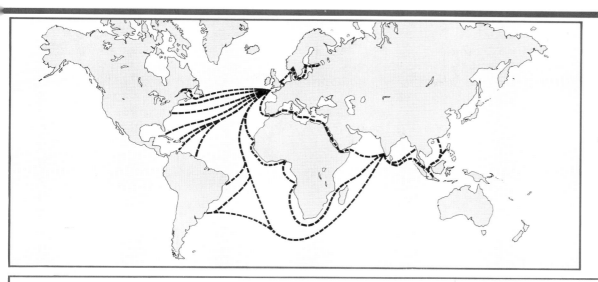

Trade and Shipping Routes of the World

The pattern of 19th and 20th century shipping was already emerging at the end of the 18th century. Although most of 'world' trade was intra-European, though the Mediterranean, North Sea, and Baltic, the amount of trade between Europe and North America was growing fast. Trade with the West Indies was declining, but trade to the Far East around the Cape of Good Hope to India and the 'country trade' between India and China was increasing. The extensive Pacific trade which exists today was virtually non-existent 200 years ago.

The situation at about 2200

4 fathoms

Dawn revealed that the first six ships of the French line were in British possession, L'Orient had blown up, the next three ships had cut their cables and were now aground.

Culloden

Culloden ran aground and took no part in the battle.

Guerrier 74 **Trulet**

Zealous 74 **Hood**

Conquerant 74

Audacious 74 **Gould**

Vanguard 74

Spartiate 74 **Emeriau**

Minotaur 74 **Louis**

Acquilon 74

Defence 74 **Peyton**

Leander 50 **Thompson**

Franklin 80 **Blanquet du Chayla**

Mutine

Orion 74 **Saumarez**

Goliath 74 **Foley**

Swiftsure 74 **Hallowell**

Alexander **Ball**

Orient 120 **Brueys**

Theseus 74 **Miller**

Majestic 74 **Westcott**

Heavily battered by the British ships around her, L'Orient caught fire near the mizzen chains. Since the fire would soon reach the powder magazines on board, ships nearby began to move away. With an explosion heard 15 miles away in Alexandria, L'Orient disappeared soon after 2200.

Peuple Souverain 74

Bellerophon 74 **Darby**

Bellerophon drifts off to leeward after engaging L'Orient which had been waiting, seventh in line, with her 120 guns double shotted.

Tonnant 90 **Dupetit-Thouars**

Heureuse 74

Timoleon 74

Mercure 74

At noon the next day Villeneuve decided to escape and got under way with the two remaining ships plus his flagship Le Guillaume Tell.

Guillaume Tell 80 **Villeneuv**

Diane 40

Justice 40

Genereux 74

Direction of Breeze

enemy van. As Nelson later explained his tactic to Lord Howe, 'By attacking the enemy's van and centre, the wind blowing directly along their line, I was enabled to throw what force I pleased on a few ships'. And thanks to Foley, Nelson's tactic was working even better than he could ever have hoped.

The battle began shortly after 1800 at a time when daylight was already failing. The French van fought stubbornly but was doomed by the overwhelming concentration of power focused on it. The lead ship, *Le Guerrier*, was engaged by the *Goliath* and dismasted within ten minutes. Her commander, Captain Trulet, refused to strike his colors for over three hours even after being reduced to sporadic fire from one stern gun and the ship finally had to be boarded. The second in the line, *Le Conquérant*, faced both the *Audacious* and the *Zealous*. As British ships began to pass down the outside of the French line, *Le Guerrier* and *Le Conquérant* were attacked from both sides but had barely enough men aboard to serve their guns on one side. Fully engaged by the *Goliath*, raked by the *Audacious* and subject to the passing fire of the *Orion* and *Theseus*, *Le Con-*

quérant had to strike after about twenty minutes. Captain Gould of the *Audacious* later wrote of *Le Conquérant* that 'the slaughter became so dreadful in the ship that the French officers declared it was impossible to make their men stand to their guns'. The *Audacious* should actually have moved farther down the French line as the *Goliath* and the *Zealous* alone could have beaten the lead ships. The *Theseus* and the *Orion* soon arrived and moved farther down the line, the *Orion* attacking the fifth French ship which was *Le Peuple Souverain*.

Moving down the outside of the French line, the *Vanguard* became locked in a heavy duel with the third French ship, *Le Spartiate*. At first the *Vanguard* suffered heavy damage and casualties from the fire of her adversary and *L'Acquilon* next in line. The *Vanguard* was in fact almost forced to break off the attack but the timely arrival of the *Minotaur* gave the battered ship some relief by diverting the fire of *L'Acquilon*. During the action with *Le Spartiate* Nelson received a nasty wound above his blind eye, rectangular and three inches long, which covered his good eye with blood and skin and gave him a concussion. But for this wound, he later said, he would have

annihilated the French fleet. As it was, the wound was messy and painful and left him 'stone blind' for a time. *Le Spartiate* put up a terrific resistance but with 49 shot holes below water line on the port side and 27 on the starboard, her magazines flooded and her guns out of action, her colors were finally hauled down. At the end Nelson refused to take Captain Emeriau's sword, saying to the officer who brought it, 'Return it to him. He has used it so well'.

While this clash was occurring, the *Defence* passed the *Minotaur* and engaged *Le Peuple Souverain* from the outside. Soon after, the *Orion* shifted from *Le Peuple Souverain* to the sixth ship in the line, *Le Franklin*, which had thus far escaped attention. The *Bellerophon* should have engaged *Le Peuple Souverain* from the outside but instead was the first ship to tackle the huge *L'Orient* which had been waiting, seventh in the line, with her 120 guns double shotted. For an hour the *Bellerophon* was blasted by a ship almost twice her size until finally, dismasted and a virtual wreck, with the captain wounded and 200 casualties, she had to cut her cable and drift off into the smoke to leeward. The *Majestic*

Below: The scene of carnage on the decks of *Le Tonnant*. Captain Dupetit-Thouars can be seen resting on his shattered stumps in a tub of bran (center) continuing to direct the hopeless fight against the British.
Overleaf: Another view of *Le Tonnant*. After her captain was killed, her crew committed his body to the waters of Aboukir Bay before surrendering.

groped its way down the blazing line and eventually engaged *L'Heureuse* but at a disadvantage. Her captain was killed, and under the command of a lieutenant the *Majestic* finally swung clear and began to fire on the bow of *Le Timoléon*, the last ship of the center division.

The first phase of the battle ended just after 2000 hours, during which time most of the ships retained their original positions and the battle moved farther down the line as more British ships came up. The arrival of the *Alexander* and the *Swiftsure* marked the next phase which revolved around the French center. The distance of these two ships from the remainder of the British squadron enabled them to function as a mobile reserve and attack the French line where it would be most effective. The last British ship, the *Culloden*, had grounded on a shoal near Aboukir Island. The frigate *Leander* and the sloop *Mutine* had been trying to help her get off but they now joined the fight with the *Alexander* and *Swiftsure*. The arrival of these fresh ships turned success into total victory.

Now that the van had been destroyed, the British ships began to move down the line to attack the center and especially to cluster around *L'Orient*. This massive ship was the keystone of the French defense and on her fate hung the victory. The *Swiftsure* anchored outside the line and the *Alexander* on the inside. Her cable cut by a shot, *Le Peuple Souverain* then drifted out of line, leaving a gap through which the *Leander* sailed to rake both *Le Franklin* and *L'Orient*. Heavily battered by the British ships around her, *L'Orient* caught fire near the mizzen chains, causing the *Swiftsure* to bring every gun to bear on that point. Early in the battle Brueys had lost both legs and was wounded in the head but he refused to be taken below, saying 'A French admiral dies giving orders'. He was seated in an armchair, tourniquets on both legs and giving orders, when a shot from the *Swiftsure* cut him in half.

The fire in the flagship spread and grew with heat so intense that sailors began to jump overboard and pitch melted in the seams of the neighboring *Swiftsure*. Since the fire would soon reach the large powder magazines on board, nearby ships began to move away and rescue *L'Orient's* sailors from the water. Still on board were Commodore Casabianca and his son, the subject of Felicia Hemans' popular poem, *The Boy Stood on the Burning Deck*. Most reliable reports state that Casabianca preferred to stay on board *L'Orient* and be blown up rather than leave the ship and abandon his wounded son, though others claim that both father and son jumped at the last minute but were drowned before they could be picked up. With a noise heard fifteen miles away in Alexandria, *L'Orient* simply disappeared in a mighty flash soon after ten. With her went half a million pounds in bullion, three tons of silver plate and the principal treasures of the Knights of Malta. At the Battle of the Nile Bonaparte lost much of his loot and financial base.

After the explosion firing ceased for almost ten minutes but was resumed by *Le Franklin*, flagship of Admiral Blanquet du Chayla. Blanquet had been severely wounded in the head

Above: Captain Dupetit-Thouars gave his final orders before he died: to nail the tricolor to the mast and to scuttle *Le Tonnant* before surrendering.

but continued to fight stubbornly. *Le Franklin* had been heavily battered in the attack on the center and at the time of the explosion the main and mizzen masts were down and all guns on the main deck dismounted. Only 80 fathoms to windward, the explosion of *L'Orient* had caused fires on *Le Franklin*, but these were extinguished and the action renewed. Nelson had now given the order for all ships to join the fighting at the center. *Le Franklin* was surrounded by enemy ships. With two-thirds of her company killed or wounded, Blanquet himself unconscious and only three lower deck guns still operational, the ship struck after an hour's fighting. Afterward Blanquet revived and inquired why the guns were silent. Informed that only three guns were still serviceable, he responded, 'Never mind, go on firing. The last shot may bring victory'.

Le Tonnant had also taken a severe pounding. At the time *L'Orient* blew up, she was razed to the deck and low in the water but still firing. Hit in both arms and with a leg shot off, Captain Dupetit-Thouars had himself placed in a tub of bran and continued shouting orders, the last of which, given just before he died, was to nail the colors to the mast and scuttle the ship before surrendering. *Le Tonnant* slipped her cable to avoid the explosion of *L'Orient* and at dawn was grounded a mile from her original position. As a gesture to his last order, the crew committed their captain's body to the deep before surrendering.

Until the explosion of *L'Orient* the last three ships in the French line – *Le Guillaume Tell*, *Le Généreux* and *Le Timoléon* – had scarcely fired a shot. Because of the thick smoke obscuring the line and his own wounds, Brueys was unable to give orders for the rear to assist the van and center. Admiral Decrès wrote in his diary, 'For four fatal hours the rear had seen nothing but the fire and smoke of the battle. It had remained at its moorings without firing a shot, waiting for signals that were not to be made, for the Commander-in-Chief had long lost the power to make his wishes known'. Villeneuve was later accused of standing by while the remainder of the fleet was destroyed, but since he was to leeward of the battle, how could his ships 'have weighed and tacked to get within range of the fighting before

the ships engaged had been disabled ten times over?' as he later wrote to Blanquet du Chayla. Had he weighed anchor, wind and current might well have carried him farther from the battle, in which case he would have been accused of flight. The only way one part of the line could have aided the others would have been for the engaged ships of the van and center to cut their cables and drift toward the rear. But when *Le Peuple Souverain* involuntarily took such an action because her cable had been shot away, it left a gap in the line through which the *Leander* then came. After the explosion of *L'Orient* Villeneuve shifted the anchorage of the rear farther to the east to wait for daylight to reveal the situation to him.

Dawn revealed that the first six ships of the line were in British possession, the seventh had blown up and there were six survivors. *Le Tonnant*, *Le Mercure* and *L'Heureuse* had all cut their cables to avoid the explosion and were aground. Of the smaller French frigates, *La Sérieuse* had run aground early in the battle, her rudder wedged by a piece of shot fired from a mortar on the poop of the *Goliath*. Although she should have kept well clear of the ships of the line, *La Sérieuse* had attacked the *Goliath*, causing Captain Foley to exclaim, 'Sink that brute, what does he here!' *L'Artémise* was sunk after the main battle. At noon Villeneuve opted for escape and got under way with the two remaining frigates, his flagship *Le Guillaume Tell*, *Le Généreux* and *Le Timoléon*. In an ineffectual attempt to turn, however, *Le Timoléon* ran aground and lost her foremast, after which her crew fired her and escaped ashore. The other four ships made good their escape.

Truly the most spectacular of Nelson's victories, the Nile virtually annihilated an entire fleet. A British sailor wrote that in the morning he '. . . went on deck to view the state of the fleets, and an awful sight it was. The whole bay was covered with dead bodies, mangled, wounded and scorched, not a bit of clothes on them except their trousers'. 'Victory is a name not strong enough for such a scene' was Nelson's comment. Of Brueys' thirteen ships of the line and four frigates, eleven of the line and two frigates were lost. Seven French captains and an admiral were killed and three captains wounded. Over 5000 French sailors were killed or missing, 3100 prisoners were put on shore and 400 others – officers, carpenters and caulkers – were carried off. Six French ships of the line were taken into British service and the rest stripped and destroyed as not worth repair. Bonaparte formed the survivors of the battle into a 'Nautic Legion' which served with his Army of the Orient but did not distinguish itself in any sense.

In the British squadron there were no ships beyond repair, but most had sustained heavy damage. Among nine of Nelson's battleships there was a total of two masts still standing but much of the loss in masts, spares and equipment was made good from the wreckage and prizes. Total British casualties were 218 killed and 677 wounded, a ratio of 1–10 in favor of the British. In addition to Nelson, three captains had been wounded and one killed.

The immediate result of the battle was to

Above: *L'Orient* in flames during the final stages of the Battle of the Nile.
Below: A contemporary broadsheet celebrating the British victory at the Nile.

ADMIRAL NELSON'S GLORIOUS VICTORY over the FRENCH FLEET off the MOUTH of the NILE on the 1st AUGt 1798.

(a) Monsr. Poussaeulque, the French Commissary viewing the Engagement from the Castle of Bequires. b.b. The French Line. c. The English Line.

ADMl. LORD NELSON.

CAPTn. BERRY.

The Leander Capt. T.B. Thompson which broke the French Line.

News my Boys from the Nile.

Christmas.

'Tis come, the day of health, the saving morn,
The Son of God, the babe of love is born.
Behold all Heaven descends upon the wing,
And choiring Angels, Glory, Glory, sing;
Glory to God, from whom such bounties flow,
And peace on Earth, good will to Men below.

An honest man is the noblest work of God.

Should some slight faults escape *my pen,*
With candor yet approve,
The boys can't reach the feats *of men,*
I'm sure at least I strove. ———

Henry Venicombe, Christmas, 1798.

Published 9th Novr 1798 by LAURIE & WHITTLE, 53 Fleet Street London.

CAPTn. DARBY.

CAPTn. WESTCOTT.
killed on board the Majestic.

The L'Orient blown up.

Success to the Jolly Tars of Old England. 64

maroon the Army of the Orient in Egypt and cut it off from supplies and reinforcements. Despite Bonaparte's reassurance, 'Come, come, gentlemen, our fate is in our own hands', the news from Aboukir Bay greatly depressed the French expeditionary force which found itself in a difficult defensive war as the people of Egypt became openly hostile. After a disastrous campaign in Syria, Bonaparte slipped back to France aboard a frigate, arriving on 9 October, 1799. The Army of the Orient finally surrendered to Britain in 1801. The Battle of the Nile thus directly rendered the Egyptian project abortive and prevented any attempts to launch attacks on India or British trade with the east.

British Supremacy in the Med.
Once again supreme in the Mediterranean, Britain's influence quickly revived and the strategic islands and bases again began to pass under her control. More important, the enemies of France were given new heart and a second coalition of Britain, Austria, Russia, Naples, Portugal and Turkey renewed the war against France. A Russo-Turkish fleet entered the Mediterranean to aid the British and while Bonaparte struggled in Syria, his country was hard-pressed with a series of military reverses. Dependent on army support and funds from conquered terri-

tories, the Directory in 1797 had hesitated to end both the war and its expansionist foreign policy, a policy to which Bonaparte was closely allied. In 1798 its policy of aggression was resumed at a moment when France had come to favorable terms with all its adversaries except Britain. The Egyptian expedition had revived the fears of the conservative monarchies about France, resulting in the 'Second Coalition' whose initial successes in turn completed the ruin of the already unpopular Directory. Although the débâcle of the Egyptian plan was the first serious reverse in his meteoric career, Bonaparte opportunely returned at a time when his beleaguered countrymen were ready to hail him as their savior and install him as First Consul of the Republic.

News of the victory was received with wild rejoicing in England. Nelson was created Baron of the Nile and Burnham Thorpe (his birthplace); he received a pension from Parliament and many other honors. By demonstrating through his own tactical genius that Bonaparte was not superhuman, Nelson had inspired the rest of Europe to continue to resist French expansion. He was now acknowledged as the greatest fighting admiral of the age, known for his swift and audacious attack and for exploiting to the fullest any success over the enemy. By his insistence on not just the defeat but the complete destruction of the enemy,

Above: Scene on the morning after the Battle of the Nile. *Le Timoleon* is ashore and burning (left); the battered *Le Tonnant* is striking her colors to *Theseus* and *Leander* (foreground)

he had revolutionized the whole concept of fleet action. The Nile also established a new tradition of leadership, for Nelson had proved another revolutionary proposition; that a resounding victory under sail could be won not through centralized command by written instructions, nor centralized command through signals, but by broad directives giving scope for independent action by subordinates. It is true that Nelson had excellent captains under his command, drawn from Jervis' Mediterranean fleet which was famed for its discipline and standards of seamanship. He was close to these men and remarked proudly after the battle, 'They are my children, they serve in my school and I glory in them'. Seven years later this same element of leadership was to be a vital factor at Trafalgar.

It would be incorrect to say that the Nile was a battle between comparable fleets. The French ships and crews were in poor condition, led by an admiral who had yet to command in battle. Pitted against him was the most brilliant and formidable sea fighter of the time in command of as fine a squadron of ships and crews as could then be had. Brueys has often been criticized for not meeting Nelson at sea and thus preventing the fatal concentration on one part of his line. Given the state of his ships and crews, however, it seems conjectural whether the French fleet would have fared any better under sail than at anchor. Where Brueys can be faulted is in not having guard frigates out and not preparing his defensive position properly. Criticism has also been leveled at Villeneuve, for had he sailed as soon as he saw Nelson's design, he could have captured the *Culloden* and prevented the *Alexander* and *Swiftsure* from entering the bay. Yet surely this was too much to expect of a thirty-five year old admiral who had been given no contingency orders. At best he could have been expected to order *L'Heureuse* and the remainder of the line to weigh at dawn, in which case five of the line might have escaped instead of two.

The Nile was the first encounter between the grandiose plans of Napoleon Bonaparte and the tactical genius of Horatio Nelson, an encounter from which the French Revolutionary Navy never really recovered. From 1798 the maritime ascendancy of Britain was definitely established and was to be one deciding factor in the struggle between France and Britain which lasted until 1815. The second encounter between the strategy of Bonaparte and the tactics of Nelson was to occur at Trafalgar in 1805, but this battle had not nearly the strategic significance of the Nile. As Bonaparte noted during his exile on St. Helena, 'I made one great mistake, my decision to invade Egypt'.

Trafalgar
1805

Early in the morning lookouts reported the masts of the enemy fleet some ten miles to leeward. Bringing with it the promise of fairer weather, daylight then revealed the enemy, now only nine miles distant. At 0540 the signal to form the order of sailing was made, followed at 0600 by 'prepare for battle'. Although he had carefully held the windward position during the night, the admiral was fearful lest the enemy decline battle as it had so often in the past and he ordered frequent signals to 'make more sail'. Having pursued this enemy fleet for almost six months, the admiral was in no mood to let it run back into Cadiz and so elude him again. His burning ambition was the complete destruction of his enemy and today, the 21st of October 1805, was the day that history had allotted. Horatio Nelson was to smash the combined Franco-Spanish fleet off Cape Trafalgar and put a final end to any notions that the usurper Napoleon Bonaparte entertained of challenging British mastery of the seas.

The encounter off Trafalgar that day was the final dénouement of a train of events set in motion seven years earlier. Finding the reputation of their brilliant young general, Bonaparte, to be 'excessive and opportune', the French Directory had tried to get him away from Paris by giving him orders to end 'the perfidy of the Cabinet of England' through invasion by the Army of England, poised on the shores of the Channel. Seven years later in 1805, this army was still waiting to cross the Channel. In the meantime, Bonaparte had abandoned the original plan to invade England as not feasible and embarked on his ill-fated Egyptian adventure. Returning to a France hard pressed by the armies of the Second Coalition in 1799, he had been welcomed as a savior by his countrymen who made him First Consul of the Republic on the fall of the unpopular Directory. An abortive royalist plot to kidnap him in 1804 had led Bonaparte to consolidate his power by establishing himself as Emperor Napoleon I.

The war between Britain and revolutionary France had been ended in 1802 by the uneasy Peace of Amiens but after a brief respite had broken out again in May 1803. By now accepting that decisive victory would not be possible until French troops were on British soil, Napoleon's immediate objective in 1803 was the invasion of England. He thus began to assemble four of his best veteran divisions, along with transports and supplies, at Boulogne. But in 1803 the plans for invasion were beset with the same problem which had caused Napoleon to declare invasion not feasible in 1797 – how to obtain control of the Channel for passage of the invasion army. It was not that France did not have adequate naval

Below: Salute to the *Victory* returning to Portsmouth under jury-rig from the Battle of Trafalgar.

forces. Ganteaume lay at Brest with 21 of the line while Latouche-Tréville, France's ablest admiral, had a further twelve of the line at Toulon. Smaller squadrons under Missiessy and Gourdon lay at Rochefort and Ferrol respectively. Already a sympathizer in 1803, Spain became a formal ally of France the following year, adding 32 of the line to Napoleon's forces. Since the Dutch fleet was also arrayed against Britain, the Royal Navy's margin of superiority was indeed slender.

At the outbreak of war Britain had adopted her traditional defense strategy which was to prevent a direct threat to the home islands, to maintain control of the Mediterranean, and to assist such allies as she may have had with her naval forces. A strong force under Admiral Cornwallis blockaded Brest and guarded the approaches to the Channel. Smaller squadrons blockaded Rochefort and Ferrol while the blockade of Toulon and other operations in the Mediterranean were directed by Nelson. The lesson of the French expedition against Egypt in 1798 which had followed the withdrawal of the British fleet from the Mediterranean had been well learned in London. As a result British naval strategy in the Mediterranean was to prevent the Toulon squadron escaping to succor the French colonies, launch a new threat against Egypt or join the Brest fleet in the Channel. Nelson's task was to check the French at sea, while Hugh Elliott,

Below: Admiral Pierre de Villeneuve, Nelson's adversary at Trafalgar.

British Minister to the Court of Naples, tried to stem their advance on land through diplomacy.

In the face of the British naval blockades, Napoleon's preparations at Boulogne stood so little chance of success that some of his contemporaries such as the Austrian Chancellor believed the whole project to be a camouflage for a contemplated struggle with Austria. In actual fact, however, the chief aim of Napoleon's naval strategy for over two years was to divert by a series of eccentric maneuvers enough British ships from the blockades to enable his naval forces to combine and concentrate in superior numbers in the Channel before sufficient British ships could re-assemble to pose a threat to the invasion flotilla. Trafalgar came at the end of the last of these maneuvers.

The core of all of Napoleon's naval plans was to have the Toulon fleet break out and combine with the Brest fleet in the Channel, along with such other ships as were able to escape the blockades. Knowing the British feared that, thwarted by the blockades in his plan to invade England, he would reopen his ambitions in the east, Napoleon encouraged their concern assiduously. Indeed, the threat was all the more effective because it was genuine; Napoleon was already looking beyond the defeat of Britain to the realization of his dreams of an eastern empire. As a first step in this deception French forces occupied Taranto, from which they could threaten Greece, Egypt and, above all, Sicily. Greece was the key to the maintenance of the Ottoman Empire, which all powers except France had a vested interest in preserving. French control of Egypt renewed the threat to India and the eastern trade routes while Sicily was essential to the maintenance of British maritime power in the Mediterranean. A series of clever intelligence plants by the French was contrived to further confirm the British in their fears for the east.

The first French maneuver to gain the Channel had been scheduled for February of 1804 but was aborted due to the royalist plot against Napoleon. A second plan had to be cancelled in the summer of that year because of the death of Latouche-Tréville, commander of the Toulon fleet, who was succeeded by Admiral Pierre de Villeneuve. A forty-two year old Provençal of aristocratic background, Villeneuve had been a pupil of Suffren, the greatest naval tactician ever produced by France. Surviving the revolutionary purges of the naval officer corps, Villeneuve had been promoted to the rank of rear-admiral at the age of 33 and had commanded the French rear at the Battle of the Nile in 1798. Initially criticized for his failure to support the center and van in that battle, his reputation had quickly shifted from goat to hero as it was realized that he was the one French admiral clever enough to have escaped the clutches of Nelson. After his brave and resolute defense of Malta against the British in 1800, his reputation was completely cleared of any stigma resulting from the Nile.

A third plan failed early in 1805 when heavy weather dismasted several of Villeneuve's ships and forced him back into Toulon only two days after his departure. Playing on the obsessive fear for the eastern Mediterranean which he

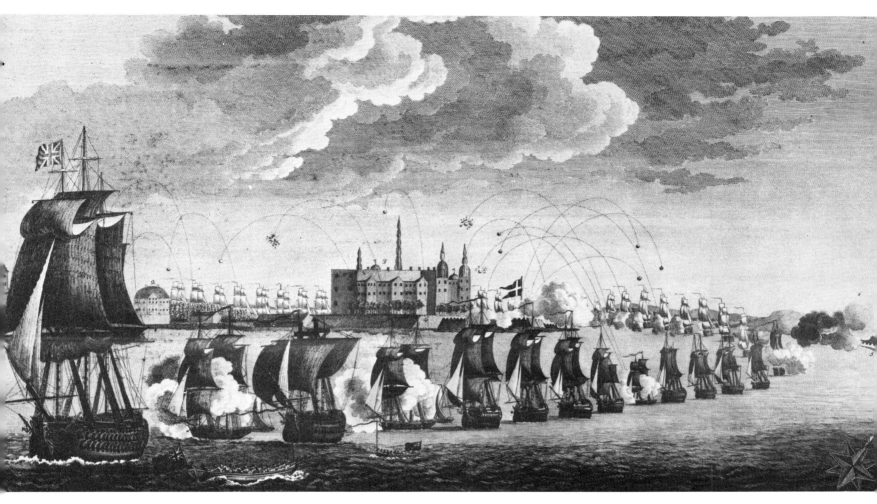

had held since 1798, strong efforts were made to convince Nelson that this expedition was headed eastward, efforts which did succeed in drawing him to Greece and Alexandria. 'I have not the slightest doubt but that the destination of the French Armament was Alexandria', Nelson wrote at this time. Although his tactics of deception had drawn Nelson to the east as planned and his fleet had been able to escape, Napoleon was becoming increasingly frustrated with his admirals. 'What is to be done with admirals who . . . hasten home at the first damage they receive?' and again, 'The great evil of our navy is that the men who command it are unused to the risks of command', he complained.

Thwarted so far in his plans to uncover Brest and launch the invasion, Napoleon conceived a last plan which is known as his 'grand design' for the campaign. Missiessy, who had already escaped to the West Indies as part of the previous plan, was ordered to remain there and in due course join other French forces off Martinique. Ganteaume was to take his fleet immediately from Brest to Ferrol where he was to drive off the blockade squadron, collect Gourdon's ships, and sail for Martinique to combine with Missiessy and Villeneuve. Returning to drive the British forces out of the Channel, he was to proceed to Boulogne where he was expected by mid-July with his combined fleet of over 40 sail. If Villeneuve failed to make the *rendezvous*, Ganteaume was to wait 30 days and then try to fight his way through to Boulogne with 25 instead of 40 sail. After breaking out of the Mediterranean, Villeneuve was to relieve the blockade of Cadiz and, having released the Spanish ships there, proceed to Martinique and wait 40 days for Ganteaume.

If Ganteaume did not appear, he was to land his 3500 troops, harass the British in the West Indies as best he could and then sail east, taking a station off the Canary Islands on the route to the East Indies. If Ganteaume had not appeared there after twenty days, Villeneuve was to return to Cadiz for further orders.

Napoleon felt that such maneuvers would draw not only Nelson's squadron but at least twenty other battleships in pursuit, if for no other reason than to save the rich West Indian sugar harvest. Thus the main point of the grand design was to create a diversion on the other side of the Atlantic to draw off enough British ships for the French fleet to gain temporary supremacy in the Channel. The grand design was a masterful plan on paper conceived by a brilliant military mind – but a mind which never understood that a

Above: Procession of the British Fleet past the Castle of Elsinore on its way to Copenhagen, 30 March, 1801. Nelson's bold stroke which destroyed the Danish Fleet frustrated Napoleon's plans to break British mastery of the seas.

Left: Admiral Sir Robert Calder, one of Nelson's few professional enemies, was nevertheless allowed to proceed home in his flagship to face court-martial on the eve of Trafalgar. Although this weakened Nelson's fleet, it was a characteristically generous gesture on the part of this great man.

Right: Rear-Admiral Cuthbert Collingwood, who led the second line in his flagship *Royal Sovereign* at Trafalgar. He was an able subordinate, much respected by Nelson.

Below: The Battle of Copenhagen, 1801. The Danish Fleet was a sitting duck which Nelson proceeded to capture and destroy. Rather than risk the destruction of their city by bombardment, the Danes capitulated immediately.

squadron of ships could not be moved about like regiments of soldiers. Ignoring the winds and obvious countermoves of the enemy, indeed the essential differences between land and sea strategy, Napoleon dismissed the possibility of serious opposition until the final combination of his forces gave him overwhelming superiority. What Napoleon's admirals thought of the grand design is not on record except for Admiral Decrès, then Minister of Marine, who wrote to the Emperor, 'It is grievous to me to know the naval profession, since this knowledge wins no confidence nor produces any result in Your Majesty's combinations'.

The scope of the grand design was not suspected by the British but the renewed activity in the blockaded French ports made them aware that some plan was afoot and hence increased their vigilance. Nevertheless, on 30 March Villeneuve again made his escape from Toulon in circumstances remarkably similar to those which had enabled Brueys to come out in 1798. A storm blew Nelson's watching frigates away from their station off Toulon just before Villeneuve came out, then by sheer luck the French admiral learned the position of Nelson's fleet from a

neutral merchantman. With eleven of the line, eight frigates and 3000 troops, Villeneuve altered his course away from Nelson and ran down the coast of Spain. At Cartagena Villeneuve found no Spanish ships ready to sail and passed Gibraltar on 8 April. Since the squadron of Sir John Orde blockading Cadiz had been shifted to the north to reinforce Cornwallis guarding the Channel, Villeneuve was able to add one French and six Spanish ships to his forces without hindrance at Cadiz. Arriving at Fort Royal, Martinique on 14 May, Villeneuve received new orders which instructed him to seize some of the British possessions in the West Indies and then return in 35 days to join Ganteaume off Ferrol. The latter had been as yet unable to leave Brest without a fight which would have contravened Napoleon's orders to avoid contact with the enemy. Shortly thereafter, Villeneuve learned of Nelson's arrival in the Caribbean and, having achieved the main objective of drawing a substantial enemy force away from Europe, decided to return at once with his eighteen sail.

Only on 4 April did Nelson learn of the French sortie, after which he lay off Sardinia waiting for more definite information. On the eighteenth he learned that the French had been seen off Cape de Gata ten days before and realized that Villeneuve was headed not east, but for the Atlantic with ten days start. On 5 May, at Gibraltar, Nelson confirmed that Villeneuve had set course for the Caribbean. Leaving a squadron of frigates and one of the line to guard the Mediterranean, he set sail for the West Indies with nine of the line, making the crossing in only ten days. Characteristically, Nelson planned to attack the French as soon as they could be located, overcoming the disparity in numbers with his tactic of overwhelming one part of the enemy line and then dealing with the disorganized and demoralized remainder. Due to misleading intelligence, the British squadron did not catch the French fleet before the latter had shaped a northerly course for Ferrol. Nelson, however, soon came to believe that Villeneuve had indeed returned to Europe but had not the slightest clue as to whether Ireland, the Channel, Ferrol or Cadiz was his adversary's destination. Since the first three possibilities lay within Cornwallis' sphere of operations, Nelson's obvious duty was to cover Cadiz and the possibility that Villeneuve might be returning to Toulon.

Sending the brig *Curieux* to England to report the latest news to the Admiralty, Nelson sailed east to Cadiz where he met Rear Admiral-Collingwood patroling with six of the line but found no sign of the enemy. Leaving Collingwood on his station, Nelson made a sweep to the west and north in the Atlantic searching for the elusive French squadron. By luck he learned from an American ship that Villeneuve had steered a northerly course, information which caused him to join Cornwallis immediately off Ushant on 15 August in case Villeneuve was making for the Channel. When he heard the latest news from Cornwallis, however, Nelson decided to return to England for some long overdue shore leave. Despite the fact that he was a relatively healthy man, 'afflicted only with seasickness, to which he was so accustomed that he did not allow it to trouble him', he had been at sea continuously for two years and desperately needed a rest.

The news given Nelson by Cornwallis was that the *Curieux* had spotted the French fleet on a northerly course for the Bay of Biscay, raising the possibility that the French objective was the Channel. When Sir Charles Barham, First Lord of the Admiralty, received this intelligence, he had immediately disposed the fleet to meet the challenge. Cornwallis was ordered to raise the blockade of Brest, leaving only a few frigates on guard, and with twenty of the line to cruise thirty leagues out to the southwest for a week to intercept the French. Sir Robert Calder's blockading force off Ferrol and Corunna was reinforced to fifteen ships. Thus two strong forces were prepared to intercept Villeneuve in the north, but these moves left Brest and Rochefort uncovered. The grand design was working, though not in the way originally planned. Napoleon was in a state of frustrated excitement and, writing to Decrès, said 'I do not understand Ganteaume's inactivity'. Messengers were sent to order the reluctant admiral to sail immediately for Boulogne. 'Hold command of this passage for three days, and you will give us the means of putting an end to British pretensions . . .' he implored Ganteaume. Unfortunately for the grand design, Ganteaume could not be persuaded to put out until 21 August, by which time Cornwallis was back on station to send the cautious French admiral running for shelter after an exchange of sporadic gunfire.

On 22 July while steering for Ferrol, Villeneuve had the bad luck to cross courses with Calder's fifteen ships 100 miles west of Cape Finisterre. The outnumbered Calder attacked but the action was inconclusive due to a thick mist. After two days of contact Villeneuve was able to make off south southeast and run into Vigo, having lost only two crippled Spanish ships which were made prizes by the hungry Calder. With many sick and seriously short of food and water, the French forces next put into Ferrol on 28 July where they were joined by the five ships of Gourdon and eleven Spanish ships. With over thirty sail at his disposal, Villeneuve was urged by Napoleon 'Leave at once. You have only to sail up the Channel to ensure our becoming masters of England'. But Villeneuve's ships were in poor condition after their long voyage and the clash with Calder while at least a

dozen of his ships were no more than floating barracks for the troops he still had aboard. His lack of enthusiasm showed in a letter to Decrès: 'When I leave here with 29 ships, I'm supposed to be capable of fighting about the same number. I don't mind telling you I shouldn't like to meet twenty'. Again prevented from trying for the Channel by northeast winds, and certain that by now the opposing forces had concentrated to block him, Villeneuve convinced himself that the grand design was no longer feasible and sailed south for Cadiz on 19 August, hoping that from southern Spain he could engage the enemy on better terms.

What a Navy! What an Admiral!

Already disillusioned with Villeneuve for retreating in the face of Calder's inferior force, Napoleon was now furious, 'What a navy! What an admiral!' As soon as word of Villeneuve's move to Cadiz reached him on 23 August, Napoleon knew that the grand design was a total failure and that the opportunity to invade England had been irretrievably lost. Even before this turn of events, however, he was aware that forces elsewhere were again combining against him and would have to be dealt with soon. English diplomacy had finally persuaded Russia and Austria to join in the Third Coalition against Napoleon. Well aware of the progress of the Third Coalition, Napoleon's 'cold and marvellous brain saw every movement; and like some gross spider he lurked in wait to dash at the first victim who should be entangled in his web'. Already quiet arrangements were being made to counter a potential Austrian attack on northern Italy and even before the naval war reached its climax, Napoleon knew that he would have to strike southeast to crush Austria before the winter. On 8 August Prussia was offered the bribe of Hanover

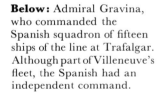

Below: Admiral Gravina, who commanded the Spanish squadron of fifteen ships of the line at Trafalgar. Although part of Villeneuve's fleet, the Spanish had an independent command.

in return for her neutrality and the order for the Imperial Guard to march from Paris to Boulogne was cancelled. News of Villeneuve's latest failure was just the last straw. The day following the receipt of this news the Grand Army began to move toward the Rhine in forced marches. 'I want to be in the heart of Germany with 300,000 men before anybody knows about it', wrote the Emperor. The War of the Third Coalition was to be decided not at sea or in England, but in Germany.

On 21 August the combined fleet of Villeneuve reached Cadiz. With only three of the line Collingwood did not dispute its entry, knowing that he would shortly be reinforced and that the combined fleet could not then escape without a battle. A hastily assembled British force established a full blockade close in. As an epidemic had ravaged the Cadiz area and food and naval supplies were known to be scarce, there was every hope that Villeneuve would come out before winter gales made maintenance of the blockade difficult. Villeneuve was in fact actually refused supplies by the local authorities until a direct order came from Madrid, and on 28 September Nelson himself arrived in the 100-gun *Victory*. Having been allowed but a short rest in England after his arduous two years at sea, Nelson had again been appointed to command in the Mediterranean since this was now the focal point of the naval war.

Since his victory at the Nile Nelson had fallen into some personal disfavor with the English establishment because of his highly visible affair with Emma, the young and beautiful wife of the elderly Sir William Hamilton, British Minister at Naples until 1800. But his rejection of his wife Fanny and Emma's unfortunate effect on his naval and diplomatic judgment in the aftermath

of the Nile tended to be forgotten even by the Establishment after his victory at Copenhagen in 1801. The battle in which he shattered a Danish fleet anchored in a well prepared defensive position and supported by strong shore batteries, Copenhagen finally established Nelson's reputation even among his enemies. From the outbreak of war in May 1803 until August 1805 Nelson was continuously at sea maintaining the blockade of Toulon and protecting the Mediterranean generally – no mean feat since the British had few bases east of Gibraltar. Hugh Elliott at Naples wrote of this period to Nelson '. . . to have kept your ships afloat, your rigging standing, and crews in health and spirits – is an effort such as was never realized in former times, nor I doubt, will ever again be repeated by any other admiral. You have protected us for two long years, and you have saved the West Indies.' Now the man of the hour in England, Nelson sailed for his post with the clamor of the populace ringing in his ears. 'I had their huzzas before – I have their hearts now!', he reportedly said to Captain Hardy of the *Victory* as they put out to sea. His reception by the bored and restive fleet off Cadiz was equally warm and sincere.

Preparations for the battle Nelson felt must soon come began on his arrival. His first act was to abandon Collingwood's close blockade and adopt his favorite tactic of the loose blockade. Regular meetings were held with the captains of the fleet, meetings at which Nelson expounded his tactics and discussed them thoroughly so that there could be no possibility of misunderstanding and a minimal need for signals. One element of Nelson's success as a commander was definitely his penchant for thorough preparation. The Admiral soon unveiled his plan for the battle which was accepted enthusiastically by his cap-

Above: The exposed Danish Fleet is destroyed by Nelson at Copenhagen in 1801.

Left: HMS *Victory*, Nelson's flagship, as she appeared at Trafalgar. A first-rate, 100-gun ship of the line, she can be seen today at Portsmouth, England, restored to her 1805 condition. It is not generally known the *Victory* fought in the American Revolutionary War, but at that time there were many differences in her appearance. **Top left:** Contemporary broadsheet giving a graphic impression of how Collingwood and Nelson used their columns to shatter the Franco-Spanish line. **Top right:** *Bucentaure* fires the first shots of the Battle of Trafalgar at *Victory* and the frigate *Euryalus*.

tains and became known in the fleet as the 'Nelson touch'. In this plan Nelson argued that the old line ahead tactic was outdated for several reasons. No day was long enough to arrange two large fleets in line ahead and still fight a decisive action. Mutual support was the aim of the line ahead but, said Nelson, mutual support could best be given by getting alongside the enemy rather than in the formal line of battle. Thus the order of sailing was to be the order of battle and the aim of the 'Nelson touch' was to break up the enemy line and force a general mêlée.

Distilling the 'Nelson touch' into a secret memorandum for his captains, Nelson wrote that he wanted to attack from the windward on an enemy in the traditional close-hauled line ahead, the standard situation confronting British admirals in actions against the French. The fleet was to attack in two, or if there were enough ships, three lines. The lee division under Collingwood was to be the main striking force, cutting through the enemy line about twelve ships from the rear and forcing a close action by the use of Lord Howe's maneuver. The weather division under Nelson was to contain the rest of the enemy fleet and prevent it from assisting the outnumbered rear which was being overwhelmed by the lee division. This was to be accomplished by threatening the van and center and then, when the lee division was fully engaged, attacking the enemy flagship and neighboring ships to paralyze the enemy command. Like the lee division, the weather division would approach in line abreast and use Lord Howe's maneuver to get close action. The goal was the capture or destruction of the entire enemy fleet.

Here Nelson was again applying his favorite tactic, that of overwhelming an inferior part of the enemy line while containing the rest, through a battle plan which was the ultimate expression of his genius. The essence of Nelson's plan was to cut the enemy line into three parts to enable him to concentrate his whole strength on little more than half of that of the enemy in a general mêlée while the remainder of the enemy lay powerless to intervene due to the wind. Collingwood was to have complete control of the lee division in accord with Nelson's belief that subordinates

should be given freedom to act within the confines of his broad plan. Nelson concluded his secret memorandum 'Something must be left to chance; nothing is sure in a sea fight beyond all others. Shot will carry away the masts and yards of Friends as well as Foes; but I look with confidence to a Victory before the Van of the Enemy can succour their Rear . . . In case Signals can neither be seen nor perfectly understood, no Captain can do very wrong if he places his ship alongside that of an Enemy.'

Crossing the 'T'.

At first glance the Nelson touch seems open to the criticism that in attacking the enemy line at right angles rather than parallel, the enemy was being given a highly desired opportunity to cross the 'T' of Nelson's two divisions. 'Crossing the T' is a naval maneuver in which a battle line sails at right angles across the head of the opposing line, thus blasting the enemy with its entire broadside from a postion at which the enemy can make little or no retaliation. In fact, however, Nelson's plan was to approach in line abreast rather than in line ahead, spreading his ships out as they approached the French line so that his 'T's' would not be crossed. As it was, however, he decided to attack with such speed that his ships never got into proper line abreast and appeared to be attacking in a disorganized line ahead. The ultimate weakness of the Nelson touch was that the first ships to attack would have some unpleasant minutes initially, taking the full brunt of enemy fire before the slower ships could come up to support them. At the time Nelson felt this was a risk worth taking to prevent the enemy from escaping, as French gunners still fired high to dismast rather than low to sink and the heavy swell that day was likely to make their aim erratic.

The British fleet consisted of three 100-gun ships including the venerable *Victory*, four 98's, one 80, sixteen 74's and three 64's. Four veterans of the Nile were among these vessels, the *Bellerophon*, the *Defence* and two captured French ships, the *Spartiate* and the *Tonnant*. Second in command was Cuthbert Collingwood, then 57, a senior and distinguished admiral who was a close friend of Nelson. He had made his reputation at the Glorious First and Cape St. Vincent. The other two flag officers in the fleet were Rear-Admirals Louis and the Earl of Northesk, Calder having been recalled to England. Shortly before the battle five of Nelson's ships under Louis had to be sent into the Mediterranean on convoy duty and to provision at Gibraltar. This left only 22 available on the day of the action, and the notion of a third group to act as a mobile reserve had to be dispensed with.

Having no further illusions about Villeneuve, Napoleon determined to replace him with Admiral Rosily. At the same time the Emperor decided he needed to take action against a joint Anglo-Russian force under General Sir James Craig which was threatening Italy from Malta. Rosily was dispatched to Cadiz bearing orders relieving Villeneuve but no advance notice of his dismissal was sent. His successor was apparently to be the bearer of the bad tidings. Instead,

Below: The day after Trafalgar remnants of the shattered French Fleet were able to make good their escape.

Villeneuve received orders to leave Cadiz immediately, pick up the Spanish squadron still at Cartagena, and then support General Saint-Cyr at Naples. Villeneuve was not to hesitate to attack any British force of equal or inferior strength. 'He reckons the loss of his ships as nothing, provided they go down in glory', wrote Decrès to which Villeneuve replied, 'As the Emperor thinks that only boldness and determination are necessary for success at sea, I shall satisfy him on that score'.

Why Napoleon did not notify Villeneuve of his dismissal is puzzling, but perhaps his contempt for the Admiral led the Emperor to believe that he would not leave port under any circumstances. Whatever the reason, it was to prove a costly error, for having heard rumors of his replacement and even talk of a court martial, Villeneuve put out to sea on 19 October after hearing that Nelson's fleet had been weakened by the detachment of Louis' squadron. In this final effort to redeem himself Villeneuve was to find that fortune dealt more harshly with him than the court martial and disgrace he feared to face. For while Napoleon was accepting the surrender of 30,000 Austrians at Ulm on 21 October, Villeneuve found Nelson waiting for him before the Straits of Gibraltar.

Villeneuve had 33 of the line, although fifteen of these were Spanish, and Napoleon allowed two of these as the equivalent of one French ship. There were command problems as well. Aside from the fact that the Spanish heartily detested the French, Admiral Gravina was not under Villeneuve's orders. He had an independent command with instructions to give the French assistance. In these circumstances it was difficult for Villeneuve to get agreement even on the order of battle. Agreement was finally reached, however, with the van to be commanded by Admiral Alava in the 112-gun *Santa Ana* and the rear by Admiral Dumanoir le Pelley in the 94-gun *Formidable*. The center was commanded by Villeneuve himself in the 80-gun *Bucentaure* with Admiral Cisneros second in command in the 130-gun *Santissima Trinidad*, the most heavily armed ship of its time. A twelve ship reserve was under Admiral Gravina in the 112-gun *Principe de Asturias*. The French forces consisted of four 80's and fourteen 74's while the Spanish had one 130, two 112's, one 100, two 80's, eight 74's and one 64; in all, a formidable fleet.

Having faced Nelson before at the Nile, Villeneuve knew what to expect of his opponent. 'The enemy will not trouble to form a line parallel to ours and fight it out with the gun', he wrote, no doubt remembering Nelson's hasty and unorthodox attack seven years earlier. 'He will try to double our rear, cut through the line, and bring against the ships thus isolated, groups of his own to surround and capture them.' As ever Villeneuve was pessimistic about his captains and the prospects: 'All we know how is to form a line, which is what the enemy wants us to do; I have neither the time nor the means to adopt other tactics, nor is it possible with the captains commanding the ships of the two navies . . .' And yet he was determined to fight, ending his written instructions to his captains with a quite Nelsonian turn of phrase, 'Captains must rely on their courage, and love of glory rather than upon the signals of the Admiral, who may be already engaged and wrapped in smoke . . . The captain who is not in action is not at his post'. On the basis of his experience at the fiasco of the Nile where he had received no orders from Brueys,

was Villeneuve in effect taking a leaf from Nelson's book and giving his captains some scope for independent action to forestall such a situation arising in his own command?

In accord with his ideas of the loose blockade, Nelson had been stationing his ships about fifty miles off Cadiz and relying on his frigates to warn him of any enemy sortie. About six in the morning of the 19th, he learned that the enemy was on the move and immediately set his own course to the southeast to get between them and the Straits of Gibraltar. Arriving off Gibraltar early in the morning of 20 October, he lay midway between Cape Trafalgar and Cape Spartel. Unfortunately for Villeneuve, the 19th had not been a very auspicious day for a sally, since light winds prevented all of his ships from clearing the harbor before dark, and the combined fleet was not really at sea before noon on the 20th. Four more hours were consumed by forming the battle order before the run toward the straits could begin.

'The Fleet is Doomed'.

After running in his regular line all night and sighting the British fleet between four and five in the morning of the 21st, Villeneuve suddenly decided about eight to reverse course to the north so that Cadiz would be under his lee if retreat became necessary. It was this maneuver which excited Nelson with the thought that the enemy might escape and caused him to sacrifice the finer points of his battle plan by rushing into action. The wind was light and the swell heavy, however, so that it was ten before the maneuver was completed. Gravina's reserve was now at the rear and Dumanoir's rear divisions had become the van. The Allied line was somewhat confused, being curved with many ships bunched two and three deep. With the enemy bearing down only five miles away, a Spanish captain was moved to remark to his first lieutenant, 'The fleet is doomed. The French admiral does not understand his business. He has compromised us all'.

The British ships in their two divisions were bearing down rapidly, as Nelson feared the enemy would deny him his battle by running for Cadiz. The growing swell suggested the approach of a storm which would be especially dangerous for damaged ships on a lee shore, so Nelson signaled to prepare to anchor at the close of the day, followed by the famous signal 'England expects that every man will do his duty'. Seeing the flags hoisted on the *Victory*, Collingwood growled impatiently, 'I wish Nelson would stop signaling, as we all know well enough what we have to do'.

His own column held back by the slower ships to the rear, Nelson was chagrined to see Collingwood in the 100-gun *Royal Sovereign* come under fire first, exclaiming 'See how that noble fellow, Collingwood, takes his ship into action. How I envy him!' And indeed, Collingwood was the picture of calm, walking the break of the poop 'with his little triangular gold-laced cocked hat, tights, silk stockings (easier to cut off in case of a leg wound) and buckles, musing over the progress of the fight, and munching an apple', as one of his lieutenants described the scene. Seeing

that the sixteenth ship from the end of the enemy line was the 112-gun *Santa Ana* of Admiral Alava, Collingwood made direct for her and gave her two broadsides at close range within five minutes which caused about one hundred casualties. The two ships were so close that they then locked yards while the French ship *Fougeux*, which had fired the opening broadside of the battle into the *Royal Sovereign*, continued a heavy assault on Collingwood's flagship which now lay between the two Allied ships. A furious muzzle to muzzle duel ensured between the three ships. Collingwood later said of the *Santa Ana* that she was a 'Spanish perfection . . . She towered over the *Royal Sovereign* like a castle. No one fired a shot at her but ourselves, and you have no conception how completely she was ruined'.

This proud assertion was not entirely accurate since the second British ship to come up, the 74-gun *Belleisle*, poured her first broadside into the *Santa Ana* and then locked yards with the *Fougeux* for an hour in another muzzle to muzzle contest. By that time the *Belleisle* was reduced to a wreck and was only saved from complete destruction by the intervention of fresh British ships. The *Fougeux* also badly blasted the 74-gun *Mars*, the next British ship to enter the battle, which was at the same time raked by the *Pluton*. Her masts and rigging destroyed, the *Mars* drifted away in an unmanageable state with heavy casualties and a dead captain. 'A cannon shot [from the *Fougeux*] killed [Captain] Duff, and two seamen who were immediately behind him. The ball struck the captain on the chest, and carried off his head. His body fell on the gangway, where it was covered with a spare colour until after the action', wrote one of the few survivors of the badly mauled vessel.

The remainder of the lee division continued to come up and one by one sail into the mass of the enemy rear. By one in the afternoon seventeen of the Allied ships had been separated from the center of their line and were assailed by the fifteen ships of the lee division in a confused mêlée. Having lost all of her masts and with Admiral Alava severely wounded, the *Santa Ana* struck at 1415. The *Royal Sovereign* was so badly damaged that she had to be taken in tow by the frigate *Euryalus* which also made the necessary signals since the flagship had not enough rigging left to hoist signal flags. The 80-gun *Tonnant* had fought a heavy action with the 74-gun *Algesiras* in which the French admiral Magon, second in command of the Allied rear, was killed and his ship captured by boarding. The flagship of Admiral Gravina, the 112-gun *Principe de Asturias*, was engaged first by the 74-gun *Revenge* and then other ships fought her assailants off. Mortally wounded, Gravina all too prophetically said 'I am a dying man, but I hope I am going to join Nelson'. The other ships fought at close range, often yard arm to yard arm, and with much boarding. At 1630 the lumbering 98-gun *Prince* finally came up to join the battle, though so late that she suffered no casualties at all. And at 1745 the French ship *Achille* blew up with most of her crew to end the battle of the rear, a battle which had gone exactly according to plan.

Fearful that the enemy would escape if he did

Opposite top: The French ship *Redoutable* under Captain Lucas engaged the *Victory* and fought with great gallantry. Her sharpshooters killed Nelson and inflicted heavy casualties on the *Victory's* crowded decks. **Opposite below:** The British 74-gun *Belleisle* was completely dismasted and sorely battered, but by 1615 hours she was surrounded by victorious British ships and captured enemies.

Above: Captain Harvey of the *Téméraire* led his seamen and marines in clearing the decks of enemy boarders.

rear, but instead of ordering Dumanoir to tack about he merely signaled that ships not engaged should get into action. Dumanoir therefore did nothing, as there were no British ships anywhere near him. Had he immediately come about, the *Victory* and the other lead ships might have been cut off and overwhelmed before the rest of the weather division could support them. As it was, the *Victory* drew heavy fire from a number of Allied ships, fire which riddled her sails and smashed her wheel so that she had to be steered by tiller from the gun room, an emergency measure requiring a number of hands urgently needed for other duties. 'This is too warm work, Hardy, to last long', remarked Nelson to his captain. Searching for Villeneuve's flagship, the *Victory* located her quarry about twenty minutes later. Passing under the *Bucentaure's* stern, the British flagship raked her with a treble-shotted broadside which sent shot crashing all the way to her bow, dismounting about twenty guns and causing nearly 400 casualties. Now being raked herself by other French ships, the *Victory* passed by the *Bucentaure*, leaving her disabled and easy prey for other British ships.

Immediately astern of the *Bucentaure* was the 74-gun *Redoutable* of Captain Jean Lucas, one of the finest fighting captains in the French navy. With a decided preference for obtaining his victories through boarding, Lucas had trained and equipped his crew well in the use of the grenade, cutlass, pistol and bayonetted carbine. At the opening of the action, Lucas had, as he wrote in his own account of the battle, 'laid the *Redoubtable's* bowsprit against the *Bucentaure's* stern, fully resolved to sacrifice my ship in defense of the

not attack immediately, Nelson ordered his faster ships to crowd on sail and engage the center. As Collingwood's division was already engaged, the columns were not even but the battle plan had always been intended to be flexible enough to meet whatever situation developed. At 1215, at the head of the weather division, the *Victory* came under fire from the *Heros*, whose gunners were aiming high in the French custom. At this moment Villeneuve in the 80-gun *Bucentaure* realized the need for his van to aid the center and

Left: The British '74 *Colossus* was heavily engaged between two Spanish 74s, the *Bahama* and the *Argonaute*, but with the aid of the *Swiftsure*, she was able to vanquish her opponents.

admiral's flag'. Although unable to prevent the *Victory* from raking the *Bucentaure* to such terrible effect, Lucas quickly closed with Nelson's now battered ship, laying his poop abeam his opponent's quarterdeck, after which the two ships became locked together by their rigging. Then, wrote Lucas, 'In this position the grapnels were flung. Those aft were cut loose but those forward held. Our broadsides were fired muzzle to muzzle, and there resulted horrible carnage'. The deck guns of the *Victory* were now almost silent from loss among their crews, but the lower deck guns were still active. Lucas ordered his lower gun ports shut and continued the battle with his deck guns. Both crews were anxious to board, but the English were prevented by French musketry and grenades which made the upper deck of the *Victory* all but untenable. The boarders of the *Redoubtable* were frustrated because both ships were rolling and by the height of the *Victory* which made it difficult to cross. They tried to lower the main yard of the *Redoutable* to serve

Below: Once Nelson and Collingwood broke the Franco-Spanish line, the battle developed into a series of individual actions. The Franco-Spanish navies were being destroyed piecemeal.

as a bridge but this attempt was foiled by the *Victory*'s marines who also wiped out a small party who got aboard by the anchors.

Having barely beaten off these boarding parties of her adversary, the *Victory* was finally saved when the *Téméraire* poured a devastating broadside into the *Redoubtable* which ended her capacity to fight. 'It would be difficult to describe the horrible carnage caused by that broadside', wrote Lucas. 'More than 200 of our brave lads were killed or wounded. I was wounded at the same instant'. A third British ship then came up and opened fire at pistol range. Locked together with the *Victory* and the *Téméraire*, whose two topmasts had fallen on the *Redoutable* in exchange for the latter's mainmast which lay on the *Téméraire*, Lucas' ship was a riddled wreck in less than half an hour. Out of control, the *Fougeux* had drifted up from the rear and also became entangled with the other ships. Having tried to prevent Nelson from passing through the Allied line and thus cutting it off from Cadiz, Lucas had precipitated the fiercest scene of the battle, but now, with all his guns dismounted or shattered and 522 of his complement of 643 killed or wounded, he struck his colors at 1420, secure in the knowledge that his ship would soon founder.

Before the battle began, Nelson had been advised to cover his uniform coat with its easily recognizable admiral's stars so that he would be less easy prey for sharpshooters but he had refused as, he said, he wanted to inspire the crew. While pacing the quarterdeck with Hardy about 1315, Nelson fell to the deck, hit by a marksman about fifteen yards away in the mizzentop of the *Redoutable* which had a contingent of Tyrolean sharpshooters aboard. The ball struck him in the chest and lodged in his spine. Groaning 'They have done for me at last. My backbone is shot through', he was carried below and died three hours later. His last words were 'Thank God I have done my duty'.

The 98-gun *Téméraire* had been the second ship of the weather division to come up and, after engaging the *Neptune* in a hot action, had drifted across the bows of the *Redoutable* and brought her port battery to the support of the hard pressed *Victory*. The *Fougeux* had drifted up from the rear but was broadsided to such effect by the *Téméraire* that she ran foul of her attacker. Unable to resist further, she was then boarded from the *Téméraire* while the four ships lay locked together. About 1415 Hardy managed to cut the *Victory* loose of the tangle and tried to head north,

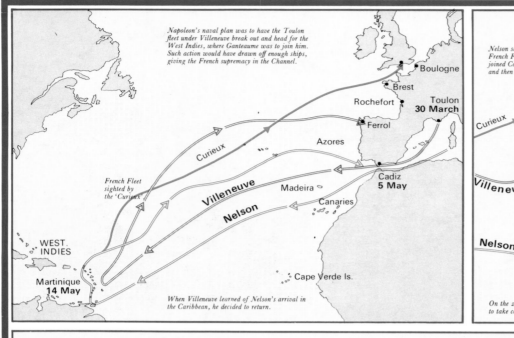

Napoleon's naval plan was to have the Toulon fleet under Villeneuve break out and head for the West Indies, where Ganteaume was to join him. Such action would have drawn off enough ships, giving the French supremacy in the Channel.

French Fleet sighted by the 'Curieux'.

When Villeneuve learned of Nelson's arrival in the Caribbean, he decided to return.

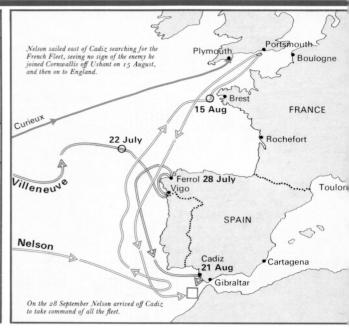

Nelson sailed east of Cadiz searching for the French Fleet, seeing no sign of the enemy he joined Cornwallis off Ushant on 15 August, and then on to England.

On the 28 September Nelson arrived off Cadiz to take command of all the fleet.

The Battle of Trafalgar, 21 October 1805

The situation at about 1200

- English
- French
- Spanish

After running in regular line all night and sighting the British fleet between 0400 and 0500 am on the 21st, Villeneuve ordered his ships to reverse course and to head north.

Collingwood, seeing that the sixteenth ship from the rear was the 112 gun 'Santa Ana' of Admiral Alava, he made direct for her and gave her two broadsides at close range within five minutes.

The French and Spanish ships was somewhat confused, being curved with many ships bunched two and three deep.

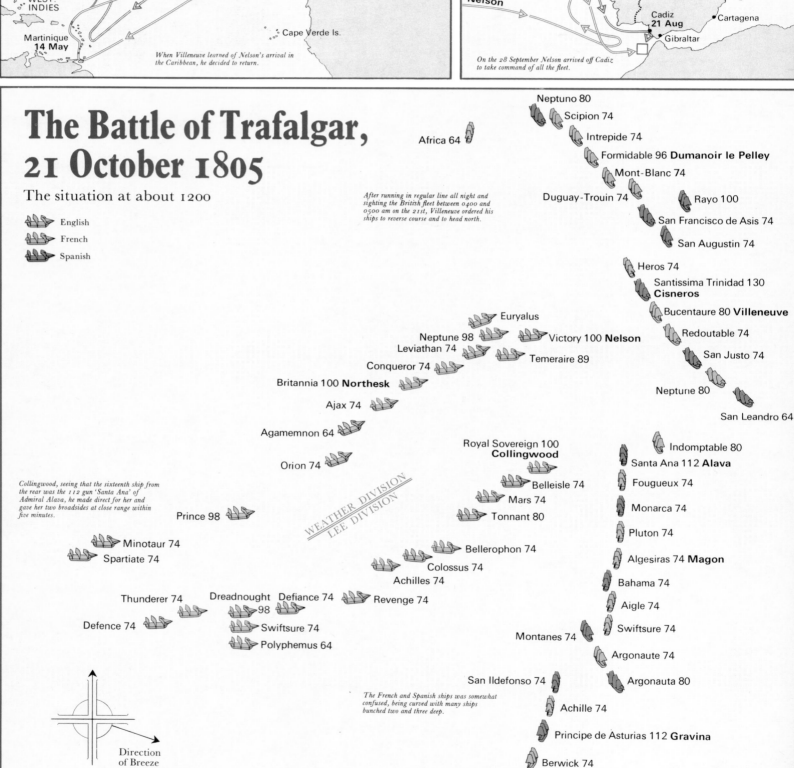

Direction of Breeze

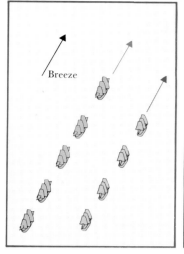

Breeze

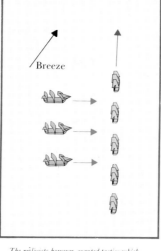

Breeze

At 1400 Villeneuve finally ordered the van, under Dumanoir, to tack around and support the centre. The wind was so light that it required two hours for the van to accomplish the manoeuver.

Neptuno 80

Scipion 74

Duguay-Trouin 74

San Francisco de Asis 74

Mont-Blanc 74

Intrepide 74

Rayo 100

Formidable 96
Dumanoir le Pelley

As Dumanoir approached the rear with five ships. Collingwood ordered six ships to form a line. Since Gravina was breaking off action and making his escape, Dumanoir decided to sail south about 1630.

The situation at about 1400

Heros 74

San Augustin 74

Africa 64

Neptune 80

Santissima Trinidad 130 **Cisneros**

Britannia 100
Northesk

Leviathan 74

Bucentaure 80 **Villeneuve**

Spartiate 74   Minotaur 74

Ajax 74

Conqueror 74

Victory 100 **Nelson**

Agamemnon 64

Temeraire 89   Neptune 98

Redoutable 74

San Justo 74

Fougueux 74

San Leandro 64

Orion 74

Santa Ana 112 **Alava**

Mars 74

Indomptable 80

Royal Sovereign 100
Collingwood

Tonnant 80

Pluton 74

Algesiras 74 **Magon**

Belleisle 74

Bahama 74

Swiftsure 74

Aigle 74

Monarca 74

Colossus 74

Bellerophon 74

Argonaute 74

Achille 74

Prince 98

Dreadnought 98

San Juan de Nepomuceno 74

Montanes 74

Argonauta 80

San Ildefonso 74

Revenge 74

Achilles 74

Thunderer 74

Principe de Asturias 112 **Gravina**

Defiance 74

Berwick 74

Polyphemus 64

Defence 74

Swiftsure 74

Direction
of Breeze

At 1735 the French ship 'Achille' blew up with most of her crew which heralded the end of the battle of the rear.

but with her masts badly damaged, her rigging in shreds and badly holed in the hull, the *Victory* could take no more part in the battle and had to anchor. Later Hardy bore the news of Nelson's death to Collingwood who took command, transferring his flag to the *Euryalus*.

By 1400 other British ships were coming up and surrounding the crippled *Bucentaure*. At this point Villeneuve belatedly realized Dumanoir's failure to support him and finally made the signal which he should have made several hours earlier. The wind, however, was so light that it required more than two hours for the van to tack around and some ships accomplished this maneuver only by using boats. Ten ships finally came around and bore down on the battle. By this time, however, the *Bucentaure* had been so badly mangled that 'her upper decks and gangways heaped with dead and wreckage . . . presented an appalling spectacle'. Displaying throughout the calmest courage, Villeneuve finally exclaimed 'The *Bucentaure* has played her part, mine is not yet over'. But unable to transfer his command to a fresh ship from the van because all of the *Bucentaure*'s boats had been destroyed, Villeneuve realized that he was trapped aboard a ship unable to defend itself while the rest of his fleet continued the fight. Accepting the inevitable, he allowed the colors to be struck rather than see his crew uselessly slaughtered.

As Dumanoir's ships approached the battle the resistance of the Allied center had already been broken, but ten fresh ships could have saved the day since many British ships were now too badly mauled to fight. The action at the rear was still hot as Gravina held his own despite the fact that he was badly wounded and the concentration of enemy ships around him increasing. Taking as his first target the last ships of the weather division to come up, the *Spartiate* and the *Minotaur*, which were heading to protect the helpless *Victory* and *Téméraire*, Dumanoir quickly found that these ships .were supported by the *Ajax*, *Orion* and *Africa*. In the face of this firepower and the fact that his commander-in-chief was now a prisoner, Dumanoir moved toward the rear with five ships. The other ships of the van moved to leeward. Seeing this new threat developing, Collingwood ordered six of his freshest ships to haul out and form a line to windward. Since Gravina was now breaking off the action and making his own escape, Dumanoir found it prudent to sail south about 1630.

The End of the Battle

With the departure of the French van, the battle was now over. The remainder of the day was given to the taking and manning of prizes and assisting the more badly damaged British ships. Of the seventeen ships engaged by Collingwood, eleven were prizes and one had blown up. Nelson's column had taken six. Dumanoir had escaped with four ships to the south while four from the van and four from the center had joined three survivors of Gravina's division and made off to the northwest. The combined Allied fleet had lost eighteen of its 33 ships and suffered 5860 dead and 20,000 prisoners. All of the prizes were totally or partially dismasted and in general

heavily damaged. By his failure to observe Nelson's earlier order to anchor at the end of the day, Collingwood saw all but four of his prizes sunk, wrecked or retaken by their own crews in the storm which blew up after the battle. No British ship was taken by the enemy but there had been heavy losses in masts and rigging, not to mention 1690 casualties. The escaping Allied ships made their way into the safety of Cadiz except for Dumanoir's four ships, which were all taken in a heavy fight with five of the line under Sir Richard Strachan off Ferrol on 2 November.

Thus ended not only the last fleet action of the Napoleonic Wars but the last major engagement between sailing fleets at sea. The radical tactics of Nelson had made Trafalgar the most decisive tactical victory ever achieved in an action in which both fleets had freedom to maneuver. But it would seem that few of Nelson's contemporaries appreciated the brilliance of the 'Nelson touch'. Although grasping that it had forced the enemy to stand and fight at a disadvantage, they tended to see it merely as a triumph for the principles of close action and support. Perhaps bemused by Nelson's last minute decision to rush into action

without forming his two divisions into proper line abreast, their lack of understanding of the 'Nelson touch' led them to carry the principle of close action to extremes in the years following Trafalgar. Not realizing how carefully tactics and gunner methods had been matched in that epic encounter, they proceeded to sacrifice the long range hitting power of their ships to make them more formidable at short range by increasingly arming them with carronades rather than cannon. Thus British ships could only develop their full fighting power in close, a fact which cost the British navy unnecessary losses in the American War of 1812. In the era of the *Permanent Fighting Instructions* tactics had been devised without regard to gunnery doctrine, but after Trafalgar new gun armaments were to be developed to a state which demanded battle conditions not always able to be provided by tactics.

Trafalgar was an excellent example of the superiority of British seamanship and gunnery in that period. In the light wind of that day, the British ships were better sailed and maneuvered and their gun crews better trained. Nevertheless

the French defeat at Trafalgar can be said to have been due as much to their own errors as to the skill of their opponents, a statement also true of the Nile. Villeneuve had failed to signal his van in time, a failure difficult to understand since he was well aware of the style of Nelson's tactics. Dumanoir exercised no initiative about getting into action and had to be ordered to fight despite Villeneuve's pre-battle admonition that captains not in action were not at their posts. Even then Dumanoir allowed his force to split into two parts, when as a compact unit it could have made a significant impression on the battle at that time. Holding the windward position, Gravina on seeing the attack developing should have brought his twelve ships up to support the center, which was Villeneuve's original concept of the reserve division, but instead he remained at the rear. The French cause was also weakened by the lack of enthusiasm of their Spanish allies about the war in general and the French in particular. Indeed, several Spanish ships had to be fired on by the French to keep them in the line and when captured, the Spanish crews offered to help their captors man their guns!

Above: The scene on board the *Victory* just after Nelson was wounded. In the foreground a marine and a midshipman take aim to kill the French sharpshooter, but all around the gun crews continue at their stations.

Left: The end of the battle. Remnants of the Franco-Spanish fleet make their escape with the British in pursuit. **Right:** Nelson was removed to the cockpit to join the scores of casualties already there Nelson already knew that he was mortally wounded. He tried to cover his decorations so that the sailors would not recognize him as he was carried below. **Below:** By the closing stages of the battle, *Victory* was heavily damaged, particularly in her rigging.

Without Nelson, however, there would have been no such victory. It was Nelson's strategy of the loose blockade which brought Villeneuve out of both Toulon and Cadiz, not the close blockade of Collingwood. With the same style of leadership he had displayed at the Nile, Nelson again inspired the best from his captains and crews. Disregarding dogma, his tactics enabled his force to engage and vanquish a numerically superior enemy. Obsessed with annihilating his enemy, he was contemptuous of what he called a 'Lord Howe victory'. He believed that the Glorious First of June had been a strategic failure and only a half-developed tactical success. His goal at Trafalgar had been the capture or destruction of twenty enemy ships, and with eighteen actually taken the goal was very nearly achieved.

In addition to a posthumous earldom, a grateful nation gave Nelson a state funeral at St. Paul's Cathedral in London and transmuted his fame into a schoolboy legend of impetuous daring. In the words of a modern historian of this period, 'The breadth and vigor of his strategic conceptions, which constituted the real proof of his genius, formed only a small part of the legend, his flashes of un-British emotionalism and theatri-cality were carefully edited, and the ill-savor of his affair with Lady Hamilton was passed over in embarrassed silence.' Collingwood took over Nelson's burdens as commander-in-chief in the Mediterranean until his own death five years later. Fate continued to deal cruelly with Ville-neuve, whose main failing had been to recognize that the French with their poorly fitted vessels and sickly and ill-trained crews could not defeat the British even when numerically superior. After four months in England Villeneuve was repatriated to France in 1806, and Napoleon ordered him not to come to Paris. Having survived the battle he could not survive disgrace and committed suicide the next day. 'He was a gallant man, although he had no talent', remarked Napoleon and ordered him buried without honors.

Trafalgar did not save England, as the instigator of the train of events leading to the battle had broken his camp at Boulogne two months earlier and rushed across Europe in forced marches to meet the threat on land of the Third Coalition. First defeating the Austrians at Ulm on 17–21 October, Napoleon decisively wrecked the coalition on 2 December at Austerlitz where in a brilliant piece of generalship and deception

he defeated the Austrians and Russians. This victory forced Austria to withdraw from the coalition and convinced Prussia, then holding the balance of power in Europe, to remain neutral for the time being. Trafalgar thus occurred months after Napoleon had accepted the grand design as a failure.

Nor did Trafalgar destroy the naval power of Napoleon: the Brest fleet was still intact and a new force was soon created at Toulon. In fact, Napoleon had at his disposal a combined total of 62 French, Spanish and Dutch ships of the line. Depending on the success of his diplomacy, more could have been added from Russia, Sweden and Denmark, a possibility which led the British to destroy the Danish fleet at Copenhagen a second time in 1807 to prevent it from falling into French hands. Already disillusioned with his admirals and the failure of his naval strategy, Napoleon was convinced by Trafalgar to end his attempts to contest supremacy of the seas with the British. The remains of the navy and the large fleet of privateers were used only for commerce raiding, which was sufficiently destructive but could not be a decisive factor in the overall struggle. After Trafalgar French arms were confined to the continent, and it was on the continent

that Napoleon would have to be defeated. Napoleon was not in fact defeated until 1814 when a Russian army marched into France, occupied Paris and captured him. Although in his last exile at St. Helena, Napoleon said 'In all my plans I have always been thwarted by the British Fleet', it was not in fact British supremacy at sea which ultimately undid him but Russian bayonets and the unpopularity of his administration in France.

Although when he read the dispatch of the victory, George III was speechless for a full five minutes, no doubt causing some consternation among his entourage. Trafalgar was probably not even fully appreciated in England at that time. The news of the victory was overshadowed by the news of the death of Nelson, who was truly a national hero. The momentous events on the continent such as Ulm and Austerlitz, the end of the Holy Roman Empire, the eclipse of Austria as a military power, and the short-lived Prussian alliance with France must have seemed far more important to the people of England. The strategic results of Trafalgar were perhaps minor compared to those of the Nile, but its effect on naval tactics and leadership made it later recognized as one of the epic events in naval history.

Below: England was plunged into grief by the death of Nelson, despite the rejoicing over the good news of his victory. His body was brought up the Thames to lie in state at the Royal Naval Hospital, Greenwich, before being taken to its final resting place in St. Paul's Cathedral.

Navarino
1827

The Battle of Navarino in 1827 is interesting not only for what it reveals about the state of naval warfare at the time, but because it marked the first successful break with the Metternich System after the Greek Revolution. Therefore it is a most significant event in political and diplomatic as well as naval history.

From 1793 to 1815 the French Revolutionary and Napoleonic wars kept Europe in an almost constant state of upheaval, upheaval which caused great dislocation in European society generally. Interrupted once by the hundred-day escape of Napoleon from his exile on Elba, the powers which had fought France for so long approached the task of reconstructing Europe through the Congress of Vienna in 1814–15. The Congress hoped to restore international stability and security by re-establishing a balance of power among the large states, imposing certain checks on France, and restoring social stability in those states disorganized by the French Revolutionary wars. Britain, Prussia, Russia, and Austria formed the Quadruple Alliance (enlarged to the Quintuple Alliance with the admission of France in 1818) to maintain the agreements reached among the powers by armed force for twenty years. Having sent Napoleon to a final exile on St. Helena, redrawn the map of Europe and provided the machinery for the perpetuation of their agreement through periodic 'congresses', the powers of the Quadruple Alliance then turned to concentrate on their respective domestic situations. After the trauma and disorder of prolonged war, the desire everywhere was less for freedom and social justice than for the restoration of social order and tranquillity. With conservative leaders firmly in control, the members of the alliance pursued a reactionary and repressive policy both domestically and internationally in the years following the peace. An international system of reaction had been established by the powers under the leadership of the Austrian Chancellor Clemens von Metternich in an effort to recreate the *status quo ante bellum*. The first successful break with this system resulted in the Battle of Navarino in 1827.

The French Revolution had stirred deep feelings of nationalism which could not easily be stemmed by the reactionary policies adopted by the conservatives. In 1820 revolutionary disturbances occurred in Spain, Portugal and parts of Italy. In addition to much political agitation in other countries, there were attempted assassinations of the heads of state in Britain and France. The conservatives became convinced that the radicals in every country were united and working jointly for revolution in much the same way that the European monarchs were united in the cause of reaction. These threats to the system moved the members of the alliance to action in the form of military intervention in both Spain and Italy. Though not without some

Below: The town of New Navarin and a French '74 in the bay three days after the battle.

strains the system proved adequate to deal with these outbreaks, but when the Greeks rose in revolt against their Turkish masters in 1821, the powers were presented with a diplomatic crisis of major proportions. For the next ten years, no political problem was more widely discussed in the chancelleries and press of Europe.

Greece had been under Ottoman domination since the fifteenth century, but this once powerful empire was in a state of advanced disintegration by the early nineteenth century. The entire administrative régime of the empire, when it functioned at all, was hardly more than one of organized brigandage. The Sultan had only the loosest hold over the outer parts of the empire such as Albania, Egypt, Syria, Arabia and North Africa. The weakness of the Ottoman Empire was well summed up by the French Ambassador to Constantinople who remarked in 1807, 'To make an alliance with Turkey is the same as putting your arms around a corpse to make it stand up'. Although Turkish exploitation of the Serbian and Greek peoples of southeastern Europe had never been thorough or uniform, it was there that the first revolts broke out. In a prolonged struggle from 1804 to 1817 the Serbs triumphed over the Turks without foreign help and established their own autonomous state. The Serbian revolt attracted little attention in Europe, but the Greek revolt of 1821 became an increasingly popular issue.

Taking the Turks by surprise in March of 1821, the Greeks enjoyed a fair measure of success militarily and soon set up their own government at Nauplia in the Peloponnese. Despite severe strife within their own ranks, the rebels con-

tinued their military advance until 1825 when a new phase of the war began. Although the Sultan Mahmud II had hoped to crush the revolt without outside help, his Turkish forces had proved hopelessly incapable and now, driven to the wall by the Greeks on land and sea, the Sultan had to ask the Pasha of Egypt for help.

An Egyptian of Albanian descent, Mehemet Ali was a man of strong character who had risen from humble origins to become Pasha by sheer merit. The British Foreign Secretary, Lord Dudley, described him in 1827 as 'wary, astute, neither a fanatical Mussulman nor a devoted servant of the Porte' and 'guided almost entirely by his personal interest and ambitions'. Mehemet Ali at this time was establishing Egypt as a kingdom virtually independent of his master in Constantinople. Having witnessed the Napoleonic invasion of Egypt, Mehemet Ali also had great respect for the military prowess of the Europeans. He actually employed many former Napoleonic officers who, glad of the chance for new careers, were advising his army and creating a modern navy which he saw as the foundation of his future power as a nationalist leader.

Although the Greeks had the same object as he – independence from Turkey – Mehemet Ali saw the Greek Revolution as a chance to extend his own power still further. He bore no grudge against the Greeks, but he still was not ready for a final break with the Sultan and decided to exploit the situation for his own benefit. His condition for aiding the Turks was governorship of the Peloponnese and command of the army and navy with 63 warships, 100 transports and 16,000 troops for his son Ibrahim. Tough, experienced, a

Left: On the left, the Turkish and Egyptian fleets; center foreground, HMS *Asia*, Codrington's 84-gun flagship. Behind *Asia* are HMS *Dartmouth*, a 44-gun ship commanded by Captain Sir T. Fellowes, the 28-gun *Talbot*, commanded by Captain Soencer, and *Zebra*, an 18-gun sloop under Captain Cotton.

severe disciplinarian and man of his word, the thirty-five year old Ibrahim was described by his father as 'the lion of the brave, whose counsel hath always proved fortunate'. By his own admission Ibrahim's one weakness was a complete lack of naval experience, but since the Greeks had only privateers and fireships, this was not seen to be a problem.

Success of Ibrahim Pasha

At first Ibrahim held control only of the land forces as the fleet was under Khosrow Muhammad, the Turkish commander-in-chief. The two commanders intrigued against each other systematically, but even so Ibrahim's campaign was very successful. Landing in January 1825 at Modon (modern Methoni), he devastated the province with both ability and ruthlessness. In May 1825 he captured the little fort on the Bay of Navarino with its excellent natural harbor on the west coast of the Peloponnese in southern Greece. With Navarino as his base, Ibrahim's object was ultimately to capture Ydra, the last Greek-held island able to man a fleet. At sea the Greeks had been fighting their Turkish enemies on more equal terms. The island captains and crews were skilled and daring, experts in the use of the fireships, and aided by a number of British officers who had joined the Greek cause. The fall of Ydra would complete the destruction of Greek power at sea and essentially finish the revolt, except for mopping-up operations. In January 1827 Ibrahim finally won the war of intrigue and displaced Khosrow, becoming himself supreme commander of both land and sea forces.

From its beginning the revolt had been marked on both sides by horrible butchery which raised sympathy in Europe, especially among the Russians who were co-religionists of the Greeks. In the belief that the Balkans were a special concern for Russia, Czar Alexander I proposed immediate intervention by armed force. Correctly suspecting that Alexander wanted to use the affair to continue the long standing Russian advance into the Balkans, Metternich insisted that the insurgents were simply rebels against the established order and that the rebellion should be allowed to burn itself out 'beyond the pale of civilization'. In this stand he had the support of the British Foreign Minister Castlereagh and, after 1822, of Castlereagh's successor George Canning who had virtually withdrawn England from the alliance in opposition to the intervention in Spain. As Foreign Minister Canning was a public champion of the cause of national self-determination, he stoutly opposed any intervention, remarking: 'Things are getting back to a wholesome state again; every nation for itself and God for us all'. The outlook of Canning tended to be quite different from that of Castlereagh and the other conservative statesmen in that Canning felt British interest was more often on the side of revolution than against it. Although the Russians tried to push toward war over it, the Greek question dragged on in European diplomacy with various negotiations, none of which produced action until 1826.

While making no progress enlisting diplomatic or military support from the European powers, the Greek rebels did capture the popular imagination in Europe and America in a powerful way. Money, supplies and volunteers poured in to give

in the conflict. The story was spread that Ibrahim was depopulating the Peloponnese so that it could be resettled with Moslem immigrants from North Africa, thereby creating a Moslem state within Europe. Known in diplomatic circles as the 'Barbarization Project', the story was soon found to have no basis in fact but not before an order had been sent to Sir Harry Neale, British commander in the Mediterranean, instructing him to inform Ibrahim that if such a project was contemplated His Majesty's Government would use force to prevent its implementation. Neale carried out the order and transferred it to his successor Sir Edward Codrington in case of a possible recurrence.

It is almost certain that Mehemet Ali and his son entertained no such notion as the 'Barbarization Project'. As good Moslems they tolerated Christians and as Ottoman administrators they saw the Greeks as subjects to be exploited in a humane way. Probably disliking the Turks even more than the Greeks did, father and son surely wanted peace and obedience rather than depopulation. It is also probable that the Egyptian break with the Sultan was already being planned. Such an action had two requirements: a strong independent navy for which European help was needed and a speedy end to the Greek rebellion which was not served best by trying to exterminate the Greeks. Ibrahim's battle orders for 1827 were thus to destroy the remaining Greek naval capacity by capturing Ydra, the one remaining island, with an effective fleet. Toward this end an Egyptian fleet of 60 warships and 40 transports left Alexandria on 5 August bound for Navarino. A Turkish force of 23 warships arrived soon after and preparations began for the expedition against Ydra.

British policy now also changed direction. Moving away from his policy of neutrality and firm opposition to any intervention, Canning came to believe it to be in Britain's commercial and political interest for the Greek question to be settled. By 1823 Britain had recognized the Greeks as belligerents and opened diplomatic relations, mainly to stop them from preying on British shipping in the Mediterranean. Convinced that the Greeks would sooner or later gain their freedom, Canning did not want their gratitude to go entirely to Russia. His policy thus became to curb Russian penetration and influence in the eastern Mediterranean, preserve the Ottoman Empire and still keep Britain out of war. Becoming impatient with the lack of response from Turkey to various proposals for mediating the issue, Canning proposed to the Czar that they take joint action to force mediation between the two contending sides, if possible with the other members of the alliance. Despite the opposition of Metternich and the Prussians, France agreed to the proposal as well.

The policy agreed upon by the three powers was formalized in the Treaty of London, signed on 6 July, 1827. In essence, the treaty called for an armistice followed by mediation by the three allies. If either the Greeks or the Turks rejected the armistice, the Allies would forcibly intervene to prevent further hostilities. If the Sultan did not accept the mediation within one month, the Allies

sustenance to the revolt. Pitting occidental against oriental, Christian against Moslem, the struggle had much appeal to a generation trained in classical studies. 'We are all Greeks', wrote Shelley. More significantly, however, it was only the Greek revolt which kept alive the liberal ideal in Europe after the other nationalist movements had failed. Romanticized in the verses of Victor Hugo and Chateaubriand in France and Shelley and Byron in England, Philhellene sentiment was a strong force in the Western countries, the more so after Byron himself was killed fighting for the Greeks at Mesolonghi in 1824. The significance of Philhellenism is that at a time when reaction prevailed domestically and memories of the interventions in Spain and Italy were still vivid, European public opinion became permeated by a liberal ideal symbolized by the Greek struggle and ultimately forced the governments of France and Britain away from the Metternich System.

The Greek guerrilla bands being no match for his disciplined troops, Ibrahim continued the systematic reduction of the country. Mesolonghi surrendered after a bloody siege in 1826 and Athens in 1827. Reduced to a few fortified towns and islands, the Greeks appealed in vain to the powers and even tried to place themselves under British protection. At the same time the new Czar of Russia, Nicholas I, who had no use for the Quintuple Alliance and no intention of taking orders from Metternich as had his predecessor, began an active anti-Turkish policy. Among other things, the Russians seized upon the devastation of the Peloponnese by the troops of Ibrahim to try to draw British policy more toward intervention would each send a consul to the Greeks which would eventually lead to recognition of the Greek state. The terms were to be communicated to the Sultan through the Allied ambassadors in Constantinople and to the Greeks by the admirals of the Allied squadrons in the Mediterranean. Although the British and French still wished to avoid conflict, the Russians were again actively thinking of war and had begun to prepare a fleet in June under Count de Heyden to join the British and French squadrons under Codrington and the French commander, Count Gauthier de Rigny.

Diplomacy Before Battle

The admirals of the Allied squadrons were ordered to agree on a means of communicating the terms to the Greeks and then to do so 'only in concert and in such a manner that none of them may seem to have the pre-eminence over the other'. If the Greeks accepted the terms the admirals were then to consider means for ending the conflict. If the Sultan rejected the terms the admirals were to treat the Greeks as friends without taking an active part in the hostilities and were to use their combined forces 'for the purpose of preventing all Turkish or Egyptian succours of men, arms, vessels, and warlike stores, from arriving in Greece or the islands of the Archipelago'. Should the Greeks refuse or break the armistice, 'the united squadrons shall endeavour to maintain the armistice without taking part in hostilities between the contending parties'. But the instructions continued, 'You are aware that you ought to be most particularly careful that the measures which you may adopt against the Ottoman navy do not degenerate into hostilities'. As Canning naively wrote, 'the spirit of that agreement was peaceful interference, recommended by a friendly demonstration'. Whatever the politicians may have thought, the admirals knew better. The Russians were frankly preparing for war. Reading these vague and contradictory instructions, both Codrington and de Rigny felt that hostilities were practically inevitable and that the Treaty of London would sooner or later lead to the independence of Greece. In accordance with their instructions, they therefore went to Nauplia to present the terms of the treaty to the Greeks and to try to persuade them to end their squabbling and prepare the rudiments of a government.

The efforts of the Allied ambassadors in Constantinople met with no success despite repeated attempts. The Sultan was angry with the interference of the European powers and could not admit that the issue involved more than some rebellious subjects, as such an admission would have been tantamount to recognition of the Greek cause. While the Greeks had accepted the armistice the day after it had been presented to them, the Sultan remained adamant in his refusal. Secretly encouraged in his resistance by the Austrians, Prussians and especially the Russians who wanted to ensure that hostilities took place, the Sultan declared that he would massacre

From left to right: Two Turkish 24s, *Mosquito* (ten guns), the 56-gun *Castor*, the 44-gun *Constantine*, the masts of the '44 *l'Armide* and the '28 *Talbot*; a 12-gun fire brig and the 10-gun *Philomel*, in flames on the far right.

all Greeks rather than give way. The ambassadors finally had no option but to order the admirals to impose the armistice.

Imposing the armistice presented many problems for Codrington and de Rigny, the Russian Count de Heyden not yet having appeared on the scene. The problem was to decide what was Greek and what was Turkish controlled territory. It was agreed that Greek held territory would be encompassed by a line drawn from the Gulf of Volo to the mouth of the River Aspropotamos and would include Euboea, Salamis, Aegina, Poros, Hydra, Spezzia and other small islands dependent on the mainland. Since the Allies had no means of enforcing the armistice on land, it was to be enforced at sea only against the Turks to counterbalance the Turkish freedom on land. In effect this was allowing the Greeks freedom of the seas and imposing the armistice only on the Turks, a solution which Ibrahim thought was excessively pro-Greek in its interpretation. A further problem was that Codrington and de Rigny disagreed over approach to their task. It was obvious that Ibrahim's fleet was intended for use against Ydra, and that the main task of the combined Allied fleet was to prevent this occurrence. Codrington thought that Navarino Bay should be blockaded to prevent the fleet from sailing but de Rigny, admitting that battle was inevitable in view of their joint orders, wanted to let the fleet out where it could be destroyed at sea.

To complicate matters further, the joint instructions to the admirals did not specify who was to

Left: From left to right: a Turkish '62 is sinking and a Turkish '76 is in flames, both having come under the fire of *Genoa*, a British '74 under Commodore Bathurst; a Turkish '26 is on the far right. **Below:** The eradication of the Turkish fleet was almost complete. In the foreground a few turbaned survivors cling to a none-too-seaworthy boat.

command the combined Allied squadrons. Codrington was senior and had orders not to place himself under a French or Russian admiral under any circumstances, while de Rigny's orders were to subordinate himself to Codrington only if the use of force became unavoidable. It was absolutely imperative that at least the British and French squadrons act in concert, since neither by itself was strong enough to attempt action against the vastly superior Turkish fleet. Only the threat of action could make the Turks give way. The weak Allied naval strength in the eastern Mediterranean was surely one factor in the failure of Allied diplomacy during the summer of 1827.

The Fleets Arrive

Codrington finally arrived off Navarino on 11 September with twelve ships with neither the desire nor the instructions to engage in an action against Ibrahim. De Rigny's squadron arrived a week later, soon followed by de Heyden's Russian ships. On 19 September Codrington warned the Ottoman commander against any hostile movement of his fleet but two days later, in accord with Ibrahim's standing orders to attack Ydra, part of the fleet put out toward that island. Badly outnumbered, Codrington still moved to intercept but the timely arrival of de Rigny's ships caused the Turks to withdraw without challenge. On 25 September Codrington and de Rigny met Ibrahim ashore to inform him of their orders. Ibrahim was extremely resentful that the armistice seemingly applied only to him but not to the Greeks and that he was not to be permitted to relieve by sea the Turkish forts, especially Patras, then under Greek attack. And indeed, in early October Ibrahim made a sortie to Patras but was turned back by Codrington's squadron and a heavy storm.

By mid-October all involved believed that battle was inevitable. De Rigny had become convinced that Mehemet Ali wanted a clash while Mehemet Ali was describing the Allies in the same terms to the Sultan and advising him of the need for concessions and avoidance of conflict. The Sultan remained adamant and on 19 October confirmed Ibrahim's original orders to take Ydra and 'in the event of aggression by the Europeans, to trust in God and to deploy the effort necessary to repulse their attacks'.

The Allied commanders were now faced with a genuine dilemma. The blockade of Navarino had temporarily bottled up the Turkish fleet, but due to the weather could not be maintained throughout the winter. Also, it was not preventing Ibrahim from ravaging the Peloponnese with his army. Codrington, de Rigny and de Heyden agreed that they had either to give up the object of the Treaty of London or enter Navarino harbor, anchor alongside the Ottoman Fleet and renew the propositions to Ibrahim from that vantage point to force some sort of decision. Although all three admirals agreed on this course of action, each did so for a different reason. Codrington wanted to force Ibrahim to stop the brutal devastation of the Peloponnese. De Heyden felt that the move into the bay would force Ibrahim to concentrate his forces at Navarino and not to undertake new operations against the Greek coast.

Above: The Russian *Azov*, a Turkish '76, and the 74-gun French *Breslau*, flanked by an Egyptian 20-gunner at Navarino.

De Rigny wanted to demonstrate to Ibrahim that his fleet should disband and return to its home bases of Constantinople and Alexandria. In fact, however, the independence of Greece hung on the decision to enter Navarino Bay.

Of the Allied squadrons, the Russian forces were in the best condition. Consisting of four ships of the line and four frigates, de Heyden's ships were new and well manned. Dutch in origin, de Heyden had served in the British navy and become a Russian in 1810. He was a fighting captain cut from the same mold as Codrington, and the two admirals found an instant affinity. The French squadron was made up of three ships of the line and four frigates, but the battleships were old and in wretched condition, so much so that de Rigny preferred to keep his flag in the frigate *Sirène* and sent a letter of protest to his superiors about the state of his command. De Rigny had five years of experience in the Mediterranean and was a good diplomat with a subtle mind concerning political matters. Codrington was always somewhat suspicious of him and said bluntly, 'the sea is not his element'.

The British contribution to the combined squadron consisted of Codrington's flagship the 84-gun *Asia* and two 74-gun ships, the *Genoa* and the *Albion*. These were supported by four frigates, two corvettes and fifteen sloops. Nor were the British ships of top quality as the Royal Navy had become a neglected and obsolescent service after twelve years of peace. The technical innovations of the day such as the steamship, the ironclad and the explosive shell had made no impact on the Royal Navy by 1827. The British Admiralty continued to rely on the fighting ability and seamanship of its captains and crews when it was already becoming apparent that these were not enough in an age of technical revolution.

As the senior officer of flag rank, Codrington was commander-in-chief of the combined squadrons. A blunt and outspoken man, he had been a lieutenant in Howe's flagship at the Glorious First of June in 1794, had commanded the 74-gun *Orion* in the van under Nelson at Trafalgar in 1805, and had participated in many lesser actions. In the words of a modern British historian, C. M. Woodhouse, Codrington was 'a fighting sailor who lacked all diplomatic finesse' who 'combined a fearful pugnacity in action with a humane and blameless private character'.

Ranged against this Allied force of ten line of

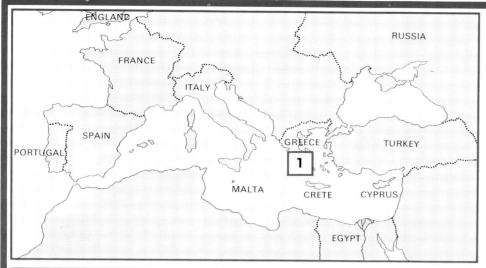

The Battle of Navarino, 20 October 1827

TURKISH
ENGLISH
FRENCH
RUSSIAN

A contingent of thirteen brigs and sloops formed a line behind the island to protect the numerous transports in the harbor.

Navarino was the last battle fought entirely between wooden sailing ships armed with smooth-bore cannon. Typical ships of the line like HMS 'Asia' continued to be built after Navarino, but within a decade revolutionary changes were soon to make these great sailing ships obsolete.

At 1400 the 'Asia' passed under the shore battery followed by the 'Genoa', the 'Albion' and the 'Dartmouth'. Next came the French contingent, led by the 'Sirene', the Russians led by 'Azov' were behind and to leeward. Each ship dropped anchor near a principal enemy ship.

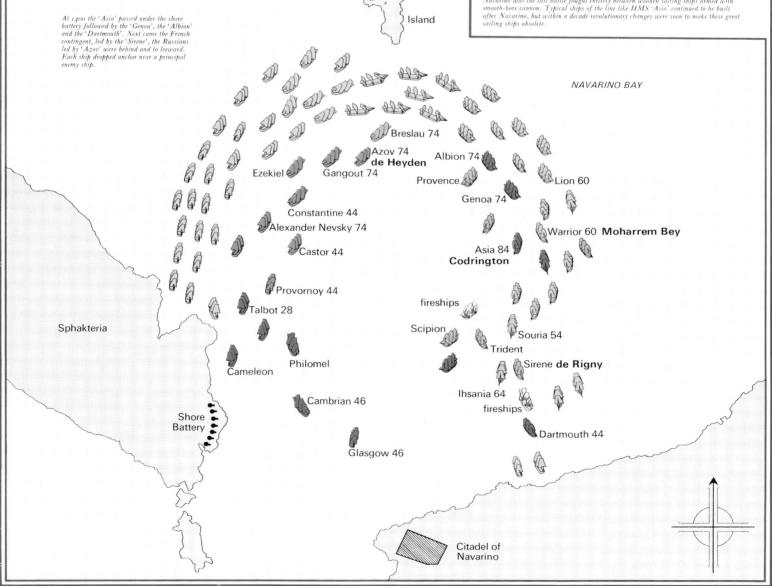

Island

NAVARINO BAY

Breslau 74

Azov 74
de Heyden

Albion 74

Ezekiel

Gangout 74

Provence

Lion 60

Genoa 74

Constantine 44

Alexander Nevsky 74

Warrior 60 **Moharrem Bey**

Castor 44

Asia 84
Codrington

Provornoy 44

fireships

Talbot 28

Scipion

Souria 54

Sphakteria

Trident

Cameleon

Philomel

Sirene **de Rigny**

Ihsania 64

Cambrian 46

fireships

Shore
Battery

Dartmouth 44

Glasgow 46

Citadel of
Navarino

battleships, eleven frigates and seventeen smaller corvettes and sloops was an Egyptian squadron, a Turkish squadron and a Tunisian squadron totalling three 74-gun ships of the line, twenty frigates, 32 corvettes, seven brigs and sloops and five fireships. Compared in terms of numbers of ships and total guns, Ibrahim's force was far superior to that of the Allies. Ibrahim's fleet also had the services of a group of French officers under Captain Letellier in the employ of Mehemet Ali. On 11 October Letellier was directed to prepare the fleet in defensive formation; he completed the task on the 15th.

The defensive disposition formulated by Letellier was to range the fleet in a crescent in the space enclosed by the citadel, the small island and the island of Sphakteria with the small island approximately on the line of the axis of the crescent. In the front line were the ships of the line and the most powerful frigates moored about two cables length apart. In a second line covering the intervals in the first line were the remainder of the frigates and the most powerful corvettes. A third line consisted of the remainder of the corvettes. At the ends of the crescent were the fireships, two on the side of New Navarin and three under the guns of the shore battery of Sphakteria.

The left wing was commanded by Moharrem Bey, Ibrahim's brother-in-law, who flew his flag in the 60-gun frigate *Warrior*. From the citadel to the island the front line was composed of the 64-gun frigate *Ihsania* and the 54-gun *Souria*.

Left: The British two-deckers *Albion* (right) and *Asia* returning to Spithead after the Battle of Navarino.

Behind the *Souria* were two 44-gun frigates, and a little behind this line was the *Warrior*. To the north of the *Warrior* and further in was a 74-gun battleship under the Patrona Bey. Behind the Patrona Bey was another 74-gun battleship and then the 60-gun frigate *Lion*. Toward the island the line was completed by a 50-gun frigate, a 74-gun battleship and another first-rate frigate. The head of this line was anchored close inshore.

Facing the entrance of the bay, the right wing was commanded by Tahir Pasha, Commander of the Turkish navy, and was less powerful than the left wing. Since the wind normally favored a move toward the right, it is probable that Letellier gambled the main attack would take advantage of the wind and not give priority to the left. From

the Sphakteria side the line consisted of two 56-gun frigates, two Tunisian frigates, two more 56-gun Turkish frigates, another Tunisian frigate, then the 60-gun frigate carrying Tahir Pasha's flag, and two 56-gun Turkish frigates. Thirteen brigs and sloops formed a line behind the small island to protect the transports in the harbor.

On 17 October de Rigny persuaded Letellier's group to withdraw from the Turkish fleet and board a neutral Austrian ship. This move severely limited Turkish options, as without the French officers the fleet could only weigh anchor for the purpose of sailing out of the harbor. Any other movement would have destroyed the utility of the defense formation. If the fleet did move out of the harbor, it had either to fight or

Overleaf: Navarino Bay on the day of the battle. It is obvious that the Turkish Navy didn't have a hope of evading the Allies once they entered the harbor.

withdraw to Constantinople and Alexandria. No Ottoman commander would dare back down without orders from above to protect him. Since Ibrahim was two days journey away at Modon with his army, it is clear that he did not expect a battle and he played no role in the engagement. The absence of Ibrahim ruled out the possibility of new orders, so the Ottoman Fleet could only remain where it was and wait the initiative of the Allies. Codrington had no conception of how provocative the move into the bay was nor did he understand the fatalism and sense of honor which would require the Ottoman officers to resist this move. Indeed, the disposition of their fleet on 18 October left them no other alternative as long as the Allies were determined to force some kind of decision.

On 19 October Codrington issued his orders to the fleet for the following day. The French squadron was to enter the bay and anchor opposite the enemy ships to the southeast because it was believed that the French officers were still aboard them. The *Asia* followed by the *Genoa* and the *Albion* was to move farther up the line opposite the heaviest enemy ships. Last in were to be the Russians on the western side of the line. The British, French and Russian frigates were to support their line of battleships respectively. The British corvettes and brigs were to neutralize the fireships. The Allied ships were to moor at their assigned places with springs on the ring of each anchor. No gun was to be fired without a signal from the admiral unless fire was received from the enemy in which case the offending ships were to be destroyed immediately. The official written orders

for the day ended 'In case of a regular battle ensuing and creating any of that confusion which must naturally arise from it, it is to be observed that, in the words of Lord Nelson, "No captain can do very wrong who places his ship alongside that of an enemy."' Only twelve years after Waterloo it might be thought that the French would object to having Nelson quoted to them but apparently they did not and, in the event, they more than followed his dictum the next day.

At 0800 on 20 October the Allied squadrons were maneuvering in company to allow the latecomers to arrive. After blowing lightly all morning the breeze strengthened and then began to drop off. Two miles off the entrance to the bay, the beat to quarters was sounded at 1100. At 1330 Codrington signaled to prepare for action. At 1400 the *Asia* passed unmolested under the shore batteries guarding the entrance to the bay. She was followed by the *Genoa*, the *Albion* and the 44-gun frigate *Dartmouth*. Next came the French contingent with the *Sirène* leading the *Scipion*, *Trident*, *Breslau* and *Provence* and the frigates *Magicienne* and *Armide*. Behind and to leeward of the French came the Russian flagship *Azov*, followed by the *Gangout*, *Ezekiel*, *Alexander Nevsky* and the Russian frigates.

The first reaction to the appearance of the Allied fleet from the Turkish side was a small boat from Moharrem Bey which requested the Allies to stand out of the harbor again. Codrington replied that he had come not to receive orders but to give them. At 1410 the *Asia* anchored near the *Warrior*, flagship of Moharrem Bey, and in range of two other Turkish ships. The *Genoa* and

Albion passed to the north of the *Asia*, each dropping her anchors within range of a principal enemy. The *Dartmouth* had been assigned to the fireships and anchored near the end of the enemy line in the southeast corner of the bay.

After the messenger from Moharrem Bey returned to shore a red flag was raised over the fort and a signal gun fired. No hostile intent had thus far been shown by the Turks. Unlike his French and Russian colleagues, Codrington still did not really expect a battle. Otherwise he would not have sailed directly into the center of the formidable enemy defenses. All the space available for guns had not even been cleared aboard the *Asia* and the marine band was assembled on the poop. From his earlier encounters with Ibrahim's ships, Codrington apparently thought there was no reason to believe that a show of force would provoke a response, even though sailing into Navarino Bay was by any standards a highly provocative action.

The Battle Begins

How the battle actually began has been subject to controversy, but the following explanation seems the most plausible. As the British and French squadrons were still entering the bay and the Russians had not yet begun, the *Dartmouth* saw a small boat sent to the fireships and preparations for action begin aboard these craft. To ships made entirely of wood, hemp, tar and canvas, fireships posed a genuine threat. Hence the *Dartmouth* put out a small boat commanded by a lieutenant to warn the fireships to move away or to evacuate their crews. As the boat approached

the fireships, it was fired on and sustained some casualties. The fireship was ignited and began to drift toward the Allied positions. The *Dartmouth* put out another small boat to tow her clear when an Egyptian corvette fired on the *Dartmouth* and on the *Sirène* which was just anchoring. At approximately 1425 the firing became general.

The Turkish point of view was that the *Dartmouth* had sent boats to seize the fireships which had justifiably defended themselves. It is certain that neither Moharrem Bey nor Tahir Pasha planned or wanted an incident as both held back their own ships for some time after the battle had become general.

Lasting until 1800 hours, the battle was stubbornly and bloodily fought and was in no way a situation calling for sophisticated maneuvers or tactical ingenuity. Letellier's plan had placed the Turkish fleet in a fixed position from which it could not move. Codrington's orders to anchor at assigned points close to the enemy had been scrupulously obeyed. Thus the battle was largely fought between stationary targets at point blank range, most of the carronades on the European ships being charged with two 32-pound shot, 32 pounds of grapeshot and sometimes a canister. Casualties were heavy on both sides and in the words of a British seaman, 'burn, sink and destroy' were the orders of the day. Only the smaller ships had a mobile role to play.

The battle was composed largely of a series of single-ship actions. After the incident between the *Dartmouth* and the fireships, the Egyptian frigate *Ihsania* engaged the *Sirène* in a heavy action which ended at 1600 when the *Ihsania* blew up.

Opposite: A Turkish ship of the line blows up under the fire of the *Albion*.
Below: As the wreck of a Turkish two-decker sinks after the Battle of Navarino, English sailors rescue some of her survivors.

Although severely damaged and with many casualties, the *Sirène* next engaged the fort at Old Navarino, supported by the *Scipion* and *Trident*.

As the fight became general the bay was obscured by a thick pall of smoke, causing the Allied ships sometimes to fire on each other by mistake. The *Asia* was the most heavily engaged ship on the Allied side, emerging from the battle a virtual wreck. When the firing started between the *Dartmouth* and the fireships, the *Asia* was anchored near the 60-gun frigate of Capetana Bey and the *Warrior* of Moharrem Bey. Capetana Bey immediately opened fire on the *Asia*, but Moharrem Bey sent an officer to say he would not fire. The *Asia* quickly disposed of the rotten and ill-manned ship of Capetana Bey, and then engaged the *Warrior* after an incident similar to the one which took place between the *Dartmouth* and the fireships. After another heavy action the *Warrior* was driven ashore a flaming wreck. The smaller Turkish ships in the second and third lines firing between the ships of the front line had the *Asia* as their particular target and caused heavy damage and casualties. Tall and easily recognizable in his admiral's uniform, Codrington himself was wounded several times during the action. Tahir Pasha later acknowledged that snipers had been particularly directed against the British admiral.

The *Genoa* was the most beleaguered ship after the *Asia*, being engaged by a 60-gun frigate and two ships of the line. Her 26 men killed in action including the captain was the highest number of deaths among the Allied ships.

The fourth French ship into the bay was the *Breslau* under Captain de la Bretonnière. Seeing the *Sirène* well supported by the *Trident* and the *Scipion*, de la Bretonnière reacted as Nelson had at the Battle of St. Vincent in 1797 and on his own initiative moved into the center of the harbor beyond the British position, placing himself between the *Albion* and the position assigned to the Russians at the head of the crescent. In concert with the *Albion* and the *Azov*, the *Breslau* played a leading part in destroying a 74-gun ship and four frigates. This initiative by de la Bretonnière was the most brilliant incident in a battle which was mainly a slogging match.

The *Albion* had sailed further into the bay than any other British ship. Becoming entangled with a Turkish frigate, the *Albion* captured its enemy by a

boarding party and then had to cut her adrift in flames. Three enemy battleships concentrated their fire on the *Albion* which was only saved by the clumsiness of her opponents, two of which actually collided, and the timely arrival of the *Breslau*. In spite of some accidental exchanges of gunfire, the *Albion* and the *Breslau* proceeded to destroy the Turkish battleships, after which the *Breslau* turned to aid the Russian squadron now joining the action on the western arm of the crescent.

The Russians were the last to join the fray, causing de Heyden to write later that 'we may have been the last to fire but we were also the last to stop'. De Heyden's ships carried out their orders to anchor at pre-determined points in the bay with a precision and discipline admired even by critical British observers. The flagship *Azov* moved into an exposed position at the apex of the crescent, supported by the *Breslau* on the right and aided by the reluctance of the Tunisian squadron in this part of the Ottoman line to join the battle. The Russian ships fought with skill and courage. The 24 killed and 67 wounded aboard the *Azov* were the heaviest total casualties of any Allied ship. The *Azov* sank two frigates, a corvette, drove a 60-gun frigate aground and destroyed Tahir Pasha's flagship. The other Russian battleships also suffered losses, but the Russian frigates came off lightly because they were kept in close support of the Russian ships of the line. De Heyden did this intentionally, as he wanted to keep his ships together in a single combat sector.

While these central actions were taking place, the British frigates *Cambrian*, *Glasgow* and *Talbot* and French frigate *Armide* had been assigned to form the farthest extension of the Allied line next to the Russian frigates and to operate against the western flank of the Ottoman line. The *Armide* and the *Talbot* had to engage the frigates of the Turkish right wing and the shore batteries on Sphakteria unsupported until joined by the *Cambrian*, the *Glasgow* and the Russians. There was much accidental firing in this sector for which the Russians were chiefly to blame.

Under the tutelage of the frigate *Dartmouth*, the British corvettes and sloops had to deal with the Turkish fireships. Although the *Scipion* came perilously close to being destroyed by a fireship early in the battle, not a single one of these attacks actually succeeded because of the effective way in which the small ships were handled. They were also constantly under fire which they were ill-equipped to return, although the six-gun cutter *Hynd* did take up a position alongside the *Asia* against the *Warrior* and fought a ferocious battle, thereby earning for herself the title 'His Majesty's Cutter of the Line'.

When the smoke cleared the victory was seen to be decisive and overwhelming. The bay was full of bodies and burning wreckage. Sixty Turkish ships had been totally destroyed with Turkish casualties estimated at 6000 killed and 4000 wounded. And not a single Turkish ship struck her colors. Although many were heavily damaged, no European ships were lost. All of the French ships except the *Trident* had to return to home ports for repairs, as did most of the British ships. Casualties on the Allied side were 75 killed and 197 wounded for the British, 40 and 141 for the French and 59 and 137 for the Russians. Codrington could accurately write to his wife, 'Well, my dear, the Turks have fought and fought well too; and we have annihilated their fleet. But it has cost us dear'.

Throughout the night Allied crews remained at battle stations but the only danger was from the burning wreckage drifting about the harbor. The following day Tahir Pasha informed Codrington that there would be no more hostile action from the few remaining Turkish warships. But he could not be certain about the forts, since Ibrahim still did not regard the armistice as applying on land. As Codrington had no other means of coercion, he was well satisfied with the day's work and naively believed that the Sultan would be made more amenable as a result. On 25 October the three squadrons sailed from Navarino and went their separate ways.

The encounter at Navarino reduced Turkey to powerlessness at sea, but Ibrahim continued the war undeterred on land and only withdrew from Greece when a French expeditionary force landed in the Peloponnese the following year. The remnants of the Turkish and Egyptian fleets sailed away unmolested in December. Having not intended to go to war with Turkey in the first place, Britain did nothing to follow up the victory, termed by Metternich a 'dreadful calamity'. Canning was now dead and his successor, the conservative Duke of Wellington, persuaded George IV to apologize and offer regrets to the Sultan 'that this conflict should have occurred with the naval forces of an ancient ally'. Russia declared war on Turkey, claiming that in accordance with the Treaty of London the war was to force mediation on the Turks, a position accepted by France and Prussia, but opposed by Austria and England. The war was ended the following year by the Treaty of Adrianople, which left the future of Greece to the three parties of the Treaty of London. By the London Protocol of 1830 Greece became a kingdom guaranteed by Britain, France and Russia. Thus one result of Navarino was the addition of the new nation-state of Greece to the political map of Europe.

The End of the Metternich System

As the first great victory for the principle of nationality since 1815, the liberation of Greece had a tremendous impact all over Europe and helped make possible the liberal victories of 1830. Already weakened by British hostility, the international system of reaction broke down completely when Britain, France and Russia intervened in Greece. The irony of the situation is that the Quintuple Alliance had been formed to intervene if necessary in the internal affairs of states in the cause of reaction. Yet at Navarino three members of this alliance intervened in the affairs of Turkey in the cause of liberal nationalism. Navarino marked the end of the Metternich System in Europe.

In naval terms Navarino was the last battle fought entirely by wooden sailing ships armed with cannon. The ships commanded by Codrington at Navarino were no different from those commanded by Nelson at Trafalgar or Howe at the Glorious First of June, which in turn were the same ships in some cases which had fought in the Seven Years War some forty years earlier. Nelson's flagship *Victory* was one such, having been commissioned in 1759. The first steam-powered warship was in fact built by Robert Fulton in 1812–1815, but was never used. There were no radical changes in naval guns from the seventeenth to the mid-nineteenth centuries, although again explosive shells were known in the eighteenth and were used by the Russians against the Turks in 1788. Thus the naval guns at Navarino remained cast-iron, smooth-bore, solid ball-throwing muzzle loaders.

The Napoleonic Wars were hardly over when the Admiralty issued new *Fighting Instructions*, which instead of recognizing the advances made by Nelson, Howe and Rodney reimposed the old rigid tactics. Future battles were to be fought as gun duels in a single line ahead parallel to that of the enemy, despite all the experience which showed such a tactic was unlikely to produce more than a marginal victory. In terms of long-range influence on tactics, Nelson might never have lived. With the exception of Navarino which was a stationary battle, the British navy was not called on to fight a major fleet action until the First World War. The test of its official tactics was delayed, therefore, for over a hundred years.

Navarino found the British and French fighting together on the same side only twelve years after Waterloo. There was initial suspicion between the officers of the two former belligerents, but it passed and did not affect the harmonious prosecution of the battle. Indeed, one unexpected result of Navarino was the revival of French naval prestige which moved Victor Hugo to write 'L'Angleterre aujourd'hui reconnait sa rivale'. The Russian government was delighted with de Heyden's conduct and later made him military governor of Revel. Similarly, de Rigny went on to become first Minister of Marine and then Foreign Minister of France. Ibrahim eventually became Pasha and later Khedive of Egypt.

Of the four major actors in the drama of Navarino, only Codrington did not fare well afterward. Although a hero to the British populace, his victory was an embarrassment to His Majesty's Government. British policy had not been to humiliate the Turks or to liberate the Greeks but to check the Russians in the eastern Mediterranean and preserve Turkey. Navarino severely compromised the government's policy and Codrington became the scapegoat for the government's embarrassment. He was soon recalled and his career forfeited, not because he had misinterpreted his instructions about blockading Ibrahim but because he had won a diplomatically inexpedient victory, a victory described by Wellington in Parliament as an 'untoward event'. Although it was of small comfort to him, Codrington did earn the official gratitude of the new Greek government and along with Byron and Canning received a place in the pantheon of the liberators of Greece.

Left: Admiral Codrington, who commanded the British squadron in the Royal Navy's last great victory of the age of sail.

Hampton Roads

1862

In the several centuries preceding Trafalgar there had been virtually no change in naval tactics or technology, but by the time of Navarino the outlines of a coming revolution in technology were clear. The adaptation of the steamship and the iron ship, both known before the end of the eighteenth century, heralded the advent of the most important innovation of the nineteenth century, the armored warship. The death knell of the old wooden warships of Nelson and Codrington had been sounded in 1853 when a Russian squadron equipped with shell firing guns had blasted a Turkish squadron to bits at the Battle of Sinope. But it was only in the American Civil War of 1861–1865 that armored vessels were first used extensively and faced each other in action. An armored warship made the first naval challenge of the South against the North at the Battle of Hampton Roads in March 1862, a challenge which, if successful, might have changed the course of the war.

In the years before the Civil War, the American navy was undergoing a transition from sail to steam in common with the European navies. At that time, steam was still generally supplementary to sail in sea-going ships since engines were very inefficient and consumed huge quantities of coal. In 1842 the American navy had acquired its first steam screw propeller warship, the *Princeton*, whose engine, propeller and main armament were designed by the Swedish engineer John Ericsson. In that same year, a commission for an armored harbor defense craft was obtained by Robert L. Stephens, but the vessel was never completed. Despite this failure, the navy was definitely aware of the growing trend toward armored ships or 'ironclads', as they were called. In the Crimean War of 1853–1856, France had used armored floating batteries with so much success that Napoleon III ordered four ironclad warships to be built. First to be completed in this group was the *Gloire*, the most powerful warship of her time. To counter this threat to her naval supremacy, Britain completed her own ironclad, the *Warrior*, a year later. With only Stephens' ship, perpetually under construction, the American navy had no ironclads at the outbreak of war. It did have, however, six new first class steam frigates, the best known of which was to be the *Merrimack*, and twelve steam sloops. All told, 42 ships were in commission.

Along with the shift to steam, new ordnance was being introduced. After some experimentation with gun barrel pressures, a young lieutenant named John Dahlgren successfully began to design guns of larger caliber after 1847. The 'Dahlgrens' were smooth bores and fired both shot and shell. Guns under eight-inch bore often had rifled barrels, making them more accurate than the smooth bores. Although Dahlgren could produce a thirteen-inch gun, the new steam frigates of the American navy were armed with nine, ten and eleven-inch guns. On the eve of the war, therefore, the navy was a small but relatively modern force, augmented by a large merchant marine and abundant shipbuilding resources.

The long-standing and deeply divisive issue of the extension of slavery to the new states being formed in the American West came to a final crisis in December 1860 when South Carolina seceded from the Union, followed by six other states. With Jefferson Davis as their president and

CHARLESTON

MERCURY

EXTRA:

Passed unanimously at 1.15 o'clock, P.M. December 20th, 1860.

AN ORDINANCE

To dissolve the Union between the State of South Carolina and other States united with her under the compact entitled "The Constitution of the United States of America."

We, the People of the State of South Carolina, in Convention assembled, do declare and ordain, and it is hereby declared and ordained,

That the Ordinance adopted by us in Convention, on the twenty-third day of May, in the year of our Lord one thousand seven hundred and eighty-eight, whereby the Constitution of the United States of America was ratified, and also, all Acts and parts of Acts of the General Assembly of this State, ratifying amendments of the said Constitution, are hereby repealed; and that the union now subsisting between South Carolina and other States, under the name of "The United States of America," is hereby dissolved.

THE

UNION

IS

DISSOLVED!

Opposite: The inauguration of Jefferson Davis as President of the Confederate States of America.

Far left: The unfinished dome of the Capitol as seen from Pennsylvania Avenue, as Lincoln's carriage proceeds to the inauguration, 4 March, 1861. **Below:** Abraham Lincoln, 16th President of the United States.

Montgomery, Alabama as their first capital, these seven formed the original Confederate States of America. By following a policy of inaction, President James Buchanan tried not to aggravate the situation but his successor Abraham Lincoln, taking office early in 1861, quickly realized force was the only means of preserving the Union. Opinion in the North was deeply divided, however, and the new president knew the first act of overt war would have to come from the South. The Confederates obligingly fired on Fort Sumter in Charleston harbor on 12 April, an act which solidly united the North, not for long, but long enough for Lincoln to act. He issued a proclamation declaring a state of insurrection and called for a volunteer army to re-establish order. Four additional Southern States then parted company with the Union.

Correctly interpreting Lincoln's insurrection proclamation to mean that the South was to be invaded, President Davis called for volunteers to defend the Confederacy. At the same time he called for privateers to sail under Confederate letters of marque with two objectives in mind. First, it was hoped that these raiders would so disrupt the commerce of the North that the European powers would intervene on the side of the South. Second, since almost all of the exports of the South went through the six ports of Norfolk, Virginia; Wilmington, North Carolina; Charleston, South Carolina; Savannah, Georgia; Pensacola, Florida; Mobile, Alabama, and New Orleans, Louisiana, the North would certainly establish a blockade, and it was also hoped that the privateers would distract the Northern Navy from the blockade.

The advantage in the war initially lay with the South as North had to be the aggressor, literally conquering and occupying the eleven states of the Confederacy one by one. Such an advantage, however, was ultimately offset by the fact that the North possessed two thirds of the nation's

population and virtually all of its industry. The economy of the South was basically agricultural and badly balanced in its heavy dependence on the export of cotton. The South had therefore to import nearly all of its iron, arms, equipment, clothing and even some food. Fully aware of their inferior economic, industrial and demographic position, Southern leaders firmly believed that the European powers and especially Britain would intervene in their favor because of Europe's need for Southern agricultural products, especially cotton. With five million people in Britain dependent on the textile industry for their livelihood and 80 per cent of Britain's cotton supplied by the South, so this view ran, the North would not dare interfere with the movement of

Above: President Lincoln, flanked by Allan Pinkerton and General McClernand, on the battlefield of Antietam, 3 October, 1862. The fight for control of northern Virginia and Maryland continued throughout the war.

Left: Lincoln's inauguration at the Capitol.

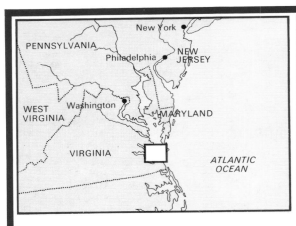

The Battle of Hampton Roads (Monitor and Merrimack), 8 and 9 March 1862

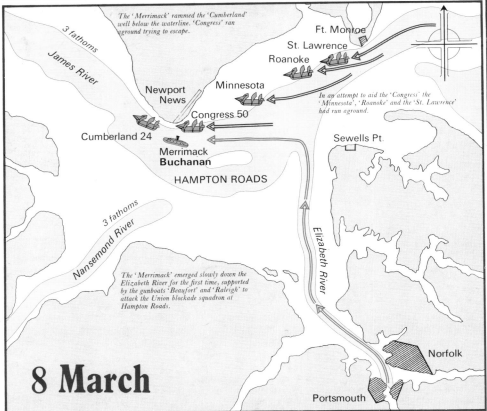

The 'Merrimack' rammed the 'Cumberland' well below the waterline. 'Congress' ran aground trying to escape.

In an attempt to aid the 'Congress' the 'Minnesota', 'Roanoke' and the 'St. Lawrence' had run aground.

The 'Merrimack' emerged slowly down the Elizabeth River for the first time, supported by the gunboats 'Beaufort' and 'Raleigh' to attack the Union blockade squadron at Hampton Roads.

8 March

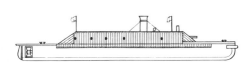

The 'Merrimack' was a 'casemate' ironclad because she had a sloping iron box superimposed on the wooden hull of a former frigate. The large single screw and rudder were under water, making her invulnerable to shell fire. Apart from her powerful guns, she had another offensive weapon — a heavy projecting ram at the bow.

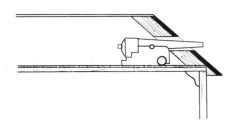

The guns of the 'Merrimack' inside the iron 'casemate' in a battery reminiscent of the ships of the line of sailing days. The sloped armor plating offered further protection, because solid shot and spherical shells tended to be deflected.

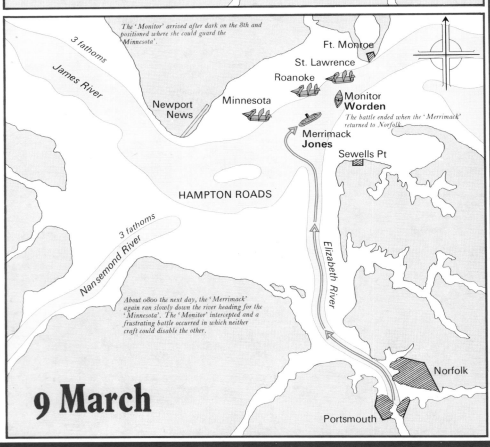

The 'Monitor' arrived after dark on the 8th and positioned where she could guard the 'Minnesota'.

The battle ended when the 'Merrimack' returned to Norfolk.

About 0800 the next day, the 'Merrimack' again ran slowly down the river heading for the 'Minnesota'. The 'Monitor' intercepted and a frustrating battle occurred in which neither craft could disable the other.

9 March

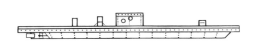

The 'Monitor' was much smaller than the 'Merrimack' and had an iron hull with an armored raft superimposed. On this raft was a cylindrical turret containing only two guns, but as the turret revolved, the same degree of firepower could be brought to bear.

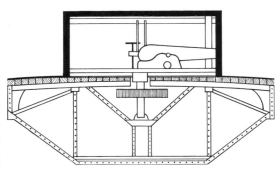

The 'Monitor's turret as designed by John Ericsson contained two 11-inch smooth-bore guns. Its armored roof and sides gave complete protection to the crew, and steam training machinery gave a 360 degree field of fire.

cotton for fear of provoking Britain to intervention on the side of the South. As Senator Hammond of South Carolina succinctly put this disastrous view in 1858, 'No power on earth dares make war on it. Cotton is King'.

But to the bitter disillusionment of Southerners everywhere, Lincoln did make war on King Cotton and Britain did not intervene. Provoked by Davis' call for privateers, the blockade was imposed immediately and within a year had become reasonably effective. King Cotton diplomacy came undone for two reasons. At the outbreak of the war in 1861, Britain already had a large oversupply of cotton on hand while during the war new sources of supply were developed in Egypt and India. A certain amount of Southern cotton also got through the blockade. At the same time, crop failures in Britain during the war years made necessary the import of Northern wheat for which Britain gladly exchanged munitions. Generally speaking, the war worked to the advantage of Britain which supplied both sides with munitions, captured most of the North Atlantic carrying trade, and imported Northern grains.

The privileged classes in Britain were basically sympathetic with the South, viewing the war as an attempt by the North to dominate the South and gladly watching the weakening of the growing power of the United States. The failure of the 'detestable' democratic experiment in America would slow down the demand for reform in Britain just as the ultimate victory of the North contributed to the ferment leading to the English Reform Bill of 1867. Seeing the North as fighting for free labor and democracy, the British working classes would never have willingly consented to intervention on behalf of slavery. Thus while the British Prime Minister Lord Palmerston was quick to assert and defend what he considered to be British rights, he proclaimed British neutrality at the outset. The formal neutrality of Britain actually worked to the advantage of the North as it forced all British trade with the blockaded states into clandestine channels and deprived such trade of official British protection. The Southern military successes early in the war led to doubts in Europe about the ability of the North to subdue the rebellious states. Britain and France made unsuccessful offers of mediation and considered intervention. The Union victory at Antietam in September 1862, however, caused Britain to be more judicious in this policy, and it was dropped completely after the Union suc-

Above: The inauguration ball held in honor of President Lincoln.

Left: The bombardment of Fort Sumter by the South Carolina batteries, 13 April, 1861. These guns heralded the start of the Civil War which was to last four years. **Above:** The interior of Fort Sumter during the bombardment. **Right:** The floating battery in Charleston Harbor during the attack on Fort Sumter. **Below:** The battered and conquered fort, with the Confederate flag waving over it.

Left; below left: Destruction of the US Navy Yard at Norfolk, Virginia involved the burning of several American ships. **Below:** A French impression of the fight between the *Monitor* (center) and *Merrimack* (left). The *Minnesota* is firing on the right. **Bottom:** The *Monitor* engaged the *Merrimack* at close range, and the clouds of powder-smoke soon obscured everything.

cesses at Gettysburg and Vicksburg in 1863. This fact became apparent even to the Confederate government, which recalled its agents from London in late 1863.

The first miscalculation of Confederate naval policy was to provoke the blockade at the outset, but having done so the primary task of the Southern navy was to break or circumvent the blockade as the Confederate Secretary of the Navy, Stephen R. Mallory, clearly recognized. Since the South had no ships of its own, Mallory decided the real answer to breaking the blockade was ironclads. In May 1861 he sent Commander James Bulloch to England to procure warships and especially ironclads. Somewhat optimistically, Mallory even hoped to buy one of the *Gloire* class from France. At the same time, a program to produce two powerful ironclads at Memphis, Tennessee and two more at New Orleans was launched despite the South's manifest inadequacies in materials and skilled workmen. When Virginia had seceded from the Union on 17 April, the Confederates happily came into possession of the Norfolk Navy Yard and with it many naval guns, a large quantity of urgently needed powder and the almost new steam frigate *Merrimack*. Fired and scuttled by the Union personnel of the yard before they escaped, this ship had only burned to the water line and was easily salvageable. Mallory authorized her con-

version to an ironclad on 11 May, thus launching the first Confederate challenge to the partly effective Union blockade.

A large wooden frigate, the *Merrimack*'s hull had only been slightly damaged. Her upper works were removed and a casement with sloping sides and curved ends was constructed. The casement was protected by two layers of iron plate, each of which was two inches thick and rolled from railroad rails. Mastless, the one-funnel vessel had an engine which could barely move her when the tide ran against her. Mounting a total of ten guns, the *Merrimack* had seven-inch rifled guns fore and aft, each of which could be trained on the keel line or on either beam. Her broadside consisted of one six-inch rifled gun and three nine-inch smooth bores. With a complement of 320 men, mostly from the army, she was under the command of Captain Franklin Buchanan. On completion in March 1862 she was renamed the *Virginia*, but this name has fallen

into disuse she remains known as the *Merrimack*.

The conversion of the *Merrimack* was no secret and had brought counter measures in the North. To the pleasant surprise of Secretary of the Navy Gideon Welles, who was very conscious of the $500,000 which had been spent on Stephens' ironclad since 1842, Congress voted funds for one or more ironclads in 1861. Three contracts were let but the first ship actually to be launched was a radically designed craft by John Ericsson who had earlier designed the *Princeton*. Using a design which had been rejected by the French during the Crimean War, Ericsson laid his ship down on 25 October, 1861 and delivered her on 19 February, 1862. The essence of Ericsson's idea was to place one or two heavy guns in a revolving turret protected by strong armor. A similar idea for a turreted ship had been unsuccessfully proposed to the Royal Navy in 1860 by Captain C. P. Coles who designed such a ship for Denmark the following year.

Left: The appearance of the famous Confederate ironclad bore little resemblance to the graceful steam frigate she had once been. The sloping iron casemate provided a shellproof battery for her guns, but she lacked maneuverability and could not have fought Federal ships on the high seas. **Below opposite:** The wooden steam frigate *Congress* was one of the victims of the *Merrimack* when she made her sortie on 8 March, 1862. **Below:** The steam frigate *Cumberland* made a gallant but hopeless stand against the *Merrimack*. Her wooden hull was soon set on fire by the ironclad's shells.

Displacing 1225 tons, Ericsson's ship was a shallow hull with one turret almost in the center. Fixed on a pivot rotated by a steam engine, the turret was twenty feet in diameter, nine feet high and protected by eight layers of one-inch iron. The deck was armored with two layers of half-inch iron plate. Above and near the waterline, the hull was secured with a belt of five one-inch layers of iron bent outwards to prevent ramming. A four foot high conning tower made of nine-inch iron logs with half-inch sight holes was placed forward and obstructed the front field of fire. The armament was two eleven-inch smooth bores which fired 166 pound shot at a very slow rate. With a length of 172 feet and a beam of 41 feet, the ship was made barely seaworthy by concentrating the heaviest armor in the turret. The crew of 65 under Lieutenant J. L. Worden were all volunteers as the ship was considered a dubious if not dangerous experiment in naval architecture. Named the *Monitor*, the strange appearance of the ship earned her the unflattering sobriquet 'cheesebox on a raft'. Like the *Merrimack*, the *Monitor* presented no unarmored target to the enemy but had two distinct advantages over her Confederate rival. She was much handier and had a draught of $10\frac{1}{2}$ feet compared to the 24 feet of the *Merrimack*, an important factor for operations in shallow coastal waters.

Merrimack Rushed into Action

Well aware of the construction of the Union ironclads, Secretary Mallory wanted the *Merrimack* in action before any Union ironclad could appear to oppose her. Hence the *Merrimack* was rushed into action with such despatch that when she got under way for the first time on the morning of 8 March, 1862, her crew thought she was going for a trial run. That bright and calm morning proved to be more than a trial run, however, as the *Merrimack* came slowly down the Elizabeth River supported by the gunboats *Beaufort* and *Raleigh* to attack the Union blockade squadron in Hampton Roads. The two wooden Union ships anchored off Newport News. The 24-gun sloop *Cumberland* and the 50-gun frigate *Congress* were the immediate targets. Intent on achieving decisive results that day, Buchanan planned to use his ram, possibly because powder and shot were scarce in the Confederacy.

As the *Merrimack* approached the *Cumberland*, both Union ships and shore batteries poured a violent fire at her. To the amazement of onlookers, projectiles bounced off her armor 'like India-rubber balls' while her own shells were smashing the two wooden ships. Undeterred by the Union fire, the *Merrimack* rammed the *Cumberland* forward well below the waterline, ripping open a gaping hole. With her crew still manning their guns, the *Cumberland* rapidly began to sink. The ram, however, wedged into her hull, trapping the *Merrimack* and taking her down with the *Cumberland*. Had the officer on the forward deck of the *Cumberland* had the presence of mind to let go her starboard anchor, it would have fallen on the deck of the *Merrimack* and ensured that she met the same fate as her victim. With water already over her forward deck, the ram suddenly broke off, freeing the attacker and

allowing the attacked to sink even more rapidly. As it was, the Confederate craft did ship some water as a result of the ramming.

While the *Cumberland* was being destroyed, the *Congress* had run aground in shoal water in a futile effort to escape. Taking up a position where she could rake the *Congress*, the *Merrimack* blasted the helpless ship for an hour until she was afire, her captain dead and had no guns operating, at which time the executive officer hoisted a white flag. By now both the day and the tide were ebbing, and Buchanan withdrew his ship, well satisfied with his day's work. While his own ship had lost her ram, had two guns disabled and suffered two killed and eight wounded, she had destroyed two enemy ships and killed 257 Union officers and ratings. Three more large wooden ships – the *Minnesota, Roanoke* and *St. Lawrence* – had run aground trying to aid the *Congress* and remained easy prey for the next day's operations. Unfortunately Buchanan himself had been wounded seriously enough for command of the *Merrimack* to pass to Lieutenant Catesby Jones.

When news of the *Merrimack*'s first raid was telegraphed to both sides there was deep rejoicing in the South but genuine panic in the North. It was feared the invincible Southern warship would raid Northern ports and even appear in the Potomac River to bombard Washington. Such fears were unfounded because of the deep draught and unseaworthiness of the *Merrimack* which had trouble just navigating Chesapeake Bay, but the results of her first day's operations seemed to more than justify this consternation to Northern observers. Even before her appearance, the news about the *Merrimack* had been so alarming that the *Monitor* had been rushed to completion and had left New York on 6 March, towed by a seagoing tug. She had had only a few days of tests and her trip south was so difficult that a less resolute person than Worden might well have turned back as the ventilation system broke down and water poured into the low beam craft. By dint of strenuous effort, however, the *Monitor* arrived at the mouth of Chesapeake Bay on the afternoon of the eighth. Hearing the sound of gunfire, Worden proceeded directly to Hampton Roads, arriving after dark, and was immediately ordered to a position where he could guard the stranded *Minnesota* against the depredations of the *Merrimack*, expected to be renewed the next day. In the light of the burning *Congress*, the Confederates also saw the *Monitor* take up her position and knew that the next day promised not easy pickings but a serious fight.

About eight the next morning, the *Merrimack* again ran slowly down the river headed for the *Minnesota*. With the guns of the Southern vessel pounding away at her, the *Monitor* crept forward to intercept and finally fired her own two guns at virtually point blank range. A frustrating encounter followed in which neither vessel could cripple the other even at close range. The *Merrimack* had been provided only with shells whereas solid shot was needed to penetrate the turret of the *Monitor* whose smooth bores were equally ineffective against the iron mail of the *Merrimack*. Worden soon grasped this fact and tried to ram his opponent but missed her propeller, the only vulnerable point at which the *Monitor* could strike, and did no damage to either ship. The sluggish duel continued, the *Merrimack* letting loose a broadside every fifteen minutes and the *Monitor* firing her guns about every seven minutes. Seeing that he was apparently doing no damage to his adversary, Jones then decided that his best course was to attack the grounded *Minnesota* rather than continuing to pound at the seemingly indestructable *Monitor*. In turning toward the *Minnesota*, however, the heavy draught of the *Merrimack* caused her to run aground for fifteen minutes. Then, abandoning any assault on the wooden ship, Jones turned again on the squat *Monitor* and determined to run her down, but his ship was unwieldy and difficult to handle in the narrow shoal channel. His nimbler opponent was able to avoid the main impact and the only result was a bad leak in the bow of the *Merrimack* caused by the sharp edge of the *Monitor*'s armored belt.

After two hours of combat, neither ship had succeeded in disabling the other, but now the *Monitor* hauled off to shallow water to replenish her empty powder and shot lockers in safety, away from the heavy draught *Merrimack*. Although thus far the *Monitor* had seemed to have the upper hand, the astonished Southerners saw this move as a retreat. When the *Monitor* renewed the action at 1130, the *Merrimack* was able to end the battle by changing her tactics. All her fire was concentrated on the conning tower of her enemy. While peering through a sight hole, Worden was stunned and temporarily blinded by a shell burst on the conning tower. Even so, he was still able to order the *Monitor* to sheer off and return to shallow water where she remained for twenty minutes. Unable to pursue the *Monitor* into her sanctuary, the Confederate ironclad assumed her adversary was finally out of action and returned to Norfolk. The *Monitor* shortly came out again to guard the *Minnesota* until the latter was afloat. The Battle of Hampton Roads was over.

Both ships had lacked the offensive power to destroy each other; hence neither suffered much damage in what was the first action between ironclad warships. The *Monitor* received 22 hits and had six wounded including Worden, while the *Merrimack* took twenty hits with two killed and nineteen wounded. Her armor was never penetrated but was broken in a few easily reparable places. Every solid hit by the heavy shot of the *Monitor* did, however, cause considerable concussion in the casement of the *Merrimack*. In retrospect, the *Monitor* should have concentrated her fire on one point to break the armor of her opponent just as the *Merrimack* finally focused her fire on the conning tower of the *Monitor* to put her out of action. But it must also be remembered that the *Monitor* had been in commission less than two weeks and with her crew not yet shaken down, she had barely enough training to operate as a ship when the battle occurred. In tactical terms, the battle was a stalemate with perhaps a slight edge to the *Merrimack* which was basically a more powerful ship than the *Monitor*. Perhaps the *Merrimack* did in fact win, since the *Monitor* declined to prevent her from resuming her raids

a month later. Thoroughly refitted and equipped now with solid shot for her guns, the *Merrimack* sallied forth again on 11 April, but the *Monitor* refused battle as Union officials were well aware that her turret could be pierced by solid shot. Had the *Merrimack* been firing solid shot on 9 March as well, the story of the battle would likely have been different.

Although a tactical stand-off, the battle at Hampton Roads on 9 March had far reaching strategic consequences. In local terms, the *Merrimack* seriously impeded the communications of General George B. McClellan's controversial Peninsula Campaign. With the object of capturing Richmond, Virginia, now the capital of the Confederacy, McClellan had planned to use the channels of the James, York, and Rappahannock Rivers for water transport of supplies and equipment while moving his troops up the peninsulas formed by the three rivers. His movements could then also be supported by Union gunboats on the rivers. While the *Merrimack* was in action, however, she controlled the James

Below: Lieutenant Catesby Jones, CSN, Commander of the *Merrimack*.

Left: General Robert E. Lee, commander of Confederate forces in Virginia and the South's greatest hero. **Bottom right:** A modern Monitor used on the Mekong River by American forces in Vietnam in 1971.

River and McClellan's main effort had to be shifted to the York River. The flow of supplies was also hindered. McClellan's forces did succeed in forcing the Confederates to evacuate Norfolk on 1 May. Because of her deep draught, always her main weakness, the *Merrimack* could escape no more than a few miles up river and had to be blown up, thus changing the local strategic situation radically. Even with control of the rivers and support of Union gunboats, including the *Monitor*, McClellan was still defeated by the Confederate General Robert E. Lee in the Seven Day Battle in June. Thwarted in his drive on Richmond, McClellan was forced to withdraw under cover of the guns of the Union ships and the Peninsula Campaign ended in failure. In the end the deep draught of the *Merrimack* proved her undoing. Unsuited for the shallow coastal waters in which she was built to operate, she was also prevented from escaping by the same weakness.

In broader terms, the North believed the *Monitor* to be the only defense it had against the awesome power of the *Merrimack*. In an effort to preserve her for a real emergency, the *Monitor* was ordered not to accept battle unless the *Merrimack* again attacked the wooden ships on blockade duty, now anchored farther out. Since the *Merrimack* contented herself with bombarding coastal installations and capturing some small craft, the *Monitor* remained watchful but did not offer a second battle. The Union Navy was most impressed with the design of the *Monitor* and ordered 21 similar ships, thus inaugurating a distinct class of ironclads known as 'monitors'. The impact of the *Monitor* itself was so great that the design was adopted by some European navies and monitors played a disproportionate role in the reconstruction of the American navy in the 1880's. Such ships were still in use in both the British and American navies until after the First World War. The last monitor was not removed from the American Navy List until 1937 while 'monitor type' ships were in use in 1974 as convoy escorts on the run up the Mekong River to the besieged Cambodian capital of Phnom Penh. Always barely seaworthy, the original *Monitor* foundered at sea on 29 December, 1862, taking sixteen of her 65-man crew down with her.

Southern naval policy as a whole was a failure. The privateers were driven off the seas within a year due to the blockade and the closure of neutral ports to them, leaving them with no place to dispose of their prizes. Bulloch found the

neutrality of England enforced enough that he had to procure ships and supplies clandestinely. He nevertheless arranged for the purchase or building of eighteen commerce raiders, the best known and most successful of which were the *Alabama*, *Florida* and *Shenandoah* which accounted for more than sixty Union ships between them. All, told, the commerce raiders took around 250 Northern ships but though highly successful, this activity did not have the desired effect of provoking European intervention though it did force the commerce of the North largely out of Northern into foreign and particularly British bottoms. Throughout the war the commerce of the North with Europe continued to increase.

The best hope of the South had rested on the ironclads breaking the blockade and here also Southern plans came to nought. The Confederacy built about 25 ironclads and bought one from France, but only half of these ever saw action. The *Merrimack* was the first and most successful of these ships, having sunk two Union ships. Other Southern ironclads were able to sink only one more ship and damage a few others. Mostly for technical reasons, the Southern ironclads never seriously impaired Union naval activity. Facing a well-equipped, efficient and numerically superior enemy, perhaps the Confederate sailors in their improvized ships experienced some feeling of awe and hopelessness as well. On the eve of the battle of Albemarle Sound in 1862, the Southern commander sighed 'Ah! If we could only hope for success . . .' as he faced sixteen Union ships mounting 54 guns with his eight ships and nine guns. The Union, for its part, ultimately had about 65 assorted ironclads.

The *Merrimack* was the first ironclad challenge made by the South to the blockade, but a second and far more serious threat appeared on the other side of the Atlantic in 1863. From the British builders of the Confederate commerce raider *Alabama*, Southern agents contracted for two powerful steam ironclad warships. These ships were fitted with iron rams to destroy the Union blockade ships while their nine-inch rifled guns could have held Northern seaports hostage to bombardment. Known as the 'Laird Rams' after their builders, the Laird Brothers of Liverpool, the ships were widely known to be destined for the use of the Confederacy. The North watched their progress with growing alarm and applied increasing diplomatic pressure on the British government to seize them. Finally the American Ambassador to Britain, Charles Francis Adams, threatened war to Earl Russell, the British Foreign Secretary, by writing 'It would be superfluous for me to point out to your Lordship that this is war . . .' Had the rams reached America, the South would probably have achieved its independence and the North would certainly have gone to war with Britain, but in the end the British government ordered the rams held and then purchased them for the Royal Navy. This ended the last chance of the South to challenge the blockade.

Despite the short lived threat of the *Merrimack*, the Southern ironclad program never really menaced the blockade. And the blockade was the main instrument of the North for causing the economic chaos which so weakened the South internally that the Union armies were able to gain ascendancy. It is significant that the major victories of the North did not occur until the South was suffering from shortages caused by the blockade. Thus the Southern failure to break or circumvent the blockade was one of the major factors leading to its ultimate defeat.

The Battle of Hampton Roads on 8–9 March, 1862 did not revolutionize naval warfare as is often asserted. That revolution had already occurred when France launched the *Gloire* in 1860. The unique feature of Hampton Roads was that on the 8th wooden ships had to oppose an ironclad for the first time while, far more significantly, the first clash of ironclads came the following day. The day of the armored ship had dawned and while it did not really come into its own until the First World War, its progressive development was to dominate the direction of naval technology for the next half century.

Left: General George McClellan, Lee's opponent in Virginia and Lincoln's challenger for the Presidency in 1864.

Manila Bay
1898

Theodore Roosevelt remarked that it wasn't much of a war but it was the only war America had. 'A splendid little war' was how John Hay, Ambassador to Britain, described it. Lasting barely four months and relatively cheap in human life, the Spanish-American War of 1898 was small in scope but large in consequences. It underlined the regeneration of the American navy and the emergence of the United States as a major world power. Fought primarily at sea, the war created an American naval legend in its opening encounter between the Pacific squadrons of Spain and the United States at Manila Bay in May 1898.

The *casus belli*, however, lay not in the Pacific but halfway around the world in the Caribbean. The island of Cuba was one of the last vestiges of the once extensive Spanish Empire in the Americas. An oppressive political system, economic domination by the mother country, and repression of all attempted reforms had brought periodic revolts against Spanish rule, the longest of which was the Ten Years War of 1868–1878. Located not a hundred miles off the Florida coast, Cuba roused intense sympathy in Americans because of their emotional, commercial and strategic ties with the island. Demands for American intervention were steady, loud and persuasive during the second half of the nineteenth century, but one President after another followed the passive policy of pressing reform on the corrupt Spanish régime.

A new revolt burst forth in 1895, a revolt which Spain was manifestly unable to suppress and which had cost her 100,000 casualties by 1898. Cuba itself was ravaged by both sides and its economy ruined. Cuban exports to the United States, its principal customer, fell by half between 1894 and 1896. Spain stopped American ships on the high seas, mistreated American citizens and destroyed American property in Cuba. The rebellion was disastrous to American commercial and financial interests in the country. To help provoke American intervention, the rebels also destroyed American property and played on American public sentiment in any way possible. The Cuban rebel lobby was very potent in the United States. American public opinion was further outraged in 1896 when Captain-General Valeriano Weyler attempted to deal with the rebellion through his policy of 'reconcentration'. Forerunner of the Briggs plan during the Malayan emergency and the American strategic hamlet program in South Vietnam, reconcentration assembled the noncombatant population in fortified cities and towns and systematically reduced the countryside so that it could not support the rebels. The American press called the inventor of reconcentration 'Butcher Weyler' while even the normally judicious President William McKinley remarked, 'It is not civilized warfare. It is extermination'.

It was apparent that Spain and the Cuban rebels could not defeat each other, and that the brutalizing war would go on until Spain, never a wealthy country, was bankrupt or another power intervened. In the meantime, the devastation of the rich island continued and the American press was filled with sensational atrocity stories. At the outset of the rebellion, President Grover Cleveland had maintained the basic American policy of demanding that Spain reform her administration in Cuba to end the rebellion but had refused to consider a more active policy. Taking office in March 1897, President McKinley continued Cleveland's policy, demanding reform

and making offers of mediation but also insisting that the problem would soon have to be solved one way or another. Intervention was always a policy alternative for him as he warned the Spanish 'The United States is not a nation to which peace is a necessity . . .' and shifted several warships to Key West to make certain his message was understood. Throughout this period the Spanish insisted that Cuba was purely their concern and that they would soon solve the problem by winning the war. If the United States remained neutral, said the Spanish, the rebels would soon lose hope and surrender. Clinging desperately to their conviction that American intervention would eventually come, the rebels under Maximo Gomez fought grimly on, hoping for liberation.

With much pressure placed upon him to intervene, Cuba was a major problem for McKinley but he continued to gather information about the situation until he was satisfied that war was the only course. Spurred on by the yellow press of William Randolph Hearst and Joseph Pulitzer, Congressional and public pressure mounted for war. In his annual message to Congress in 1897 McKinley finally stated that Spain must act at once or he would intervene. By now thoroughly disillusioned with Spanish inability to deal with the situation in Cuba, and angered by the de Lôme letter to Spain which insulted McKinley by calling him a 'spineless weakling', a letter which was intercepted and received wide publicity, the last straw for McKinley and America was the mysterious explosion which sank the US battleship *Maine* in Havana Harbor on 15 February, 1898. It did not matter how the *Maine* was sunk. This incident had to lead to war. Even more rabid than usual, the yellow press screamed 'Remember the *Maine* and to hell with Spain!' In his war message to Congress in April, McKinley himself said '. . . the destruction of the *Maine*, by whatever exterior cause, is a patent and impressive proof of a state of things in Cuba that is intolerable'. The United States had been rapidly arming since the *Maine* incident but, though he did not really believe in them, McKinley still tried a flurry of last minute diplomatic maneuvers to try to gain his ends peacefully and avoid war. These failed at the end of March, and war came on 21 April, to the jubilation of most of the country.

During this period deeper forces were at work in the United States which smoothed the path to war. The reconstruction of the American Navy had begun in the 1880's while at the same time new ideas of naval strategy and defense were being propounded. The old naval theory had been that the two wartime functions of the navy were coastal defense and commerce raiding requiring monitors for the former and fast unarmored cruisers for the latter. And in fact the first new ships authorized in the 1880's were monitors and cruisers. In 1890, however, Captain Alfred Thayer Mahan, a lecturer in naval tactics and history at the Naval War College, published his classic book *The Influence of Sea Power on History, 1660–1783* which took the admiralties of the world by storm and profoundly affected civilian policy and thinking in the United States,

Above: President William McKinley in 1898. This former Senator from Ohio did his best to avoid war, but public opinion forced him to ask for a declaration of war from Congress after the de Lôme Letter was published which called him a 'spineless weakling'.

Europe and even the Far East. The essence of Mahan's argument was that a major power must have a strong fleet of capital ships to drive off enemy blockading fleets and give it battle supremacy in a wide zone contiguous to its coasts. For national prosperity, a strong mercantile fleet, colonies and a large navy to protect both were all necessary. These were not novel ideas, for Britain had been following the same type of policy for two hundred years. Mahan further pointed out, however, that although the United States had no colonies, competed in only a few world markets and had only a modest merchant marine, the country was obviously entering a period of commercial competition and would need colonies and a strong fleet as it came in conflict with the interests of other nations.

At a time propitious for its adoption as the basic doctrine of American naval policy, Mahan thus reformulated what came to be known as the 'capital ship' theory and became the ideologist for American naval expansion. Even before publication of his book, Mahan's ideas were known in the Navy Department and demonstrably influenced policy. The American naval construction program from 1890 increasingly endorsed the capital ship theory as battleships and armored cruisers were requested from Congress, which voted the funds for construction without much protest. Further impetus was given by the Sino-Japanese War of 1894–1895, which was widely interpreted as proving the fighting value of capital ships. By 1897 the United States was completely committed to seizing absolute command of the sea in a wide zone extending out from the Atlantic, Pacific and Gulf seaboards and had a formidable, modern battle fleet which went far towards realizing this objective.

The 'Mahan School'

Outside the sphere of naval policy, however, Mahan was only one of a small but potent group of intellectuals preaching a new doctrine of expansion, linking it with the old American notion of 'manifest destiny' and the acquisition of foreign markets. Others in this group were Whitelaw Reid, publisher of the *New York Tribune*, Theodore Roosevelt, soon to be Assistant Secretary of the Navy, Senator Henry Cabot Lodge, and John Hay, Ambassador to Britain, all men of stature and men with access to the president. In their view, the new navy was to be the spearhead of American commercial expansion, to advance and protect American interests in the Far East, the South Seas, and Central and South America. From there it was but a small step to Mahan's thesis that colonies were essential to sustain the naval power necessary for the support of American diplomacy, prestige and commerce abroad. Although there were others arguing America's imperial destiny in the 1890's, it was Mahan and his politically influential friends Henry Cabot Lodge and Theodore Roosevelt who really sounded the call to action, marshaling the ideas of national security, commercial expansion, cosmopolitan philanthropy and national honor in support of a major program of imperial and naval expansion.

This program received a more active voice in

the government when Theodore Roosevelt was appointed Assistant Secretary of the Navy in 1897. A convinced follower of Mahan long before his own entrance into government, Roosevelt was restless by temperament, an advocate of the physically vigorous life, and naturally disposed toward military and naval affairs. A rabid 'jingo', the Assistant Secretary was a strong advocate of a big navy, an aggressive foreign policy, armed intervention in Cuba and territorial expansion overseas. Genuinely seeking a peaceful solution to the Cuban problem, McKinley was nervous about appointing this bellicose man, who believed that insufficient power invited aggression and that was not an unmitigated evil, to such an influential position.

In 1896 the Navy Department had developed a comprehensive plan for operations against Spain in the Caribbean, Europe and the Far East. Roosevelt quickly espoused the view that war should be waged vigorously in three theaters and worked day and night to weld men, ships and supplies into a workable fighting organization. To cut off Spain from her revenue and colonies in the Far East, the navy plan called for an attack on the Spanish squadron stationed at Manila to prevent its use against American shipping and territory in the Pacific, followed by seizure of Manila as a base to control the trade of the Philippines. In 1898 the American Navy had five battleships, six monitors, two armored cruisers, eight protected cruisers, nine smaller cruisers and ten gunboats ready. Usually only half a dozen cruisers and gunboats were on the Asiatic station to guard the lives and property of American merchants and missionaries in China and Korea. Certain that war would come, Roosevelt selected Commodore George Dewey to organize the Asiatic squadron for its role in the coming drama.

An enterprising officer receptive to Roosevelt's plans, the sixty-year-old Dewey out-maneuvered a rival for the post of Asiatic commander with Roosevelt's aid and left for the Far East in Decem-

Above: Senator Henry Cabot Lodge of Massachusetts. Lodge preached the doctrine of sea power; he was one of the war hawks of 1898. He later became President Woodrow Wilson's arch-enemy and opponent of America's participation in the League of Nations after World War One.

Left: President William McKinley (left) honors Admiral George Dewey in a victory parade in New York after the Spanish-American War. **Right:** Samuel Ferguson, apprentice signal boy, John McDougall, Marine orderly, Commodore George Dewey and Merrick Creagh, Chief Yeoman on board USS *Olympia* during the Battle of Manila Bay. **Far right:** The Spanish ships *San Juan de Ulloa* and *Reina Cristina* were destroyed by the USS *Boston*, USS *Baltimore* and USS *Olympia*.

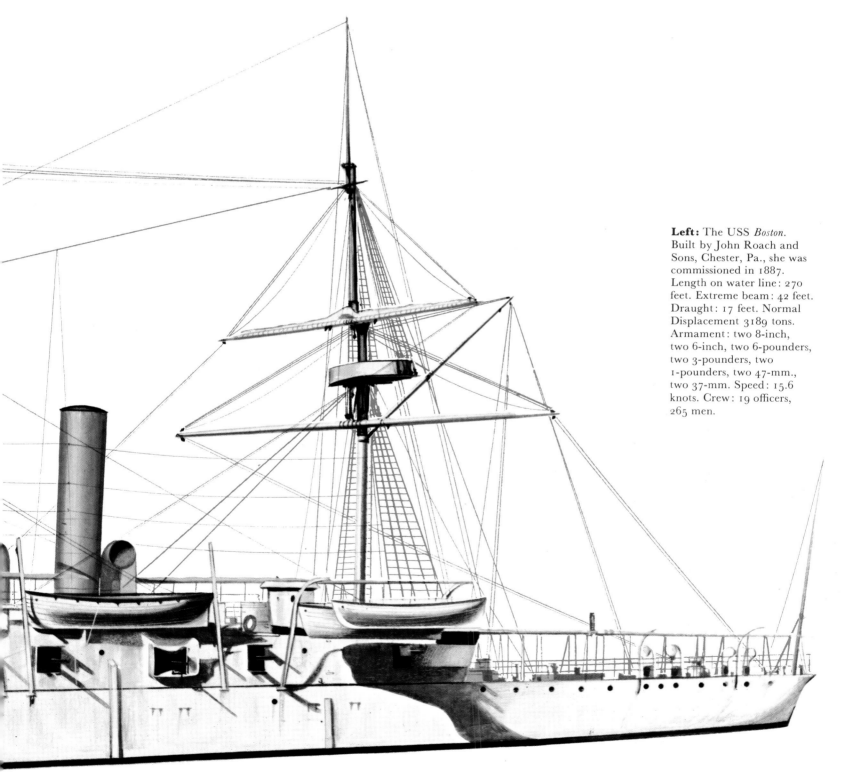

Left: The USS *Boston*. Built by John Roach and Sons, Chester, Pa., she was commissioned in 1887. Length on water line: 270 feet. Extreme beam: 42 feet. Draught: 17 feet. Normal Displacement 3189 tons. Armament: two 8-inch, two 6-inch, two 6-pounders, two 3-pounders, two 1-pounders, two 47-mm., two 37-mm. Speed: 15.6 knots. Crew: 19 officers, 265 men.

ber 1897. He had already had long and respectable service, mostly in shore assignments, and presumably wished to crown his naval career by raising his flag in command of a squadron. Under Roosevelt's direction he had collected the Asiatic squadron at Hong Kong and was ready to strike when war was declared in April 1898. As war approached, Dewey's main worry was that his squadron might be stranded in the Far East without coal, ammunition or supplies. Britain, Japan and China had already made clear their neutrality in the event of war which precluded obtaining supplies from them but Dewey was assured that supplies could always be obtained at Shanghai since China, then being carved up into 'spheres of influence' by the European powers and Japan, was helpless to enforce strict neutrality. Then it was discovered that other naval commanders, anticipating possible trouble in China, had bought up all available stocks of good Welsh coal. Dewey was, however, able to purchase the British collier *Nansham* with 3000 tons of coal aboard and later acquired the steamer *Zafiro* as a provision ship. The ammunition problem was alleviated when the cruiser *Baltimore* arrived with a special consignment from Hawaii on 22 April.

Dewey finally mustered four unarmored cruisers, two gunboats and three auxiliaries as his squadron. He flew his commodore's flag in the *Olympia*, the finest unarmored cruiser of the navy. Laid down in 1890, the 5800-ton ship could do twenty knots and mounted twin eight-inch guns in hooded barbettes of four-inch steel fore and

aft. In her superstructure, mounted to fire ahead or astern, were four five-inch quick firers with five more such guns on the broadside. There were also two fixed and four trained torpedo tubes. With a partial double bottom, she had a protective steel deck varying from two to four and three quarter inches and a thirty-three-inch cellulose belt around the waterline. The *Boston* was a partially protected cruiser of 3200 tons laid down in 1884, fully rigged without poop or forecastle but with a superstructure amidships. Fore and aft was mounted a single eight-inch gun in a barbette of two-inch steel, but the aft gun was on the starboard and the fore gun on the port side to make room for a six-inch gun with axial fire at each end of the superstructure. This design was, however, thought to strain the ship and was not repeated on any other ships. Four more six-inch guns were mounted in the superstructure as well. The *Boston* also had a one-and-a-half-inch steel deck all over, a double bottom, nine watertight compartments and a speed of $15\frac{1}{2}$ knots.

The third cruiser was the 4600-ton *Baltimore*, laid down in 1888, mounting two four-inch guns fore and two more aft, two eight-inch and two six-inch firing axially and three six-inch on the broadside. Her speed was twenty knots and her deck varied from two and a half to four inches of protective steel. The last cruiser was the 3200-ton *Raleigh*, laid down in 1889 and capable of 19 knots. She mounted one six-inch and two five-inch quick firers aiming forward, four five-inch quick firers aiming astern, and five more five-

Below: The Spanish cruiser *Reina Cristina* was driven ashore and became a burning wreck.

inch guns on the broadside. This ship was heavily criticized by contemporary naval officers because her bunkers were too small, her machinery too delicate for hard work and the heat in the engine and boiler rooms excessive. The remainder of Dewey's fighting force consisted of the gunboats *Petrel* and *Concord*. The former was 800 tons, mounted four six-inch guns and could make thirteen knots while the latter was 1700 tons, mounted six six-inch guns and did seventeen knots. In addition to the *Nanshan* and *Zafiro* there was also the armed revenue cutter *McCulloch*. The entire squadron was repainted slate grey instead of the customary snowy white of American warships in peacetime.

On 23 April the squadron was requested to leave Hong Kong within twenty-four hours, as the blockade of Cuba had been proclaimed and hostilities began. The following day Dewey received orders from Secretary of the Navy John Long to proceed to Manila and capture or destroy the Spanish fleet there. His first thought was to leave immediately but then the Commodore learned that the American Consul at Manila, Oscar Williams, was en route to Hong Kong, so the squadron waited to obtain such information as the consul could give about Manila and its defenses. Williams arrived on the 27th at 1100 hours and the squadron sailed for Manila at 1400.

Spain had entered the war in a near hopeless position. She had been unable either to defeat the Cuban rebels (or those in the Philippines, for that matter), make any genuine reforms,

or accede to American demands because of the deep conservatism in the Spanish government and among the Spanish population of Cuba. As McKinley steadily tightened the diplomatic screws in 1897 and early 1898, some Spanish officials realized that Cuba was lost. But Spanish honor demanded that she be lost in a face-saving manner. Court circles, conservative politicians and nationalists preferred defeat in war to any surrender to American demands. Even Spanish moderates feared that any compromise over Cuba would lead the conservatives and nationalists to threaten the throne of the young Spanish king, then under the regency of his Austrian mother. 'They know Cuba is lost', Ambassador Stewart Woodford cabled McKinley, 'but they will seek honorable defeat in war'. And defeat was certain since the Spanish Navy was entering the conflict with only four armored cruisers, twelve old cruisers, five torpedo gunboats, three destroyers and some gunboats. Of this force only the armored cruisers, three destroyers and a few gunboats were actually in an efficient state, the remaining ships being in serious disrepair and of little use. The navy was especially weak in heavy armored ships of the battleship class without which there was no hope in sea battles.

The Spanish Navy faced other major problems from the outset. There was a serious shortage of personnel, and Spanish ships were undermanned. Due to shortages of coal and ammunition, the navy did no training in gunnery or maneuvering. As a Madrid newspaper put it, 'The Americans

The Battle of Manila Bay, 1 May 1898

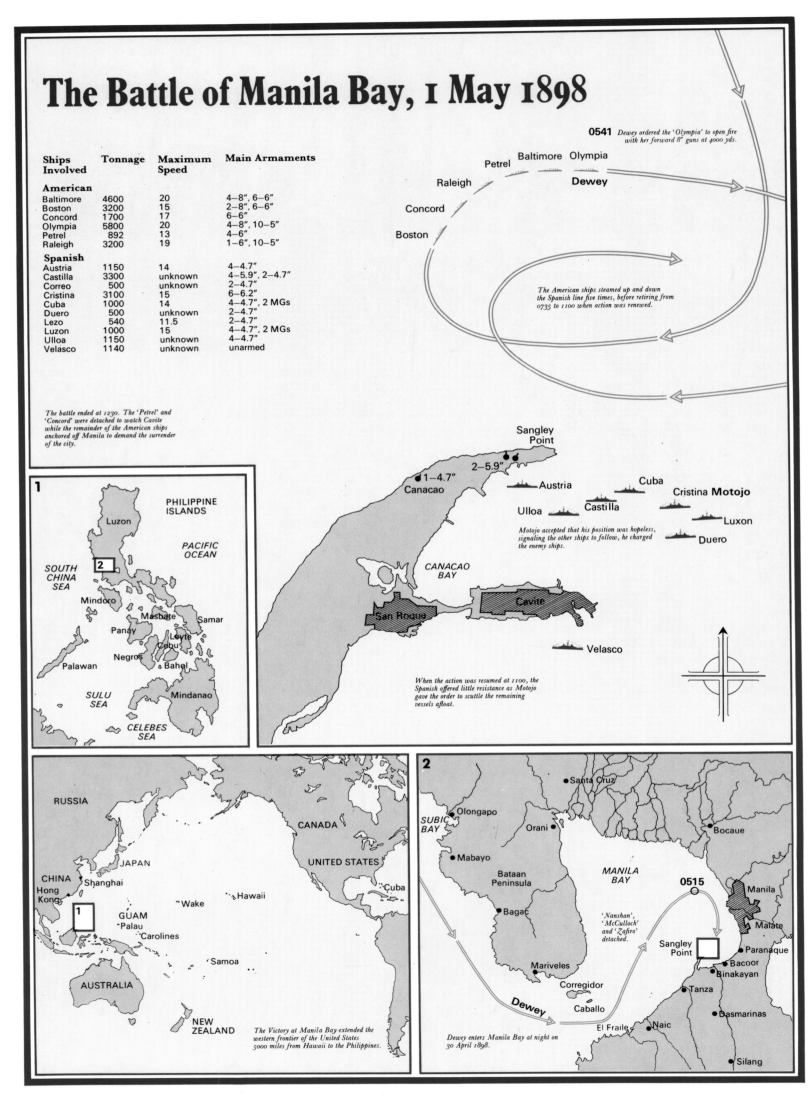

0541 *Dewey ordered the 'Olympia' to open fire with her forward 8" guns at 4000 yds.*

Ships Involved	Tonnage	Maximum Speed	Main Armaments
American			
Baltimore	4600	20	4–8", 6–6"
Boston	3200	15	2–8", 6–6"
Concord	1700	17	6–6"
Olympia	5800	20	4–8", 10–5"
Petrel	892	13	4–6"
Raleigh	3200	19	1–6", 10–5"
Spanish			
Austria	1150	14	4–4.7"
Castilla	3300	unknown	4–5.9", 2–4.7"
Correo	500	unknown	2–4.7"
Cristina	3100	15	6–6.2"
Cuba	1000	14	4–4.7", 2 MGs
Duero	500	unknown	2–4.7"
Lezo	540	11.5	2–4.7"
Luzon	1000	15	4–4.7", 2 MGs
Ulloa	1150	unknown	4–4.7"
Velasco	1140	unknown	unarmed

The American ships steamed up and down the Spanish line five times, before retiring from 0735 to 1100 when action was renewed.

The battle ended at 1230. The 'Petrel' and 'Concord' were detached to watch Cavite while the remainder of the American ships anchored off Manila to demand the surrender of the city.

Sangley Point

2–5.9"
1–4.7"
Canacao

Austria   Cuba
Ulloa   Castilla   Cristina **Motojo**
Luzon
Duero

Motojo accepted that his position was hopeless, signaling the other ships to follow, he charged the enemy ships.

CANACAO BAY

Cavite
San Roque

Velasco

When the action was resumed at 1100, the Spanish offered little resistance as Motojo gave the order to scuttle the remaining vessels afloat.

Inset 1

1

PHILIPPINE ISLANDS
Luzon
PACIFIC OCEAN
SOUTH CHINA SEA
2
Mindoro
Masbate   Samar
Panay   Leyte
Cebu
Negros   Bohol
Palawan
SULU SEA
Mindanao
CELEBES SEA

Inset world map

RUSSIA
CANADA
JAPAN
UNITED STATES
CHINA   Shanghai
Hong Kong
Cuba
Wake   Hawaii
1   GUAM
Palau
Carolines
Samoa
AUSTRALIA
NEW ZEALAND

The Victory at Manila Bay extended the western frontier of the United States 5000 miles from Hawaii to the Philippines.

Inset 2

2

Santa Cruz
Olongapo
SUBIC BAY
Orani   Bocaue
Mabayo
Bataan Peninsula   MANILA BAY
0515
Manila
Bagac
'Nanshan', 'McCulloch' and 'Zafiro' detached.   Malate
Sangley Point   Paranaque
Mariveles   Bacoor
Binakayan
Corregidor   Tanza
Dewey   Caballo
Dasmarinas
El Fraile   Naic
Silang

Dewey enters Manila Bay at night on 30 April 1898.

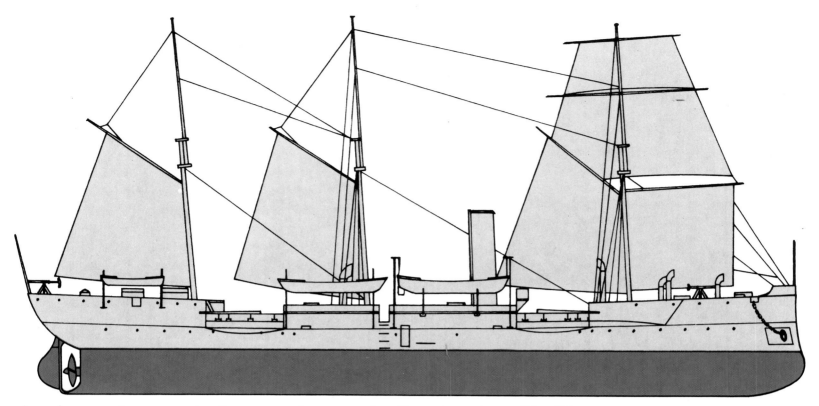

have for a year been preparing for war . . . there was not a day that they did not fire their guns. We have had but one target practice and that was over a year ago'. There were defects in some of the guns, while the country was simply too poor to keep its ships well-supplied or in good repair. No plan of operations had been prepared, especially for re-coaling the fleet. In vain did Admiral Pascual Cervera point out that even a victory would only postpone the inevitable disaster since Spain had no resources to repair or refit damaged ships. And counter to any concept of sensible strategy, the Spanish authorities weakened their already weak forces by deciding to send a squadron to the Caribbean under Cervera and a smaller squadron under Admiral Manuel Camara to reinforce the Philippines. It is little wonder that Cervera had a sense of impending disaster and wrote to Admiral Bermejo, Minister of the Marine, '. . . I hesitated exceedingly before accepting my command, but having accepted it I will face all the consequences which it involves . . .'

The sorry state of Spanish preparations for war generally was reflected in microcosm at Manila. Admiral Patricio Montojo was in command of a squadron of cruisers and gunboats but the cruisers were old, of little fighting value, had much wood about them, little or no armor protection and low speed. The best ship in the squadron was Montojo's flagship. the 3100-ton *Cristina* which had been laid down in 1887, could make sixteen knots and had as her main armament six 6.2-inch guns supplemented by seventeen smaller guns. The main support of the *Cristina* was the 3300-ton *Castilla*, a wooden ship with iron upper works and armed with four old 5.9-inch Krupp guns and two 4.7-inch guns. But the *Castilla* was no more than a floating battery, as she had bad boilers and a hull with leaks so bad that they could not be stopped if her engines were running. Although classed as cruisers, the *Cuba* and *Luzon* were iron ships of 1000 tons, fairly armed with six 4.7-inch guns each but barely

equal to Dewey's gunboats. The *Velasco* was an old ship of 1140 tons which was undergoing repairs and had neither guns nor boilers aboard. The 1150-ton *Ulloa* carried four 4.7-inch guns as her main armament but was also under repair and had most of her machinery ashore. The *Austria* was an old ship of similar size and armament to the *Ulloa*. The *Duero*, *Correo* and *Lezo* were ancient 500-ton gunboats mounting two or three 4.7-inch guns and suffering from low speed, lack of range and no protection. The total weight of the Spanish broadside was about one-third that of the American squadron but was less in actuality, since the Spanish ships were equipped with few quick fire guns. The Spanish did have nineteen torpedo tubes among their ships but no torpedoes with warheads.

Given this state of affairs, four courses of action were open to the Spanish at Manila. First, they could have landed the men, guns and ammunition from their ships to be employed in the defense of Manila and prepared the hulls of the ships to be blown up or scuttled on the appearance of the Americans. This was probably the most sensible plan and the one reportedly favored by Montojo, who was overruled by the military governor. Second, Montojo could have met Dewey under steam with his four serviceable ships, perhaps attacking at night or as the American ships passed Corregidor. Considering the condition of the ships, this was a dubious idea. Third, Montojo could have dispersed his ships among the islands and harassed the Americans as best he could. Such a plan would have caused Dewey considerable embarrassment and might have preserved the Spanish squadron. Lastly, Montojo could fight at anchor in Manila Bay with the support of shore batteries. This was the plan which he finally adopted.

Montojo moored his fleet in an irregular line with its west end in Cañacao Bay close to the Cavite Arsenal, protected by the guns of Fort St. Philip and Sangley Point. The east end composed of the *Correo*, *Lezo* and the transport *Mindanao*

Above: The American gunboat *Petrel*. Length: 176 feet; Beam: 31 feet; Draught: 11.6 feet; Displacement: 892 tons; Armament: four 6-inch, two 3-pounders, one 1-pounder, two 37-mm., two Gatlings; Speed: 11.55 knots; Crew: ten officers and 122 enlisted men.

Above: From left to right: *Isla de Cuba, Isla de Luyon, Reina Cristina, Boston, Raleigh, Olympia, Concord* and *Baltimore.*

was anchored in Bakor Bay within distant range of the Malate battery at Manila. Within the line, the stationary *Castilla* had her wooden hull protected with sand bags and lighters filled with sand on the side facing the enemy. The *Velasco* was moored off Cavite Arsenal with no guns aboard. The *Ulloa* was anchored in Cañacao Bay behind Sangley Point with starboard battery bearing, her port guns having been removed and placed in shore batteries.

The shore batteries should have been a valuable asset to Montojo but most of these were close to Manila and in an effort to save the city from American shells, the Spanish Admiral had moored his fleet too far away for the batteries to be effective. The Sangley Point battery with two 5.9-inch guns and three 64-pound muzzle loading Pallisers could not use the latter as the range was too great for them, while the 9.4-inch Krupp guns of Fort St. Antonio were five to eight thousand yards from the American squadron during the action. Thus the support of the most powerful batteries was largely neutralized by distance.

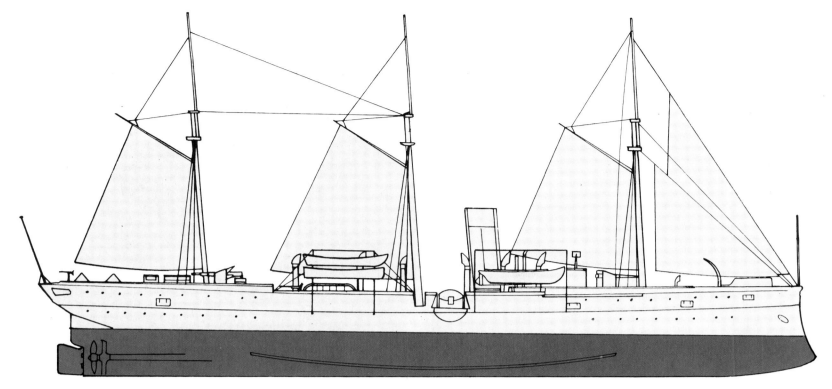

At seven in the evening of 30 April Montojo was informed that American ships had been seen earlier that day at Subic Bay. At midnight he heard the sound of gunfire and sent his men to quarters with the order to clear for action. Dewey had decided on a bold course of action after Consul Williams had provided him with detailed information about the forts and Spanish ships at Manila and told him of the state of unpreparedness there. Slowing his fleet to six knots and with only one screened light on the taffrail of each ship, Dewey determined to enter Manila Bay at night despite rumors of formidable shore batteries and heavy mining of the bay. The entrance to the bay had in fact been extensively mined but the water was so deep that the mines were well below the draught of any ship. Dewey also wisely attacked at night when the Spanish thought that navigation of the channel into the bay would be impossible for foreigners. By attacking immediately in the fashion of Nelson, Dewey robbed Montojo of any further time for preparations.

The American squadron entered the bay in single line ahead with the *Olympia* in the lead,

Above: The US gunboat *Concord*. Length: 230 feet. Beam: 36 feet. Draught: 14 feet. Displacement: 1710 tons. Armament: six 6-inch, two 6 pounders, two 3-pounders, one 1-pounder, two 37-mm, two Gatlings. Speed: 16.14 knots. Auxiliary sailing rig.

Left: A rather fanciful portrayal of the *Olympia* (left) hammering the Spanish lead ship, *Reina Cristina*.

followed by the *Baltimore*, *Petrel*, *Raleigh*, *Concord*, *Boston*, *McCulloch*, *Nanshan* and *Zafiro*. Dewey had placed his weaker fighting ships – the *Petrel* and the *Concord* – between the more powerful. In the channel to the bay were the islands of Corregidor, Caballo and El Fraile, all of which mounted batteries. Ships normally used the channel between Corregidor and the northern coast which was all the Spanish had mined. Dewey went in by the channel between El Fraile and Caballo, drawing only a few ineffective rounds from the El Fraile battery. With their crews considerably relieved by the unchallenged passage into the bay, the ships steamed slowly towards Manila, now 22 miles distant. Next, as they were to take no part in the fighting, the *McCulloch*, *Nanshan* and *Zafiro* were detached. By about 0515 on 1 May the squadron was off Manila and the first ranging shots were fired by the battery on Cavite.

Manila Bay was quiet as a mill pond on that warm and misty morning. Both the shore batteries and the Spanish fleet had opened fire at extreme range, dropping a hail of shells well ahead of the

American line steaming along at eight knots. The strain on the nerves of his squadron was so great, however, that at 0541 Dewey ordered the *Olympia* to open fire with her forward eight-inch guns at 4000 yards. He later recalled that he turned to the captain of the *Olympia* and gave the order by saying 'You may fire when you are ready, Gridley'. The ships astern quickly followed suit. The *Olympia* steamed slowly along the Spanish line as close as her heavy draught would allow, followed by the rest of the line, guns ablaze. Though it was still early in the day, the

Left: Admiral George Dewey on board USS *Olympia*. **Below:** Lithograph depicting all the ships in the US Navy at the time of the Spanish-American War. The ill-fated *Maine* appears top right.

THE · MAINE
DESTROYED BY EXPLOSION FEBRUARY 15TH 1898

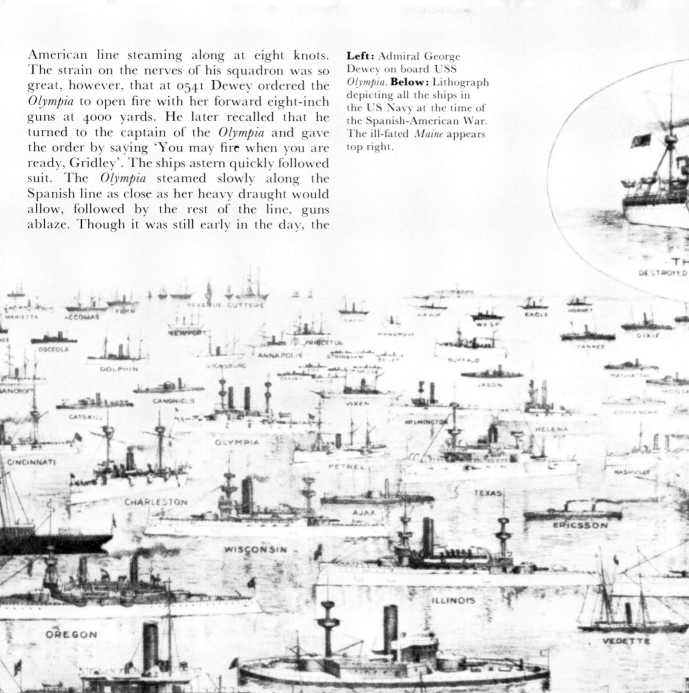

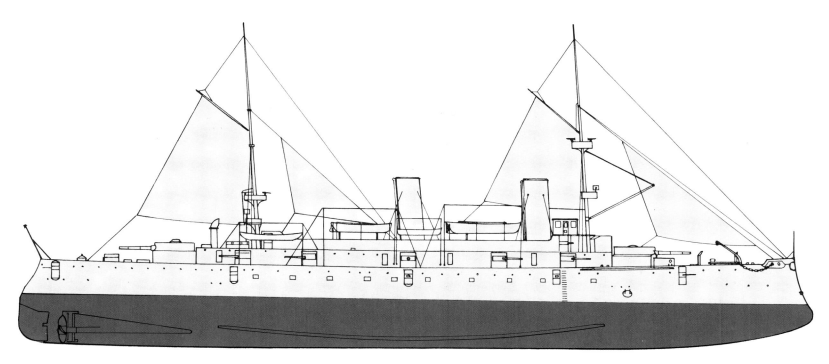

Above: USS *Olympia*. Length: 340 feet. Beam: 53 feet. Draught: 21½ feet. Displacement: 5870 tons. Armament: four 8-inch, ten 5-inch, fourteen 6-pounders, six 1-pounders, four Gatlings. Speed 21.69 knots.

heat and smoke were already very hard on the American crews. As the sun rose, temperatures of 116 degrees were reached in some of the magazines, prompting one sailor to remark 'We don't have to worry, for hell ain't no hotter than this!'

Dewey's ships ran down the Spanish line well handled and broadsides thundering, then turned and came back. The Spanish were firing heavily but ineffectively, their shots mostly falling long or short. The Manila forts also opened a fierce fire, but the range was too great to menace the American line. At ranges of 5000 to 2000 yards, the American ships steamed up and down the Spanish line five times, using mainly their heavy guns and adding the six pounders and smaller calibers when the range shortened. Before the fifth pass, Montojo had already accepted that his cause was hopeless unless he could close with or ram one of the enemy. Signaling the other ships to follow, he slipped his cables and charged the enemy. As the *Cristina* advanced a fearful fire was aimed at her and she was literally shot to pieces. One shot started a fire on the orlop deck, another swept the bridge and destroyed the steering gear, still another smashed the stern while yet another exploded in the sick bay, putting the wounded out of their misery for good. Finally an eight-inch shell exploded in or near the ammunition room and caused such an uncontrollable fire that the magazines had to be flooded. Burning furiously and with only two men left to fight the broadside guns, the ship managed to turn to shore where the crew was ordered to scuttle and abandon ship. Of the crew of 400, 200 were casualties including Montojo who was wounded in the leg by shell splinters.

The demise of the *Cristina* left the *Cuba*, *Luzon*, *Ulloa*, *Castilla* and *Duero* in the battered Spanish line. Moored with her port broadside bearing and protected by sand bags and lighters on that side, the *Castilla*'s forward cables were shot away so that she swung around and had her defenseless starboard bearing. With only one gun still in action, riddled with shot and afire repeatedly, her captain finally ordered her sunk and abandoned. The *Ulloa* had only two serviceable guns left when she was struck at the water line by a

shell which killed her captain and disabled half her remaining crew. The *Luzon* had three guns out of action but was otherwise unharmed while the *Duero* had only one engine functional and one of her three guns still firing. In the midst of this desperate situation, the Spanish suddenly realized to their amazement that the American ships had ceased fire and were steaming out into the bay. Montojo seized the opportunity to order the remaining Spanish ships into the inmost recesses of Bakor Bay where they were to resist to the end and scuttle when the battle was hopeless.

Dewey had been genuinely startled and alarmed when Captain Gridley of the *Olympia* informed him that only 15% of the ammunition remained for the five-inch battery. Fearing the other ships were equally short, the Commodore had ordered an immediate withdrawal, since little damage was apparent in the Spanish line and his gunners appeared not to have been very effective in their aim. 'It is true', later reported an observer aboard the *Olympia*, 'at least three of his (Spanish) ships had broken into flames but so had one of ours – the *Boston*. These fires had all been put out without apparent injury to the ships. Generally speaking, nothing of great importance had occurred to show that we had seriously injured any Spanish vessel . . . The gloom on the bridge of the *Olympia* was thicker than a London fog in November'. But a conference of captains held aboard the *Olympia* revealed no serious damage or men killed on any ship despite the fierce Spanish fire. Even more surprising was the discovery that the original message concerning ammunition had been garbled and only 15% of the ammunition had been expended rather than spared. While the captains were considering the happy news that more than sufficient ammunition remained for a vigorous renewal of the action, they were also informed that strong blazes had been sighted in the *Cristina* and *Castilla* and the sounds of exploding ammunition heard in the distance. It was apparent now that the main Spanish resistance had been broken and that essentially a mopping up operation remained.

Opposite: Dewey aboard the *Olympia* at the Battle of Manila Bay.

To avoid demoralizing the crews, Dewey had informed them that the halt had been called for breakfast. The sailors in the stokeholds and magazines were surely grateful as temperatures of 120–160 degrees Fahrenheit had been registered during the battle but the gun crews had wanted to continue the fight and shouted 'To hell with breakfast!'

When the action was resumed at eleven the Spanish offered little further resistance, as Montojo soon gave the order to scuttle the remaining vessels afloat, first carefully taking their papers and the breech blocks of their guns ashore. Dewey's ships again approached in line ahead, the *Baltimore* now in the lead. At a range of 2800 yards she engaged the battery on Sangley Point and the *Ulloa* which was lying just behind the point. The battery was speedily silenced and the *Ulloa* just as speedily sunk, although the water was so shallow that her upper works projected with the Spanish flag still flying. The *Olympia* and *Boston* also blasted the battery, although the latter was hampered by the heating of her guns which made the breach plugs hard to work. Burning in her upper works the *Cristina* was rocked by constant explosions off Cavite while the *Castilla* was a mass of flames in Cañacao Bay. The *Raleigh* had been directed to attack the ships in Bakor Bay but could not enter because of the shallow water, so the *Concord* and *Petrel* were sent in behind Sangley Point. The *Concord* fired on the transport *Mindanao* whose crew immediately fired and abandoned her. Attempting to attack the enemy ships behind Cavite, the *Petrel* pushed around the peninsula and fired on the government offices near the arsenal. These shots caused a white flag to be raised over the arsenal and all firing ceased. The *Petrel* then sent a boat to burn the *Austria*, *Cuba*, *Luzon*, *Lezo* and *Duero*, most of which were already aground and full of water.

The battle ended at 1230. The *Petrel* and *Concord* were detached to watch Cavite while the remainder of the American ships anchored off Manila to demand the surrender of that city. Dewey sent a message to the governor saying that if the Manila batteries fired another shot, the American squadron would bombard the city. The governor replied that the batteries would remain silent 'unless it was evident that a disposition of the American ships to bombard the city was being made'. With this half-truce, naval operations came to an end. Since Dewey had no troops with which to take possession of the city, the governor called his bluff on surrender. The American ships could only blockade the city by water to cut off supplies from the sea while the Filipino nationalist liberation forces of Emilio Aguinaldo besieged it by land.

A Total Disaster

With their entire fleet either sunk or burned, Manila Bay was a total disaster for the Spanish. Only two small gunboats, some steam launches and a small surveying ship were left to be captured by the Americans. Spanish casualties were 58 killed and 381 wounded out of a total of 1151 officers and men in the fleet. The remains of the *Cristina* showed 39 hits, including thirteen from eight-inch shells, although Montojo estimated that his ship took about 70 hits all told. The *Ulloa* showed 33 identifiable hits, while 40 were counted on the *Castilla* with probably twice as many in actuality. The *Cristina* and *Castilla* were so riddled with shells that an American journalist with the fleet wrote 'The *Castilla* after the action was so littered with pieces of our shells that it was impossible to walk there without displacing some of them'.

The American squadron had suffered no appreciable damage or casualties. With three hits on her hull and ten in the rigging, the *Olympia* had no damage worth mentioning and no casualties from enemy fire. She actually suffered more damage from the concussion of her eight-inch guns than from the fire of the enemy. The *Baltimore* had eight lightly wounded from splinters from a 4.7-inch armor piercing shell and one six-inch gun temporarily out of action but her total of five hits also rendered her no appreciable damage. The *Boston* was hit four times by six-pounders, while the *Raleigh* and the *Petrel* each took one hit and the *Concord* none at all. Total American casualties were eight lightly wounded in the *Baltimore*, one man grazed in the *Boston* and two injured by gun recoil in the *Olympia*. The American ships did, however, suffer a number of technical problems. Some of the guns tended to overheat slowing the rate of fire, some of the ammunition was unsatisfactory, and the electric firing mechanisms failed in many

Below: The Spanish admiral, Pascual Cervera.

ships which meant that the old percussion gear had to be used. Range finders were not available, and ranges had to be obtained by taking cross bearings and measuring off the distances on charts of the bay.

Despite the outcome of the battle, the Americans were agreed that the Spanish had fought bravely. 'The Spaniards lacked only the skill to make a good fight', wrote one officer from the *Boston*, while Dewey sent a personal message to Montojo that he would be glad to shake him by the hand and congratulate him on the gallantry of his fight. Responsibility for the defeat must be laid on both the governments in Madrid and Manila and on Montojo himself. The Madrid government had given Montojo a rusty, decrepit fleet and left him exposed to attack by a powerful enemy. The Spanish authorities in Manila were too distracted by the insurrection and the irresolution of the government in Madrid to order the retreat which prudence dictated. As the captain of the *Boston* remarked to the Spanish naval chief of staff, 'You have fought us with four very bad ships, not warships', and therein lies most of the tale.

Despite the admittedly wretched condition of his fleet, however, Montojo can still be faulted for lack of vigilance and for poorly preparing his defensive position. Had he defended the entrance to Manila Bay with strong shore batteries and his better ships, he could have kept Dewey's ships outside the bay and forced them into a blockade situation thousands of miles from the nearest American bases. Such a blockade could not long have been maintained for Dewey would quickly have run out of coal and supplies and been forced to leave. As it was, Montojo's main mistake was to allow Dewey to steam into the bay unopposed, the same mistake made by the Turks at Navarino. In his own report, Montojo laid the blame: 'The inefficiency of the ships composing the small Spanish squadron, the lack of all classes of personnel, especially of gun captains and seamen-gunners, the ineptitude of some of the provisionally engaged engineers, the want of quick-firers, the strong crews of the enemy, and the unprotected nature of the greater part of the Spanish ships, all contributed to make more decided the sacrifice which the squadron offered for its country.' His report notwithstanding, the Spanish government still saw fit to court martial Montojo, but he was acquitted. His defense included a letter from Dewey testifying to the Spanish admiral's gallant conduct of the battle.

News of the victory did not reach the world until 7 May because the Manila-Hong Kong cable had been cut. America went wild at the news and Dewey became the first and greatest hero of the war. Henry Cabot Lodge enthusiastically but inaccurately rated Manila Bay above the Nile as an epic victory. Most Americans had never heard of the Philippines, one wit remarking that he had thought they were canned goods, while even McKinley after being shown a chart of the islands said 'It is evident that I must learn a good deal of geography in this war . . .' Under the impact of the victory, the appetites of the expansionists were ravenous and even McKinley, having already used the war emergency to annex Hawaii, thought that 'the general principle of holding onto what we get is wise'. McKinley inclined from the beginning toward retaining all of the islands and in his usual manner began deftly to develop public opinion in this direction. An expeditionary force under General Wesley Merritt was immediately despatched to support Dewey, while the Spanish island of Guam was also seized to provide a base between Hawaii and Manila. Thus the route which was the principal American strategic line of communication across the Pacific until the Second World War was established.

The war with Spain was a milestone in the development of the American Navy and of American foreign relations. After its decade of reconstruction, the new navy successfully passed the test of war and emerged with enhanced prestige abroad and vast popularity at home. The importance of armor and the dependence of modern warships on coaling and supply was demonstrated by the American Asiatic squadron which without Manila as a base and constant resupplying could not have remained in the Far East. The acquisition of the Philippines, Hawaii and Guam, to which Wake Island and Eastern Samoa were added the following year, were all designed to assure the navy of adequate facilities in the Pacific. To keep them out of German or Japanese hands, Britain agreed to the American acquisition of the Philippines, while Japan made no diplomatic protest but did render some unofficial aid to the forces of Aguinaldo resisting the American occupation. Germany had tried to prevent war between Spain and the United States as the Germans wanted to purchase or seize the Philippines but finally settled for purchase of the Carolines, Marianas and Palau islands from Spain. The acquisitions of 1898–1899 constituted the American empire in the Pacific for the next forty years and launched the United States as an imperial power. Thus the war which had begun for the freedom of Cuba and the end of the Spanish empire in the Americas ironically ended with the subjugation of the Philippines by the United States and the establishment of an American empire in the Pacific. As a further irony, by acquiring the Philippines, the United States also acquired the insurrection, since the Filipinos were no more disposed to accept American than Spanish rule. But Cuba soon became independent, albeit as a sort of American protectorate, and the US took Puerto Rico from Spain as well.

Dewey's victory at Manila Bay extended the western frontier of the United States 5000 miles from Hawaii to the Philippines which soon came to be regarded as a center, second only to the Caribbean in strategic value, from which the navy could support American diplomacy in the Far East. Thus Dewey ended the time when the United States could remain aloof as a mildly interested spectator of events in East Asia. The United States was now forced into big power diplomacy to defend her interests and possessions in the Caribbean as well as the Far East. The seeds of the future conflict with Japan were sown on 1 May, 1898, seeds which eventually sprouted 43 years later.

Tsushima

It was a perfect night. A full moon lit the smooth sea rendering excellent visibility. Within the harbor the fleet lay anchored in three lines with a row of five battleships on the outside. The ships and harbor installations were fully illuminated by electric lights since the Viceroy had thought it would be 'premature' to put them on a war footing. Twenty miles out, two guard destroyers had not interfered but had run into the harbor at full speed to raise the alarm which arrived simultaneously with the first torpedoes. Nine attacking destroyers ran along the line of battleships, each destroyer in succession firing its torpedoes and turning away at full speed. Searchlights vainly pierced the night while hastily manned guns banged away at an enemy no longer there. It was the night of 8 February, 1904, the night when Admiral Heihachiro Togo opened the Russo-Japanese War with a surprise

attack on the Russian fleet at Port Arthur. As the war opened with this only moderately successful attack, so it was to end in a much different fashion a year and a half later at the Battle of Tsushima. The largest naval battle between Trafalgar and Jutland, Tsushima had a profound influence upon naval warfare and radically changed the structure of power in the Far East as a whole.

The war grew directly out of the competing imperialisms of Russia and Japan in Korea and Manchuria. In 1894–1895 Japan had fought China for primacy of influence in Korea and won Port Arthur and the Liaotung Peninsula by the Treaty of Shimonoseki. Russia had been pursuing a vigorous Far Eastern policy for decades and was now moving into Manchuria and Korea to compete with Japan. With the support of France and Germany, Russia had been able to force Japan to return her gains in the Sino-Japanese War to China, after which she then obtained a long lease on Port Arthur from China and began to develop it as the basis of her power in that area. During the Boxer Rebellion of 1900 in China, Russia took the opportunity to occupy much of Manchuria, from which she refused to withdraw. The Russian drive into Manchuria alarmed not only the Japanese, but also the British and Americans. The Russian threat brought Britain and Japan together in the Anglo-Japanese Alliance of 1902, the essence of which was that if Japan was at war in the Far East, Britain would intervene on the Japanese side if another power entered the war against her. The effect of the alliance was that Russia could not rely on French and German support against Japan as had been the case in 1895. Generally speaking, at this time Japan, Britain and the United States supported each other against Russia and France in the contest for power in the Far East.

It was not Manchuria, however, but Russian penetration into Korea that Japan found intolerable. Control of Korea was correctly seen as vital to the security of Japan or, as one Japanese statesman put it, Korea was 'an arrow pointed at the heart of Japan'. The Japanese had fought the Sino-Japanese War to remove the Chinese as rivals in Korea, only to see Chinese influence replaced by Russian. Russia in fact was virtually running the country. There had always been a strong 'war party' in Japan which advocated settling the Korean question by invasion and occupation, but as tension increased in 1903, the Japanese government first tried negotiations with

Opposite, above and below: Two Japanese portrayals of the attack at Port Arthur which inaugurated the Russo-Japanese War in 1904. The Japanese surprise attack which preceded a formal declaration of war effectively wiped out the entire Russian Far Eastern Fleet the first day. This forced Russia to send her Baltic Fleet to Asia if she were to combat Japanese naval power in the war.

Above: The capitulation of
Port Arthur took place
after several months of
siege. The Russian garrison
left the city as Japanese
forces entered to occupy it.

its rival. The Japanese suggested what amounted
to a mutual recognition of their respective spheres
of interest in Manchuria and Korea, but Russia
dragged out the talks in the belief that she was
strong enough not to have to accept any compromise. Also, Russia did not believe that Japan
would dare to fight a European power. When
asked if Russian policy might not provoke war
with Japan, the Russian Foreign Minister replied
'One flag and one sentry; Russian prestige will do
the rest'. Admiral Alexeiev, the Viceroy of the
Far East and rumored illegitimate son of Czar
Alexander II, was prominent among the 'hard

liners'. While negotiations limped along, Japan
saw Russian influence in Korea increasing even
more as Russians obtained land, timber and
business concessions. Since it was obvious that no
change in Russian policy was under consideration, Japan declared war on 10 February, 1904.

Japan was well aware of the role of naval power
as her lines of communications depended on it.
Possessed of a compact and modern fleet, it was
only in 1892 that she decided to look outward by
increasing her naval budget at the expense of the
army. The one naval encounter of the Sino-
Japanese War, the Battle of Yalu, had revealed
Japanese sailors as disciplined and well trained
while the victory had won the navy the enthusiasm of the nation. The officer who had fired
the first shot in the Sino-Japanese War was
Heihachiro Togo, now vice-admiral and head of
the fleet. Of samurai origin, Togo was highly
intelligent and experienced and as a young
officer had trained in Britain with the Royal
Navy. Japanese officers were often reported by
their foreign contemporaries to be highly professional. This, coupled with the battle experience
of the Sino-Japanese War, made the Japanese
navy a modern and efficient fighting force.

Always attentive to British naval policy, Japan
had decided to adopt its own 'two power standard' which meant that her navy should be
stronger than the combined Pacific squadrons
of any other two powers, excluding Britain. 'Any
other two powers' meant Russia and France,
and in 1896 a new naval program was launched.
Armored cruisers and battleships were built in
Britain but a fair number of light cruisers and
torpedo craft were constructed at the Yokosuka
and Kure dockyards. Japan was also largely
dependent on Britain for guns, ammunition and
coal. By 1904 the Japanese battle fleet was new

Right: Court ladies at
St. Petersburg make
garments for the Russian
soldiers at the front in the
Far East. **Opposite top:**
Officers of the Imperial
Russian Guard leave
St. Petersburg for the front.
The journey on the
recently-completed
Trans-Siberian Railway
sometimes took weeks.
Opposite bottom:
Admiral Heihachiro Togo,
head of the Japanese Fleet
and victor at Tsushima.

and homogenous due to Japan's late start in capital ship construction. All of Togo's battleships were less than ten years old and had similar speeds, turning circles and optimum gun ranges.

The two oldest battleships were the *Fuji* and *Yashima*, launched in Britain in 1896. Each was 12,500 tons, had a speed of eighteen knots and mounted four twelve-inch and ten six-inch guns. The *Hatsuse*, *Shikishima*, *Asahi* and *Mikasa* were new modern ships of 15,500 tons which could make eighteen knots and mounted four twelve-inch and fourteen six-inch guns. The *Mikasa* in particular had improved protection for her secondary armament and was one of the best of the world's pre-dreadnought battleships. To support her six battleships, Japan also had half a dozen armored cruisers – the *Asama*, *Tokigawa*, *Yakumo*, *Idzumo*, *Iwate* and *Adzuma*. These were 10,000 ton ships with twenty knot speed and mounted four eight-inch and fourteen six-inch guns. During the growing tension with Russia in 1903, Japan bought two new armored cruisers from Argentina with British aid. The *Kasuga* and *Nisshin* were both 7700-ton ships with twenty knot speed. The main armament of the *Kasuga* was one ten-inch gun forward and two eight-inch guns aft while the *Nisshin* mounted four eight-inch guns. The navy also had fourteen lighter cruisers and during the war armed 27 merchantmen as auxiliary cruisers.

Russia actually possessed three fleets – the Baltic, Black Sea and Pacific fleets. The Black Sea fleet was an instrument in Russia's age-old rivalry with Turkey and by the terms of the Treaty of London of 1870 was not permitted to pass through the Dardanelles, so it was not a factor in the Russo-Japanese War. Based at Port Arthur, the Pacific fleet contained seven battleships, six cruisers and several dozen destroyers

西京丸の敵彈蝟集

明勇ある樺山同令長官、
更ふ意ふ止せず益々猛進するや清
艦等の甲鐵艦定遠鎮遠の二大艦
驚愕せしが、再び水雷と分
魚形水雷艇を放ちて突進せしめ
通過せく令中せず大膽にも樺山中將の艦底深
射せん一兩艦、驚愕せし
とて西京丸の艦後に深上り
水を清り艦後に水雷と分

我驅逐艦隊於旅順港外近接敵艦激戰大破敵隊

Opposite left:
Transporting Russian soldiers across Lake Baikal on sledges. The problem of supplying an army thousands of miles away from the centers of population and industrial production proved insurmountable in the end.
Left: A Japanese version of the night attack at Port Arthur in 1904.

於黃海我軍大捷圖第一

Left: A Japanese artist's portrayal of the Battle of the Yalu River against China in 1894. The Sino-Japanese War of 1894–95 was the first time Japan put her fleet into action, surprising the world with the ability of an Asian nation to construct an effective, modern fleet. The world was shocked even more in 1904–05 when Japan was able to thoroughly defeat a major European state.

125

Top left: Japanese barbers and their clients aboard the *Mikasa*. **Top right:** The Japanese battleship *Hatsuse* in 1905. **Above center:** The Japanese battleship *Fuji* was built, like much of the Japanese Navy, in British shipyards. **Above:** The Japanese cruiser *Asama*, commanded by Admiral Uriu, which sank the *Variag*.

and torpedo boats. By itself it was more than a
match for Togo's fleet in terms of gun power and
numbers of ships. In 1898 Russia had begun a
capital ship program which made her the world's
third power in battleships behind Britain and
France by 1904, although the United States and
Germany were rapidly catching up. Well aware
of the progress of Russian naval expansion, the
naval factor was a major reason why Japan
elected to attack at the time and in the manner
that she did. A Japanese naval delegation had
visited Russian navy yards in the Baltic area in
the autumn of 1903 and knew that an additional
half-dozen battleships were destined for the
Pacific within a year's time. Already outnumbered in terms of battleships in the Pacific, Japan
had to act soon or war would not be possible in
naval terms.

Japanese war strategy was to secure Korea
and Port Arthur and then advance into Manchuria. To put troops into Korea, however, the
Russian superiority in seapower had to be
neutralized. Therefore Togo's plan was to destroy
as many Russian ships as possible in three simul-
taneous actions at Port Arthur, the nearby
Russian civil port at Dalny (Dairen), and
Chemulpo (modern Inchon), the port of Seoul.
Japanese intelligence had reported Russian ships
at all three places but on the night of 8 February
no ships were found at Dalny and only a cruiser
and a gunboat were destroyed at Chemulpo
where 2500 Japanese troops were also landed
under naval cover. With the surprise attack on
Port Arthur Togo had hoped to rob the Russians
of their battleship supremacy, but the attack
succeeded only in damaging two battleships and a
cruiser. These were minor losses which were
soon repaired, but Togo had seized command of
the sea and forced the Russian fleet on the
defensive, a position from which it never recovered. He had also insured that there would be
a land battle for Korea and perhaps Manchuria

浦潮港海軍之攻撃

八雲艦の砲撃ハ敵ニ散ス多大

の損害を加ヘ大勝利を以て引揚

露艦氷結困却の圖

as well. There was outrage in Russia at the immorality of the 'sneak' attack, but in Britain and the United States such a 'smart' move was generally admired.

Apart from three cruisers which raided from Vladivostok and were soon eliminated, the entire Russian Pacific Squadron was now bottled up in Port Arthur protected by formidable shore batteries. Togo made a number of efforts to destroy the fleet in the harbor but other than some skirmishing off Port Arthur, the Russian ships made no attempt to interfere with Japanese troop landings or communications. The Russian ships lay inert until the energetic Admiral Stephan Makarov arrived and rapidly began to whip them into fighting shape. Unfortunately in April Makarov's flagship, the *Petropavlovsk*, was sunk by a mine with no survivors. Without Makarov, the fleet took no further part in the war beyond several unsuccessful attempts to escape to Vladivostok. For their part, the Japanese lost the battleships *Hatsuse* and *Yashima* to mines in May but even so, the Russian squadron at Port Arthur showed no inclination to challenge Japanese control of the sea.

Japan prosecuted the war vigorously on land as well as sea. One Japanese army pushed south across the Liaotung Peninsula and soon had Port Arthur under siege while two other armies fought their way north into Manchuria. Although the Russians were pushed back to Mukden, the Russian Army remained intact and was receiving steadily increasing reinforcements. Then the

Japanese learned that their worst fears were about to be realized. The Russians had been giving some consideration to sending part of their Baltic fleet to reinforce the Pacific Squadron, but the news of the death of Admiral Makarov, the loss of the *Petropavlovsk* and the inactivity of the Port Arthur ships moved Czar Nicholas II and his advisors to make a final decision in this matter. The Russian plan was to relieve Port Arthur by sea, overwhelm the Japanese Navy with the now combined squadrons and thus delay the Japanese advance into Manchuria until enough reinforcements could arrive via the Trans-Siberian Railway for General Kuropatkin's army in Manchuria to turn the tide on land as well. In view of this turn of events, the main Japanese objective became to capture Port Arthur as soon as possible and destroy the Russian fleet there without risking their own fleet too much in the process.

The 'Second Pacific Squadron'

The man entrusted with command of what was called the 'Second Pacific Squadron' was the 56-year old son of an aristocratic and well to do family. Sinovie Rozhestvensky had joined the navy at 17, fought in the Turkish War of 1877–1878, served as Naval Attaché in London and after service in the Far East had become Naval Chief of Staff. He was a taciturn personality who rarely confided in his staff. In addition to his lack of command experience at sea, he combined a modest sense of tactics with a lack of imagination.

It is not clear what Rozhestvensky's views on the mission of the Second Pacific Squadron were, but it is known that he rightly felt the venture was extremely dangerous and that it was his duty to lead it in person. Others had higher hopes. 'The Czar with his habitual optimism expected Rozhestvensky to reverse the war situation' wrote the Minister of Finance.

The five divisions of the Second Pacific Squadron did not weigh anchor until 15 October. The first division consisted of four new first class battleships – Rozhestvensky's flagship *Suvorov*, *Alexander III*, *Borodino* and *Orel*. These were 15,000-ton ships with eighteen-knot speed and mounting four twelve-inch guns. The six-inch armament was mounted in turrets which was an improvement over the sea drenched casemates still used by

other navies. Their speed and stability was reduced, however, by the extra ammunition, provisions and coal which they carried on the voyage east; they had to be handled carefully and it was dangerous for them to turn at more than twelve knots with their gun ports open. The second division was led by the *Oslyabya*, flagship of second in command Admiral von Felkerzam, a modern ship of the same class as the ships of the first division. Then there were two old battleships of 10,000 tons armed with four twelve-inch guns – the *Sisoi Veliky* and the *Navarin*. The division was completed by the *Nakhimov*, an old armored cruiser of 6000 tons built in 1882. With the exception of the *Oslyabya*, these ships were no longer suitable for front line service in 1904. With his flag in the *Oleg*, Admiral

Enkvist led the third division of eight cruisers. The remaining two divisions were made up of light cruisers and destroyers.

The heart of Rozhestvensky's squadron was obviously the five modern battleships which compared very favorably with the best Japanese ships. There were a few differences, however, which were to be significant. Aside from their slower speeds, the Russian ships had a slower rate of fire per minute on their big guns which were still fired by lanyard rather than electrically. Russian shells were also lighter than Japanese shells, a twelve-inch Russian shell weighing 732 pounds versus 850 pounds for a comparable Japanese shell. This gave the former a greater muzzle velocity and hence greater penetrating power and a flatter trajectory, which in turn

Opposite: Rozhestvensky's fleet in the Straits of Malacca. Apart from incidents with British in the Dogger Bank, along the African coast and near Malaya, the trip was 'uneventful'. **Left:** The Russian battleship *Orel* shortly after her capture by the Japanese in the Battle of Tsushima. **Above:** Admiral Rozhestvensky, commander of the ill-fated Baltic Fleet, which became the 'Second Pacific Squadron'.

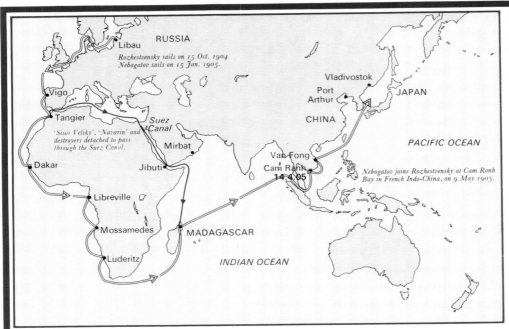

RUSSIA

Rozhestvensky sails on 15 Oct. 1904
Nebogatov sails on 15 Jan. 1905.

Libau

Vigo

Tangier

Suez Canal

'Sisoi Veliky', 'Navarin' and destroyers detached to pass through the Suez Canal.

Dakar

Mirbat

Jibuti

Libreville

Mossamedes

MADAGASCAR

Luderitz

INDIAN OCEAN

Vladivostok

Port Arthur

JAPAN

CHINA

PACIFIC OCEAN

Van Fong
Cam Ranh
14.4.05

Nebogatov joins Rozhestvensky at Cam Ranh Bay in French Indo-China, on 9 May 1905.

The Battle of Tsushima, 27 May 1905

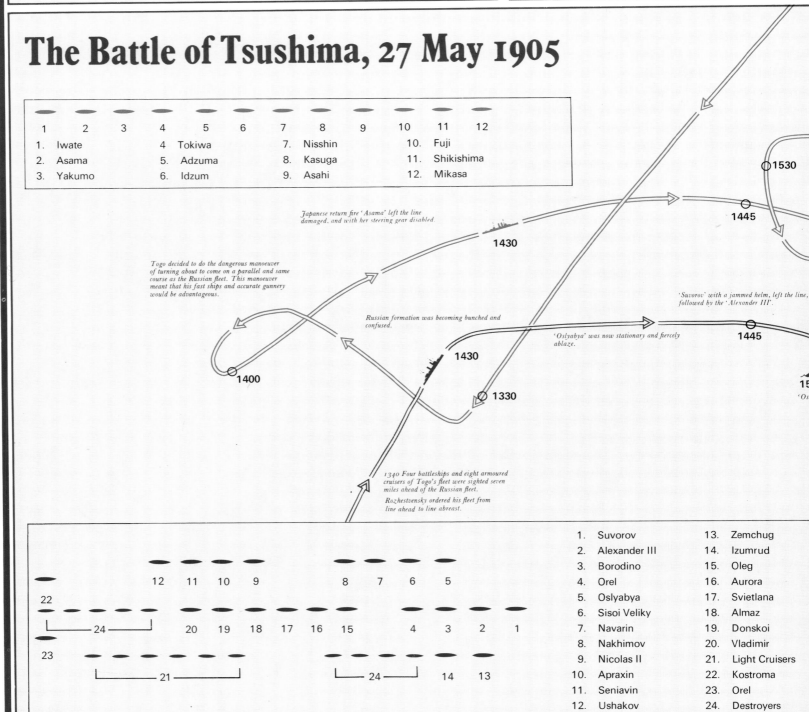

| 1 | 2 | 3 | 4 | 5 | 6 | 7 | 8 | 9 | 10 | 11 | 12 |

1. Iwate	4. Tokiwa	7. Nisshin
2. Asama	5. Adzuma	8. Kasuga
3. Yakumo	6. Idzum	9. Asahi

10. Fuji	
11. Shikishima	
12. Mikasa	

Japanese return fire 'Asama' left the line damaged, and with her steering gear disabled.

1530

1445

1430

Togo decided to do the dangerous manoeuver of turning about to come on a parallel and same course as the Russian fleet. This manoeuver meant that his fast ships and accurate gunnery would be advantageous.

'Suvorov' with a jammed helm, left the line, followed by the 'Alexander III'.

Russian formation was becoming bunched and confused.

'Oslyabya' was now stationary and fiercely ablaze.

1445

1430

1400

1330

150

Osly

1340 Four battleships and eight armoured cruisers of Togo's fleet were sighted seven miles ahead of the Russian fleet.
Rozhestvensky ordered his fleet from line ahead to line abreast.

12	11	10	9		8	7	6	5
22								
24	20	19	18	17	16	15	4	3	2	1
23								
21			24	14	13

1. Suvorov	13. Zemchug
2. Alexander III	14. Izumrud
3. Borodino	15. Oleg
4. Orel	16. Aurora
5. Oslyabya	17. Svietlana
6. Sisoi Veliky	18. Almaz
7. Navarin	19. Donskoi
8. Nakhimov	20. Vladimir
9. Nicolas II	21. Light Cruisers
10. Apraxin	22. Kostroma
11. Seniavin	23. Orel
12. Ushakov	24. Destroyers

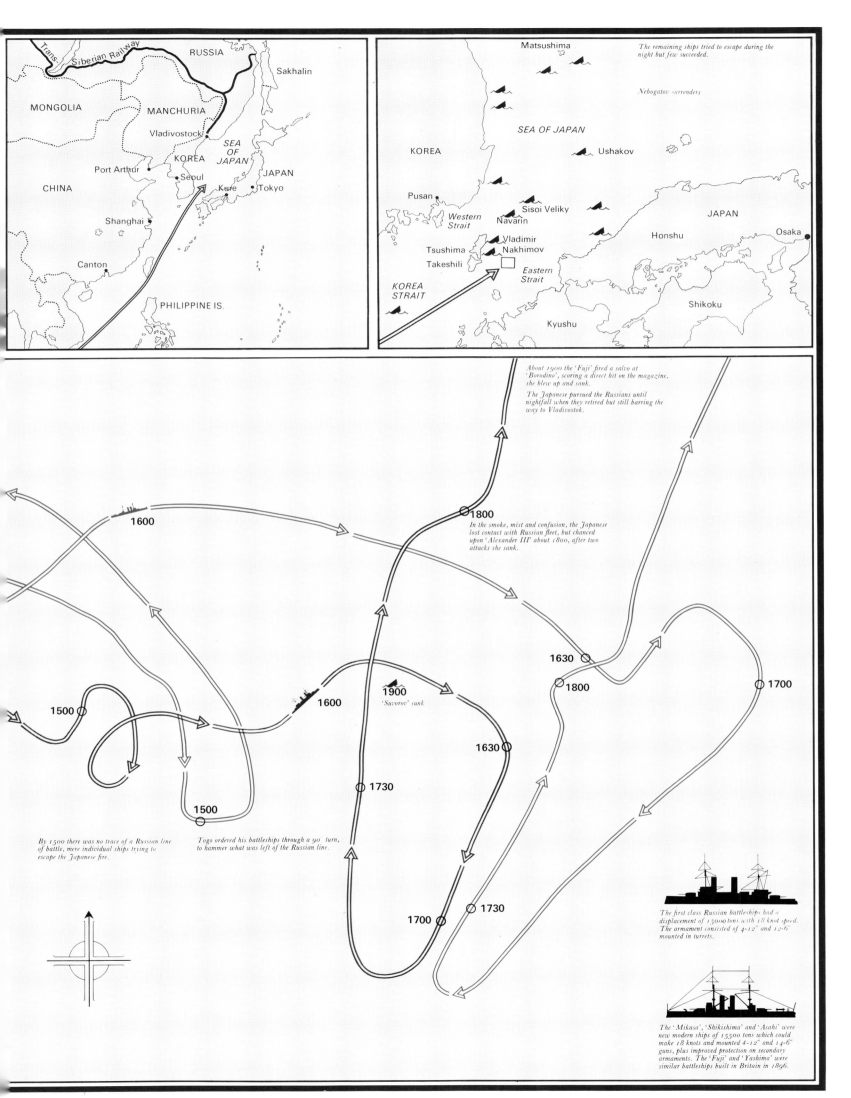

Trans-Siberian Railway

RUSSIA

Sakhalin

MONGOLIA

MANCHURIA

Vladivostock

SEA OF JAPAN

CHINA

KOREA

Port Arthur

Seoul

Kure

Tokyo

JAPAN

Shanghai

Canton

PHILIPPINE IS.

Matsushima

The remaining ships tried to escape during the night but few succeeded.

Nebogatov surrenders

SEA OF JAPAN

KOREA

Ushakov

Pusan

Western Strait

Sisoi Veliky

Navarin

JAPAN

Osaka

Tsushima

Vladimir

Nakhimov

Honshu

Takeshili

Eastern Strait

KOREA STRAIT

Shikoku

Kyushu

About 1900 the 'Fuji' fired a salvo at 'Borodino', scoring a direct hit on the magazine, she blew up and sank.

The Japanese pursued the Russians until nightfall when they retired but still barring the way to Vladivostok.

1600

1800

In the smoke, mist and confusion, the Japanese lost contact with Russian fleet, but chanced upon 'Alexander III' about 1800, after two attacks she sank.

1630

1800

1700

1500

1600

1900

'Suvorov' sunk

1630

1500

1730

By 1500 there was no trace of a Russian line of battle, mere individual ships trying to escape the Japanese fire.

Togo ordered his battleships through a 90° turn, to hammer what was left of the Russian line.

1730

1700

The first class Russian battleships had a displacement of 15000 tons with 18 knot speed. The armament consisted of 4-12" and 12-6" mounted in turrets.

The 'Mikasa', 'Shikishima' and 'Asahi' were new modern ships of 15500 tons which could make 18 knots and mounted 4-12" and 14-6" guns, plus improved protection on secondary armaments. The 'Fuji' and 'Yashima' were similar battleships built in Britain in 1896.

133

meant a greater margin of permissible error in estimating range. Since naval thought at that time assumed that battles would be fought between lines of battleships trying to force shells through the armor of their opponents, the duel between gun and armor was the dominant concept. The plain armor of the ironclads had first been superceded by compound armor, then Harvey (American) armor and finally Krupp (German) plate which was by far the hardest and was specified in all new Russian ships. At Tsushima the five modern Russian battleships all had Krupp armor, whereas only a few of the Japanese ships were so equipped.

All navies were at that time searching for an efficient armor-piercing shell and here the Russians were the most advanced with their AP shell which had a special cap to aid penetration. The shell had a relatively small bursting charge, however, which caused little damage and produced little smoke to help the gunlayers judge the fall of their shot. The British Navy was slow in this field and still used a 'common' shell with less penetrating power but a sizable bursting charge. Since the Japanese bought most of their ammunition from Britain, they also lacked a good AP shell but compensated by using a new explosive called *shimose* (after its Japanese inventor), which was more powerful than gun cotton with none of its disadvantages. *Shimose* had great explosive force which shattered the shell case into minute splinters (a single Russian sailor was wounded in 160 places by one shell burst) and also produced clouds of incapacitating smoke which caused headaches and giddiness and made it easier for Japanese gunners to gauge their accuracy.

The Dogger Bank Incident

Rozhestvensky's squadron faced severe problems from the outset. The crews had received no training and he was expected to remedy this lack en route. His new battleships had not completed their sea trials, while many of the remaining ships were simply too old for such a long trip.

Thus most of his ships suffered from engine trouble. Three ships were actually sent back as unfit once the voyage had begun. One Russian captain later wrote 'Our long voyage was a prolonged and despairing struggle with boilers that burst and engines that broke down. On one occasion, practically every ship's boilers had to be relit in the space of twenty-four hours'. And it was a long voyage, an impossible 18,000-mile route from the Baltic to Port Arthur along which there was not one Russian base. Coaling was to be done from 70 colliers chartered from the Hamburg-Amerika Line of Germany and the fleet included a number of stores and repair ships. After Rozhestvensky had talked the Navy Board out of giving him more antiquated ships, the fleet finally sailed in mid-October. Tension was high as rumors were rife of Japanese torpedo boats lying in wait along the route. After sailing all day on 24 October in mist and fog and keeping in bad contact, the ships of the first division saw small craft ahead and heard gunfire. Thinking their fears were realized, the ships opened fire and saw cruisers to the west also firing at them. After fifteen minutes of gunfire Rozhestvensky and Enkvist realized that they were firing on each other's ships. The small craft had been the Hull fishing fleet trawling the Dogger Bank, one of the busiest fishing grounds in the world. Felkerzam's ships had passed without incident, but Enkvist's ships had panicked and fired on the main fleet. One trawler was sunk and five more damaged while the Cruiser *Aurora* had taken five hits as well. Due to the rumors of the torpedo boats, Rozhestvensky had ordered his fleet to fire on any unidentified vessels which came too close.

What came to be known as the 'Dogger Bank Incident' caused an international uproar and raised the possibility of war between Britain and Russia. The British press called Rozhestvensky 'the mad dog' while Count Reventlow, naval correspondent of the *Berliner Tageblatt*, wrote trenchantly: 'The officers commanding the Russian ships must be all the time in an abnormal state of mind, and it is therefore not altogether

Below: Rozhestvensky's lost squadron. *Orel* (captured), in foreground, *Suvorov* in the center (sunk). Every ship in this illustration was either captured or sunk at Tsushima.

Above: The Baltic Fleet bombarding English fishing boats in the Dogger Bank Incident which created an international uproar.

unjustifiable to ask . . . whether a squadron led as this squadron is led, ought to be allowed to sail the seas'. Britain put all its squadrons on a war footing and sent a strong force of heavy cruisers to shadow the Russian fleet all the way to North Africa. In his own report Rozhestvensky maintained that there had been at least two torpedo boats among the trawlers, although why these boats had fired shells rather than torpedoes and how they managed to find the Russian fleet which was thirty miles off its expected course in a fog remained unexplained. The Russian government had to accept this weak explanation and later adjudicated the matter with Britain at the International Court at The Hague.

After this less than auspicious start the fleet arrived at Tangier where Felkerzam with the *Sisoi Veliky*, *Navarin* and the destroyers were detached to transit through the Suez Canal while the remainder of the fleet went down the west coast of Africa and around the Cape of Good Hope to reunite off Madagascar. During the voyage Rozhestvensky attempted to drill his fleet in maneuvers and deployment, but the results revealed confusion and incompetence and brought the Admiral to a scarcely veiled contempt for some of his captains and officers. As the voyage progressed he became increasingly taciturn which made communication between him and his officers even more difficult than usual. Morale among the crews sank to very low levels from hard work and boredom, the breakdowns and defects in the ships, and the failures of seamanship but especially from the news the fleet received on arrival in Madagascar in early January.

At the siege of Port Arthur the Japanese had finally succeeded in capturing a key hill overlooking the city from which artillery fire could be directed into the harbor. With eleven-inch howitzer shells from enemy siege guns dropping on them, the ships of the First Pacific Squadron had come to an ignominious end within four days, never having properly engaged the slightly inferior enemy fleet. With the demise of the Port Arthur fleet, Russian naval strength in the Far East was reduced to one armored cruiser and some small craft at Vladivostok. Later in the month came the news that Port Arthur had capitulated after a five-month siege. The people of Russia were deeply shocked and believed that nothing was left. Whatever Kuropatkin's growing army in Manchuria or the vaunted Second Pacific Squadron could accomplish seemed almost irrelevant. Serious disturbances broke out in Russia which signaled the start of the Revolution of 1905, news of which further depressed Rozhestvensky's crews.

The loss of the Pacific fleet and the fall of Port Arthur changed the position of the Second Pacific Squadron. The relief of Port Arthur was no longer an objective nor could a junction be made with the Port Arthur ships to overwhelm the Japanese fleet. If the Japanese were to be confronted in battle, the Second Pacific Squadron would have to do so alone. The only reasonable course left was to proceed to Vladivostok and use that as a base from which to disrupt Japanese sea communications. The assumptions upon which the Baltic fleet had been dispatched to the Far East were now largely unfounded.

At Madagascar Rozhestvensky found that Felkerzam's ships needed at least two weeks for repairs, though Rozhestvensky wanted to push on and attack the Japanese fleet before it recovered from the long and wearing blockade of Port Arthur. The Japanese in fact were so worried about this very possibility that, fearful of a reverse

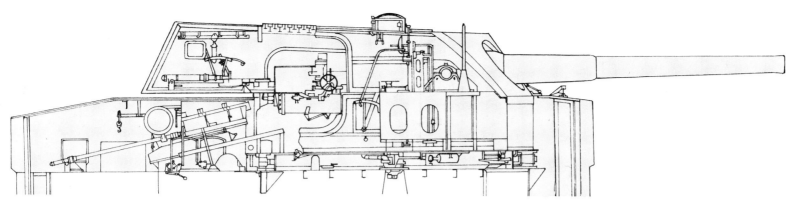

Far left: Admiral Togo on duty. **Above left:** A Japanese 12-inch gun turret.

Left: The Russian battleship *Potemkin* which mutinied in Odessa harbor during the Revolution in 1905 which accompanied the Russo-Japanese War.

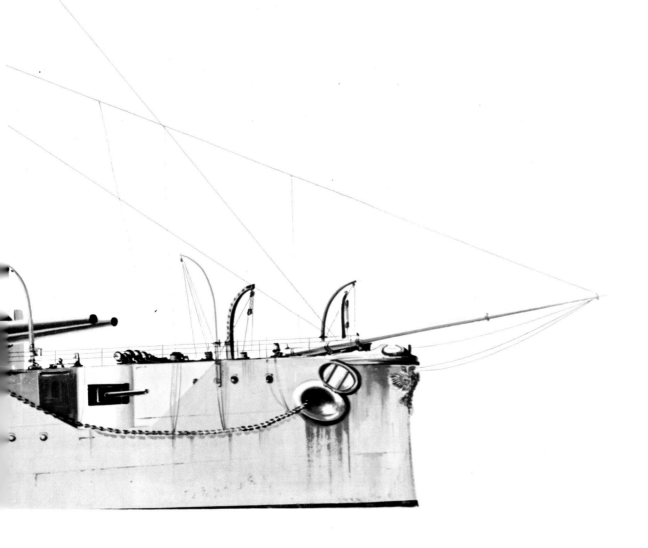

Left: *Potemkin*. Weight: 12,600 tons. Length: 115.3 meters. Beam: 22.3 meters. Range: 2816 km at 16 knots; 5471 at 10 knots. Armor: 150mm–254mm. Armament: four 304mm, sixteen 152mm, fourteen 76.2mm, torpedo tubes: five 45cm. Crew: 26 officers and 715 men.

at sea they began to stockpile matériel in Manchuria for a vigorous five-month campaign to prevent a disastrous peace settlement. In the event, however, Japanese fears were groundless as Rozhestvensky was also informed at Madagascar that another squadron had been despatched from the Baltic to reinforce him and that he was to await its arrival.

The reinforcement consisted of the same ancient ships which Rozhestvensky had persuaded the Navy Board not to send with him in the first place. Under the command of Admiral Nebogatov, the squadron consisted of the *Nicolas II*, an 1882 second-class battleship of 10,000 tons; the *Vladimir Monomakh*, a rigged cruiser of 6000 tons and equally ancient vintage; and three coastal defense ships, known derisively as 'flat-irons'. The *Apraxin*, *Seniavin* and *Ushakov* were small ships of 4500 tons, moderate armor and speed but large guns, the *Apraxin* having three ten-inch guns and the other ships four nine-inch guns. Among their crews these relics were termed the 'sink by themselves class'. After waiting until 16 March, Rozhestvensky sailed without Nebogatov, possibly hoping that the reinforcements would not catch up to him at all. Just before its departure, however, the Second Pacific Squadron suffered a further blow to its morale with the news of the Battle of Mukden. In the last great land battle of the war, 207,000 Japanese had attacked 276,000 Russians and forced them to retreat from Mukden at the end of February. The Japanese objective had not been the capture of territory but the destruction of the Russian Army in order to force Russia to the peace table. In this they had failed but the effect of the defeat, coming so soon after Port Arthur, was

shattering to Russian morale and brought the downfall of General Kuropatkin.

From Madagascar the fleet sailed across the Indian Ocean and on 14 April arrived at Cam Ranh Bay in French Indochina, having made a non-stop voyage of 4500 miles – the longest ever for a coal-fueled squadron without refueling. Probably with fresh orders about the reinforcements, Rozhestvensky tarried there long enough for Nebogatov to catch up and then the combined fleet of over forty ships sailed on into the South China Sea. Three possible routes to Vladivostok were now open to the Russian admiral. One route lay through the Korean Straits, passing the west coast of Japan into the Sea of Japan. The other two routes meant sailing around the east coast and using either the Tsugari or Soya Straits to the north of Japan. Had Rozhestvensky wished to attempt to avoid battle, he should have chosen one of the latter two straits, but instead he set his course for the Korean Straits, probably reasoning that avoiding battle served little purpose at this point.

Rozhestvensky apparently made few if any preparations for the battle he knew must lie ahead. He never consulted his three junior flag officers nor raised any discussion of contingencies. After the long voyage he apparently had a very low opinion of his subordinates and refused to consult them. In this event, however, they were even more in need of his detailed direction since they lacked initiative and skill. Also, signaling was chancey under the best of circumstances, so full orders were needed as Rozhestvensky would be unable to control his divisions in the heat of battle. But full orders were not given and a disorganized fleet approached the enemy. To

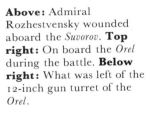

Above: Admiral Rozhestvensky wounded aboard the *Suvorov*. **Top right:** On board the *Orel* during the battle. **Below right:** What was left of the 12-inch gun turret of the *Orel*.

make matters worse, Felkerzam died on 23 May but the death of the second in command was kept from the rest of the fleet, which meant that it would have to turn to an already dead commander if Rozhestvensky had been put out of action.

Although he had mined and was patroling the Tsugari and Soya Straits, Togo was certain that his enemy would try the Korean Straits and had made his defensive dispositions accordingly. His heavy cruisers under Admiral Kamimura were based at Masampo, while his other ships were at Takeshii on the island of Tsushima. Tsushima lay in the middle of the Korean Straits and gave its name to the coming battle. Armed with squared maps of the area, four armed merchantmen and two old cruisers formed an outer guard line. Behind these were the four light cruisers of Admiral Dewa. The last concrete intelligence Togo had received was that the Russians had been sighted off the mouth of the Yangtse River on 25 May, but now he was worried as there had been no further news of them. As the Russian fleet approached the straits on the 26th, Rozhestvensky had ordered all wireless activity to cease and slowed his fleet so that their passage would be made in daylight as the night still held the terror of torpedo attacks. As daylight began to fade, Rozhestvensky gave the signal: 'Prepare for action. Tomorrow at the hoisting of the colors, battle flags will be flown'.

Around 0300 on the 27th, the auxiliary cruiser *Sinano Maru* almost ran down a Russian hospital ship in the mist and soon sighted more ships. At 0500 she sent the urgent message 'Enemy fleet in sight in square 203. Is apparently making for the eastern channel' (between Tsushima and the Japanese mainland). At 0634 Rogo wired the Emperor 'I have just received news that the enemy fleet has been sighted. Our fleet will proceed forthwith to sea to attack the enemy and destroy him', after which the entire Japanese fleet put to sea. Around seven the first contact was made by the cruiser *Idzumi* which followed the Russians through the thinning mist for an hour until the *Suvorov* trained guns on her at 9000 yards. At nine the four cruisers of Admiral Kataoka's division appeared on the port side on a parallel course but later moved off. At eleven four light cruisers appeared again on the port side but quickly made off when the Russians sent a few rounds in that direction. The weather was now definitely poor with a heavy rolling sea and thickening mist.

By noon the Russian fleet was sailing at eight knots off the southern point of Tsushima. Hidden now from the watching enemy cruisers by the mist, Rozhestvensky made his only real tactical

Above: Looking forward from the hurricane deck of the shattered *Orel* after her capture.

canary yellow funnels which made them better targets than the slate grey Japanese ships on that dull day. Togo's line consisted of his battleships *Mikasa*, *Shikishima*, *Fuji* and *Asahi* supported by the armored cruisers *Kasuga* and *Nisshin*. Then followed Kamimura's armored cruisers *Idzuma*, *Adzuma*, *Tokigawa*, *Yakumo*, *Asama* and *Iwate*. As the Japanese line reversed its course, the *Suvorov* and *Oslyabya* opened fire, followed by the other ships in the still somewhat confused Russian formation. The Japanese line returned the fire more selectively, six ships concentrating on the *Oslyabya* and four on the *Suvorov* with telling effect. 'Shells seemed to be pouring upon us incessantly, one after the other' recalled one officer aboard the *Suvorov*. Serious fires broke out on the Russian flagship and the *Alexander III* but the *Oslyabya* was the hardest hit with fires, her fore turret out of action and a great hole in her bow at waterline where two twelve-inch shells struck simultaneously. In the opposing line, Togo's flagship *Mikasa* took a number of hits while the *Asama* left the line holed and with her steering gear entirely disabled.

The Japanese line was now curving around to starboard and ahead of the slow moving Russian formation. At about 1430 Rozhestvensky could have out maneuvered Togo by turning to port and passing astern of the Japanese, concentrating his fire on the ships of the enemy rear. But with three of his battleships already battered, Rozhestvensky instead allowed himself to be pushed around by the faster fleet and veered to starboard, throwing his gunners off-target in the process. With the enemy now almost in a semi-circle ahead of it, the Russian formation was becoming bunched and confused, the *Oslyabya* and *Suvorov* again the main targets of what was becoming a cross fire. The *Oslyabya* was now stationary and fiercely ablaze while the bridge of the *Suvorov* had been cleared by shell splinters. Rozhestvensky himself had been wounded in the head, back and legs. Moved to the conning tower, he was again wounded in the foot and lost consciousness. He was later evacuated aboard a destroyer. Now a burning ruin with an eight degree list to port and both funnels collapsed, the *Suvorov* had a jammed helm and turned a complete circle, followed by the *Alexander III*. The remainder of the formation was now in complete confusion with little semblance of a line. The ships behind the *Oslyabya* now pressed past that stricken vessel and watched in horror as she turned turtle and sank, a few frantic figures clinging to her keel. A destroyer was sent to inform Nebogatov that he was now in command.

Togo Finishes the Job

Taking his battleship division through two successive ninety-degree turns, Togo returned to hammer what was left of the Russian line. Kamimura's cruisers moved in to pound the hulks of the *Suvorov* and *Alexander III* at 3000 yards. By three o'clock there was no trace of a Russian line of battle, merely individual ships trying to escape the ring of Japanese fire. In the smoke, mist and confusion, the Japanese lost contact with the disintegrating Russian fleet but chanced upon the *Alexander III* about six

maneuver for the battle by ordering his fleet from line ahead to line abreast, possibly thinking that he could cross the Japanese T by turning to starboard or port as Togo arrived from the north in the traditional line ahead. The execution of the maneuver failed, however, and left the fleet in two parallel but unequal columns. At 1340 the four battleships and eight armored cruisers of the enemy were sighted seven miles ahead to starboard. Since noon the Japanese battle force had been cruising ten miles north of Okino-shima and with the enemy now in sight, Togo made the Nelsonian signal 'The Empire's fate depends on the result of this battle. Let every man do his utmost duty'. On its present bearing the Japanese fleet would have passed its enemy on an opposite and parallel tack, but Togo decided on the dangerous maneuver of turning about to come on a parallel and same course as the Russians. This maneuver meant that his ships would mask each others' guns temporarily. But afterwards his faster ships and more accurate gunnery would be in a position to inflict maximum damage for a longer period than if the fleets passed each other on opposite courses.

One line of four battleships was led by the *Suvorov*, while the remaining seven armored ships were led by the *Oslyabya* in a line to starboard. All the Russian ships were painted black with o'clock, low in the water but with her fires under control. After two attacks, she sank with but four survivors from her complement of 830. Subjected to repeated attacks by torpedo boats and destroyers, the *Suvorov* went down at seven with all hands. At the same time, the *Fuji* fired the last salvo of the main battle, scoring a direct hit on the magazines of the *Borodino*, which immediately blew up and sank leaving only one survivor.

By the end of the day the Russians had lost five battleships, three auxiliaries and suffered considerable damage to most of their other ships. Admiral Enkvist with the cruisers *Oleg*, *Aurora* and *Zemchug* had disappeared to the southwest and weeks later were interned in Manila. Nebogatov had collected the *Nicholas I*, *Orel*, *Apraxin*, *Seniavin* and cruiser *Izumrud* and remained undetected through the night by running without lights. At daybreak the Japanese battle line was north of the recent battle area, the fleet having withdrawn to allow attacks on the remaining Russian ships by torpedo boats and destroyers during the night but still barring the way to Vladivostok. As Nebogatov steamed toward the enemy in the morning he knew that a further clash was futile and hoisted the international signal of surrender. 'I'm an old man of sixty', he told his crew before going to surrender his sword to Togo. 'I shall be shot for this but what does that matter? You are young and it is you who will one day retrieve the honor and glory of the Russian navy. The lives of the 2400 men in these ships are more important than mine'.

The remaining ships tried to escape during the night but few succeeded. The *Ushakov*, *Navarin* and *Sisoi Veliky* were sunk while the *Nakhimov* and *Vladimir Monomakh* were scuttled off Tsushima. The destroyer to which Rozhestvensky had been evacuated was captured and the still unconscious admiral became a prisoner of Togo. Only one cruiser and two destroyers reached Vladivostok intact while a few other ships managed to make neutral ports where they were interned.

The battle was an utter disaster for Russia which lost 34 of 37 ships, 4830 dead, 5917 captured and 1862 interned in neutral ports. Japanese losses were one armored cruiser and two light cruisers badly damaged, three torpedo boats sunk, 110 killed and 590 wounded. When news of Tsushima reached Russia, it produced numbed despondency among the people and for the first time sentiment to end the war among the aristocracy. After Tsushima the war for all intents and purposes was over, although the Russian and Japanese armies continued to face each other in Manchuria. What the Japanese Army had failed to achieve had finally been accomplished by the navy at Tsushima: the annihilation of a major Russian force to bring Russia to the peace table. Tsushima made a profound impression in St. Petersburg precisely because it was so complete a disaster that Russia had no alternative but to pursue peace.

Immediately after the battle, the Japanese government asked President Theodore Roosevelt of the United States to use his good offices as mediator. After quietly sounding out the Russians, on 8 June Roosevelt formally wrote to each of the belligerents offering mediation. Russian and

Right: The doomed *Borodino*. There was only one survivor. **Below:** The body of the commander of the *Orel* is committed to the sea.

Japanese delegates met in August at Portsmouth, New Hampshire where the Treaty of Portsmouth was signed on 5 September. By this treaty, Japan received Russian railway rights in southern Manchuria and the ports of Dairen and Port Arthur in the Liaotung Peninsula. Russia recognized Japan's 'paramount political, military and economic interests' in Korea and also ceded the southern half of the island of Sakhalin to Japan, thus giving her complete control of the approaches to the Sea of Japan. With the loss of southern Manchuria, Russia was forced to give up her ambitious plans in the Yellow Sea area and concentrate on consolidating her remaining position. Japan became established as a continental Asiatic power and immediately proceeded to develop southern Manchuria. Japan also derived such prestige from being the only Asian nation to have defeated a western power that many Asians were ready to overlook her expansive ambitions and see her as the best available leader in the struggle against Western imperialism.

As Tsushima brought to an end a war which gave Japan increased territorial strength and prestige, so the battle also directly affected Japan's relationship with the United States. Up to 1904 American interests in the Far East had been largely assured by a system of competing powers in which no nation had military or naval preponderance. This system was further supported by the fact that the two leading naval powers in Asia – Britain and Japan – worked with the United States to counter the interests of Russia and her allies. The preservation of a balanced antagonism between Russia and Japan had become an essential ingredient of Roosevelt's Far Eastern diplomacy. The total destruction of Russian naval power in the Far East at Tsushima and the consequent diverting of her interests elsewhere destroyed this balanced antagonism. Roosevelt in fact had tried to get Russia and Japan into peace talks before Tsushima to preserve at least some of the naval balance which was changed still further as Britain increasingly withdrew her ships from the Far East to meet the rising challenge of German naval power in Europe. Of the half dozen major powers present in the Far East in 1904, only the United States and Japan remained to share or contend for mastery of the Pacific a few years after Tsushima.

This fact was quickly recognized by each government. In 1908 the Root-Takahira Agreement made an attempt to delineate the general position of the two powers in the Far East. Each government agreed to respect the 'existing status quo' in the Pacific, implying that America would give Japan a free hand in Korea while Japan would respect the American position in the Philippines. With the balanced antagonism between Russia and Japan destroyed at Tsushima, however, the United States had to redress the balance of naval power in the Far East shattered by Russia's defeats. Japan passed from being a 'sure' friend to a 'possible' enemy in American strategic planning, so a battle fleet had to be sent to the Pacific. Pearl Harbor in Hawaii was made the principal American base in the Pacific rather than Subic Bay in the Philippines, which was now exposed to a hostile Japan. The Philippines in fact had become a source of weakness rather than a strategic point from which American naval and diplomatic influence could be exerted in Asia. The powerful American fleet needed to defend the Philippines was as threatening to Japan as Japanese defenses were to the Philippines. After 1909, therefore, neither Japan nor the United States could assure protection for their territories by military or naval means without compromising the defenses of the other, a problem which defied solution by either side until 1941. Thus it could be argued that the consequences of Tsushima were hardly less important for the United States than those of Manila Bay.

The Lesson of Tsushima

The navies of the world drew an important lesson from the action at Tsushima. It was noted that the capital ships had been sunk by big guns while secondary armaments had been of little use due to the range and modest damage which they could inflict. Even before Tsushima, naval thinkers in Britain and the United States had been considering a new battleship design termed the 'all-big-gun' type. As a result of the experiments in America of Commander William S. Sims and his colleague Admiral Sir Percy Scott in Britain, the effectiveness of large guns at long range had been greatly increased. It was recognized that a main battery of large guns of the same caliber could concentrate a far heavier fire more accurately at greater distances than the mixed batteries of existing ships. The first all-big-gun ship to appear was the HMS *Dreadnought* in December 1906. Her 17,900 tons, 21 knots, heavier armor and above all her ten twelve-inch guns gave the *Dreadnought* twice the offensive power of any ship in existence and made every capital ship afloat obsolete. President Roosevelt saw the new design of battleship as necessary for the maintenance of American power in the Atlantic and Pacific, and in 1905 committed the United States to constructing dreadnoughts, the first of which was the 20,000-ton *Delaware*. With the HMS *Dreadnought* a new era in naval warfare was launched.

Coronel and Falkland

1914

Opposite left: Lord 'Jackie' Fisher, the British First Sea Lord whose prompt action insured that the two battlecruisers arrived at the Falklands in time for the arrival of Admiral Spee's squadron.
Opposite right: Graf Spee talking to German consular officials in Valparaiso after the Battle of Coronel.
Below: British battlecruisers in pursuit of German cruisers.
Bottom: British battlecruiser *Invincible* works up to full speed as she leads the chase.

While the configuration of power in the Far East was being altered dramatically by the Russo-Japanese War of 1904–1905, the balance of power in Europe after 1900 was undergoing a fundamental re-alignment as well. The unification of the North German states in 1867 had produced a young and vigorous nation state which was challenging the status quo on the continent. Eventually the Triple Alliance of Germany, Austria-Hungary and Italy came to be one focus of power while Britain, France and Russia provided another. The conflict between the interests represented by these two centers resulted in the First World War which lasted from August 1914 to November 1918. World War I was a land war, with only two encounters of note between the German and British navies. Early in the war, small squadrons of German and British ships clashed in what came to be known as the Battles of Coronel and the Falklands, and midway through the war the controversial Battle of Jutland took place. Described by First Sea Lord Winston Churchill as 'the saddest naval action of the war', Coronel and its sequel off the Falkland Islands were the first time that the British Navy had been challenged in open battle since Trafalgar.

After 1815 Britain had been undisputed master of the seas but during the latter part of the nineteenth century its fleet had slipped into a sad state due to neglect and parliamentary parsimony.

In 1889, however, the large task of reconstruction was begun with the Naval Defence Act. From 1900 Britain began to accelerate the expansion of her fleet in specific response to a perceived threat from her neighbor across the North Sea. Germany was undergoing rapid growth industrially, commercially and militarily and becoming a major power in Europe. The ambitious new state had also embarked on a program of naval expansion in the belief that a strong navy was necessary to protect German shipping, commerce and colonies throughout the world and that a strong battle fleet in particular was essential to German foreign policy. Not only would it increase Germany's alliance value and strengthen her diplomacy but combined with her formidable land power, the new fleet would give her a commanding influence in the world. It is clear that the Germans had taken the blue-water theories of Alfred Thayer Mahan to heart.

Anglo-German Naval Rivalry

Although Germany steadfastly maintained that her fleet was not intended for aggressive use, Britain came to view the German battle fleet as its main security problem. Between 1900 and 1905 Germany had launched fourteen battleships against sixteen for Britain, a fact which indicated to the British that Germany would be the second naval power in the world by 1906. The belief grew in the public domain and government circles that Germany aimed first at continental domination and then world hegemony. What other reason could there have been for her strong fleet and massive army? Thus Anglo-German relations deteriorated from 1900, not only due to naval rivalry but to political, commercial and colonial tensions as well. In Britain war came to be regarded as inevitable. In the words of First Lord of the Admiralty Sir John Fisher, '. . . that we have eventually to fight Germany is just about as sure as anything human can be, solely because she can't expand commercially without it'. In 1904 the German Ambassador to Britain reported 'Most of the papers regard every step in the progress of our Fleet as a menace to England'. The reaction was to end the long policy of British isolation, forming in 1902 the Anglo-Japanese alliance, in 1904 the *Entente Cordiale* with France and in 1907 affecting a rapprochement with Russia. Thus after 800 years of enmity and rivalry, Britain and France were brought together by the threat of Germany. The alliance with Japan and the destruction of Russian naval power in the Pacific during the Russo-Japanese War enabled Britain to bring most of her ships back from the east while a subsequent agreement with France left the French fleet with responsibility for the Mediterranean. As a result Britain was able to concentrate most of her battle fleet in home waters against the German threat.

The threat in fact was far more perceived than real. There was no basic conflict between German and British colonial and commercial interests. On the contrary, they were each other's best customers. Real German aspirations lay in Eastern Europe and it was as a result of events in Eastern Europe that war broke out. The basic problem was that due to her geographic position athwart Ger-

many's sea approaches, any increase in German sea power posed a potential security problem for Britain, which is why she felt it necessary to concentrate her fleet in home waters after 1900. As the German naval attaché noted, 'The steadily increasing sea power of Germany constitutes the greatest obstacle to England's freedom of political action'. The war resulted from the various rivalries and aspirations of the continental powers, but when it did break out in August 1914, the Anglo-German naval rivalry had ensured on which side Britain would be. But the naval side of the First World War was almost entirely a non-contest between the British Grand Fleet and the German High Seas Fleet.

In 1906 Britain had 53 battleships to Germany's 20, a superiority which Germany would never have been able to overcome even with the most ambitious naval construction program. But in that year an event occurred which wiped out British superiority at the stroke of a bottle of champagne and rekindled the naval race on far more even terms. In December the HMS *Dreadnought* was launched, a launching which rendered every battleship then afloat or under construction obsolete. In the words of her creator, Admiral Fisher, the *Dreadnought* marked the 'beginning of a new naval epoch . . . today all nations start *de novo* . . .' Fisher had built the *Dreadnought* with such speed and secrecy that until she was launched it was not known what a radical design she embodied. The new ship caused a furor in Britain because she destroyed British superiority in battleships. The high cost of these new ships meant that fewer of them could be built compared to the old battleships. Fisher was severely criticized for this act, but he had had no choice. Not only was the technology available to build ships of this design, but it was known that the Americans, Russians and Japanese were all designing similar ships. By moving so rapidly and secretly, Fisher had given Britain almost a two-year lead in the dreadnought race.

The essential characteristics of the *Dreadnought* were gunpower and speed. The Spanish-American War of 1898 had convinced most navies that the big gun was the most important asset of the capital ship, a fact thought to have been confirmed in the Russo-Japanese War. At the same time, long-range firing was being developed. Until 1900 the effective battle range had been considered to be about 2000 yards with most captains expecting to come within a mile of the enemy and 'smother him with superior fire'. With the introduction of smokeless powder, new systems of fire control and more sophisticated range finders, accuracy at longer ranges advanced, until by 1914 16,000 to 18,000 yards was normal. Another reason for the increase in battle range was the increasing range and accuracy of the torpedo. Previously, battleships had only been vulnerable to other battleships, but now submarines and torpedo craft could launch torpedoes from distances up to 14,000 yards. The development of long range firing had an important effect on battleship design, as the varied armament of battleships had made fire control and accuracy at long range difficult due to different sizes of shell (and therefore splash), different rates of fire, and

Above: SMS *Dresden* flying the white flag before her sinking.

mutual interference from blast and smoke. At long range lighter guns were useless while the heavy guns reached their peak accuracy. Speed was another essential in a battleship, since it was widely believed that in a fleet action both sides would use the line ahead, in which case the line 'with the superior speed must win . . .'. Speed was 'the first desideratum in every type of battleship' wrote Fisher. Superior speed was the equivalent of having the weather gauge in Nelson's time, as it enabled a fleet to engage at the most advantageous moment.

The *Dreadnought* was a ship of 17,900 tons with 21 knots speed, two knots faster than any capital ship afloat or under construction. Ten twelve-inch guns were arranged so that six could fire ahead or astern, and eight on the broadside. Previous battleships could fire only two ahead or astern and four on the broadside; the *Dreadnought* was, therefore, equal to three battleships ahead or astern and two on the broadside. The only other armament was 27 twelve-pounders to repel torpedo boat attacks. Advances in gunnery had made the *Dreadnought* inevitable, for in the words of Admiral Jellicoe, 'The recent development of the prospect of hitting frequently at long ranges is the all important fact which has brought the value of the heaviest gun forward, and which culminates in the design of the *Dreadnought*'. The main armor belt of the new ship was eleven inches thick, while its hull had a large number of watertight compartments as a safeguard against torpedo and mine damage. Another innovation was the use of turbine as opposed to reciprocating engines. The former could operate at full speed for long periods whereas the latter tended to break down regularly. With its primary armament of eight to twelve

large guns of the same caliber, the *Dreadnought* set the pattern for all subsequent capital ships of every navy. Awesome in its overwhelming power, the *Dreadnought* was the Edwardian ultimate deterrent.

Another of Fisher's brainchildren was the battle cruiser, the first of which was the *Invincible*. At 17,200 tons the *Invincible* was virtually identical to the *Dreadnought*, except that armor protection had been sacrificed for a 25-knot speed and there were only four turrets mounting eight twelve-inch guns plus anti-torpedo boat armament. 'Indeed, these Armored Cruisers are battleships in disguise' commented the Admiralty committee on ship design. The battle cruiser was to function as a super scout, forcing its way through the enemy screen of lighter ships to get information on the size and disposition of the opposing battle fleet, and then to act as a fast wing of the battle fleet in action. With the 23-knot German liners in mind, another use Fisher considered was the pursuit and destruction of armed merchant raiders.

With Germany now less than two years rather than decades behind Britain, the *Dreadnought* and *Invincible* ushered in the most intensive period of Anglo-German naval rivalry. Other countries were also in the race. The United States had let contracts for its first dreadnoughts – the *South Carolina* and the *Michigan* – in July 1906 while Japan had laid down the keel of an all-big-gun ship even before the Russo-Japanese War was over. The first German dreadnoughts and battle cruisers were laid down in 1907 and an ambitious naval program was launched in 1908, aiming at thirteen dreadnoughts to Britain's eighteen by 1912. As the race went on, size escalated as well as numbers. From the 17,900 tons and ten twelve-inch guns of the original *Dreadnought* in 1906, Britain had gone to the 28,000 tons and ten fourteen-inch guns of the *Canada* by 1915. The first German dreadnoughts were 18,800 tons with twelve eleven-inch guns, while the largest German ships at Jutland were 25,800 tons and ten twelve-inch guns. At the outbreak of war in 1914, Britain had twenty dreadnoughts and nine battle cruisers with twelve dreadnoughts and one battle cruiser under construction. To these must be added one Chilean and two Turkish dreadnoughts confiscated while under construction in Britain and 39 pre-dreadnought battleships. In addition to her 22 pre-dreadnoughts, Germany had thirteen dreadnoughts and five battle cruisers with seven of the former and three of the latter on the stocks. Thus Britain had maintained a decisive superiority in the new naval race, a superiority to which it could add one more advantage. The British Navy had confidence and the German Navy did not. With centuries of tradition behind it, the Royal Navy was better trained, more experienced and spent far more of its time at sea. Soldiers at sea rather than sailors, the Germans lacked a certain offensive spirit, even though they were hardworking and better educated. The German High Seas Fleet spent much of its time in harbor and usually trained in sheltered waters. While the opening naval encounter of the war at Coronel had little effect on British morale, it had a significant effect on that of the High Seas Fleet.

Left: Rear-Admiral Sir Christopher Cradock, who lost his life at Coronel.

The German Navy's Passive Role

Well aware of British naval superiority, the German General Staff cast its navy in a passive role. The war was to be won by Christmas by Germany's incomparable army. The navy was to attack British commerce with submarines and surface raiders and prevent a landing on the German coast. But the war was not over by Christmas. In the first six months of the war, before the U-boat campaign began in earnest, the commerce war was carried on by detached cruisers and armed merchantmen. These ships were limited by coal and supply problems, and were a short-lived problem for the British, as the German bases from which they could operate soon fell. At the beginning of the war the Royal Navy immediately placed a distant blockade on the German ports to deny German naval forces and shipping access to the high seas. Since the German cruisers already on foreign stations had little chance of returning to Germany, they were ordered 'to carry on cruiser warfare against enemy merchant vessels and against contraband carried in neutral vessels, raid the enemy's coasts, bombard military establishments and destroy cable and wireless stations'. As the far-flung British empire was especially vulnerable to this sort of attack, these detached forces would assist the main fleet 'by holding many of the enemy's forces overseas'. The chief duty of these vessels was thus to damage the enemy as much as possible at the discretion of their captains since there was no way for orders to reach them from Germany. Nine cruisers were in foreign waters and were put to this use. The most successful was the light cruiser *Emden* which sank seventeen British ships in the North Pacific and Indian

Ocean in the first three months of the war before being sunk herself. In the Atlantic the *Karlsruhe* accounted for fifteen more ships. These losses were negligible when measured against total British shipping at this time, but public opinion demanded that action be taken.

The most dangerous threat, however, was the German China Squadron commanded by the aggressive Count Maximilian von Spee, a dangerous and resourceful adversary who had been in the Far East for almost two years. At the start of the war the 53-year-old von Spee had been on a training cruise at Ponapé in the Caroline Islands. Since Japan entered the war on the side of Britain on 23 August, it was obvious that his squadron could not long remain in the Pacific in the face of the Japanese Fleet. He therefore decided to operate off

Below: The British armored cruiser *Good Hope* was the flagship of Rear-Admiral Cradock and was lost with all hands at Coronel.

the west coast of South America where there were important British trade routes protected by only a weak cruiser squadron and where he could use the friendly ports of Chile for coaling. Von Spee knew that the effectiveness of his force would be short, writing to his superiors, 'I must plough the seas of the world doing as much mischief as I can, until my ammunition is exhausted, or a foe of far superior strength succeeds in catching me'. But to the British, von Spee's existence presented a genuine threat. In the words of Churchill, 'He had no lack of objectives. He had only to hide and strike . . . So long as he lived, all the Allied enterprises lay under the shadow of a serious potential danger'. So Graf Spee made his way across the Pacific and arrived off the coast of Chile toward the end of October with two armored cruisers and three light cruisers. The armored cruisers were the *Scharnhorst* and the *Gneisenau*, 11,000-ton, 23.8-knot ships manned by the pick of the German Navy and renowned for their accuracy with the six 8.2-inch and six 5.9-inch guns of each ship. These were supported by the light cruisers *Nürnberg*, *Leipzig* and *Dresden*, each mounting ten 4.1-inch guns and capable of 23 to 24.5 knots.

At first the Admiralty was misled into believing that Graf Spee was heading west rather than east. But on 5 October, on the basis of an intercepted message from the *Scharnhorst*, they informed Rear Admiral Sir Christopher Cradock, commanding the South Atlantic station, that the German ships were definitely on their way to South America and instructed him to 'be prepared to meet them in company . . .'. On receiving this information Cradock proposed the formation of two forces, each strong enough to face von Spee independently, to operate on the east and west coasts of South America. This would counter the possibility of von Spee slipping past Cradock and raiding in the Atlantic. The Admiralty agreed and formed an east coast squadron under Rear Admiral A. P.

Stoddart consisting of the powerful armored cruiser *Defence*, three other cruisers and two armed merchantmen. But Cradock received no reinforcements other than the old battleship *Canopus*. His west coast squadron was thus composed of the 14,000-ton armored cruiser *Good Hope* mounting two 9.2-inch guns and sixteen 6-inch guns, the 9800-ton armored cruiser *Monmouth* with fourteen 6-inch guns, and the modern light cruiser *Glasgow* with two 6-inch and ten 4-inch guns. In addition, Cradock was lumbered with the *Otranto*, an armed merchant cruiser never intended for battle. Manned mainly by reservists, the *Good Hope* and *Monmouth* had been hurriedly commissioned at the start of the war and rushed off to the South American station without even having

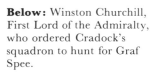

Below: Winston Churchill, First Lord of the Admiralty, who ordered Cradock's squadron to hunt for Graf Spee.

had time to fire their guns. A further problem was that the armor piercing shells for the armored cruisers were obsolescent. So were the fuses of the lyddite common shells of all the ships.

The Admiralty knew that Cradock's ships were not fast enough to force an engagement with von Spee but assumed that at least the force was in no danger from the enemy as long as it had the *Canopus* to serve, in Churchill's words, as 'a citadel around which all our cruisers in those waters could find absolute security'. It was recognized that without the *Canopus* Cradock stood no chance against Graf Spee, but there was no alternative in the eyes of the Admiralty since all the dreadnoughts and battle cruisers were needed in home waters. Vice-Admiral Sir Doveton Sturdee, Director of Naval Operations, had proposed sending additional ships but this had been vetoed by Churchill and First Lord of the Admiralty Louis Battenberg. Cradock's order for the *Defence* to join him was also countermanded by the Admiralty on the grounds that the *Canopus* was sufficient reinforcement. Lightly armored even for a pre-dreadnought, the *Canopus* was in fact an old second-class battleship which had been scheduled for scrapping but was reprieved by the war. The maximum range of her four 12-inch guns was only 14,000 yards compared to the 13,500-yard range of the German 8.2-inch guns. Her crew consisted largely of untrained reservists whose gunnery efficiency was very low. As her chief engineer later said, 'Our fighting value was very small – our two turrets were in charge of Royal Naval Reserve Lieutenants who had never been in a turret before . . .'

The Admiralty's first mistake had been to use the British and Australian naval forces in the Far East to capture the harmless German colonies of Kaiserwilhelmsland in New Guinea, Yap, Nauru and Samoa instead of hunting Graf Spee down in the first days of the war. After belatedly recognizing the elimination of the German squadron as a high priority, their second mistake was the failure to concentrate enough force to deal with

Above: *Scharnhorst* and *Gneisenau* (left and right in background) leave Valparaiso with a light cruiser for their rendezvous in the Falklands. The ships in the foreground are Chilean cruisers.

the situation. The *Canopus* had arrived on 18 October with engines that needed overhauling, able only to make twelve knots. Cradock cabled this fact to London but then added, 'but shall trust circumstances will enable me to force an action'. Although Cradock apparently believed that he was expected to seek out a superior enemy force and bring it to action, Churchill placed his faith in the *Canopus* and made no effort to clarify what action Cradock was or was not expected to take. On 22 October another cable was received from Cradock stating that he was starting a sweep around the Horn and was leaving the slow *Canopus* to convoy his colliers. Again Churchill made no comment on the detachment of the *Canopus* or Cradock's course of action. Thus the Admiralty's third mistake was its failure to clarify its intentions to Cradock. In the last days of October Admiral Fisher replaced Battenberg as First Lord and immediately apprehended the situation. The *Defence* was dispatched to join Cradock posthaste while Cradock himself was ordered not to seek battle without concentrating all of his forces including the *Canopus*. But Cradock had already rounded the Horn and never received the cable.

Given the fact that his opponent was known to be superior in speed, gunpower, efficiency and numbers, Cradock's motivation for seeking an engagement is puzzling. Described by Fisher as 'one of our best officers', the 52-year-old admiral may have felt that he had to fight after being refused the *Defence* and told that he had sufficient force. The Nelson tradition of aggressively seeking out the enemy was still very strong in the Royal Navy, and a colleague of Cradock's was at that time up for court martial for not engaging a marginally superior enemy. One widely accepted explanation among his colleagues was that Cradock was 'constitutionally incapable of refusing or even postponing action, if there was the smallest chance of success'. Another common view was that Cradock, knowing his mission was impossible, wanted to damage Spee far from any German repair yards and force him to use up his irreplaceable ammunition. Whatever the reason, with good sea-room and plenty of time to escape on 31 October off Coronel, Cradock instead turned toward the enemy and engaged.

Cradock had sent the *Glasgow* to call at Montevideo for any messages from the Admiralty, but when the light cruiser touched at Coronel, von Spee learned of her presence and came south from Valparaiso to dispose of her. In response to the news from the *Glasgow* that she was intercepting wireless traffic from a German cruiser, Cradock in turn sailed north. Each thought that his quarry was a single ship, and neither admiral discovered the truth until the squadrons sighted each other at 1640 the following day fifty miles west of Coronel. With his dream come true – an inferior enemy cruiser force looking for a fight – von Spee immediately altered course so as not to be maneuvered into a lee position and to cut Cradock off from neutral waters.

The ensuing battle was hopeless for the British ships: 'the most rotten show imaginable' as one survivor described it. In single line ahead, Cradock tried to close the enemy to force the

The Battle of Coronel, 1 November 1914

Ships	Tonnage	Maximum Speed	Main Armament
British			
Glasgow	4800	25	2–6", 10–4"
Good Hope	14000	23	2–9.2", 16–6"
Monmouth	9800	18	14–6"
Otranto	12128	18	8–4.7"
German			
Dresden	3600	24.5	10–4.1"
Gneisenau	11000	23.8	6–8.2", 6–5.9"
Leipzig	3250	24.5	10–4.1"
Nürnberg	3450	24.5	10–4.1"
Scharnhorst	11000	23.8	6–8.2", 6–5.9"

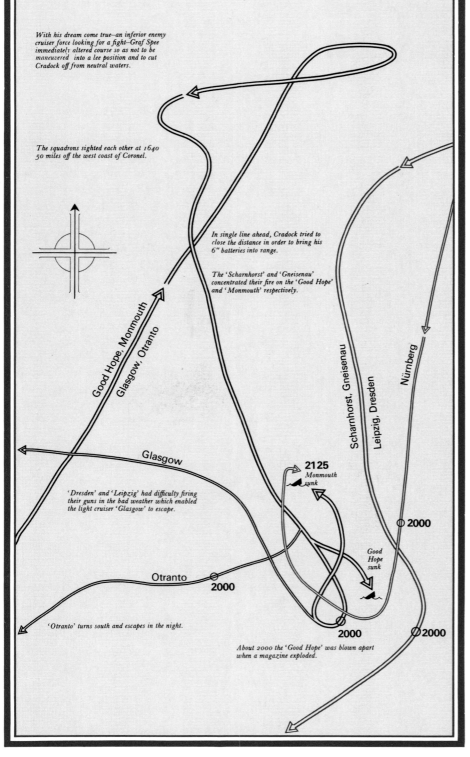

With his dream come true—an inferior enemy cruiser force looking for a fight—Graf Spee immediately altered course so as not to be maneuvered into a lee position and to cut Cradock off from neutral waters.

The squadrons sighted each other at 1640 50 miles off the west coast of Coronel.

In single line ahead, Cradock tried to close the distance in order to bring his 6" batteries into range.

The 'Scharnhorst' and 'Gneisenau' concentrated their fire on the 'Good Hope' and 'Monmouth' respectively.

Good Hope, Monmouth

Glasgow, Otranto

Scharnhorst, Gneisenau

Leipzig, Dresden

Nürnberg

2125 Monmouth sunk

'Dresden' and 'Leipzig' had difficulty firing their guns in the bad weather which enabled the light cruiser 'Glasgow' to escape.

Glasgow

Otranto

2000

2000

2000

2000

Good Hope sunk

'Otranto' turns south and escapes in the night.

About 2000 the 'Good Hope' was blown apart when a magazine exploded.

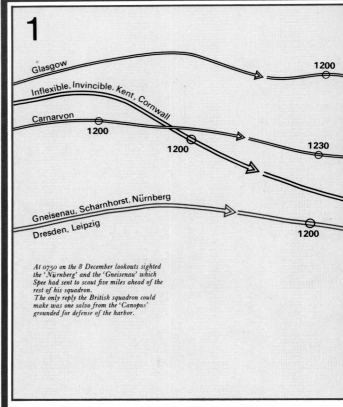

1

Glasgow

Inflexible, Invincible, Kent, Cornwall

Carnarvon

1200

1200

1200

1230

1200

Gneisenau, Scharnhorst, Nürnberg

Dresden, Leipzig

1200

At 0750 on the 8 December lookouts sighted the 'Nürnberg' and the 'Gneisenau' which Spee had sent to scout five miles ahead of the rest of his squadron.
The only reply the British squadron could make was one salvo from the 'Canopus' grounded for defense of the harbor.

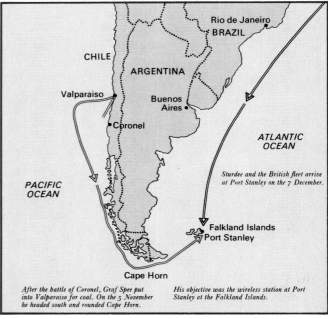

Rio de Janeiro
BRAZIL

CHILE

ARGENTINA

Valparaiso

Buenos Aires

Coronel

ATLANTIC OCEAN

PACIFIC OCEAN

Falkland Islands
Port Stanley

Cape Horn

After the battle of Coronel, Graf Spee put into Valparaiso for coal. On the 5 November he headed south and rounded Cape Horn.

Sturdee and the British fleet arrive at Port Stanley on the 7 December.

His objective was the wireless station at Port Stanley at the Falkland Islands.

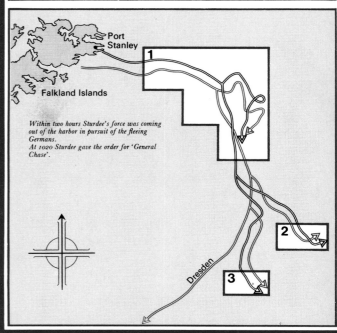

Port Stanley

1

Falkland Islands

Within two hours Sturdee's force was coming out of the harbor in pursuit of the fleeing Germans.
At 1020 Sturdee gave the order for 'General Chase'.

2

3

Dresden

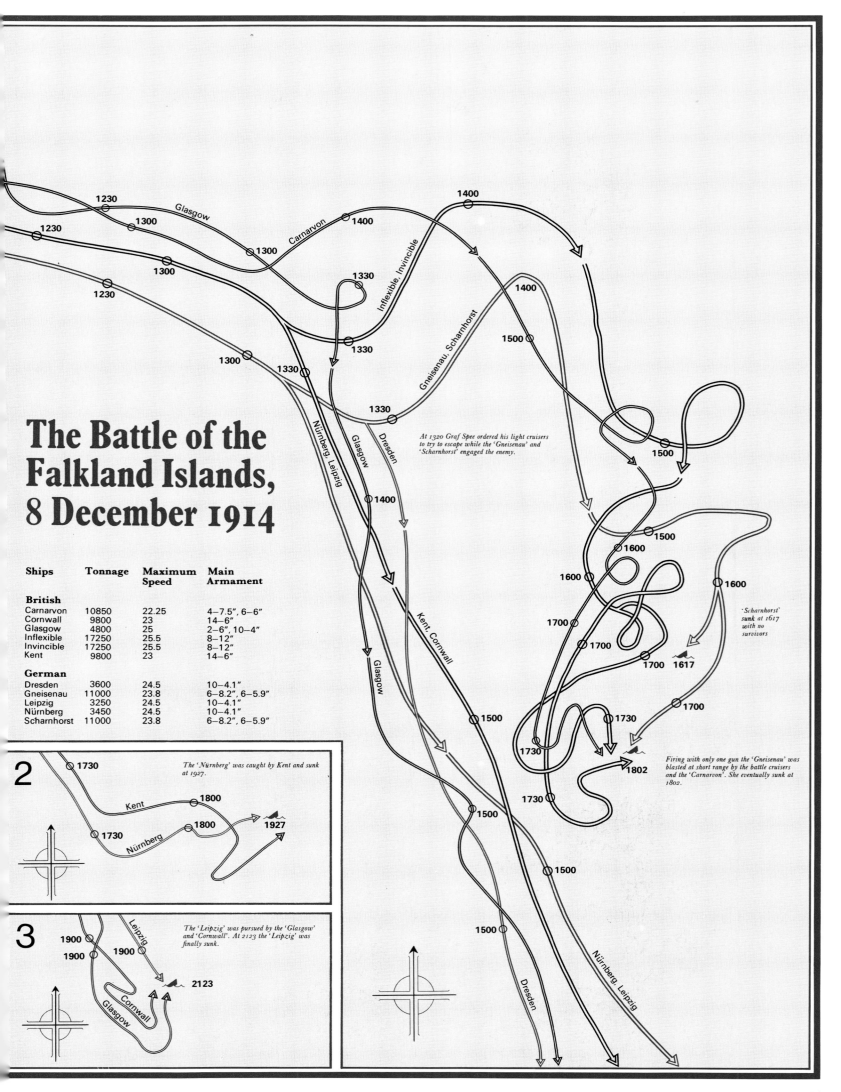

The Battle of the Falkland Islands, 8 December 1914

Ships	Tonnage	Maximum Speed	Main Armament
British			
Carnarvon	10850	22.25	4—7.5", 6—6"
Cornwall	9800	23	14—6"
Glasgow	4800	25	2—6", 10—4"
Inflexible	17250	25.5	8—12"
Invincible	17250	25.5	8—12"
Kent	9800	23	14—6"
German			
Dresden	3600	24.5	10—4.1"
Gneisenau	11000	23.8	6—8.2", 6—5.9"
Leipzig	3250	24.5	10—4.1"
Nürnberg	3450	24.5	10—4.1"
Scharnhorst	11000	23.8	6—8.2", 6—5.9"

At 1320 Graf Spee ordered his light cruisers to try to escape while the 'Gneisenau' and 'Scharnhorst' engaged the enemy.

'Scharnhorst' sunk at 1617 with no survivors

Firing with only one gun the 'Gneisenau' was blasted at short range by the battle cruisers and the 'Carnarvon'. She eventually sunk at 1802.

2 The 'Nürnberg' was caught by Kent and sunk at 1927.

3 The 'Leipzig' was pursued by the 'Glasgow' and 'Cornwall'. At 2123 the 'Leipzig' was finally sunk.

action before sunset. With the British between him and the sun, Spee was in a bad position and used his superior speed to keep the range at 18,000 yards until sunset. Then, with the enemy silhouetted against the horizon, von Spee quickly closed to 12,000 yards and opened fire. The two squadrons were on parallel courses but at this range only the two 9.2-inch guns of the *Good Hope* could answer the twelve 8.2-inch guns of the enemy so Cradock closed to 5500 yards to bring his six-inch batteries into range. A heavy sea was making it almost impossible to fight the main deck guns of the *Good Hope* and *Monmouth* which considerably reduced the gun power of the British line. The power of the British attack was further weakened by the poor quality of their shells, some striking and failing to explode.

The *Scharnhorst* concentrated her fire on the *Good Hope* while the *Gneisenau* blasted the *Monmouth*. Within five minutes decisive hits had been scored on each British cruiser. At 1930 the *Monmouth* veered out of line burning furiously and half an hour later the *Good Hope* was blown apart by an exploding magazine after taking more than 35 hits. Spee's crews had lived up to their reputation for excellent gunnery. By 2100 the *Nürnberg*

closed with the *Monmouth* which was then almost incapacitated and had only a few guns still in action. When the *Monmouth* refused to strike and made as if to ram, the *Nürnberg* dispatched her with shell fire at the point blank range of 600–1000 yards. Never intended to face warships, the *Otranto* had earlier turned south while the *Glasgow* also escaped because her adversaries – the small cruisers *Dresden* and *Leipzig* – had difficulty fighting their guns in the bad weather.

By superior force, skilful tactics and first class gunnery, von Spee had sunk two second-class enemy cruisers with the loss of all their crews and a rear-admiral while his own ships had suffered only six hits and two wounded. But the encounter had been costly in another way, for the German cruisers had used almost half of their 8.2-inch shells and these could only be obtained from Germany. After the battle Graf Spee put into Valparaiso to coal, and then received orders to try to break through to Germany with his ships. On 5 November he steered south with the intention of doing as much damage as possible on the way. His first objective was the wireless station at Port Stanley in the Falkland Islands where he also hoped to find a weak British cruiser squadron taking on coal.

The strategic gains reaped from Coronel by the Germans were practically nil – at best a temporary suspension of nitrate, copper and tin shipments from Chile and Peru. But the battle had been a blow to British prestige. Even though the losses at Coronel were negligible, they were still the first losses in battle in over a hundred years. Although the Admiralty blamed Cradock for disobeying orders by failing to concentrate his force, public reaction felt that the Admiralty had

Below: Rear-Admiral A. P. Stoddart commanded the cruiser squadron at the Battle of the Falklands.
Right, above and below: Two pictures of the German cruiser *Dresden*, sunk by the *Glasgow* five months after the Battle of the Falklands. The British ship violated Chilean neutrality to make certain of sinking the last survivor of Spee's squadron.

bungled by placing Cradock in a position where he had to face a superior enemy force. The setback also had its effect on the balance of neutral opinion. The news of the battle was received with great enthusiasm in Germany where Admiral Reinhard Scheer wrote that 'this news filled us in the fleet with great pride and confidence'.

The Search for Graf Spee

Within a day of learning of Coronel, Churchill and Fisher had developed plans to eliminate von Spee. The best course for the Germans would be to pass into the South Atlantic for operations there off the east coast of South America. Fisher therefore determined to create a powerful force to annihilate the raiders. He somewhat unjustly blamed the Director of Naval Operations, Vice-Admiral Sir Doveton Sturdee, for the faulty dispositions which had led to Coronel and fired him. The only post which was acceptable to Sturdee was command of the South Atlantic and South Pacific station. So ironically the man whom many held responsible for Coronel was charged with avenging it. The 55-year-old Sturdee was ordered to incorporate Stoddart's force and, using the Falklands as a base, to hunt and destroy the German squadron. The battle cruisers *Invincible* and *Inflexible*, identical 17,250-ton, 25.5-knot ships mounting eight 12-inch guns, were the core of his force; the remainder was Stoddart's armored cruisers *Defence*, *Cornwall*, *Kent*, *Carnarvon*, the light cruisers *Glasgow* and *Bristol*, and the armed merchant cruiser *Macedonia*. The two battle cruisers sailed on 11 November and arrived at Port Stanley on 7 December, having collected Stoddart's ships off Brazil on the way. Sturdee intended to leave the following day after coaling his

squadron, as the available intelligence still placed the Germans off the coast of Chile.

At 0750 the following morning, however, lookouts were surprised to sight two unidentified warships approaching from the south. Spee had sent the *Gneisenau* and *Nürnberg* to scout five miles ahead of the rest of his squadron. The British ships were still coaling and none had steam up, so if Graf Spee had come up with his entire force, he could have blasted each British ship as it emerged from the harbor. As it was, the only response the British could make was one salvo from the *Canopus*, now grounded for defense of the harbor. Aware neither of the unprepared state in which he had caught the British nor of the presence of two battle cruisers, von Spee decided not to risk an action and to use his superior speed to escape. The salvo from the *Canopus* had caused the two scouts to veer off while the British ships frantically got up steam. Within two hours Sturdee's force was coming out of the harbor in pursuit of the fleeing Germans. It was a calm, clear day with excellent visibility, ideal conditions for a shooting match. With plenty of sea-room and eight hours of daylight, Sturdee gave the order for 'General Chase' at 1020.

Von Spee fled southeast but at 1247, when the range had narrowed to 16,000 yards and his hindmost ship, the *Leipzig*, was coming under fire, the German admiral knew that the 12-inch guns and greater speed of the battle cruisers spelled the doom of his squadron. At 1320 he ordered his light cruisers to try to escape while the *Scharnhorst* and *Gneisenau* engaged the enemy. The three small cruisers scattered in the direction of the South American coast with three British cruisers hard on their heels. The *Nürnberg* was

Below: At about 1 p.m. the battlecruiser *Inflexible* opened fire on the German ships with her forward 12-inch guns.

Below: SMS *Scharnhorst*, which was launched in 1906. Displacement: 11,600 tons. Length: 474 feet. Beam: 71 feet. Draught: 24.5 feet. Speed: 22.5 knots. Armament: eight 8.2-inch, six 5.9-inch, eighteen .4-inch guns and four 18-inch torpedo tubes. Crew: 764 officers and men. **Opposite left:** A shell from the *Nürnberg* carried away the topmast of the *Kent*. The funnels are blistered from the intense heat generated during the chase. **Opposite right:** A six-inch casemate in HMS *Kent* after the Battle of the Falklands. The shell hole was caused by a hit from the *Nürnberg*. **Opposite center:** The armored cruiser *Kent* was hit several times by German shells during the battle. This is a hole in the engine room artificers' bathroom made by a 4.1-inch shell.

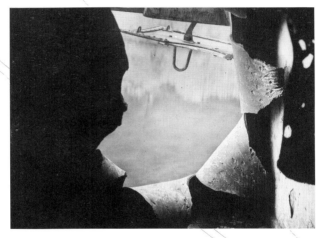

caught by the *Kent* and sunk after an unequal but fierce short range duel. The *Glasgow* and *Cornwall* ran down and destroyed the *Leipzig* which sank at 2123 while the *Bristol* and *Macedonia* sank two of the three German colliers. The third collier and the *Dresden* escaped, the former to be interned in Argentina and the latter to be sunk by the *Glasgow* five months later.

While the light cruisers were making their bids for survival, the armored cruisers were confronting the battle cruisers in another unequal struggle. Each admiral was maneuvering to get the range most suitable for his guns. Sturdee tried to keep a position where his 12-inch guns could outrange the 8.2-inch guns of the enemy, while von Spee tried to close the range to bring his 5.9-inch batteries into action and thus gain some advantage over the battle cruisers which had no intermediate armament. By 1500 von Spee had reduced the range to 11,000 yards and was hammering the battle cruisers with an accurate fire. Sturdee tried to counter by using his superior speed to open the range again and also to get clear of the battle smoke which was reducing his

gunnery efficiency. Even so, the 12-inch guns of the battle cruisers had already scored serious hits, for within half an hour the *Scharnhorst* was listing heavily and on fire. Disregarding signals to strike, she went down at 1617 with no survivors. Fighting with only one gun, the *Gneisenau* was blasted at short range by the battle cruisers and the *Carnarvon*, absorbing at least fifty 12-inch shells. She was listing, her upper deck a shambles and burning fiercely, but her captain refused to surrender, preferring instead to open his valves and blast out the sides of the ship with charges. The *Gneisenau* was finally abandoned at 1800 and 200 survivors were picked up.

Graf Spee had fought to the bitter end against hopeless odds, losing four of five ships and 2200 men as well as his own life. Sturdee's force had suffered little damage and few casualties, which only increased the jubilation in Britain over the victory. The Battle of the Falklands stilled public criticism of the Admiralty and reassured Britain's allies that the Royal Navy was still master of the seas. Even though he had achieved the Royal Navy's nearest approach to a smashing victory in the war, Sturdee still had his critics who pointed out that a weaker enemy had literally sailed into his backyard. Even Sturdee had to acknowledge this when he said of von Spee '. . . he gave our squadron a chance by calling on me the day after I arrived'. Fisher and Churchill were also cool toward him for allowing the

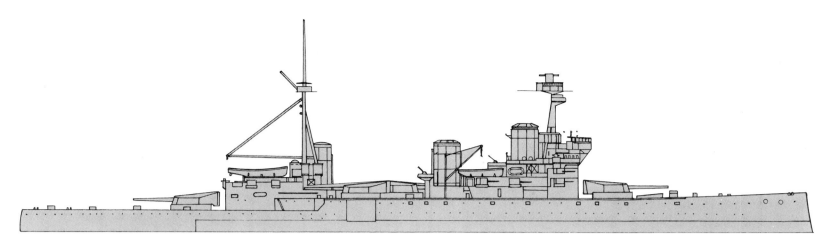

Dresden to escape. Being simply a stern chase, the action at the Falklands has no particular tactical interest, but it did have major strategic consequences. The stain of the defeat at Coronel was wiped out and morale in the service and the country received a substantial boost. A grave menace to British commerce and trade had been removed. Except for the *Dresden* and two armed merchant raiders, the Royal Navy was again in complete command of the seas. Within five months all of the surface raiders had been sunk or interned, but at that point the German submarine offensive began and was to bring Britain to the brink of starvation in a short time. After the Falklands, the Admiralty was able to strengthen the home fleet by recalling many ships from foreign stations, thus completing what Churchill termed the first phase of the naval war, the 'clearance of the seas and recall of foreign squadrons'. The consequent phases were the closing of the Elbe and the domination of the Baltic Sea.

The Battles of Coronel and the Falklands represented the first blow to British naval prestige and confidence in the war. The losses on each side were insignificant, but it was now clear the Germans could fight and fight well at sea. The British Navy could no longer afford to be overconfident. The two navies were to have only one more serious encounter during the war. Nineteen months after Coronel and the Falklands, Jutland was to be the second blow to British prestige.

Above: A battlecruiser of the *Invincible* class, armed with eight 12-inch guns and capable of $25\frac{1}{2}$ knots. They were designed with a battle like the Falklands in mind, but were never used again with such striking success.

Opposite: The battlecruiser *Inflexible* stops to rescue German survivors of the *Gneisenau*. **Below:** The *Scharnhorst* (above left) has already sunk, but the *Gneisenau* is still firing all her guns at the *Invincible* (foreground).

Jutland

1916

The British Grand Fleet and the German High Seas Fleet met only once during the First World War. The result was the Battle of Jutland, a battle which has stirred controversy for over 50 years since its occurrence on 31 May, 1916. From Coronel and the Falklands to Jutland, there were only minor skirmishes between British and German surface units; the British blockade kept the High Seas Fleet in port while German U-boats kept the Royal Navy strained trying to cope with their highly successful attacks. Each side, however, kept a wary eye on the enemy battle fleet, hoping for the opportunity to strike a major blow. The British, who were already much superior materially at the outbreak of the war in 1914, had increased their margin of superiority by 1916. Jutland was the result of one German effort, not to defeat the Grand Fleet, but to reduce that margin of superiority.

In 1916 the Royal Navy had 33 dreadnoughts and ten battle cruisers, having added thirteen dreadnoughts since the war had begun. The German navy had added but five dreadnoughts, giving it a total of eighteen dreadnoughts and six battle cruisers. The two fleets which met at Jutland – the Grand Fleet and the High Seas Fleet – showed a similar disparity in strength.

The Grand Fleet put 28 dreadnoughts, nine battle cruisers, eight armored cruisers, 26 light cruisers, five destroyer leaders and 73 destroyers into the battle while the High Seas Fleet had 16 dreadnoughts, five battle cruisers, eleven light cruisers, six pre-dreadnought battleships and 61 destroyers. Thus during the battle the Grand Fleet had a 37:21 superiority in dreadnoughts and battle cruisers and a 102:78 edge in other ships. On paper the two fleets were roughly equal in speed at 24 to 25 knots, but in fact the British had an advantage of which they were unaware. The pre-dreadnought battleships limited the High Seas Fleet to eighteen knots but these ships had been included at the last minute thanks to the pleas of their officers. In the German fleet they were known as 'five minute ships', because that was how long they were expected to last in action against dreadnoughts.

The Grand Fleet also enjoyed a considerable superiority in gun power with 272 heavy guns in its battle fleet against 200 for Germany's and 72 against 44 in the battle cruiser squadrons. British capital ships almost always carried larger caliber guns than their opponents. Laid down in October 1912, the *Queen Elizabeth*, for example, mounted eight 15-inch guns with a broadside of 15,600

pounds while the *Kronprinz Wilhelm*, a comparable German dreadnought laid down in May 1912, mounted ten 12-inch guns with an 8600-pound broadside. Heavier shells are more accurate at long ranges than lighter shells and battle ranges were now 14,000 to 16,000 yards. The lighter German shells achieved the same penetrating power as the British shells, however, due to higher muzzle velocity. The Germans also had a better armor piercing shell. Although British armor piercing shells had a larger bursting charge, they were 'lamentably weak' for 12-inch guns and above when striking armor at oblique impact, but this was not recognized until after Jutland.

A new and far more effective system of fire control had been introduced in the Royal Navy in 1912. Termed 'Electrical Director Fire Control', it enabled all the guns of the broadside to be aimed and fired by one man using one sight in the conning tower. The result was a remarkable increase in accuracy. At Jutland all British dreadnoughts and battle cruisers had this system but only for their main armament. Fire control

on German capital ships relied on an electrical 'follow the pointer' system which aimed and fired the broadside. The turret guns followed the lateral movement of the gunnery officer's periscope while elevation was determined by a 'range pointer'. Since they attached great importance to the initial estimation of range, the Germans had developed a stereoscopic range finder which was far more sophisticated and accurate than the British 'coincidence' range finder. The former was particularly superior in poor visibility and hence was a major factor at Jutland.

Because of the British preference for heavier guns, German ships were better armored than British, a fact which was made possible by their greater displacement. In the later classes of German dreadnoughts the armor belt was almost fourteen inches thick, while comparable British ships carried ten to twelve inches of armor. British battle cruisers had only nine inches of armor compared to twelve inches in German battle cruisers. German armored protection was also more comprehensive than that of British ships, whose turrets and magazines in particular were not properly protected; only the bows of German ships were inadequately armored. This British deficiency was the result of sacrificing some armor for heavier guns in dreadnoughts and a few knots extra speed in battle cruisers. Another significant difference was that German ships had a more complete watertight division below the waterline which gave better protection against mines and torpedoes.

Other weapons which were to influence the conduct of the fighting at Jutland were mines and especially torpedoes. After sinking eighteen ships in the Russo-Japanese war the mine had come into its own, especially in Germany. German mines were far in advance of British, since the Royal Navy had shown no interest in mines until after 1914. After registering its first successes in the American Civil War, the torpedo had had a checkered career. The Japanese had scored only four per cent hits in their war with the Russians, but further advances in technology had given the torpedo a 14,000-yard range and 45-knot speed, while the development of the gyroscope gave it far more accuracy. Delivery systems also improved with the advent of larger and faster sea-going destroyers and the submarine. Because of these developments, battleships now had to be screened by squadrons of destroyers to guard them against torpedo attacks by submarines and other destroyers. Thus the needs of the battleship increasingly shifted the role of the destroyer from offensive to defensive.

On the eve of Jutland, the German Navy was equal to the British in quality of ships, guns and gunnery, while in armor, shells, mines and torpedoes it was superior. At that time, however, British complacency was such that only the Admiral of the Fleet, Sir John Jellicoe, appreciated this fact, writing that 'it is highly dangerous to consider that our ships as a whole are superior or even equal fighting machines'. British naval superiority rested squarely and simply on the disparity in the size of the two fleets and on the confidence and experience of the British officers

and ratings. A further British advantage was that at the beginning of the war, British naval intelligence had acquired captured German cipher and signal books and squared maps of the North Sea from the Russians. Thus through intercepted and decoded messages, the British often had advance knowledge of enemy movements. Eventually the Germans became suspicious and introduced variations in their codes, but this was offset by the development of directional wireless as a means of locating ships.

The tactical ideas underlying the dispositions for battle did not differ markedly from those of Nelson's time. The twin fetishes of the line ahead and centralized command had survived unchallenged down to 1916 because the nineteenth century had been devoid of occasions for testing them. Senior British officers, such as First Lord of the Admiralty Sir John Fisher, Admiral of the Fleet Sir John Jellicoe and others were firm believers in the line ahead while more junior officers such as Vice Admirals Sir Doveton Sturdee and Sir David Beatty argued for divided tactics, attack by divisions and using part of the battle fleet in an independent role so as to concentrate superior force on a part of the enemy. Tactics had not been much studied in the Royal Navy during the nineteenth century, while after 1900 most officers felt that technology had so changed naval warfare that the past had little to offer. For its part, the Admiralty preferred to leave strategy and tactics to those in command.

Above: The German battlecruiser *Seydlitz* was very badly damaged at Jutland.

Below: British battleships *Royal Oak* and *Hercules* deploying into the line as the Grand Fleet comes into action at Jutland.

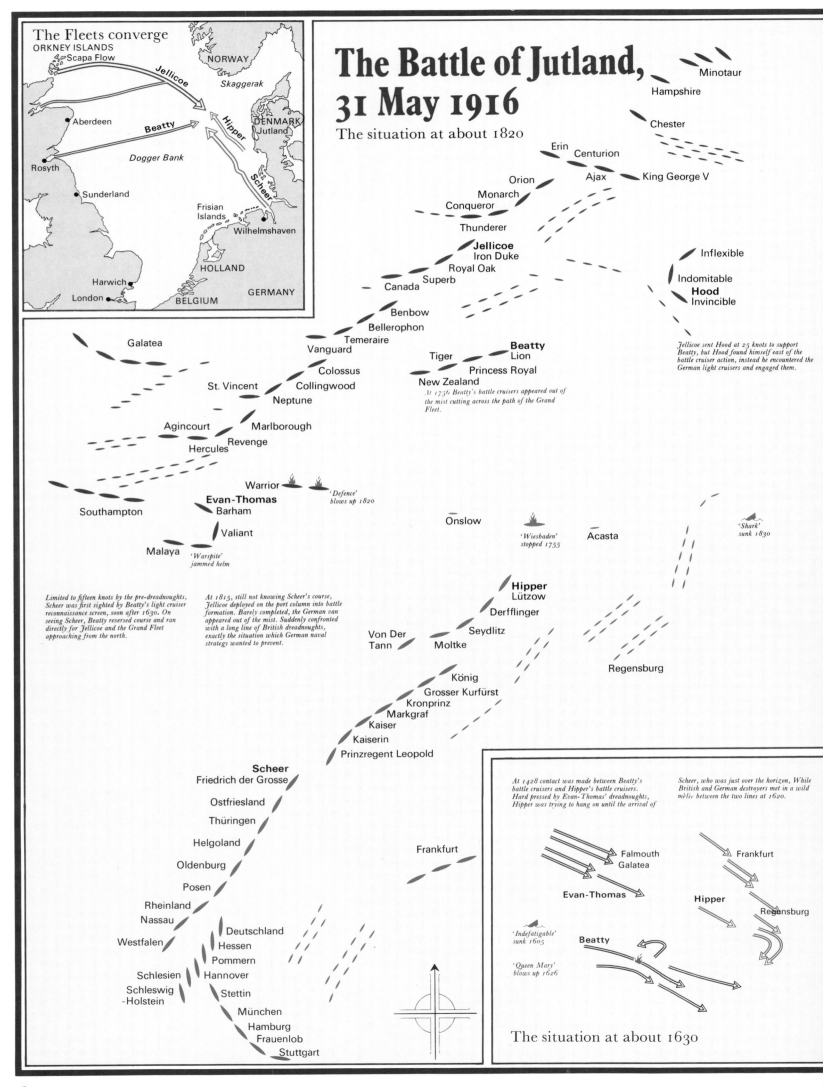

The Battle of Jutland, 31 May 1916

The situation at about 1820

The Fleets converge

The situation at about 1630

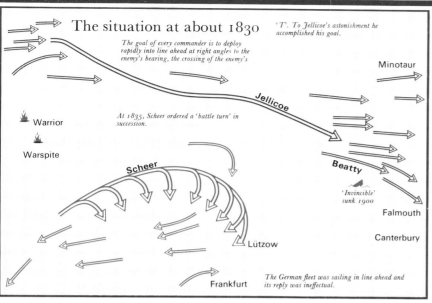

The situation at about 1830

'T'. To Jellicoe's astonishment he accomplished his goal.

The goal of every commander is to deploy rapidly into line ahead at right angles to the enemy's bearing, the crossing of the enemy's

Minotaur

Jellicoe

At 1835, Scheer ordered a 'battle turn' in succession.

Warrior

Warspite

Scheer

Beatty

'Invincible' sunk 1900

Falmouth

Canterbury

Lützow

Frankfurt

The German fleet was sailing in line ahead and its reply was ineffectual.

Ships	Tonnage	Maximum Speed	Main Armaments
British			
Barham	31000	24.5	8–15", 12–6"
Chester	5200	25.5	10–5.5"
Defence	14600	23	4–9.2", 10–7.5"
Galatea	3512	28.5	2–6", 6–4"
Invincible	17250	25.5	8–12", 16–4"
Iron Duke	26400	21	10–13.5", 12–6"
Lion	26350	28	8–13.5", 16–4"
Orion	22500	21	10–13.5", 16–4"
Shark	935	30	3–4"
Tiger	28500	29	8–13.5", 12–6"
Tipperary	1300	32	6–4"
Warrior	13550	23	6–9.2", 4–7.5"
German			
Derfflinger	26180	27	8–12", 12–5.9"
Kaiser	24380	23	10–12", 14–5.9", 8–3.4"
König	25390	23	10–12", 14–5.9", 8–3.4"
Moltke	22640	28	10–11", 12–5.9", 12–3.4"
Pommern	13200	18	4–11", 14–6.7", 20–3.4"
Rostock	4900	28	12–4.1"
Stettin	3550	25	10–4.1"
Von der Tann	19400	24.8	8–11", 10–5.9", 16–3.4"
V25	812	33	3–3.4"

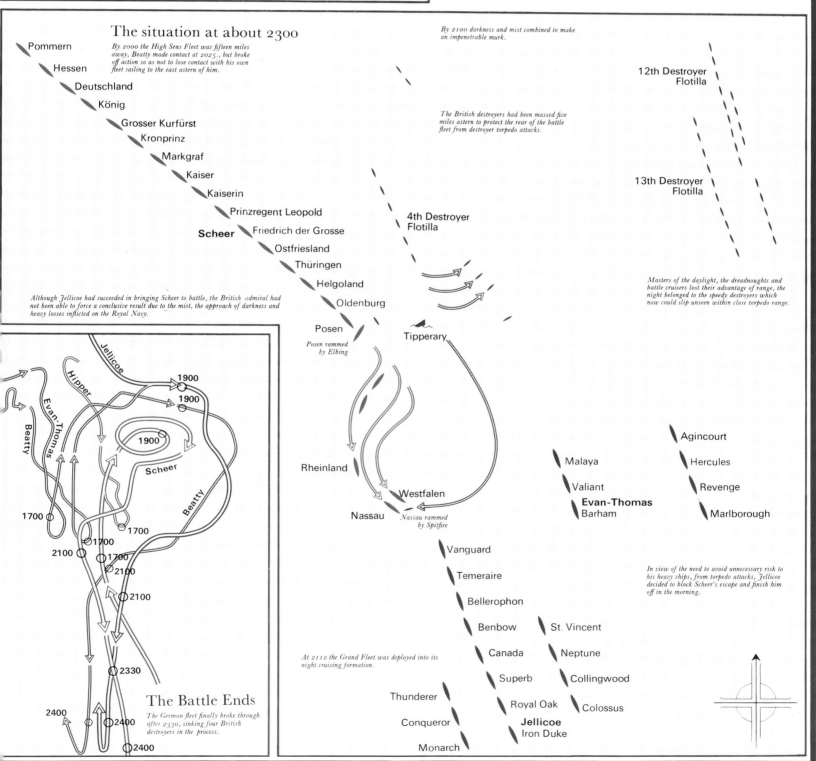

The situation at about 2300

By 2000 the High Seas Fleet was fifteen miles away, Beatty made contact at 2025., but broke off action so as not to lose contact with his own fleet sailing to the east astern of him.

By 2100 darkness and mist combined to make an impenetrable murk.

Pommern

Hessen

Deutschland

König

Grosser Kurfürst

Kronprinz

Markgraf

Kaiser

Kaiserin

Prinzregent Leopold

Scheer Friedrich der Grosse

Ostfriesland

Thüringen

Helgoland

Oldenburg

Posen

Posen rammed by Elbing

The British destroyers had been massed five miles astern to protect the rear of the battle fleet from destroyer torpedo attacks.

12th Destroyer Flotilla

13th Destroyer Flotilla

4th Destroyer Flotilla

Masters of the daylight, the dreadnoughts and battle cruisers lost their advantage of range, the night belonged to the speedy destroyers which now could slip unseen within close torpedo range.

Although Jellicoe had succeeded in bringing Scheer to battle, the British admiral had not been able to force a conclusive result due to the mist, the approach of darkness and heavy losses inflicted on the Royal Navy.

Tipperary

Rheinland

Westfalen

Nassau

Nassau rammed by Spitfire

Agincourt

Malaya

Hercules

Valiant

Revenge

Evan-Thomas
Barham

Marlborough

Vanguard

Temeraire

Bellerophon

Benbow St. Vincent

Canada Neptune

In view of the need to avoid unnecessary risk to his heavy ships, from torpedo attacks, Jellicoe decided to block Scheer's escape and finish him off in the morning.

Superb Collingwood

Thunderer Royal Oak Colossus

Conqueror **Jellicoe**
Iron Duke

Monarch

At 2112 the Grand Fleet was deployed into its night cruising formation.

The Battle Ends

The German fleet finally broke through after 2330, sinking four British destroyers in the process.

Jellicoe

Hipper

Evan-Thomas

Beatty

1900
1900
1900

Scheer

Beatty

1700

1700

1700

2100

1700

2100

2100

2330

2400

2400

2400

Some discussion had been generated by divided tactics but it was generally agreed that these offered too many problems. Coordination was one such problem. Wireless had not yet been developed for tactical use and even in the best visibility signaling was sometimes difficult, so that a commander-in-chief would be unable to keep control of a modern high speed fleet in a smoke-filled battle zone. Then there was the prospect that the enemy might turn the tables and achieve his own concentration of force against a division or independent squadron. And if the battle fleet minus its independent squadrons came up against the enemy, it would be too weak to achieve a decisive victory and might even be in danger. Tactical maneuvering by detached squadrons was also not feasible at ranges of 14,000 to 16,000 yards because the enemy could start a counter-maneuver before a maneuver of the attackers was completed. On the other hand, the line ahead still brought the greatest number of guns on the battleships in action, creating a blanket of fire, and was the best formation for maintaining the coherence of the fleet. What the advocates of divided tactics had failed to realize was that the development of long range gunnery made the concentration of ships of Nelson's tactics unnecessary, because all of a battle fleet's heavy guns could focus on any part of the enemy fleet without the ships themselves changing relative positions. Modern tactics relied not on tactical but on gunnery concentration.

Thus the general conception was that 'of an artillery duel in one long line on parallel courses', wrote a British officer. The goal was to 'deploy rapidly into line at right angles to the enemy's bearing' to achieve that dream of every commander, the crossing of the enemy 'T'. The Grand Fleet Battle Orders read: '. . . the ruling principle is that the "Dreadnought" fleet as a whole keeps together . . . the squadrons should form one line of battle'. The British strategy was to rely on superior numbers and a heavier broadside to defeat the enemy. No fundamental or comprehensive tactical doctrine united the commanders of the Royal Navy beyond general acceptance of crossing the enemy 'T'. This tactical conception only made sense if it was assumed that the enemy wanted to engage and would do so in line ahead. Although the Germans did normally use the line ahead, at Jutland the last thing they wanted was an action between the battle fleets.

The dominant tactical concept of the line ahead was related to a firm belief in the need for centralized command. Every movement of each squadron or division was initiated by the fleet admiral from his flagship. 'Devolution of authority was interpreted either as weakness or laziness' wrote an officer. Centralization was carried to such extremes that on occasion British ships had been known to collide with each other because orders to turn had not been received. Yet the system had its critics for, as Admiral Sturdee wrote, 'The system of signalling every movement from the fleet flagship tended to develop an acute

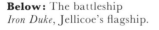

kind of tactical arthritis . . . valuable opportunities were frequently missed because no one would act without an order'. One of the main weaknesses of the British fleet at Jutland was the amount of centralization contained in the Grand Fleet Battle Orders. The Germans practised a much greater degree of centralization with a corresponding increase in the initiative of their officers.

The man responsible for containing the High Seas Fleet was 57-year-old Vice-Admiral Sir John Jellicoe, Commander-in-Chief of the Grand Fleet. With a long and distinguished career, Jellicoe was a genius in his own way and the officers of his fleet had absolute faith in him. In addition to his firm belief in the line ahead and the big gun, Jellicoe's strategy for the Grand Fleet emphasized defense. The main duty of the fleet was to stay 'in being' and in superior force; at all times, therefore, it was to be handled with caution. Sailing toward Jutland on 31 May, Jellicoe had virtually the entire British capital ship force under his command and was uncomfortably aware that, in the apt words of Churchill, he was 'the only man on either side who could lose the war in an afternoon'. Those who unfavorably compare Jellicoe's cautious tactics at Jutland with Nelson's bold stroke at Trafalgar should remember that Nelson commanded less than a third of the British battle fleet and thus could afford to take risks. To add to Jellicoe's concern, disaster could come to the Grand Fleet in ways other than from the guns of the enemy. To compensate for their inferiority in numbers, the Germans were making good use of mines, torpedoes, and submarine traps. One great fear of the British was that the balance of naval power would be suddenly and dramatically altered by these cheap means. The only way known in 1916 to neutralize mines, torpedoes and especially submarines was simply not to fight on the enemy's prepared ground. This forced Jellicoe to stifle his natural desire to bring the rival fleet to battle under any circumstances whatever.

A further reason for Jellicoe's caution lay not with the High Seas Fleet but on the other side of the Atlantic. In 1916 Britain was faced with the possibility of war with the United States over the blockade question and the taking of American ships into Allied harbors for contraband searches. 'One circumstance was in my mind throughout the action . . . This was the possibility of the United States coming into the war on the side of our opponents, a possibility which increased the desirability of not running unnecessary risks with the Grand Fleet', Jellicoe wrote in his own account of the battle.

Jellicoe's Strategic Concept
Jellicoe's strategic concept was that the Grand Fleet would be used to nullify any aggressive action by the High Seas Fleet, to cover its own vessels maintaining the blockade or protecting commerce, and to block invasion or landing raids. The elimination of the High Seas Fleet would be the ultimate fulfillment of these objectives but since they were also accomplished when the Germans lay at anchor in harbor, it made little sense to risk the Grand Fleet, especially in view of the danger of attrition from submarines and

mines. As Jellicoe himself expressed it, 'There is no doubt that, provided there is a chance of destroying some of the enemy's heavy ships, it is right and proper to run risks with our own heavy ships, but unless the chances are reasonably great, I do not think that such risks should be run, seeing that any real disaster to our heavy ships lays the country open to invasion, and also gives the enemy the opportunity of passing commerce destroyers out of the North Sea'. Thus from the beginning British naval strategy recognized the fact that the maintenance of sea supremacy was far more vital than the defeat of the German Fleet. The entire British war effort – supply of home islands, communications with the Empire, support of the British Expeditionary Force in France, and the blockade of the German coast – hinged on this supremacy. However appealing the defeat of the High Seas Fleet may have appeared, it always remained secondary.

German naval strategy also was built on caution and defensive concepts but for entirely different reasons. The German General Staff had assigned the role of guarding the country from assault by sea to the navy. It was confidently expected that the German army would win the war on land in a short time, and the Kaiser himself had specifically ordered that the fleet was not to be risked. The German concept was that confrontation was unnecessary in any event since mines and submarines would take their toll of British ships. By 1916, however, the swift victory on land was yet to be attained. The balance of manpower was turning against Germany, and the pressure of the British blockade was becoming painful. In view of their deteriorating position, the Germans began to reassess their naval strategy in order to gain some relief from the blockade. The initial step in January 1916 was the appointment of Reinhard Scheer as commander-in-chief, the first genuinely able German fleet admiral of the war. Knowing full well that he lacked the ships to engage in the pitched battle envisaged by the British, Scheer's strategy was to try to reduce the

Below: Prince Henry of Prussia (with field glasses) and Admiral Scheer, Commander-in-Chief of the German High Seas Fleet.

Grand Fleet's margin of superiority. His basic approach was to create a situation in which the entire High Seas Fleet could overwhelm a part of the Grand Fleet, by enticing the Grand Fleet out with a sortie by the High Seas Fleet. Submarines and mines positioned off the British bases would account for some capital ships, while the High Seas Fleet itself would intercept and destroy any detached squadrons.

A specific operation was devised for mid-May. Submarines were to be stationed off the main British bases, especially the Grand Fleet base at Rosyth, to provide reconnaissance for Scheer and to cut down the British advantage with some well placed torpedoes. Admiral Franz von Hipper's First and Second Scouting Groups were to bombard Sunderland to bring Admiral David Beatty's battle cruisers out of the Firth of Forth. Hipper would then lead the battle cruisers to their destruction by the dreadnoughts of the High Seas Fleet, waiting 50 miles off Flamborough Head, before Jellicoe and the Grand Fleet could reach the scene. The key to this plan was extensive zeppelin reconnaissance to ensure that the Grand Fleet was not already in the North Sea. On 25 April the U-boats were recalled from their anti-commerce operations and dispatched to their battle stations on 17 May. With 30 May the last day that the submarines could remain on station – submarine endurance was barely two weeks in 1916 – Scheer experienced various delays until 29 May. Then bad weather ruled out the use of zeppelins, so an alternate plan was initiated. Hipper was to make a bold appearance in the Skaggerak as if searching for commerce and British patrol cruisers, in the hope of drawing part of the Grand Fleet to drive him off. The High Seas Fleet would then overwhelm this British force in waters close to home, with its retreat assured. The one exposed German flank could be guarded by cruisers and destroyers against surprise. With his flag on the battle cruiser *Lützow*,

Hipper sailed at 0100 on the 31st with the five battle cruisers of the First Scouting Group and the four light cruisers and three flotillas of destroyers of the Second Scouting Group. His orders were to show himself off the Norwegian coast before dark so that the British would discover part of the German fleet was at sea and sent out a force to chase it. An hour and a half later, Scheer and the sixteen dreadnoughts of the battle fleet followed, the admiral's flag in the *Friedrich der Grosse*.

After 17 May the suspicions of British naval intelligence had been roused when the U-boat fleet put to sea followed by no reports of sinkings. On 30 May it was known that the High Seas Fleet was assembling off Wilhelmshaven. At 1740 that day the Admiralty informed Jellicoe that 'Germans intend some operations commencing tomorrow' and ordered him to concentrate his ships 100 miles east of Aberdeen 'ready for eventualities'. With his flag in the *Iron Duke*, the Admiral sailed with 24 dreadnoughts, three battle cruisers, eight armored cruisers, twelve

Far left: Despite heavy damage which put most of her guns out of action, the battlecruiser *Seydlitz* continued in action. **Left:** German battleships plow through shell bursts from the battleships of the Grand Fleet.

Left: The battleship *Warspite* was in action against seven battleships when her steering jammed at a crucial moment, but she survived with superficial damage. **Below:** The British battlecruiser *Lion* was the flagship of Sir David Beatty.

light cruisers, five destroyer leaders, 46 destroyers and a minelayer. One of the more colorful figures of the war, Vice Admiral Sir David Beatty, flying his flag in the *Lion*, led his battle cruiser force of six battle cruisers, four dreadnoughts, fourteen light cruisers, and 27 destroyers from the Firth of Forth with orders to join the battle fleet 90 miles west of the entrance of the Skaggerak. This flamboyant Irishman had a meteoric career in the service, becoming at 38 the youngest flag officer since Nelson. Married to a daughter of the Chicago millionaire Marshall Field, Beatty had a solid grasp of strategy and tactics and a passion for victory. As a result of the alertness of British intelligence in anticipating Scheer's sortie, the Grand Fleet was already at sea awaiting its rival. But due to a mix-up at the Admiralty between the intelligence branch and the Operations Division, Jellicoe was then informed that the German batttle fleet was still in harbor. The result was that Jellicoe later had little confidence in the subsequent information he received from the Admiralty and no immediate sense of urgency in making a junction with Beatty. Beatty's opinion of the mix-up was, 'What am I to think of [Operations Division] when I get that telegram

and in three hours time meet the whole German fleet well out to sea'.

Early on the afternoon of the 31st Beatty was sailing in two columns toward his rendezvous with Jellicoe with the four dreadnoughts of Rear-Admiral Evan-Thomas' Fifth Battle Squadron five miles to the rear. At 1415 the British ships swung around to the north, coming onto a converging course with Hipper's battle cruisers. A small Danish steamer was sighted simultaneously by the respective left wings of the cruiser screens of the two fleets. When each came to investigate, contact was made and firing began at 1428. Had it not been for this accidental contact, Jellicoe's Grand Fleet would have been in a position to intervene quickly, but at that time he was still 65 miles to the north and coming south while Scheer and the High Seas Fleet were 50 miles to the south coming north. At 1432 Beatty turned southeast to cut off the enemy's retreat, thinking that only German light cruisers were involved. Five miles to the rear, Evan-Thomas missed Beatty's signal and only turned at 1440, thus placing himself ten miles behind the battle cruisers. Still, the situation did not seem urgent. There was no reason to expect that the

Opposite above: The heavily damaged battle-cruiser *Seydlitz* lies half-submerged at the dock in Wilhelmshaven after the battle. **Top left:** The battlecruiser *Indefatigable* going into action minutes before she blew up. **Top right:** The British battleship *Valiant* at Rosyth. **Above left:** Shell damage to the German battlecruiser *Derfflinger*. **Above right:** The British battleship *Barham*, flagship of the 5th Battle Squadron, at Scapa Flow.

Bottom: The German battlecruiser *Moltke*.

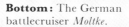

Right: One artist's misconception of the way the day battle of Jutland was fought. In reality ships never got so close to one another. The days of such close ship-to-ship conflict were long since past since the departure of the great sailing fleets. **Center:** A little closer to reality, this painting shows the battleship *Thüringen* sinking the British cruiser *Black Prince*. This only happened because the British ship had lost her way in the dark and blundered into the German Fleet. **Far right:** Another fanciful view of the night action. Although at times the ships drew close to one another, there was never a large-scale mêlée as depicted here. **Below:** A graphic representation of the British battle line firing. Clouds of coal and cordite-smoke rapidly obscured visibility.

German cruisers related to a larger force, since the Admiralty had placed the German fleet still at anchor.

A Misread Signal

After receiving a misread signal from his cruisers concerning 24 to 26 British dreadnoughts, Hipper had turned northwest to investigate. With the same intentions of joining the light cruiser action, Hipper and Beatty were now steaming toward each other at a combined speed of 45 knots. Sighting two columns of British battle cruisers coming over the horizon at 1520, Hipper reduced speed to eighteen knots and held his course, confident that he could hold his own without falling back on Scheer. After informing Scheer that the 'Enemy battle fleet is in sight' he then saw how the enemy was cutting between him and Scheer and turned 180 degrees southeast to catch Beatty between his battle cruisers and Scheer's dreadnoughts. With his destroyers and light cruisers in defensive position to beat off any destroyer torpedo attacks, Beatty now had his battle cruisers in single line ahead and ordered Evan-Thomas' squadron to come east at 25 knots from its position six miles to port. Although it was a windless day with excellent visibility, the smoke of the ships was already beginning to obscure the vision of the gunnery officers. As the range came down to 18,000 yards, Beatty turned east-southeast to clear the smoke and bring all of his guns to bear. With their superior range finders, Hipper's gunners found the range of the enemy some minutes before their own ships were sighted. As his guns were slightly outranged by those of the enemy, however, Hipper waited for the range to shorten to 16,500 yards. At 1548 both battle cruiser squadrons opened fire simultaneously.

The German gunners had the British ships neatly bracketed, scoring two hits each on the *Lion* and *Princess Royal* and four on the *Tiger* within the first three minutes. The fore turret of the *Princess Royal* and two turrets of the *Tiger* were knocked out of action temporarily. The range had narrowed to 12,900 yards before the British made their first hit with two shells from the *Queen Mary* which struck the *Seydlitz* at 1555. After over-estimating the range initially, British gunnery remained poor and somewhat confused in the coordination of targets. At 1600 both flagships were hit simultaneously, but the *Lützow* suffered no serious damage. The midship turret on the *Lion* was burst by a heavy shell, starting a cordite fire which would have blown up the ship had not a dying officer given the order to flood the adjacent magazine. The *Lion* took six more hits from the exceptionally accurate German fire and suffered more fires and flooding. The fight had become so hot by then that Beatty turned south and Hipper southeast. As the Germans continued to pound the British line with a deadly fire, Beatty was forced to shift a few degrees to starboard to alter the range. At the end of the two battle lines, now on more or less parallel courses, the *Indefatigable* and the *von der Tann* were matched in an unimpeded ship-to-ship duel. Within the space of fourteen minutes, the eleven-inch guns of the German ship sent

three shells crashing through the decks of its British adversary to explode a magazine, then hit her with another salvo which sank her. The *von der Tann* received not a single hit from the twelve-inch guns of the *Indefatigable*.

The British battle cruiser squadron was so badly mauled that it drew away to deal with its damage and put out the fires in the *Lion*. To keep Hipper occupied, Beatty ordered a flotilla of twelve destroyers to the attack, but before these could get into action Evan-Thomas' dreadnoughts appeared on the scene and turned onto a course parallel to Beatty's. Although the targets were obscured by smoke, the dreadnoughts smothered the rear of the enemy line with accurate salvoes of fifteen-inch shells, scoring serious hits on the *von der Tann* and the *Moltke* which were only saved because the inferior British shells were breaking up on impact instead of penetrating and bursting. Although the *Lion* still had fires, Beatty brought the battle cruisers back into the fray. At 1626 the *Queen Mary* was struck by five shells from the *Seydlitz* and the *Derfflinger* which either penetrated the armor of the British ship to explode in a magazine or ignited a magazine by the flash from their bursts. Whichever was the case, the ship was blown apart by her

was first sighted by Beatty's light cruiser reconnaissance screen which was two miles ahead of the battle cruisers. Just after 1630 Scheer sighted the two battle cruiser forces coming toward him, still hotly engaged. On seeing Scheer, Beatty reversed course and ran directly for the Grand Fleet approaching from the opposite direction. In order to become Scheer's advance force, Hipper also reversed course but in the process the *Seydlitz* was torpedoed in the side under her armor by a British destroyer. She was able to stay in line, however, due to her watertight compartments.

Beatty now steamed toward Evan-Thomas' squadron which was eight miles away and still blasting Hipper's rear to cover the retreat of the British battle cruisers. As the battle cruisers passed the dreadnoughts on an opposite course, Beatty signaled that the latter should turn in succession (one after the other rather than simultaneously) and follow him. Turning in succession requires considerably more time than turning simultaneously, and Scheer's approaching van was able to give the dreadnoughts a good dose of fire, the *Barham* and *Malaya* both taking hits. The dreadnoughts retaliated, however, with the

magazines and went down with all of her 1266 man crew. Just afterward, the *Princess Royal* was briefly obscured by smoke and spray, causing a signalman on the *Lion*'s bridge to report '*Princess Royal* blown up, sir'. Whereupon Beatty turned to his flag captain and said matter-of-factly, 'Chatfield, there seems to be something wrong with our damned ships today. Turn two points to port' – which was toward the enemy.

Hard pressed by Evan-Thomas' dreadnoughts, Hipper was trying to hang on until the arrival of Scheer who was just over the horizon. While Hipper considered easing his situation by ordering his destroyers to attack, the German flotilla leaders led their ships into action on their own initiative. The British destroyers had now got their attack underway and the two forces met in a wild *mêlée* between the two lines at 1620, a struggle in which two German ships were sunk and one British vessel disabled. The British dreadnoughts had turned away from the destroyer attack, and the longer range gave some relief to Hipper's outnumbered and outgunned battle cruisers. The British destroyers made several ineffectual attacks and then retired.

Limited to fifteen knots by the 'five minute ships' he had unwisely included in his fleet, Scheer

Right: A German battleship fires a salvo. **Below:** German torpedo boats come under fire from British ships during the opening stages of the battle.

Barham and the *Valiant* getting hits on the *Lützow* and *Derfflinger* while the *Warspite* and *Malaya* did the same to the leading German dreadnoughts, the *Grosser Kurfürst* and *Markgraf*. The faster British ships managed to retire out of range by 1730. The ships of Hipper's force had suffered greatly in the engagement thus far: the *von der Tann* had no guns operational, the *Lützow* and *Seydlitz* were heavily damaged and only the *Moltke* remained relatively unscathed. Still believing that Beatty's force was only an isolated squadron, Scheer signaled 'General chase'.

Despite the heavy damage to his four remaining battle cruisers, the speed of Beatty's force was unimpaired and he began to cut north-northeast across Hipper's path to get into position to cross the German 'T', signaling his ships 'Prepare to renew the action'. After this turn, however, Beatty lost touch with Scheer and even with Hipper who was steaming roughly parallel with him in the mist. Evan-Thomas was still in contact with Scheer but sent out no reports. At 1740 Hipper's ships appeared out of the mist 14,000 yards to the southeast. With the visibility advantage now on their side, the British battle cruisers and dreadnoughts laid down a heavy fire which the Germans could not return with any effect. Hit forward, the *Derfflinger* began to sink but was saved by her watertight compartments, while the hapless *Seydlitz* was struck many times by British shells and set afire. This fire forced Hipper to move to increase the range, a move which prevented him from seeing the approach of the Grand Fleet. His wireless was out in any event so that he could not have reported it nor was he able to report that Beatty and Evan-Thomas were still full of fight.

With its dreadnoughts in a six-column cruising formation screened by destroyers and light cruisers, the Grand Fleet had been steaming south toward its junction with the battle cruiser force. Eight miles ahead were the eight armored cruisers in line abreast as scouts in the increasingly poor visibility, while twenty miles ahead was the Third Battle Cruiser Squadron of Admiral Hood, composed of the *Invincible*, *Indomitable* and *Inflexible*. On receiving the first news of contact with the enemy, Jellicoe had sent Hood east to cut off the German light cruisers' escape through the Skaggerak in the belief that only a light enemy force was out. When news of the clash of the battle cruisers arrived Jellicoe sent Hood at 25 knots to support Beatty, but Hood found himself east of the battle cruiser action because Beatty had miscalculated his position by seven miles to the west. Instead, Hood's three ships encountered the German light cruisers and engaged them, an action which Hipper then came upon after he had swung east to escape from Beatty. Thinking that Hood was the van of the British battle fleet, Hipper fell back on Scheer and took his place at the head of the German battle line before 1900.

Visibility and Daylight Fade

Since only a few hours of daylight remained, it was now urgent that the Grand Fleet be deployed in battle formation. The already poor visibility was getting worse, raising the risk that the fleet might encounter the enemy in battle formation while it was still in cruising formation. To get his six columns into single line ahead, Jellicoe had to wheel them to the right or left, a maneuver which took at least four minutes. The position of the enemy determined which way and in what order the columns wheeled, and Jellicoe's main problem was his lack of information about the position of the enemy. Then a report from his cruisers, 'Large amount of smoke as though from a large fleet bearing east-south-east', caused Jellicoe to increase speed to eighteen knots. At 1630 his cruisers sighted Beatty's cruiser screen, but faulty signaling left the admiral no better informed about events to the south, although gunfire could now be heard in the distance. The wireless of the *Lion* had been shot away so any reports from Beatty to Jellicoe would have had to be sent through a third ship and no officer took initiative in this respect in the heat of battle. At 1750 Jellicoe's own cruisers sighted gun flashes and from that point he began to get regular reports. After receiving a signal from Jellicoe that a battle was imminent, the Admiralty realized its earlier mistake and from intercepted wireless traffic gave Jellicoe the enemy speed, course and position. With Beatty actually eleven miles northwest of his reported position, it now transpired that the Grand Fleet had miscalculated its own position as well; Jellicoe needed to know his position relative to Scheer before deploying the fleet. Hood was engaging the German light forces ahead and to port of the Grand Fleet when suddenly at 1756 Beatty's battle cruisers appeared out of the mist cutting across the path of the Grand Fleet and engaging an unseen enemy. When no response was received to his signal 'Where is the enemy's battle fleet?' Jellicoe repeated it and this time received answers from both Beatty and Evan-Thomas that Scheer was to the southwest. Still not knowing Scheer's course, which had always been northwest, Jellicoe deployed on the port column at 1815. His thought was to give his ships better visibility by firing toward the sunset, to cross the German 'T' if Scheer headed southeast, and to cut off the German retreat north to the Skaggerak or south to the Heligoland Bight. This deployment was barely completed as the German van appeared out of the mist. Suddenly confronted with a long line of British dreadnoughts, Scheer recoiled in amazement. Exactly the situation which German naval strategy was concerned to prevent was occurring – the High Seas Fleet was meeting the Grand Fleet in pitched battle.

The pall of heavy smoke over the battle area combined with the mist had masked the approach of the Grand Fleet and the Germans were taken completely by surprise. The dreadnought *Marlborough* opened fire at 1817, quickly followed by other British ships. The German fleet had been sailing in line ahead and, unable to turn to a more tactically advantageous course, Scheer could see that Jellicoe was crossing his 'T'. The *Lützow*, *Derfflinger*, *König*, *Grosser Kurfürst* and *Markgraf* all took hits while the Germans were unable to make an effective reply – a classic tactical situation. The seven battle cruisers of Hood and Beatty now combined to blast Hipper's five ships, hitting the *Lützow* nine times and the *Derfflinger* four. Although in a bad position for gunnery due to the light, the German ships found a target in the *Invincible* at 1831 and sank her with a salvo from the *Derfflinger* which exploded her magazines. Hipper's ships also sank an armored cruiser and left another sinking. The *Lützow* was in such battered condition that she could only manage low speed and Hipper was taken off in a destroyer intending to transfer his flag, but the other battle cruisers were also too badly damaged with the exception of the *Moltke*, which Hipper finally succeeded in boarding around 2100.

In a desperate situation, at 1835, Scheer ordered a 'battle turn' in which each ship put its helm over hard and reversed course in succession beginning from the rear. Under cover of a smoke screen and a torpedo attack by German destroyers, this was the quickest way Scheer could get his line out of range. The German battle line followed by the battle cruisers and light cruisers, had disappeared into the mist heading west by 1845. Thinking that the German ships were momentarily hidden by the mist, it was over eleven minutes before Jellicoe realized that Scheer had withdrawn. The ships toward the rear of the British line saw the German maneuver but failed to report it, nor did the light cruiser squadrons inform the Admiral that the enemy had fled. For fear of destroyer torpedo attacks and possible mines laid by the retreating enemy and with only two hours of daylight remaining, Jellicoe declined pursuit and put his fleet into its six-column cruising formation. At first setting his course southeast, he then made two partial turns, edging close to Scheer while cutting off his retreat. Although Jellicoe had skilfully trapped Scheer into action, the poor visibility and the failure of his captains to keep him informed allowed the German admiral to escape.

After ordering his destroyers to the attack, Scheer did another battle turn to the east at 1855, probably thinking that he could cross the tail of the British fleet, hammer it in passing and regain his path home. But, mistaking Beatty's battle cruisers for the van of the Grand Fleet and thus misjudging its position, Scheer came directly against the center of the British fleet still heading south at 1910. This meant that the surprised Jellicoe was again crossing the equally surprised Scheer's 'T' at a range of only five miles. At 1912 the hapless *Lützow* was blasted by two dreadnoughts, bursting into flames and sheering off in a hopeless condition only to be sunk later by the merciful torpedoes of German destroyers. The entire British battle fleet then opened up on the lead ships of the German line, scoring many hits with an accurate fire. At 1920 Beatty's battle cruisers began scoring many hits on the German battle cruisers at 14,000 yards. The German reply was ineffectual: only the dreadnought *Colossus* was struck by a salvo of twelve-inch shells. Many of the German ships were heavily damaged, especially the *König* and *Grosser Kurfürst*. Facing annihilation for the second time that day, Scheer decided that the only way to extricate his battle fleet from this peril was to sacrifice his already battered battle cruisers. Receiving the signal 'Close the enemy and ram', the battle cruisers without Hipper to lead them charged the

British fleet only to be met by a heavy curtain of fire. After suffering heavy damage, the battle cruisers were reprieved from their 'death ride' at 1917 when Scheer signaled 'Operate against the enemy's van'. This signal allowed the battle cruisers to cover the retreat of the battle fleet as it performed yet another battle turn. At 1935 the German dreadnoughts were again heading west into the mist, followed by the battle cruisers, all of which survived the suicide attack, and the light cruisers.

At the same time the German destroyers had come in to make their attack but this was partly broken up by British destroyers and light cruisers so that only twenty destroyers were able to launch 31 torpedoes at a range of 8000 yards. The standard maneuver to counter such an attack was to turn away, so as Scheer was turning west, Jellicoe's ships turned east and continued in that direction for fifteen minutes until the attack was over. Again, due to the mist, Jellicoe failed to realize that Scheer had reversed course. 'No report of this German movement reached me' he later wrote, although some of his ships had witnessed it. As the Grand Fleet had once more lost contact with its adversary, it again turned on a southerly course, having missed its one chance of closing with the Germans after their second battle turn. By 2000 the High Seas Fleet was fifteen miles away. The still aggressive Beatty made contact at 2025, but after scoring some hits and driving the Germans farther west he broke off so as not to lose touch with his own fleet. Although Jellicoe had succeeded in bringing Scheer to battle, the British admiral had not been able to annihilate his adversary due to the mist, the approach of darkness, and Scheer's agility in refusing action. As night fell, the strategic advantage lay with the Grand Fleet, for it barred the German escape to the east and had only to wait less than six hours before it could renew the encounter in daylight.

An Impenetrable Murk

By 2100 darkness and the mist had combined to make an impenetrable murk. Masters of the daylight, the dreadnoughts and battle cruisers lost their advantage of range; the night belonged to the speedy destroyers which now could slip unseen within close torpedo range. In line with orthodox British naval thought concerning night fighting, Jellicoe did not consider a night engagement which would expose his heavy ships to torpedo attacks by Scheer's destroyers. In view of the need to avoid unnecessary risks to the Grand Fleet, it made far more sense to block Scheer's escape and finish him off in the morning.

The Heligoland Bight was protected from intruders by minefields through which there were a number of swept channels. Scheer had three possible routes leading to these channels. One route was past the Horn Reefs and down the Frisian coast while a central route was past Heligoland. A southwest route would have taken the High Seas Fleet near the German coast and past the mouth of the River Ems, but at 180 miles this was the longest and the least probable since the British had a speed advantage. Jellicoe prudently elected to take a middle course south which covered all three possible escape routes, making Scheer's best chance to cut behind the Grand Fleet and run for the Horn Reefs passage. At 2112 the Grand Fleet was deployed into its night cruising formation. On a course due south at seventeen knots, the dreadnoughts were in three columns. The destroyers had been massed five miles astern to make the barrier larger and to protect the rear of the battle fleet from destroyer torpedo attacks. Separating the destroyers from the heavy ships also removed the possibility of confusion in the darkness. The battle cruisers had been stationed ahead and on the west flank of the battle fleet, which meant that the Germans could neither outrun nor get past the British to the south.

With the superior Grand Fleet blocking his escape and only waiting for daylight to annihilate him, the desperate Scheer decided that a night action offered his best chance. The losses from breaking through the British line would be preferable to certain destruction in the morning, so he opted for the shortest route home through the Horn Reefs passage. Covering its van with destroyers and light cruisers and placing the old battleships and limping battle cruisers in the rear, the High Seas Fleet made its bid for escape.

At 2200 British destroyers made contact with and fired on several light cruisers but were uncertain as to their identity. Between 2220 and 2230, the German fleet made various attempts to shove its way through the British destroyers and light cruisers in the rear bringing about repeated actions. Two German dreadnoughts were rammed by British destroyers, but after sheering off to the west the German fleet renewed its effort and finally broke through after 2330, sinking four British destroyers in the process. At 2215 a report of the beginning of these encounters was sent to Jellicoe, but it did not reach him until 2338. After that one message, the British rear sent no more reports to inform their commander that the quarry was

attempting to escape. The Fifth Battle Squadron of Admiral Evan-Thomas was stationed as an intermediate link between the rear and the battle fleet and was well aware of the action astern. Its two hindmost ships even saw the leading German dreadnoughts coming through, but neither of these ships reported the fact to Evan-Thomas, leading in the *Barham*, on the assumption that he also had sighted the Germans. Thus Jellicoe was left in ignorance as the enemy made good its escape.

Yet unmistakable clues that Scheer was making a break for the Horn Reefs were available to the British. From its directional wireless the Admiralty sent Jellicoe two messages on the German position. The first message contained an error and was obviously incorrect, but the second accurately gave the disposition, course and speed of the High Seas Fleet, adding that at 2114 it had been ordered home. What the message neglected to include was that Scheer had requested a dawn zeppelin reconnaissance over the Horn Reefs area. This message was received at 2330, the same time as a signal was received from the light cruiser *Bir-*

Above: The British light cruiser *Southampton* undergoes repairs after the battle. Note that the Zeppelin menace has already resulted in the fitting of an anti-aircraft gun (left).

Below: Torpedo boats and a battleship of the High Seas Fleet. Even moderately rough weather made the torpedo boats roll violently.

Above: The German battleship *Pommern* blew up after being hit by a single torpedo during the night action.

mingham that 'Battle cruisers probably hostile' were in sight and steering south. The British cruiser had seen the enemy as it was turning away from a British destroyer torpedo attack, and had got the course incorrectly but for Jellicoe, already distrustful of intelligence received from the Admiralty, this sighting confirmed his doubts and no action was taken. Inexplicably, Jellicoe made only one attempt at 2246 to inquire about the firing astern. Thus to the lack of initiative of his subordinates in transmitting vital information must be coupled the admiral's inertia.

The Last Contact
The last contact of the battle came just before dawn on 1 June. The Twelfth Destroyer Flotilla sighted the Germans, sent a contact report to Jellicoe at 0152 and then sank the dreadnought *Pommern*, thus accomplishing more than the entire battle fleet had so far managed. Probably due to wireless failure, the contact report never reached Jellicoe. When day broke around 0240, Jellicoe turned north with every expectation of meeting the High Seas Fleet. He then learned from the Admiralty that directional wireless placed the enemy near the Horn Reefs. On receipt of this disappointing news, a fruitless sweep for stragglers was made and then the Grand Fleet went home.

It was then that the second Battle of Jutland began, a battle which lasted until the British public was distracted by the advent of the Second World War some twenty years later. As one historian of the First World War has noted, no battle in all history has spilled so much ink as Jutland. Convinced of British superiority, both public opinion and the navy had been complacent and the navy even above criticism. Coronel had been explained away as due to the weakness of pre-

dreadnought ships, while the Falklands had demonstrated the superiority of the Royal Navy and proved the worth of the battle cruiser. Jutland thus came as an unpleasant surprise. The first British communiqué, issued before full details had been received from the returning fleet, was an honest attempt to give the known facts. And the facts were that Britain had lost three battle cruisers, three armored cruisers, eight destroyers and 6097 officers and ratings against German losses of one dreadnought, one battle cruiser, four light cruisers, five destroyers and 2545 casualties. The public reacted first with horror, then disbelief and finally outrage. Then a second communiqué was issued in which the estimates of German losses included all possibles and doubtfuls listed as probables so that on paper, British losses appeared to be slightly less than German ones. Public opinion was mollified still further when it became clear in the following weeks that Jutland was not a decisive German victory since the Royal Navy was still in command of the seas.

There also developed considerable discussion of the conduct of the battle, centering around Beatty's handling of the battle cruiser force and Jellicoe's failure to smash an inferior force which he had trapped. It is true that Beatty allowed his superior force of battle cruisers to be lured within range of the High Seas Fleet and lost a third of his ships in the encounter. He also committed two tactical errors which were then compounded by signaling mistakes. Initially Beatty had denied himself the support of Evan-Thomas's dreadnoughts by stationing them too far astern, and he then endangered these ships by waiting too long to signal his retreat so that they were exposed to the full force of the guns of the German van, only escaping serious damage by their excellent shooting. But to offset this, Beatty had then out-maneuvered Hipper so that Scheer was unaware of the approach of the Grand Fleet. Thus Beatty enabled Jellicoe to enter the battle at 1800 with the full strategic advantage on his side.

Given British naval strategy and the tactical assumptions of the day, Jellicoe handled the Grand Fleet cautiously but ably. He had his enemy at a severe tactical disadvantage twice and inflicted heavy damage. Where he can be faulted is in allowing Scheer to escape. The main reason lies in the execrable communications within the Grand Fleet, for if there was one factor which allowed the German fleet to survive, it was surely that Jellicoe's officers repeatedly failed to inform him of the movements of the enemy at vital moments. This factor characterized the action on the British side from beginning to end, from the initial difficulty which Jellicoe had in learning the position of the enemy to the end when the ships of the Fifth Battle Squadron watched the Germans make their escape without reporting it. This was surely the most damaging aspect of the lack of initiative – Sturdee's 'tactical arthritis' – which resulted from the preoccupation with centralized command. If one man was to control the fleet, however, then Jellicoe must also bear the blame for ignoring the signs and for his lack of suspicion that Scheer was making his escape.

On the German side, Jutland was quickly announced as a victory. Easily the best admiral on either side, Hipper had decisively beaten Beatty with superior gunfire, but then Scheer had been ambushed by Jellicoe in the confrontation of the battle fleets. Scheer in turn had out-maneuvered Jellicoe during the night to make his escape almost unscathed. Superior British strength forced Scheer to repeatedly break off the action. In tactical terms, therefore, an inferior force generally out-maneuvered a superior enemy and inflicted greater losses on it. Jutland can fairly be judged as a tactical victory for the Germans, a victory which demonstrated their skill and helped to dissipate their feeling of inferiority. Nor did Jutland discourage further initiative by the High Seas Fleet. Twelve weeks later, on 19 August, Scheer again tried to trap a part of the Grand Fleet by bombarding *Sunderland* as bait, but Jellicoe displayed his customary caution, Beatty lost another cruiser and no battle resulted. After this episode, it was fairly apparent that Scheer's strategy was not effective and the resources of the navy were increasingly thrown into the highly successful U-boat campaign. A last sortie by the High Seas Fleet was planned for 29 October, 1918 but by then morale in the German navy was poor and the crews mutinied and refused to sail. When the armistice came a few days later on 11 November, part of the terms were that all U-boats must surrender and the surface fleet be interned in an Allied harbor. On 21 November five battle cruisers, nine dreadnoughts, seven light cruisers and 49 destroyers were turned over to the Allies at Aberlady Bay inside May island. On that day Beatty said to his crew, 'I always told you they would have to come out'. Just before the Treaty of Versailles was signed the High Seas Fleet was scuttled by the Germans themselves.

Measured in terms of the goals of the two antag-

Left: All that was left of the battlecruiser *Queen Mary* after a cordite fire detonated her magazines.

onists, however, Jutland emerges as a strategic victory for Britain. Germany failed to weaken the Grand Fleet or shake its sea supremacy while it placed its own carefully husbanded battle fleet in mortal jeopardy. The Grand Fleet, on the other hand, 'nullified' the initiative of the High Seas Fleet and avoided any serious losses, precisely the defensively oriented strategy enunciated in Jellicoe's Grand Fleet Battle Orders. Thus neither the balance of naval power nor the strategies of the war were even slightly affected by Jutland. The battle could just as well have never taken place and indeed it might have been better for the Royal Navy had it not. The Navy lost great prestige in the eyes of the British public and the Allies and had their own complacency thoroughly shaken. The standard of German gunnery had been far higher than the British had expected and this by comparison reflected to some extent on British gunnery. Material deficiencies were also made manifest by the battle – the inferior armor piercing shell, the insufficient armor of British ships against plunging fire, and the lack of protection to prevent the flash of an explosion in a turret passing into the magazine. The latter was the most probable reason for the sudden demise of the *Queen Mary* and the *Indefatigable*. The utility of Fisher's beloved battle cruisers was questionable as well, since it appeared that skimping on armor for marginal extra speed was a dubious benefit. It must be remembered, however, that Jutland was only the second major naval battle of the steam age (Tsushima being the first), and therefore that the navies of the world had had little opportunity to experiment and to learn. After Jutland, no main fleet actions were to take place until the Second World War when battles would be fought under considerably different conditions as technology continued to revolutionize naval warfare.

Matapan

1941

The first big naval battle of World War II was fought off Cape Matapan in southern Greece on 28 March, 1941. Since the European war was composed mainly of land operations for geographical reasons, Matapan was the only large fleet action in the war which took place outside the Pacific theater. Matapan also marked a transition between the naval actions of World War I, fought with gun and ship-borne torpedo and the subsequent great carrier actions of the Pacific war. Indeed, the British fleet at Matapan contained two veterans of Jutland but at the same time assigned a crucial role to an aircraft carrier. The genesis of Matapan was a chain of complex and sometimes haphazard events which changed the Mediterranean from a backwater of the war to a major theater of operations for both sides.

As a result of Adolf Hitler's decision to invade Poland, Britain and France had declared war on Germany in 1939, but the German blitzkrieg had swept across Europe, bringing the capitulation of France in June 1940 and leaving Britain to stand alone against Hitler's European empire. At the same time, Benito Mussolini had brought Italy into the war against Britain, transforming the Mediterranean into an arena of war, for Britain had a Mediterranean fleet, large bases at Gibraltar, Malta and Alexandria, and vital interests to protect in that part of the world. After the capitulation of France, Hitler's main interest was the launching of Operation Barbarossa – the invasion of the Soviet Union – after which he planned to revert to the problem of Britain. The adventures of his erstwhile Italian ally, however, drew him into major commitments in the Balkans and North Africa on which he had not counted.

Although generally considering Europe south of the Alps to be Mussolini's domain, Hitler's relations with the Italian dictator were usually touchy. Neither Hitler nor Mussolini were by nature cooperators and it was also no secret that

the latter resented his subordinate role. By 1940 the relationship between Der Führer and Il Duce was already losing some of its strength. If Hitler was going to create an empire from the Atlantic to the Urals, Mussolini intended to build an Italian empire in the Mediterranean world. The German defeat of Britain and France gave him an opportunity to attempt to seize what he wanted: Corsica, Malta, Tunisia, part of Algeria, an Atlantic port in Morocco, French Somaliland and the British position in Egypt and the Sudan. First on his shopping list was the Adriatic coast of Greece. Knowing full well that Hitler would try to restrain him, Mussolini gave the German leader no advance notice of the invasion of Greece on 28 October, 1940, sending a letter antedated by five days at the last minute. Undertaken against the advice of all three Italian chiefs of staff, the attack struck through Italian-held Albania and was a complete failure. Within three weeks the counterattacking Greeks had driven the invaders off Greek soil. Mussolini had launched a war he could not finish, the first of a long series of disasters for Italy, and had seriously distorted Hitler's strategy, as the Germans were forced to intervene to retrieve the situation.

Mussolini had not planned to go to war to attain his objectives before 1942, but the fall of France forced him to advance his schedule. Except in naval terms, Italy was not a strong power. Her air force was obsolescent, her army poorly equipped and low in morale. But her navy ranked fifth in the world. In 1937 two modern battleships – the *Vittorio Veneto* and the *Littorio* – had been launched, while four others of World War I vintage had been rebuilt. There were nineteen modern cruisers, 120 destroyers and torpedo boats, and 100 submarines. There were, however, no aircraft carriers. During the great naval debate over aircraft carriers in the 1920's and 1930's, Mussolini had said that Italy itself was an unsinkable air-

Below: One of Italy's new battleships, the *Vittorio Veneto*. She was fast and well-armed with nine 15-inch guns.

craft carrier and had not commissioned one for his navy. The Italian view was that a good air force could support their ships all over the Mediterranean, but unfortunately Italy did not have such an air force. With only the Mediterranean in which to operate, the Italian Navy was in fact a formidable force, so much so that in April 1940 France concentrated most of her naval strength in the Mediterranean. In May the French and British began combined naval operations and swept the Mediterranean while the Italian fleet prudently lay low. But in June France made armistices with both Germany and Italy, leaving Britain with but a small and overworked fleet in the Mediterranean. On 7 July Admiral Sir Andrew Cunningham, naval commander in the Eastern Mediterranean, completed negotiations with Vice Admiral R. E. Godfroy for the demilitarization of the French ships at Alexandria, thus sparing himself the need to fire on his former comrades-in-arms as had Admiral James Somerville at Oran.

Matched against the British Mediterranean fleet, the Italian Navy was superior in numbers while its ships were newer, faster and better armed. The Italians were, however, untrained in night operations, believing these to be impracticable for heavy ships, and were completely lacking in radar, which admittedly was a scarce and relatively untried instrument in 1940. Strengthening their Mediterranean fleet by the addition of a battleship and a carrier, the British shifted their main base from exposed Malta to Alexandria. The battle fleet consisted of three battleships, a carrier and a number of cruisers and destroyers. But even with the additions, the Italians would have been far superior materially had they wished to put to sea. The British ships were always in a poor state of repair due to constant use and no replacements. Destroyers and to a lesser extent cruisers suffered in terms of speed and operational efficiency as a result. On the other hand, the crews were experienced and morale high in the British ships, whereas the Italian sailors had logged little sea time and had no war experience.

As the British position in the Middle East was dependent on control of the eastern Mediterranean, the focus of British strength lay in Egypt where the Eastern Mediterranean Fleet under Admiral Cunningham and the Army of the Nile under General Sir Archibald Wavell were based at Alexandria. Facing Wavell across the Libyan desert was an Italian force of 215,000 men under Marshal Graziani, who was finally prodded into action by Mussolini in the fall of 1940. In December Wavell's mixed force of 30,000 British, Australian, New Zealand, French and Polish units counterattacked all the way to Benghazi in a brilliant campaign and in the process destroyed an Italian army six times its own size. Undertaken by the British largely to sustain morale on the home front, the campaign was the second major Italian disaster of the war. It forced Hitler to send General Erwin Rommel and his Panzer units to North Africa to support the Italians, and also caused him to take a closer look at British support of Greece, scene of the first Italian disaster, and at the need for German involvement in that campaign as well. Operation Barbarossa would have to wait until the Mediterranean had been tidied up.

Since the Italian entry into the war in June 1940 there had been skirmishes between the British and Italian fleets but no full scale action. Even with their superiority, the Italians were not challenging the British strongly since their operational aim was to maintain strong control in the central Mediterranean and to keep the sea route to Libya open. On 11 November, 1940 the British made a carrier based air strike on the Italian naval base at Taranto which put half of the Italian battle fleet out of action. For their part, the Italians made surprisingly successful torpedo boat attacks on British ships in various harbors. With German intervention in North Africa in February 1941, 400 German planes were based in Sicily and Rhodes to protect Rommel's supply lines between Sicily and Tripolitania. British shipping and bases came under heavy air attack. Malta was cut off and all but the eastern Mediter-

ranean became impassable to British convoys. The task of the British fleet had originally been to keep the lines of communication with Malta open and subsequently to attack Rommel's supply lines as well. At the same time the Royal Air Force had been giving modest assistance to the Greeks against the Italians. The Greek plight was raising strong Philhellene sentiment in Britain, but Churchill's proposal to increase aid to Greece in February 1941 had deeper political motivations. To maintain Britain's honor, he wished to uphold its 1939 guarantee of Greece. Successful British support of Greece would also encourage Turkish leaders to bring their country into the war against Germany. But perhaps most important, the Greek cause was very popular in the United States, and any aid, successful or otherwise, would add to British virtue in American eyes. Churchill's main goal was the creation of an alliance strong enough to defeat the Nazis, a goal to which American participation was essential. German intervention in Mussolini's Greek debacle was also expected imminently, and it was hoped that with British help the Greeks could clear out the Italians before Hitler struck. Thus on 4 March, 1941 Operation Lustre began the transport of British, Australian and New Zealand troops from Egypt to Greece, mostly in merchant ships. With the cruisers *Orion*, *Ajax*, *Perth* and *Gloucester*, Admiral H. D. Pridham-Wippell covered this traffic through operations in the Aegean Sea, thus adding yet another task to the burden of the Eastern Mediterranean Fleet. While British convoys ran north from Alexandria to Piraeus in support of the Greek campaign, German and Italian convoys went south from Sicily to Tripolitania in support of Rommel at the other end of the Mediterranean.

Believing two of the three British battleships to be out of action as a result of raids on Alexandria harbor, the German liaison staff suggested to the Italian Naval High Command on 9 March that the intensive traffic between Alexandria and the Greek ports carrying reinforcements and supplies

Above: The light cruiser *Orion*, Pridham-Wippell's flagship in the Aegean.
Left: Vice-Admiral Henry Pridham-Wippell, commander of the cruisers at Matapan.

Above: Admiral Andrew Cunningham, Commander-in-Chief of the Mediterranean Fleet, aboard his flagship *Warspite* in Alexandria.

was a particularly worthwhile target: 'The German naval staff considers that the appearance of Italian units in the area south of Crete will seriously interfere with British shipping, and may even lead to the complete interruption of the transport of troops, especially as these transports are at the moment inadequately protected'. The Italian Chief of Naval Staff, Admiral Riccardi, planned a reconnaissance in force to the island of Gavdo south of the western end of Crete, the first initiative of the Italian navy in the war thus far. With Admiral Angelo Iachino, Commander-in-Chief Afloat, in overall command, the force was divided into two groups. With his flag in the new 30-knot battleship *Vittorio Veneto*, mounting nine modern fifteen-inch guns, Iachino commanded the first group composed of the three cruisers *Trieste*, *Trento*, and *Bolzano* and seven destroyers. Within this group Admiral Sansonetti commanded the three cruisers and three destroyers while the remaining ships were under the direct orders of Iachino. Group two was Admiral Cattaneo's force of the cruisers *Zara*, *Fiume*, *Pola*, *Abruzzi* and *Garibaldi* and six attendant destroyers. Six of Iachino's eight cruisers were new 10,000-ton ships mounting eight eight-inch guns and capable of 32–35 knots.

Iachino was ordered to sail on 26 March to carry out an offensive reconnaissance to a point twenty miles south of Gavdo Island, while Cattaneo's force made a sweep 50 miles to the north into the Aegean. Having destroyed all enemy convoys which could be found, they were then to rendezvous and return to base. Enemy warships were to be engaged only if conditions were entirely favorable to the Italian squadron. Air support, so crucial to modern naval operations, was problematical since it was not under the orders of Iachino who had to make requests for Italian planes to his own naval high command and for Luftwaffe support to the German liaison officers aboard his flagship. While at sea on 27 March, the *Vittorio Veneto* intercepted a message to Alexandria from a British reconnaissance plane reporting three Italian cruisers 80 miles east of Sicily and heading toward Crete. Both Iachino and Riccardi knew that the element of surprise was now gone and with it any chance of meeting a convoy, but Riccardi ordered the sweep to continue to avoid offending the Germans at whose instigation the operation had been mounted in the first place. Cattaneo was ordered not to penetrate the Aegean but merely to meet Iachino twenty miles off Gavdo Island at dawn on the 28th of March.

By 26 March the British Eastern Mediterranean Command had noted the increase in Italian air reconnaissance and concluded that a major Italian operation was imminent in view of the expected invasion of Greece by the Germans. A naval diversion to cover a landing in Cyrenaica or Greece or an attack on Crete might be in the offing but the most likely objective was the convoys of Operation Lustre. When the report of the Italian cruisers was received on the 27th, the Aegean was cleared of shipping and north and south bound convoys cancelled. If the enemy force could be located and if the British fleet could get to sea early enough, it might be able to bring the enemy to battle. The Italian cruisers were a source of much worry to the British command since these ships were faster and more heavily gunned than the old six-inch British cruisers. Known to his fleet as 'ABC', Admiral Andrew Brown Cunningham would have dearly loved to bring the Italian fleet to a decisive action and he thought it was just possible that there were battleships out in support of the Italian cruisers. He therefore hoisted his flag in the battleship *Warspite* and put out to sea with his fleet on the night of 27 March, having waited until after dark to deceive the ever present Italian reconnaissance planes. Admiral Pridham-Wippell with his force of cruisers was to meet Cunningham's squadron at 0630 on the 28th, 30 miles south of Gavdo Island.

The British Battle Squadron

The British battle squadron consisted of the *Warspite*, a modern ship mounting eight fifteen-inch guns and with 24-knot speed. The battleships *Valiant* and *Barham* had similar armament but both were veterans of Jutland and while the *Valiant* had been modernized, the *Barham* had not and could only manage 22 knots. The guns of these ships were inferior in range to those of the *Vittorio Veneto*. The *Formidable* was an armored aircraft carrier capable of $30\frac{1}{2}$ knots and carrying 27 planes – thirteen Fulmar fighters, four

Swordfish torpedo bombers and ten Albacore torpedo bombers, only five of which were fitted with long range tanks. The Fulmars were new and well-armed fighters, but the Swordfish and Albacores were old, slow biplanes. This fleet was screened by eight destroyers, each mounting from four to eight 4.7-inch guns and capable of 36 knots, whereas the Italian destroyers carried five or six 4.7-inch guns but could do 39 knots. Pridham-Wippell's Aegean cruiser force was composed of the *Orion*, *Ajax*, *Perth* and *Gloucester*, supported by four destroyers. The *Gloucester* was a 9600-ton vessel mounting a dozen six-inch guns, while the other three cruisers ranged between 6900 and 7200 tons and carried eight six-inch guns. All had 32-knot speeds compared to the 35 knots of their Italian counterparts. To add to the speed advantage already enjoyed by the Italians, the *Warspite* passed too near a mud bank as she left the harbor, fouling her condensers and reducing her speed to 20 knots. The battle fleet was thus limited to this relatively low speed. One advantage enjoyed by the British, however, was the fact that the *Formidable*, *Valiant* and *Ajax* were all equipped with the newest radar which had a range of 40–50 miles.

At dawn on the 28th, the British fleet was 150 miles south of the east end of Crete, at which time the *Formidable* turned into the wind and launched a dawn air search. At 0720 a report came in of four cruisers and four destroyers, followed a few minutes later by another report of four cruisers and six destroyers. The two forces were about 100 miles north of Cunningham's position and about twenty miles apart from each other. Hence it appeared that one force must be Pridham-Wippell but that the other must be the Italian cruisers. Then Pridham-Wippell reported Italian cruisers eighteen miles north of his position and heading east. Cunningham increased speed to 22 knots, the maximum then for the *Warspite* and the *Barham*, hoping to reach the scene and engage the enemy in two hours. In fact Pridham-Wippell had reached his assigned position, which was virtually identical with the scheduled rendezvous of Iachino and Cattaneo, and had then been sighted by an Italian reconnaissance plane.

All day on the 27th, Iachino had correctly believed the British battle fleet to be still at Alexandria. At dawn on the 28th, his own squadron was in three separate groups. Forty miles northwest of Pridham-Wippell was the *Vittorio Veneto* and four destroyers, ten miles to port was Sansonetti with three cruisers and three destroyers, while twenty miles to his port was Cattaneo with five cruisers and six destroyers. The *Vittorio Veneto* had catapulted a plane for a dawn air search and at 0643 this plane had reported the position of Pridham-Wippell's ships. Feeling that a convoy might be near, Iachino pressed on at 30 knots and ordered Sansonetti ahead to identify and then retire to the main force. At 0758 Sansonetti sighted Pridham-Wippell and reported him as thirteen miles away 'Evidently bound for Alexandria', but instead of retiring he pursued and shortly after 0800 opened fire with his eight-inch guns. With their superior speed, the Italian cruisers closed the British ships rapidly and concentrated their fire on the *Gloucester*. The British

ships were in line abreast, retiring at full speed since their six-inch guns were outranged, making smoke, and evading the enemy fire by 'snaking the line' or making alternate 30-degree turns. As the range shortened, the *Gloucester* opened fire but the Italians turned away out of range on a parallel course and continued their fire. Pridham-Wippell set his course straight for the main British force a hundred miles to the southeast, trying to draw the Italians with him, unaware that a second Italian force, that of Cattaneo, was also close by. At 0855 Sansonetti was recalled by Iachino who thought that he was already farther east than orders warranted. The Italian cruisers withdrew to the northwest, but Pridham-Wippell had drawn them 50 miles nearer to the British battleships and within range of an air strike from the *Formidable*. He then turned and began to shadow the Italians so as not to lose contact.

Cunningham had ordered the *Valiant* and two destroyers forward to support Pridham-Wippell, but when the action ceased they rejoined the main force without making contact with the British cruisers. An air strike had also been prepared by the *Formidable* but Cunningham did not want to launch it and reveal his strength until he was sure of the presence of the Italian battle fleet and close enough to overtake any enemy ship crippled by the strike. His general plan was to launch an air

Top: The Italian heavy cruiser *Zara*, which was sunk at Matapan. **Center:** The Italian heavy cruiser *Pola*, sister ship of the *Zara*. She suffered the same fate. **Above:** The Italian heavy cruiser *Fiume* firing her 8-inch guns. She ended up with her other two sisters at the bottom of the Aegean.

strike to slow or stop the Italians long enough for his battle squadron to get within range and make the kill. Although the engineers had now made the *Warspite* capable of 24 knots, the fleet was still limited to 22 by the old *Barham*. A variety of air reports were coming in but the picture was still confused for Cunningham, since there were three separate Italian forces. At 0905, for example, a report of three Italian battleships was received but Pridham-Wippell was only seven miles from their reported position at the time and would have made a visual sighting, so the report was discounted as 'manifestly incorrect'. This was actually Sansonetti whose three large cruisers had been mis-identified as Cavour class battleships to which they did bear some resemblance.

Italian air reconnaissance reports appeared confused to Iachino who also tended to discount them, assuming that the British fleet was still comfortably at rest in Alexandria harbor and that he was dealing only with a convoy escort. At 0900

he turned east to get north of Pridham-Wippell, after which he intended to order Sansonetti to reverse course and come back on his pursuers, catching them between his three cruisers and the *Vittorio Veneto*. Hard on the heels of Sansonetti, Pridham-Wippell sighted the *Vittorio Veneto* as the first fifteen inch salvo splashed around his ships from a range of twelve miles. Sansonetti had altered course according to plan and with his superior speed would shortly be in range. Once more in a desperate situation, Pridham-Wippell again headed toward Cunningham at full speed, making smoke furiously. Eighty miles away, Cunningham now knew the presence of at least one enemy battleship and launched the air strike from the *Formidable*, although he would have preferred to wait until his ships were closer. At the same time, he requested a strike from the naval air station at Maleme on the west end of Crete. The fire of the *Vittorio Veneto* was concentrated first on the *Orion* and then on the *Gloucester*. From a safe

Left: Fulmar fighters ranged on the flight deck of the carrier *Illustrious* with the battleship *Valiant* carrying out gunnery practice in the background.

Left: The battleship *Barham* was a sister ship of the *Warspite* and another veteran of Jutland which fought at Matapan. She had not undergone the same drastic modernization as her sister ship. **Below:** The aircraft carrier *Formidable* approaching Gibraltar.

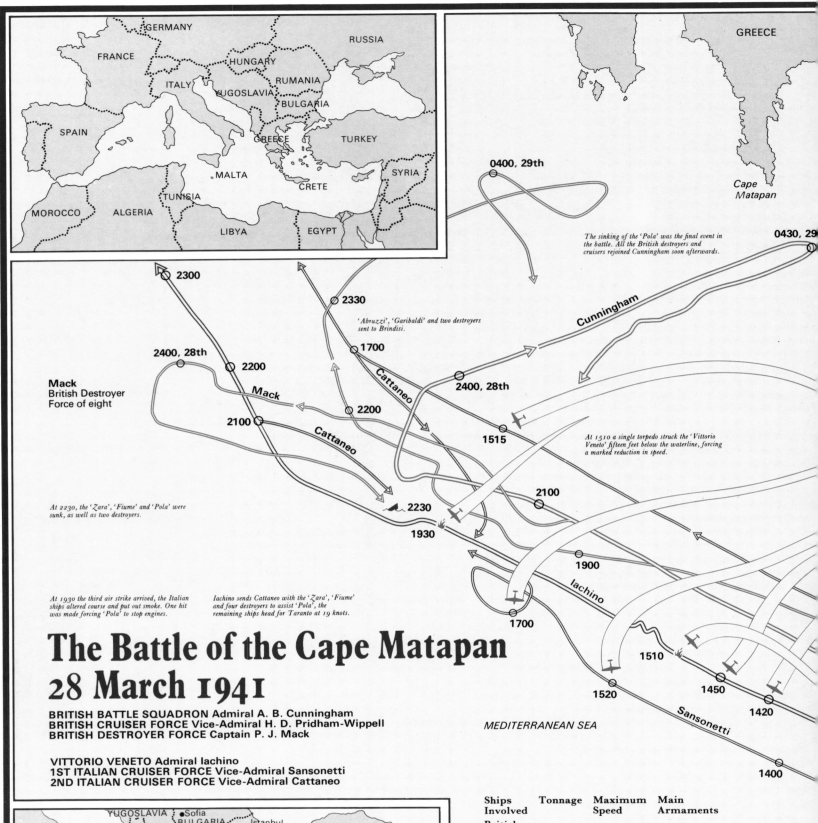

0400, 29th

Cape Matapan

0430, 29

The sinking of the 'Pola' was the final event in the battle. All the British destroyers and cruisers rejoined Cunningham soon afterwards.

2300

2330

'Abruzzi', 'Garibaldi' and two destroyers sent to Brindisi.

Cunningham

1700

2400, 28th

2200

Mack
British Destroyer
Force of eight

Mack

2200

Cattaneo

2400, 28th

2100

Cattaneo

1515

At 1510 a single torpedo struck the 'Vittorio Veneto' fifteen feet below the waterline, forcing a marked reduction in speed.

At 2230, the 'Zara', 'Fiume' and 'Pola' were sunk, as well as two destroyers.

2230

2100

1930

1900

At 1930 the third air strike arrived, the Italian ships altered course and put out smoke. One hit was made forcing 'Pola' to stop engines.

Iachino sends Cattaneo with the 'Zara', 'Fiume' and four destroyers to assist 'Pola', the remaining ships head for Taranto at 19 knots.

Iachino

1700

1510

1450

1520

1420

Sansonetti

MEDITERRANEAN SEA

1400

The Battle of the Cape Matapan
28 March 1941

BRITISH BATTLE SQUADRON Admiral A. B. Cunningham
BRITISH CRUISER FORCE Vice-Admiral H. D. Pridham-Wippell
BRITISH DESTROYER FORCE Captain P. J. Mack

VITTORIO VENETO Admiral Iachino
1ST ITALIAN CRUISER FORCE Vice-Admiral Sansonetti
2ND ITALIAN CRUISER FORCE Vice-Admiral Cattaneo

Iachino left Taranto on 26 March on an offensive reconnaissance to a point twenty miles south of Gavdhos Island, Crete.

MEDITERRANEAN SEA

Ships Involved	Tonnage	Maximum Speed	Main Armaments
British			
Ajax	6900	32	8–6", 8–4"
Barham	31000	22	8–15", 12–6", 8–4"
Formidable	23000	30.5	27 planes, 16–4.5"
Gloucester	9600	32	12–6", 8–4"
Orion	6900	32	8–6", 8–4"
Perth	6830	32.5	8–6", 4–4"
Valiant	31000	24	8–15", 20–4.5"
Warspite	31000	24	8–15", 8–6", 8–4"
Italian			
Abruzzi	7874	35	10–6", 8–3.9"
Bolzano	10000	32–35	8–8", 12–3.9"
Fiume	10000	32	8–8", 12–3.9"
Garibaldi	7874	35	10–6", 8–3.9"
Pola	10000	32–35	8–8", 12–3.9"
Trento	10000	32–35	8–8", 12–3.9"
Trieste	10000	32–35	8–8", 12–3.9"
Vittorio V.	35000	30	9–15", 12–6", 12–3.5"
Zara	10000	32	8–8", 12–3.9"

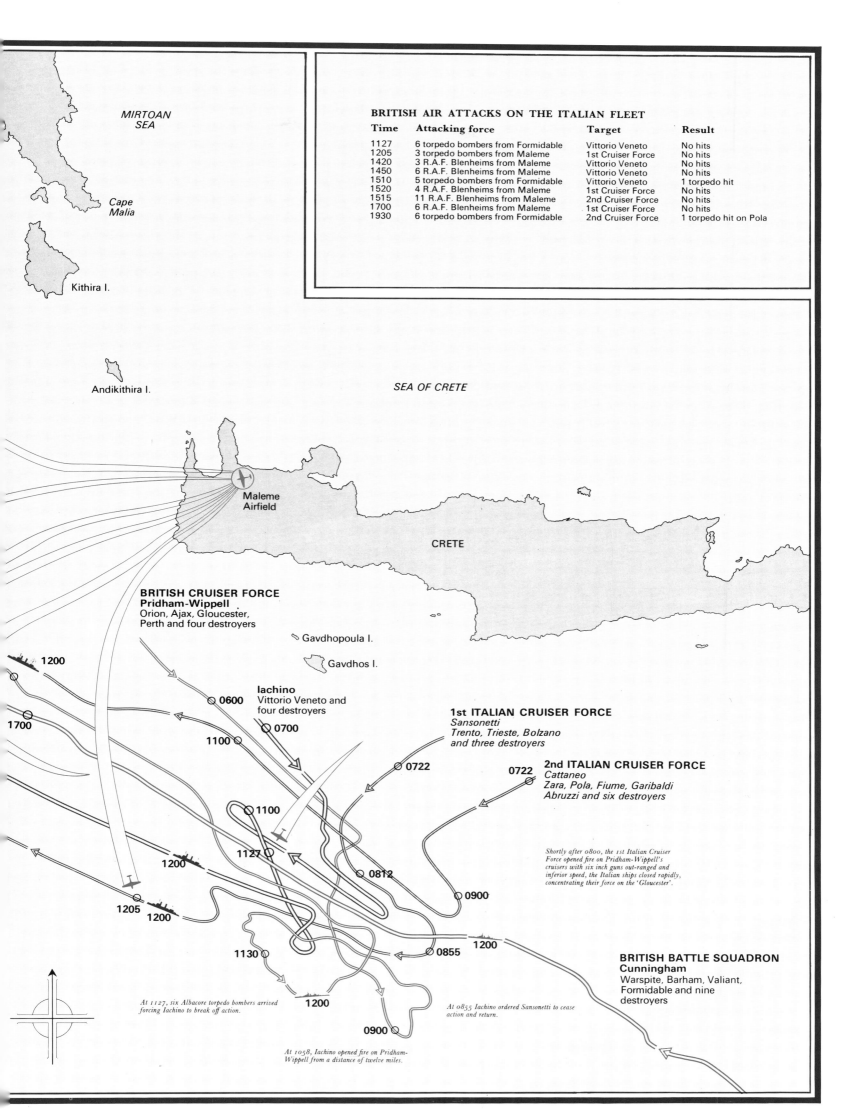

MIRTOAN
SEA

Cape
Malia

Kithira I.

Andikithira I.

SEA OF CRETE

Maleme
Airfield

CRETE

BRITISH AIR ATTACKS ON THE ITALIAN FLEET

Time	Attacking force	Target	Result
1127	6 torpedo bombers from Formidable	Vittorio Veneto	No hits
1205	3 torpedo bombers from Maleme	1st Cruiser Force	No hits
1420	3 R.A.F. Blenheims from Maleme	Vittorio Veneto	No hits
1450	6 R.A.F. Blenheims from Maleme	Vittorio Veneto	No hits
1510	5 torpedo bombers from Formidable	Vittorio Veneto	1 torpedo hit
1520	4 R.A.F. Blenheims from Maleme	1st Cruiser Force	No hits
1515	11 R.A.F. Blenheims from Maleme	2nd Cruiser Force	No hits
1700	6 R.A.F. Blenheims from Maleme	1st Cruiser Force	No hits
1930	6 torpedo bombers from Formidable	2nd Cruiser Force	1 torpedo hit on Pola

BRITISH CRUISER FORCE
Pridham-Wippell
Orion, Ajax, Gloucester,
Perth and four destroyers

Gavdhopoula I.

Gavdhos I.

1200

1700

Iachino
Vittorio Veneto and
four destroyers

0600

0700

1100

1st ITALIAN CRUISER FORCE
Sansonetti
Trento, Trieste, Bolzano
and three destroyers

0722

0722

2nd ITALIAN CRUISER FORCE
Cattaneo
Zara, Pola, Fiume, Garibaldi
Abruzzi and six destroyers

1100

1127

1200

0812

Shortly after 0800, the 1st Italian Cruiser
Force opened fire on Pridham-Wippell's
cruisers with six inch guns out-ranged and
inferior speed, the Italian ships closed rapidly,
concentrating their force on the 'Gloucester'.

0900

1205
1200

1130

0855
1200

BRITISH BATTLE SQUADRON
Cunningham
Warspite, Barham, Valiant,
Formidable and nine
destroyers

At 1127, six Albacore torpedo bombers arrived
forcing Iachino to break off action.

1200

At 0855 Iachino ordered Sansonetti to cease
action and return.

0900

At 1058, Iachino opened fire on Pridham-
Wippell from a distance of twelve miles.

191

distance the battleship could have picked off the British cruisers one after the other, but at 1127 the strike force of six Albacores from the *Formidable* arrived. All aimed their torpedoes at the *Vittorio Veneto*, forcing her into evasive maneuvers, after which the entire Italian force broke off the action and headed northwest toward their home base. Although the British pilots thought that they had scored a hit, the *Vittorio Veneto* combed the tracks of the torpedoes successfully. Pridham-Wippell saw neither the air strike which saved him nor the retreat of the enemy. When the smoke cleared, there was only an empty horizon, and the cruiser force joined the main force at 1230. When signaled 'Where is the enemy?', Pridham-Wippell had to reply 'Sorry don't know; haven't seen them for some time'.

Cunningham's united force was now an estimated 45 miles east-southeast of Iachino, but unless the *Vittorio Veneto* had been slowed by a torpedo the lumbering British battleships would never catch the swift Italians. The air strike from Maleme had also missed their target; if the battleships were to get into action, a second strike from the *Formidable* would have to slow up the Italians. A force of three Albacores and two Swordfish with two Fulmars for cover was ready by noon. To launch and recover, however, the *Formidable* had always to turn into the wind, slowing the whole fleet. With two destroyers for a screen, the carrier was detached for independent operations while the remainder of the squadron steamed on at 22 knots. Launching its strike after noon, the *Formidable* rejoined the main force, which now had Pridham-Wippell's four cruisers sixteen miles in front as the van, at 1400.

After being attacked by carrier planes, Iachino had deduced that a carrier, four cruisers and attendant destroyers were at sea but he still believed the enemy battleships to be in port. Using air reconnaissance reports, he also calculated that the British were 170 miles behind him. With his superior speed and better gunned ships, he did not have to worry about a gun battle, but he was concerned about attacks from land-based planes. Several times that afternoon his ships had suffered high altitude bomb attacks by Blenheim bombers but were not hit. Unhappy about his vulnerability to air attack, Iachino later wrote in his account of the battle, 'I felt pretty well deceived by the lack of cooperation. We remained for the rest of the day without fighter cover'. Shortly after 1500 his fears were realized when the

second air strike arrived and scored a single torpedo hit on the key ship in the Italian squadron. Struck fifteen feet below the waterline near the port screw, the *Vittorio Veneto* immediately shipped a large amount of water and stopped engines. 'Enemy has made a large decrease in speed' was the jubilant report received at 1558 by Cunningham, who ordered Pridham-Wippell's cruisers to press on at full speed to make contact. A third air strike was launched at 1735. Six Albacores and two Swordfish were to take advantage of the cover of dusk to try to achieve a surprise attack. The 1830 air report placed the enemy 50 miles in front of Cunningham, making only twelve to fifteen knots. Even at that speed it would take the battleships four hours to get within gun range.

The Crippled *Vittorio Veneto*

Damage control and repair parties had worked hard on the *Vittorio Veneto*, however, and by 1700 she was able to make nineteen knots. Iachino still believed that the British surface forces were too far behind to catch him and that the main threat remained air attack. He therefore detached his two smaller cruisers, the 7800-ton *Abruzzi* and *Garibaldi*, and ordered them to Brindisi with two destroyers. Since his reduced speed had removed one of his biggest advantages and reduced his ability to maneuver, he arranged his fleet in five columns. The middle column was the *Vittorio Veneto* with two destroyers ahead and two astern. Three cruisers were ranged on each side and the flanks were covered by the remaining destroyers. Such a formation made any form of air or surface attack extremely difficult.

Spotted before its attack began at 1930, the third air strike met a furious curtain of anti-aircraft fire as the Italian ships altered course and put out smoke. Only one hit was made, but it forced the cruiser *Pola* to pull out of line with stopped engines. Iachino remained uninformed of this fact for another half-hour and then sent Cattaneo with the *Zara*, *Fiume* and four destroyers back to assist the stricken *Pola*, believing that the situation called for the presence of a flag officer to assess the damage and make decisions. 'It never occurred to me that we were within relatively short distance of the entire British force', he later wrote. 'I thought the British cruisers had decided to turn back leaving only two destroyers to deal with us'. The remainder of the fleet headed for Taranto at nineteen knots, then altered course at 2048 directly for Cape Colonne.

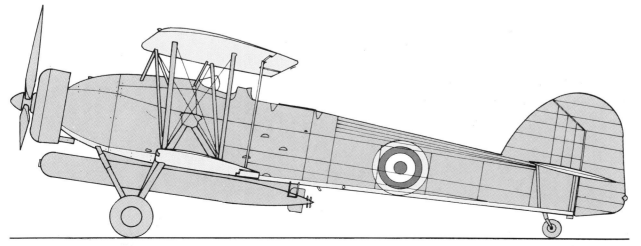

Right: The Supermarine Walrus amphibian was carried on board British cruisers and battleships for spotting and reconnaissance duties.

Below: British battleships firing their 15-inch guns. The *Valiant*, followed by the *Barham* and *Warspite*, shown here on a gunnery exercise, were all later at Matapan. Their guns could fire a 1900-pound shell a distance of over twenty miles. **Below right:** The first intimation that the Italian cruisers had of the British presence at Matapan was a blaze of searchlights.

Pridham-Wippell's cruisers had pressed ahead and at 1918 they made visual contact with the enemy ten miles away. A few minutes later the force was witness to the third air strike. With the enemy crippled and in striking range, the hazards of a night attack were debated by Cunningham's staff, all of whom tended to be opposed. The essence of the dilemma was whether to risk the battle fleet in a night action with an enemy heavily screened by cruisers and destroyers, thus exposing the British heavy ships to night torpedo attacks, or to wait until morning and risk an attack by land-based German dive bombers. Although Cunningham wrote in his memoirs that he paid 'respectful attention' to the opinions expressed by his staff officers, one of these later said that in fact 'ABC' just looked at them and said 'You're a pack of yellow livered skunks. I'll go and have my supper now and see after supper if my morale isn't higher than yours'. The night orders were, predictably, 'If cruisers gain touch with damaged battleship, second and fourteenth destroyer flotillas will be sent to attack. If she is not then destroyed, battle fleet will follow in'. Four destroyers were left to screen the battleships and carrier while the remaining eight under Captain P. J. Mack went forward to attack the Italians who were now estimated to be but 33 miles ahead. Due to the increase in the speed of the *Vittorio Veneto* at 1700, however, the Italian squadron was actually 57 miles ahead. At the same time Pridham-Wippell's cruisers picked up a large ship dead in the water on their radar. Assuming it to be the *Vittorio Veneto*, Pridham-Wippell reported the position of the crippled *Pola* to Cunningham and gave her a wide berth as he continued his search for the rest of the enemy. Mack did not intercept this message and, unaware of the *Pola* and the easy target she would have made for his destroyers' torpedoes, swung to the north in an attempt to get ahead of the point where he had been told the Italian fleet was, in the hope of cutting it off.

Pridham-Wippell's report of a stopped ship caused Cunningham to think that the *Vittorio Veneto* had been left for the battlefleet to handle. In line ahead with the *Warspite* followed by the *Valiant*, *Formidable* and *Barham*, Cunningham headed straight for the target twenty miles distant. An hour later look-outs reported a large ship six miles ahead off the port bow. Ten minutes later

the excited look-outs pointed out more ships crossing the bows of the British line only two miles away. In blissful unawareness Cattaneo's squadron was passing under the guns of three British battleships. 'Never in my life have I experienced a more thrilling moment . . . The enemy was at a range of no more than 3800 yards – point blank' wrote Cunningham, who was a great believer in the gun as a weapon. At 2227 the British destroyers turned their searchlights on the *Fiume* which then received broadsides of fifteen-inch shells from the *Warspite* and *Valiant* at 2900 yards. Five of the six shells in the *Warspite's* first salvo hit at intervals along the *Fiume's* length below her upper deck, while the sixth blew the aft turret completely over the side. 'One saw whole turrets and masses of other heavy debris whirling through the air and splashing into the sea . . . in a short time the ships themselves were nothing but glowing torches . . .' was the way Cunningham described the scene in his memoirs.

When suddenly fired on, Cattaneo's ships were paralyzed with surprise and unable to fight back. The Italians had no radar and could not use their main armament because they had no anti-flash ammunition and no means of gun laying and fire control at night. In any event, their main guns could not be brought into action on the spur of the moment. The attack was so overwhelming and unexpected that the Italian cruisers were completely shattered before resistance could begin. The *Fiume* was burning from stem to stern and listing heavily to starboard. While the *Warspite* continued to blast her with both her main and secondary armaments, the *Valiant* turned its guns on the *Zara* and poured in five broadsides in three minutes. The *Barham* then came up and gave her six more broadsides. Completely ablaze and with Cattaneo dead, the *Zara* was listed to port and heeled over in that direction. The *Fiume* sank at 2315 hours.

The *Formidable* had already hauled out of the battle line and steered north when three Italian destroyers counterattacked the battleships with torpedoes, forcing the latter to take evasive action and lift their fire from the hapless cruisers. Since his own destroyers had already been fired on mistakenly by his larger ships in the dark, Cunningham ordered his four destroyers to finish off the enemy ships with torpedoes, turned his battle line 90 degrees starboard on a northward course,

Left: The battleship *Warspite*, flagship of Admiral Cunningham at Matapan. This ship was a veteran of Jutland, but had been modernized twice and completely altered in appearance. She had eight 15-inch guns in four twin turrets and could steam at 24 knots. She saw the most arduous service of any battleship in World War Two. Built in 1914 *Warspite* served throughout World War Two.

and signaled the remainder of his forces that 'all forces not engaged should retire to the northeast'. At that moment Pridham-Wippell's cruisers were 35 miles east-southeast of Iachino's main force, unaware of the position of the elusive Italian admiral. Interpreting the message to include his force as well, Pridham-Wippell broke off his search and set course northeast as ordered. Mack's destroyers were 30 miles south-southeast of Iachino but continued their search, since for them the order had been qualified with 'after your attack'.

After their torpedo attack the three Italian destroyers were engaged by two British destroyers but with their superior speed, all three made good their escape by 2320, suffering only a few shell hits in the process. The remaining two British destroyers sank the other Italian destroyer. At midnight these two ships – the *Havock* and the *Greyhound* – discovered the abandoned *Zara* and the *Pola*. With no torpedoes left, they opened fire with their guns, then mistook the *Pola* for a battleship in the dark and hurriedly withdrew. A frantic signal concerning the sighting of a battleship 'undamaged and stopped' was received by Cunningham and also intercepted by Mack who was then, at 0030, sixty miles west-northwest of the battle area and 25 miles south of Iachino due to the latter's course change and increase in speed. Mack immediately raced toward the battle area at his full speed of 36 knots. Later the message was corrected from a battleship to a cruiser, but by then Mack had been steaming away from Iachino for almost an hour. Still not certain where the *Vittorio Veneto* really was, Mack decided to continue east and arrived at the battle zone after 0200 on the morning of the 29th. Drawn to the *Zara* by the light of her fires, Mack dispatched the abandoned ship with torpedoes. The *Pola* was then discovered and when illuminated by the searchlights of the British destroyers, was shown to have her guns trained fore and aft and her flag flying. On the upper deck was a thoroughly demoralized group of men which one British officer described as 'longing to surrender' and showing 'definite signs of inebriation'. These were apparently the non-swimmers of the *Pola's* crew, the others having gone over the side long before. After taking off this company, the *Pola* was sunk with torpedoes. The British officers who interrogated these prisoners wrote in their report 'Prisoners when asked why they failed to fire at us replied that they thought if they did we would fire back'. In fact, however, the electric power of the *Pola* was out and with it all her turrets.

The sinking of the *Pola* was the final event in the Battle of Matapan. All the British destroyers rejoined their main force soon afterwards, while Pridham-Wippell's cruisers arrived some hours later. At the time the British fleet was lying some thirty miles off Cape Matapan which gave its name to the battle. A dawn air search was sent out but found no sign of any Italian ships. The destroyers then returned to the battle area and picked up more than 900 survivors but were forced to break off this work as attacks by land-based German planes were expected. Cunningham sent a message to the Italian high command concerning the remainder of the survivors who were picked up two days later by the Italian hospital ship *Gradisca*. Later that day, as it returned to Alexandria, the British fleet was attacked by German Ju-88's, but no damage was sustained.

The Italian navy had lost the *Zara*, *Pola*, *Fiume* and two destroyers as well as Admiral Cattaneo and 2400 men. Unaware of these events when he reached Taranto with the remainder of his force, Iachino only learned of the disaster the next day in Rome when his superior, Admiral Riccardi showed him the British communiqué concerning the action. The stunned admiral blamed the disaster on the Italian and German air commands for not providing him with air cover and air reconnaissance reports, but he had in fact been operating most of the time at the extreme range of the Italian planes based at Rhodes and Scarpanto and to the east of the area normally covered by German planes. When Italy had entered the war, Iachino had felt that local air and sea superiority should have been immediately established by an all-out attack on Malta, which would have confined the British to the eastern Mediterranean. But as the Italian fleet stayed in port, its morale and ability to take the initiative fell drastically. The reinforcement of Cunningham's command and the air raid on Taranto caused the Italians virtually to relinquish any ideas of aggressive naval action until prodded by their German allies. Thus, the first fleet initiative of the Italian Navy was also its last. It did not engage the British again but stayed quietly in port until Italy made an armistice with the Allies in September 1943, after which it sailed to Malta and surrendered.

Although they were pleased to have further reduced the Italians' naval superiority by the elimination of three of the fast heavy cruisers which were such a threat to the older, slower British cruisers, there was considerable disappointment in the British fleet over the escape of the *Vittorio Veneto*. Iachino's ships had been saved by their increase in speed after the torpedoing of the *Vittorio Veneto* and their change of course. The British had simply been too slow to have had much chance of catching the Italians and what chance

there was had been nullified by British mistakes. Cunningham's order, which he himself later termed 'ill considered', for the fleet to withdraw to the northeast had caused Pridham-Wippell to break off his search while the mis-identification of the *Pola* had ended the search of the destroyer force. Yet in the darkness and confusion of Italian and British torpedo attacks, it was imperative for Cunningham to extricate his capital ships, for a hit on any of them would have reduced its speed and left it easy prey for German dive bombers the next day. It had been a cheap victory for Cunningham as it had cost only the Albacore which had torpedoed the *Vittorio Veneto*, shot down with its two-man crew.

Taranto followed by Matapan tipped the strategic situation in the Mediterranean in British favor, but this was all too brief. Preceded by a renewed and again unsuccessful Italian offensive in Albania, the anticipated German invasion of Greece began on 6 April. Operation Lustre, which the Italian Navy had tried to disrupt with such disastrous results for itself, had brought 50,000 British, Australian, and New Zealand troops to Greece. But British military cooperation with the Greeks was a series of muddles and misunderstandings. By the end of April resistance on the Greek mainland had ceased and the survivors of the Greek and Commonwealth forces had withdrawn to Crete which Britain had occupied six months previously. The defense of Crete was bungled as well, so the

Below: The battleship *Valiant* at anchor at Alexandria surrounded by nets to protect her against torpedo attack.

evacuation of that island began on 1 June. The British Navy suffered heavily in these operations: three cruisers and six destroyers were sunk, and two battleships, three cruisers and a carrier were damaged by German air attacks. In fact the navy had to suspend further operations around Crete with the evacuation only half-completed as further losses would have jeopardized its control of the eastern Mediterranean. More serious losses were suffered toward the end of the year when the old *Barham* was sunk by a German submarine and Italian midget submarines audaciously entered Alexandria harbor to put the battleships *Valiant* and *Queen Elizabeth* out of action for many months.

The strategic significance of Matapan is that it removed the potential threat of the superior Italian surface fleet to the British position in the eastern Mediterranean. While the Italians had no intention of using their fleet to dispute British control and did so only under German pressure, the British could not know this fact. For them the threat was real. Matapan secured Operation Lustre and made certain that the Italians would not try to interfere with the evacuation of Greece or Crete. Had the Italians made their sortie with the full support of the Luftwaffe during the evacuations of Greece and Crete, it might have been more than Cunningham's overextended force could have handled at that point. 'There is little doubt that the rough handling given to the enemy on this occasion served us in good stead during the subsequent evacuation of Greece and Crete. Much of these later operations may be said to have been conducted under cover of the Battle of Matapan' wrote Cunningham in his final dispatch. By midsummer Germany was in control of the Balkans. The North Africa campaign between Rommel's Afrika Corps and Wavell's Commonwealth forces then became the main focus of fighting in the Mediterranean until May 1943 when the Allies' Italian campaign began.

Matapan entailed a number of firsts in terms of naval warfare. It was the first time that carrier planes played a main role in a fleet action. For the first time, radar was used in a sea battle. It was also the first main fleet action of the British Navy since Jutland. It was, however, also a 'last' in the sense that it was the last fleet action in the European theater of war. Naval forces tended to play supporting roles in the European theaters, while the Pacific with its vast expanses of ocean and island fortresses was a naval war par excellence. Epic sea battles were to follow Matapan, but they took place in the Pacific. Thus Matapan was the last main fleet action of the Royal Navy.

Coral Sea

1942

While the European war grew out of the grand designs of Adolf Hitler and was primarily a continental European land war with the various navies playing a supporting role, the Pacific war stemmed from the adventures of the Japanese army first in Manchuria and then in China. By the time the Western powers became directly involved, however, it was already clear that China was a static theater and that the real struggle between Japanese and Western imperialism was to take place in the vast expanses of the Pacific Ocean. The Pacific war was thus a naval war, the greatest naval war in history, with mastery of the Pacific as the prize. It centered around a series of epic naval actions which involved a different style of warfare from the traditional gun and ship-borne torpedo actions. The Battle of the Coral Sea in May 1942 was the first of these new style actions, fought entirely between aircraft carriers, in which no ship on either side sighted the enemy.

Emerging from the Russo-Japanese War of 1905 with no serious rival in Korea or southern Manchuria, Japan had soon developed a practical alliance with Russia to safeguard both their interests on the Asian mainland against Japan's other Pacific rival, the United States. American policy from the early twentieth century opposed the creation of imperialist monopolies in China and Manchuria in favor of opportunities for all comers; in other words, the 'Open Door' policy. Having annexed Korea in 1910, Japan continued its pressure in Manchuria until 1931, when the expansionist faction of the Japanese army presented its government with a *fait accompli*, and the puppet state of Manchukuo was created. By 1937 the Japanese Army had turned covetous eyes on North China and engineered a war with the weak government of Chiang Kai-shek. The Japanese were able to seize the main population areas but were unable to dislodge Chiang from the mountainous interior to which he had retreated. The China war thus became a stalemate in which little territory changed hands until late 1944.

The United States had watched the expansion of Japanese influence on the East Asian mainland with disquiet and in particular protested against Japanese military moves against China. American-Japanese relations deteriorated until in December 1940 the United States tried to use

economic pressure to gain its political ends by imposing an embargo on the sale of scrap iron and war materials to Japan. With its supply of vital materials thus threatened, Japan decided in 1941 that she must gain control of the supplies of oil, tin and rubber in the European colonies in Southeast Asia. The aims of this move were to obtain freedom from pressure by the Western powers, who had been applying economic sanctions in an effort to control Japanese expansion; to crush China's hopes and force her to make peace by attacking her western allies, and to build up a Japanese empire in Asia by defeating the Western colonial powers. This last goal did not envision a simple military operation but was touted as a great enterprise to join the peoples of Southeast Asia and China under the beneficient hegemony of Japan in what was termed the 'Greater East Asia Co-Prosperity Sphere'. The object was to end Western imperialism in Asia by Britain, France, the Netherlands and the United States. In a radical departure from her traditional foreign policy, Japan ceased to regard Russia as her main enemy and signed a non-aggression pact with the Soviet Union in April 1941 so that she could shift her focus to the south. Japanese leadership in the struggle against western imperialism was generally welcomed by many Southeast Asian nationalists, but as the war went on it became obvious that Japan was not launching a crusade of Asians against the West but was embarked on the simple predatory business of transferring to herself the benefits previously enjoyed by westerners in Asia.

As a first step, Japan occupied French Indo-China in 1940 and 1941 to gain the bases necessary for reducing Southeast Asia. President Franklin D. Roosevelt responded by stepping up the economic war, freezing Japanese assets in the United States and imposing a virtual embargo on oil and steel trading with Japan. With only two years of oil stockpiled, the issue was now clearcut for Japan: capitulate to American demands or go to war. Both sides believed that war was inevitable but each continued to test the diplomatic possibilities through negotiations while Imperial General Headquarters hurriedly devised a war plan. By November 1941 negotiations were completely deadlocked over the issue of Japanese withdrawal from China, Manchuria and Indochina in return for the lifting of the assets freeze and the oil embargo. War came early in the morning of 7 December with the classic Japanese attack on the big American base at Pearl Harbor and resulted from the inability of the Japanese government to find any other means of resolving a situation already beyond its control. The war was a desperate venture, hastily undertaken and conducted not with elaborate planning and systematic operational schemes but by improvisation.

The surprise attack on Pearl Harbor was planned by a man who had lost two fingers at Port Arthur in 1904. Since that time Admiral Isoroku Yamamoto had risen high in the Japanese navy by industry and original thinking. In 1939 he had been made Commander-in-Chief of the Combined Fleet and was one of three or four men responsible for planning naval operations. Yamamoto's fleet had not been in a serious action since the Battle of Tsushima in 1905 and was untested by current standards. As long as the Washington Naval Limitation Treaty had been in force, a great deal had been known in the West about Japanese naval construction. When Japan withdrew from the naval limitation agreement in January 1936, however, the West found these links severed and knew only obliquely of the subsequent burst of capital ship construction in Japan.

Below: Pearl Harbor, the 'day that will live in infamy', brought the United States into World War Two with a vengeance. Much of the Pacific Fleet was destroyed on the morning of 7 December, 1941, but luckily the American aircraft carriers were at sea and were not affected by the Japanese surprise attack.

Right: Admiral Yamamoto, who was opposed to Japan's attack on the United States. He privately predicted defeat for Japan. **Far right:** Admiral Hara later realized that Japan's initially easy conquests made them overconfident, which led them to believe that after Pearl Harbor and the conquest of Southeast Asia the US might negotiate a compromise peace.

Between 1921 and 1941 the combat tonnage of the Japanese Navy doubled, while that of the British and American navies registered but modest increases. In 1941 the Japanese fleet was more powerful than the combined Pacific fleets of Britain and America and was far better prepared for combat. With well-designed and well-armed ships, the fleet was fully and rigorously drilled and exercised. The number of carriers and battleships in the fleet was substantially increased after 1936. Last additions to the battle fleet before the war were the *Yamato* and *Musashi*, 63,000-ton behemoths mounting eighteen-inch guns, which were completed in 1941. A comparison of the Japanese with the American Pacific Fleet in 1941 shows ten Japanese battleships to nine American, ten carriers to three, eighteen heavy cruisers to twelve, seventeen light cruisers to nine, 111 destroyers to 67, and 64 submarines to 27, leaving Japan superior in every category.

Since the 1920's only one clique in the Imperial Navy had been interested in naval air warfare, but its most prominent member was Yamamoto, who had early been attracted to the various theories of air power and was sceptical of the value of battleships. Yamamoto became commandant of a naval school and trained many pilots but his views were not popular with the other Japanese admirals. In a characteristically Japanese solution to this conflict, the fleet as a whole was not reformed but a separate fleet oriented toward air tactics was created in addition to the traditional battle fleet. This development within the Japanese Navy was not noted by western intelligence services, which thought that the Japanese were weak in skilled naval pilots. How wrong they were was demonstrated at Pearl Harbor.

The Japanese Navy was more conservative than the army which was deeply involved in the government and had involved Japan in a gigantic adventure on the Asian mainland. Until Pearl Harbor the war had been largely an army affair, but the navy was captivated by the thought of an ocean empire in the south. Enlarging the war to Southeast Asia and the South Pacific meant that the navy would have its own ocean theater in which to operate. Within the navy Yamamoto was a moderate who agreed to war only when the situation was desperate. His plan was to prevent the American fleet from sailing to engage Japan in the western Pacific by destroying it before it could get into action. The Japanese had warned the Americans many times that an attack on Pearl Harbor was not excluded from their plans but due to the unbelievable negligence of the United States, Yamamoto's six carriers were able to score a stunning success. This occurred despite the fact that Japan had tried to observe customary usage by warning the United States thirty minutes before the attack, but had failed to get the message through in time. The American battleship force was put out of action, though four carriers escaped. Yamamoto's bold stroke had given Japan almost two years in which to consolidate its gains or to make peace. Concurrently, Japanese forces began an offensive which by the spring of 1942 had gained them Hong Kong, the Philippines, Wake, Guam, Malaya, Burma and the Netherlands East Indies.

The first offensive had been so successful yet so cheap in casualties, and American and British power had proved so ineffectual, that Imperial General Headquarters determined to embark on a second grand offensive. Tulagi in the Solomon Islands and Port Moresby in Papua were to be seized to give Japan air mastery of the Coral Sea. The Combined Fleet was then to cross the Pacific to annihilate the remains of the American fleet and capture Midway Island and the Western Aleutians. A 'ribbon defense' anchored at Attu, Midway, Wake, the Marshalls and the Gilberts would be set up, followed by the invasion of New Caledonia, the Fijis and Samoa to isolate Australia. The reasoning was that with the American Fleet wiped out, the Japanese conquests could be organized and the ribbon defense made impregnable. Tiring of a futile war, the Americans would negotiate a peace which would leave Japan master of the Pacific. These moves had been part of the Japanese Basic War Plan since 1938, but new elements were added in 1942: the major fleet action with the Americans and the advancing of the timetable.

The 'Victory Disease'

After the war Rear-Admiral Chuichi Hara called this plan the result of 'victory disease'. Success had come so easily that contempt for and underestimation of the Americans had grown in Japanese minds. Imperial General Headquarters failed to understand that continued success depended on an adequate sea supply system to support its far-flung defense perimeter and on superior sea power to protect its lines of communication. Japan's merchant tonnage was insufficient and too inefficiently organized to meet the first requirement while she did not have the industrial capacity or manpower for the second. Sea power meant carrier-borne air forces, and while Japan had initially displayed clear superiority in planes, pilots and techniques, by April 1942 she had already lost 315 naval planes in combat while a further 540 had been lost 'operationally'. These losses were not yet irreplaceable but already the quality of air crew replacements was noticeably lower. Thus the second offensive was to fatally overextend Japanese military capabilities. The sound part of the plan was Yamamoto's insistence that the American Pacific Fleet must be destroyed by 1943. He was well aware of the superior economic and industrial might of the United States and knew that once this might began to be translated into warships, the American Navy would be irresistable.

As a prelude to the second offensive, the navy made a successful sweep of the Indian Ocean in early April to neutralize the small British naval forces. The navy then turned to its primary objective, dominance of the Coral Sea. Bounded on one side by 1500 miles of the Great Barrier Reef of Australia and on the others by New Caledonia, the New Hebrides and the Louisiades, the Coral Sea was crucial to Australia's security. Since early 1942 the Japanese had dominated the bight of the Coral Sea, the Bismarck Sea, from their big base at Rabaul. The plan was that from Rabaul a force under Rear Admiral Shima would occupy Tulagi in the lower Solomons and establish a seaplane base from which Nouméa could be neutralized. Another force of twelve transports carried the Port Moresby Invasion Group, covered by four heavy cruisers and the light carrier *Shoho*, with twelve 'Zero' fighter planes and nine 'Kate' torpedo bombers. Under the command of Rear Admiral Goto, this force was to strike at Port Moresby from Rabaul through the Jomard Passage. Another squadron of two light cruisers and a seaplane tender under Rear-Admiral Marushige was to operate in support of Goto and establish a seaplane base in the Louisiades. The Carrier Striking Force under Vice-Admiral Takagi was to come south from the Carolines, circle the Solomons and enter the Coral Sea from the east to destroy any Allied resistance. This force was built around the carriers *Shokaku* and *Zuikaku*, both veterans of Pearl Harbor, supported by two heavy cruisers and six destroyers. Overall command was the responsibility of Vice-Admiral Inouye, Commander-in-Chief of the Fourth Fleet. Any Allied naval force was to be caught between Takagi's planes and Goto's cruisers, after which Takagi's group would attack the Allied bases at Thursday, Coen, Cooktown and Townsville in Queensland. With Port Moresby and its airfield in their hands, the Japanese could menace the ports and airfields of Australia. The more optimistic among them thought that this might even force Australia out of the war.

It was a typically Japanese plan which relied on an elaborate organization of various forces following different routes on a set schedule to trap the enemy in an unequal battle. The Japanese also believed that the Americans had only one carrier available in the South Pacific, which made their own force that much superior. It was strategically unwise to divide their forces to such an extent but the Japanese were relying heavily on the element of surprise. The plan might well have been successful but for one factor which the Japanese could not take into account. The vital

Left: Vice-Admiral Shima's force occupied Rabaul and Tulagi in the Solomons, which threatened Australia.

The Battle of the Coral Sea, 3-8 May 1942

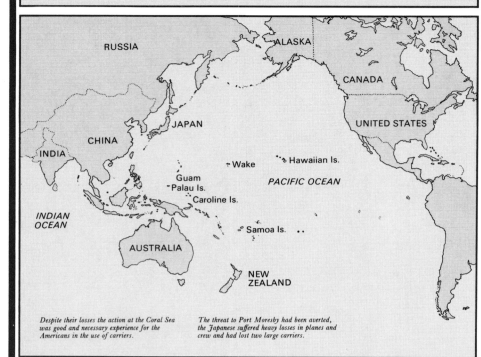

On 1 May Shima's force sailed from Rabaul for Tulagi while the American carrier forces made their rendezvous north of New Caledonia.

When informed of the loss of the 'Shoho', on the 7th, and Crace's position south of the Jomard Passage Admiral Inouye ordered 'Shima' to hold his force north of the Louisiades.

BISMARCK SEA

New Britain

NEW GUINEA

Due to intense activity by South West Pacific Command planes Inouye postponed the Port Moresby expedition while Takagi began to retire to Truk.

SOLOMON SEA

PAPUA

Port Moresby

Despite their losses the action at the Coral Sea was good and necessary experience for the Americans in the use of carriers.

The threat to Port Moresby had been averted, the Japanese suffered heavy losses in planes and crew and had lost two large carriers.

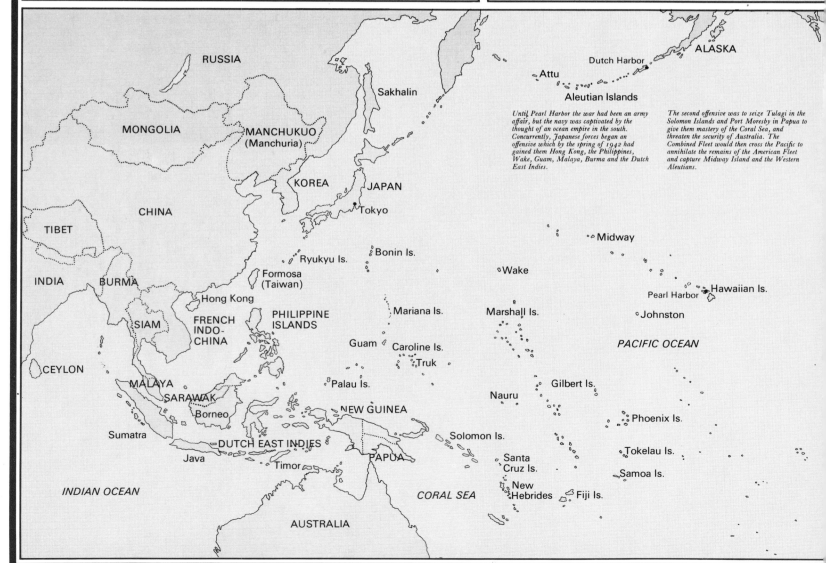

RUSSIA

Sakhalin

Dutch Harbor   ALASKA

Attu

Aleutian Islands

MONGOLIA

MANCHUKUO
(Manchuria)

Until Pearl Harbor the war had been an army affair, but the navy was captivated by the thought of an ocean empire in the south. Concurrently, Japanese forces began an offensive which by the spring of 1942 had gained them Hong Kong, the Philippines, Wake, Guam, Malaya, Burma and the Dutch East Indies.

The second offensive was to seize Tulagi in the Solomon Islands and Port Moresby in Papua to give them mastery of the Coral Sea, and threaten the security of Australia. The Combined Fleet would then cross the Pacific to annihilate the remains of the American Fleet and capture Midway Island and the Western Aleutians.

KOREA

JAPAN

CHINA

Tokyo

TIBET

Midway

Ryukyu Is.

Bonin Is.

INDIA   BURMA

Formosa
(Taiwan)

Wake

Hong Kong

Hawaiian Is.

Pearl Harbor

SIAM

FRENCH
INDO-
CHINA

PHILIPPINE
ISLANDS

Mariana Is.

Marshall Is.

Johnston

Guam   Caroline Is.

PACIFIC OCEAN

CEYLON

Truk

MALAYA

Palau Is.

Gilbert Is.

SARAWAK

Nauru

Borneo

NEW GUINEA

Phoenix Is.

Sumatra

DUTCH EAST INDIES

Solomon Is.

Tokelau Is.

Java   Timor

PAPUA

Santa
Cruz Is.

Samoa Is.

INDIAN OCEAN

CORAL SEA

New
Hebrides   Fiji Is.

AUSTRALIA

RUSSIA   ALASKA

CANADA

JAPAN

CHINA

UNITED STATES

INDIA

Wake   Hawaiian Is.

Guam
Palau Is.

PACIFIC OCEAN

Caroline Is.

*INDIAN
OCEAN*

Samoa Is.

AUSTRALIA

NEW
ZEALAND

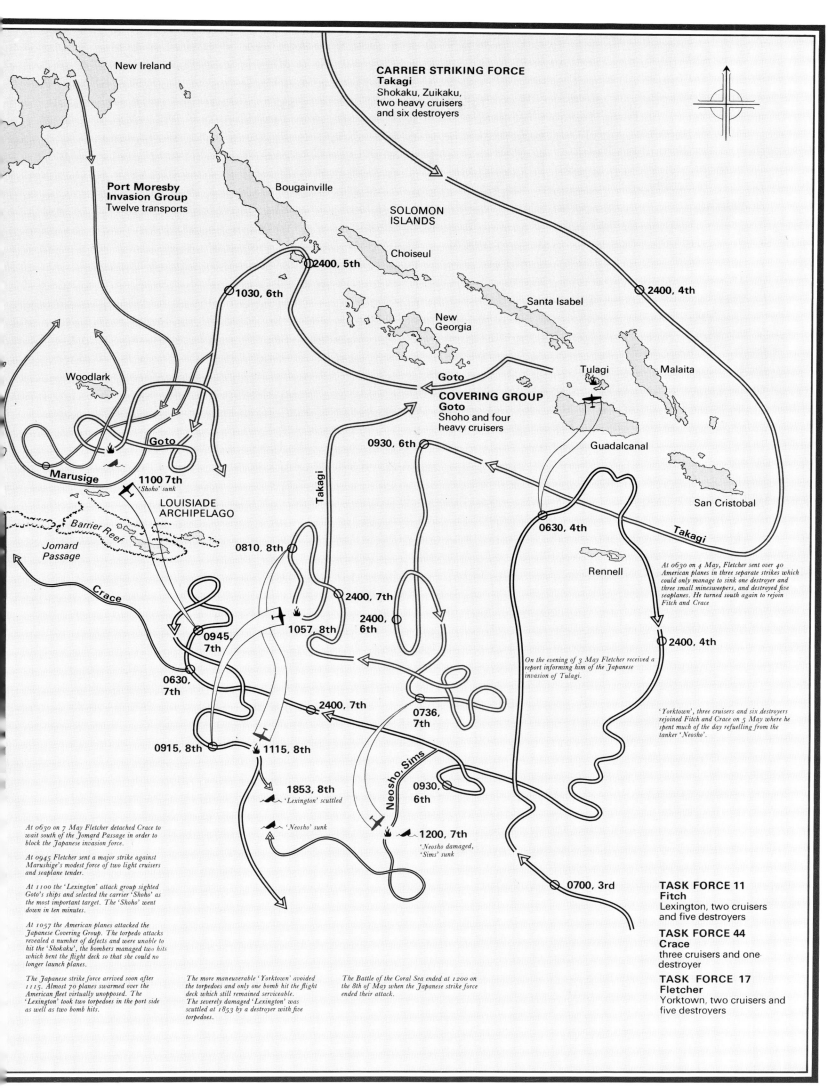

New Ireland

**Port Moresby
Invasion Group**
Twelve transports

CARRIER STRIKING FORCE
Takagi
Shokaku, Zuikaku,
two heavy cruisers
and six destroyers

Bougainville

SOLOMON
ISLANDS

Choiseul

2400, 5th

1030, 6th

Santa Isabel

2400, 4th

New
Georgia

Woodlark

Goto

COVERING GROUP
Goto
Shoho and four
heavy cruisers

0930, 6th

Tulagi

Goto
Marusige

1100 7th
'Shoho' sunk

LOUISIADE
ARCHIPELAGO

Guadalcanal

Malaita

Takagi

San Cristobal

Barrier Reef

Jomard
Passage

0810, 8th

0630, 4th

Takagi

Rennell

Crace

2400, 7th

At 0630 on 4 May, Fletcher sent over 40
American planes in three separate strikes which
could only manage to sink one destroyer and
three small minesweepers, and destroyed five
seaplanes. He turned south again to rejoin
Fitch and Crace

0945,
7th

2400,
6th

2400, 4th

1057, 8th

0630,
7th

On the evening of 3 May Fletcher received a
report informing him of the Japanese
invasion of Tulagi.

2400, 7th

0736,
7th

'Yorktown', three cruisers and six destroyers
rejoined Fitch and Crace on 5 May where he
spent much of the day refuelling from the
tanker 'Neosho'.

0915, 8th

1115, 8th

Neosho, Sims

0930,
6th

1853, 8th
'Lexington' scuttled

'Neosho' sunk

1200, 7th
'Neosho' damaged,
'Sims' sunk

0700, 3rd

At 0630 on 7 May Fletcher detached Crace to
wait south of the Jomard Passage in order to
block the Japanese invasion force.

At 0945 Fletcher sent a major strike against
Marushige's modest force of two light cruisers
and seaplane tender.

At 1100 the 'Lexington' attack group sighted
Goto's ships and selected the carrier 'Shoho' as
the most important target. The 'Shoho' went
down in ten minutes.

At 1057 the American planes attacked the
Japanese Covering Group. The torpedo attacks
revealed a number of defects and were unable to
hit the 'Shokaku', the bombers managed two hits
which bent the flight deck so that she could no
longer launch planes.

The Japanese strike force arrived soon after
1115. Almost 70 planes swarmed over the
American fleet virtually unopposed. The
'Lexington' took two torpedoes in the port side
as well as two bomb hits.

The more maneuverable 'Yorktown' avoided
the torpedoes and only one bomb hit the flight
deck which still remained serviceable.
The severely damaged 'Lexington' was
scuttled at 1853 by a destroyer with five
torpedoes.

The Battle of the Coral Sea ended at 1200 on
the 8th of May when the Japanese strike force
ended their attack.

TASK FORCE 11
Fitch
Lexington, two cruisers
and five destroyers

TASK FORCE 44
Crace
three cruisers and one
destroyer

TASK FORCE 17
Fletcher
Yorktown, two cruisers and
five destroyers

Above: Admiral Chester W. Nimitz, Commander-in-Chief of the US Navy in the Pacific.

command of Fletcher. Fitch and Fletcher were to meet on 1 May in the approaches of the Coral Sea to the west of the New Hebrides. Fletcher's orders were simply to stop the enemy however possible. His force was further strengthened by the addition of most of the ships of 'MacArthur's Navy', two Australian and one American cruiser, and two destroyers under the command of Rear-Admiral J. G. Crace of the Royal Navy. These ships joined Fletcher on 4 May.

At this point the Americans could only conduct a strategic defense, the object of which was to protect the Hawaiian Islands and communications with Australia and New Zealand by way of Palmyra, Samoa, Fiji and New Caledonia. General Douglas MacArthur's Southwest Pacific Command was organizing the meager American and Australian forces for the defense of northern Australia and Papua. A former chief of staff of the American Army, MacArthur had an outstanding record in World War I and was on loan to the Philippine Commonwealth when called to command in the Southwest Pacific. He was already a controversial figure, in conflict with both Roosevelt and Army Chief of Staff George Marshall on a number of issues. On a larger scale, the high commands of the army and navy were scarcely on speaking terms with each other and often displayed a lamentable lack of cooperation. This sometimes led to disastrous results, as at Pearl Harbor. The main responsibility for this sad state of affairs lay with the navy which existed in peculiar isolation from American society, self-sufficient and self-contained, with its own politics and ethos. The navy in war was apt to think that the enemy was really the rival services with which it had to cooperate. In particular it hated MacArthur, the army general with whom it unwillingly shared the Pacific war. An intense rivalry quickly developed between Nimitz of the navy and MacArthur of the army, a rivalry which determined the course of American strategy in the Pacific.

On 1 May Shima's force sailed from Rabaul for Tulagi while the American carrier forces made their rendezvous north of New Caledonia. On 2 May a reconnaissance plane of the Southwest Pacific Command sighted Shima's ships but the reports which reached Fletcher were not clear and certainly did not seem to indicate a force bound for Port Moresby. Giving Fitch a position for reunion at dawn on 4 May, Fletcher rushed northwest with the *Yorktown* group in order to be able to use his own reconnaissance planes. On the evening of 3 May one of MacArthur's reconnaissance planes reported Japanese troops disembarking on Tulagi; having been warned of Japanese intentions, the Australians had withdrawn their modest garrison on 1 May to save it from being pointlessly annihilated. On the basis of this report Fletcher tried to catch the enemy ships with a dawn strike. Over forty American planes made three separate strikes the following day but the pilots were inexperienced and, despite glowing reports of damage, sank only one destroyer and three small minesweepers, and destroyed only five seaplanes. These meager results were not known to Fletcher as he went south again to rejoin Fitch. The economically

element of surprise was lost because by 17 April the American Pacific Command already knew the gist of the plan and had taken countermeasures. In fact, American intelligence had broken the Japanese codes long before the war had begun and could decipher many of the Japanese fleet messages. This was to cost the Japanese heavily on a number of occasions during the war.

The Americans and Australians also felt that the fall of Port Moresby would be of major import since that base was essential to General MacArthur's strategic plans. The general intended to develop this advanced outpost as a major air base to block Japanese penetration of Australia and as one of the bases for his return to the Philippines. Thus all available force was mustered to resist the Japanese threat. Rear-Admiral Frank Fletcher was already in the South Pacific with Task Force 17 built around the carrier *Yorktown*. Admiral Chester W. Nimitz, Commander-in-Chief of the Pacific Fleet, immediately dispatched his other available carrier group, Task Force 11 centered on the carrier *Lexington*, from Pearl Harbor with Rear-Admiral Aubrey Fitch, to be under the minded Takagi had diverted his two carriers to deliver a few planes to Rabaul, missing his first opportunity to strike the Americans and do so while their forces were divided. Both carrier forces thus began their encounter on an ineffectual note.

Having rejoined Fitch and the Lexington group, Fletcher's Task Force spent much of 5 May refueling from the tanker *Neosho*. The American admiral was receiving many reconnaissance reports of various Japanese forces but to him the picture was confused. That night he set course northwest toward the probable route of any enemy force bound for Port Moresby. That same night Takagi's Carrier Striking Force rounded San Cristobal and turned northwest into the Coral Sea. Like his American counterpart, the Japanese admiral had no information on the size or position of the enemy fleet. The following day the fall of the Philippines was completed when General Jonathan Wainwright surrendered the American garrison on Corregidor. Waiting for more information about his foe, Fletcher turned southeast while refueling. That morning Takagi had set a southerly course which if continued would have brought contact with the American fleet, but in the evening he again turned north when the two forces were only 70 miles apart. For some reason Takagi had not sent out an air search but Fletcher's force was sighted by a Rabaul-based plane. This information did not, however, reach Takagi until the following day. Fletcher's air search had missed the Japanese ships which later in the day were hidden by low lying clouds generated by a cold front which lay east-west across the Coral Sea.

Takagi reversed course at 0200 on the seventh and at dawn launched an air search while 200 miles east of the enemy. At 0736 there was a report of one carrier and one cruiser 200 miles south-southwest. Certain that this was the one American carrier in the South Pacific, Takagi launched a major strike of 36 'Val' dive bombers and 24 'Kate' torpedo bombers with 18 Zeroes as cover. Arriving over target, the chagrined pilots found nothing but the tanker *Neosho* and its escort, the destroyer *Sims*. Both were quickly sunk but the reconnaissance pilot's error meant that Takagi had sent a major part of his force against a minor target and in so doing had left his carriers vulnerable to air attack. To add to the admiral's discomfort, a reconnaissance plane catapulted from one of Goto's cruisers soon reported the actual position of the American carriers. All Takagi could do was to wait for his planes to return, rearm and refuel, and launch a second strike.

'MacArthur's Navy' Detached

Still concerned about the elusive Port Moresby invasion force, Fletcher began the seventh of May by detaching 'MacArthur's Navy' under Crace to wait south of the Jomard Passage in order to be doubly certain that the Japanese invasion convoy was blocked. The American carriers then turned north and launched a major air search, which failed as the Japanese were still protected by bad weather. At 0815 a search plane from the *Yorktown* reported 'two carriers and four heavy cruisers' 175 miles northwest of the American force. Fletcher not unnaturally assumed that this was the Japanese main force and immediately launched 28 Dauntless dive bombers, twelve Devastator torpedo bombers and ten Wildcat fighters from the *Lexington*, while the *Yorktown* contributed 25 dive bombers, ten torpedo bombers and eight fighters. But when the search plane returned to the *Yorktown*, it was discovered that the pilot's code contact pad had been disarranged and that the message should have read 'two heavy cruisers and two destroyers'. Fletcher was now in the same situation as Takagi. Due to a reconnaissance error, he had sent a major strike against a minor target, accompanied by a large

part of his defensive fighters. His forces were now vulnerable to any massive attack from shore-based planes or the enemy carriers. The strike was not recalled, however, for another report placed an enemy carrier and other ships near the original target.

The first erroneous report had actually located Marushige's modest force of two light cruisers and a seaplane tender while the second located Goto's covering force for the Port Moresby invasion convoy. At 1100 the attack group from the *Lexington* discovered Goto's ships and selected the *Shoho* as the most important target. Starting their dives at 18,000 feet and releasing their bombs at 2500 feet, the dive bombers made their attack while the *Shoho* took violent evasive action. The Japanese Combat Air Patrol was airborne but was unusually ineffective, bagging but one American dive bomber while losing eight of its own fighters. The *Shoho* went down in ten minutes. 'Scratch one flattop', jubilantly signaled the strike leader. The strike had cost Fletcher three planes but by 1338 his force was back on deck refueling and arming. By the time this process was complete, however, it was too late to consider another strike even if Takagi's position had been known. As the American carriers were not yet capable of night flying operations Fletcher decided to wait for shore-based planes to locate the enemy.

When informed of the loss of the *Shoho* and of Crace's position south of the Jomard Passage, Admiral Inouye in Rabaul ordered Shima not to take the Port Moresby invasion convoy through the passage but to hold it a safe distance north of the Louisiades. Goto followed with his covering force. Inouye then sent 31 bombers from Rabaul to eliminate Crace. Although subjected to repeated attacks, Crace handled his ships so well that not one received a scratch. Maintaining his position, he also beat off an attack by three of MacArthur's B-17's which thought his ships were Japanese.

Toward evening Takagi, bolder than his American adversary, sent out a search-attack mission of twelve Vals and fifteen Kates. There could be no fighter cover as the Zero was not capable of night operations. At the end of a fruitless search, the pilots jettisoned their bombs and torpedoes and were heading for home when they were suddenly attacked by American Wildcats. Their homeward course had taken them directly over Fletcher's fleet. With his Combat Air Patrol already in the air on routine patrol over the fleet and twenty minutes warning from his radar, Fletcher had scrambled the remainder of his

fighters to pounce on the unsuspecting Japanese. The lumbering Kates made easy victims and eight went down. The highly maneuverable Vals fought back and lost only one of their number against two Wildcats. With night now falling, the American fighters were recalled and began landing. It was then noticed that three strange planes had joined the circuit, switching on their lights and signaling. Recognition burst simultaneously on both sides. Followed by a burst of gunfire, the three Japanese planes which had mistakenly tried to land on the *Yorktown* beat a hasty retreat into the gloom. Twenty minutes later the *Yorktown* underwent a similar experience as three more Japanese planes tried to land on her. With no radio homing beacons or radar, the Japanese carriers had to switch on their searchlights to guide their planes in. Only seven landed safely. All in all, it had been a disastrous day for Takagi. He considered seeking a night action with his cruisers, but the loss of the *Shoho* had denuded the Port Moresby invasion convoy of its air cover and Takagi felt it necessary to turn north to protect it.

Each side now knew the strength and relative position of its opponent and anticipated major action the following day. Fletcher placed Fitch in tactical command of the fleet as he was the most experienced carrier officer of flag rank in the navy. For a similar reason, Rear-Admiral Chuichi Hara was given tactical command by Admiral Takagi.

Early on the 8th Hara launched an air search 200 miles southeast and southwest. A strike force of 33 Vals, 18 Kates and 18 Zeroes took off at dawn through a series of rain squalls. By the time the strike force was fully airborne, the sighting report on which Hara had counted came in. The American force lay 180 miles to the south and had launched its own air search. As Hara's attack groups flew south, a reconnaissance plane from the *Lexington* sighted the Japanese fleet. By 0915 the *Lexington* and *Yorktown* had sent 46 dive bombers, 21 torpedo bombers and fifteen

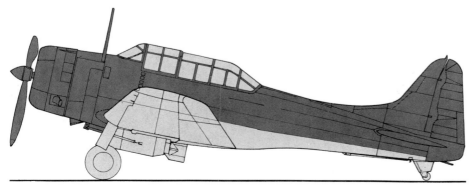

fighters on their way. After searching for each other for three days and three nights, the two fleets were finally to join battle on even terms. The Japanese had two carriers with 121 planes, four heavy cruisers and six destroyers opposed to the Americans' two carriers, 122 planes, five heavy cruisers and seven destroyers. Hara and Takagi still had the advantage of being covered by a belt of clouds while Fitch and Fletcher lay under clear sunny skies.

Although launched an hour later than the Japanese force, the 41 planes of the *Yorktown* attack group were the first on target. The *Zuikaku* was hidden in a rain squall, so the attack was focused on the *Shokaku* at 1057. Both carriers were in the process of launching their Combat Air Patrol and threw up a heavy anti-aircraft barrage. In their first real torpedo attack of the war, the American pilots discovered a number of problems. The Devastator torpedo bomber proved to be a low performance plane, unequal to the demands made on it. The torpedoes themselves were slow and unreliable and many ran wild. It was necessary for them to be launched at low speed only a few feet above water. Facing heavy anti-aircraft fire, most of the American pilots released their torpedoes at too great a distance so that the *Shokaku* easily avoided them all. The dive bombers fared better, landing a 500-pound bomb which bent the flight deck of the *Shokaku* so that she could no longer launch planes. Many of the planes from the *Lexington*'s attack group became disorganized in the rain clouds, failing to locate the target and returned home. Only four dive bombers and eleven torpedo bombers actually attacked. The attack scored another bomb hit which started a fire forward in the *Shokaku* and killed 100 men. Overall the strike cost the Americans five dive bombers, five torpedo bombers and three fighters.

The Japanese strike force had a far better morning than the Americans. Almost 70 Japanese planes swarmed over the American fleet virtually unopposed. The American Combat Air Patrol was caught when it was low on fuel. Although radar had again given a twenty-minute warning of the approaching attack, the nine Wildcats launched in that interval did not yet have enough altitude to meet the attack. Facing their first major air attack, the anti-aircraft gunners proved inexperienced and unpracticed. When the Japanese pressed home their attack, the American defense was too ineffectual to hinder let alone repulse it. The *Lexington* was surrounded by torpedo tracks and, unable to avoid them all, took two in the port side as well as two bomb hits. With a shorter turning circle, the *Yorktown* took no torpedoes and only one bomb hit the flight deck which still remained serviceable.

The End of the Battle

When this attack was over at noon, the battle had ended. The *Yorktown* had lost 66 men from its solitary bomb but was in good shape and was recovering its planes. The *Lexington* was listing seven degrees to port and had three major fires but her power plant was intact. The fires were being contained, the list corrected by transfering oil and returning planes were being landed. At 1247, however, she was shaken by a violent internal explosion. Because they must transport large quantities of aviation fuel, carriers with bomb or torpedo damage are especially susceptible to the build-up of gasoline fumes between decks. The ignition of these fumes can make otherwise reparable damage lethal and proved to be the Achilles heel of carriers in battle. The *Lexington* was wracked by a series of such explosions until 1707 when the ready bomb storage was threatened by fire and the order was given to abandon ship. At 1853 the coup de grace was administered by a destroyer with five torpedoes. The carrier had suffered 216 casualties and took 35 planes down with her.

Due to intense activity by Southwest Pacific Command planes, Inouye postponed the Port Moresby expedition while Takagi began to retire toward Truk. On the 8th, incensed that Takagi had allowed an American carrier to escape, Yamamoto ordered his subordinate south to 'annihilate' the remains of the enemy. But it was already much too late to renew contact with Fletcher, and Takagi was permitted to retire the next day. Fletcher was also ordered to withdraw

Right Japanese Val dive bombers ready to take off from a carrier in the Coral Sea. **Below:** The Japanese aircraft carrier *Shokaku* was heavily damaged in the Coral Sea and had to return to Japan for extensive repairs.

Above: Sailors leap overboard just before the *Lexington* blows up and sinks.

by Nimitz on the 8th since the Port Moresby expedition had been thwarted and since the *Yorktown* was urgently needed at Pearl Harbor to meet the next Japanese threat.

In tactical terms the Battle of the Coral Sea was a drawn action. The Japanese had lost the *Shoho* against the *Lexington* which gave them the edge in tonnage sunk. The *Yorktown* was operationally out of action and had to be dispatched to Pearl Harbor for repairs. The *Shokaku* was so heavily damaged that she endured a perilous journey back to Japan for two months of repairs, while the *Zuikaku* had lost so many planes and crews that she also had to return to Japan until

12 June for a new complement. Overall the Japanese had lost three-quarters of their bombing planes and pilots. In battle the Japanese airmen had shown themselves unused to night operations and had also revealed faults in their tactics and intelligence. It was clear that the high standards demonstrated at Pearl Harbor were possessed by only a minority of Japanese pilots, a minority that was dwindling as casualties took a toll. The Japanese Navy was also hampered by its lack of radar, an astonishing lack since Yamamoto eagerly espoused everything connected with modern air warfare. The British had been using radar for two years and a form of it was also known

Below: An American destroyer leaves the listing *Lexington*, after having rescued some of her crew.

in Germany. The Germans had in fact sent two sets to Japan by submarine, but either technicians did not accompany them or they were not good enough to make any impact on the Japanese military. This was but one more costly indication of the slight cooperation between the two Axis partners.

Despite their losses the action at the Coral Sea was good and necessary experience for the Americans in the tactical use of carriers. The threat to Port Moresby had been averted, the Japanese had suffered heavy losses in planes and crews and had operationally lost two large carriers at a crucial moment. Although it was not

known to the Allies at the time, the Battle of the Coral Sea set a limit to Japanese expansion southward. It was also the first setback which the Japanese had suffered. It served to confirm Yamamoto in his belief that the further acquisition of territory was not only pointless but wasted Japan's precious resources. Using the prestige from his victory at Pearl Harbor to impose his ideas on his more conservative colleagues, Yamamoto argued that top priority must be given to the destruction of the remnants of American sea power in the Pacific. The second part of the offensive had to be undertaken. Thus Yamamoto set the stage for the Midway campaign.

Above left: A huge pall of smoke towers over the doomed *Lexington* as her gasoline tanks finally explode. **Above:** Crewmen crowded the topsides of the *Lexington* after the order had been given to abandon ship.

Midway

1942

Opposite right: General
Hideki Tojo, Premier of
wartime Japan who made
the ultimate decision to go
to war against the United
States.

Below: The raids of Jimmy
Doolittle on Tokyo and
other Japanese targets in
1942 came as a welcome
tonic to Americans at
home, who had heard
nothing but bad news for
months after Pearl Harbor.
B-25s took off from the US
carrier *Hornet* to get within
range of Japanese cities.
The showdown at Midway
was yet to come.

The Midway campaign had been planned as the most important part of the second general offensive by the Japanese. On 5 May even before the Battle of the Coral Sea was fully underway, Imperial General Headquarters issued the order: 'Commander-in-Chief Combined Fleet will, in cooperation with the Army, invade and occupy strategic points in the Western Aleutians and Midway Island'. After the blunting of the Japanese southward thrust at the Coral Sea, Yamamoto pressed his view that any actions diverting the Japanese from their main problem – the American fleet – were dangerous. The Japanese admiral was under no illusions about Japan's position if the war was prolonged. The United States was mobilizing for war at full speed and if it was allowed to bring its might into play it would be irresistible. Japan had to strike again and at

once. Over the protests of many of his colleagues, Yamamoto gained acceptance of his view that the next move must be the conquest of Midway Island. The objectives of the Midway campaign were to gain bases in the Aleutians as the northernmost anchors of the proposed 'ribbon defense' and to gain Midway for a similar purpose but especially as a base for raids on the main American Pacific base at Pearl Harbor. The ribbon defense would thus have its anchors north to south at Kiska, Midway, Wake, the Marshalls, the Gilberts, Guadalcanal and Port Moresby. The main goal, however, was to draw out and destroy the remains of the American fleet, especially the carriers that had escaped at Pearl Harbor, before new construction replaced the initial losses. Yamamoto counted on Nimitz accepting that Midway was vital to American defense and send-

ing out his weakened fleet where Yamamoto could destroy it. Success in this battle was central to the entire Japanese strategic concept of the war. Victory would leave Japan master of the Pacific Ocean.

There were other reasons for seizing Midway. Lying only 2500 miles from Tokyo, the island could be used as a base for air raids on Japan. As a result of the raid by B-25 bombers led by Col. James Doolittle in April 1942, the Japanese were very sensitive about this prospect and had assigned hundreds of planes to defend Tokyo. The origin of the raid (actually the carriers *Hornet* and *Enterprise*) had never been discovered and Roosevelt's remark that it had come from Shangri-la had not illuminated the matter. Some Japanese officers suspected that Midway had been the base, and felt the capture of that island would protect the Emperor from the indignity of being bombed again. The island had also become an important base for the refueling of American submarines which were beginning to harass Japanese shipping. Thus Midway appeared to be the most appropriate target from several points of view.

Yamamoto was an undisputed genius, perhaps the only one Japan possessed in the war, with that rare combination of original ideas and the ability to translate them into action. He had, however, never been sanguine about Japan's ability as an island country, totally dependent on overseas supply, to wage war against an industrial giant like the United States. Before the war he had

frankly warned his Premier that 'If I am told to fight regardless of consequences, I shall run wild for the first six months or a year, but I have utterly no confidence for the second and third years'. After Pearl Harbor he wrote to his sister 'Well, war has begun at last. But in spite of all the clamor that is going, we could lose it. I can only do my best'. If he gained the annihilating victory he was seeking at Midway, Yamamoto planned to press on the Premier, General Hideki Tojo, the need for a negotiated peace with the United States, even to the point of proposing terms disadvantageous to Japan. In Yamamoto's eyes, victory at Midway was not only central strategically but essential for the survival of Japan.

However strongly Yamamoto felt about the Midway campaign, other Japanese had grave doubts concerning it for a number of reasons. Due to the speed Yamamoto was demanding, there was insufficient preparation and briefing of officers, and no time to digest the lessons of the action at the Coral Sea and the wisdom of the tactics used there. There was friction between Yamamoto's air wing and the rest of the navy which was beginning to suffer from general morale problems. More responsible officers particularly criticized Yamamoto for the speed which he was demanding as this required their two most powerful carriers to be excluded: the *Shokaku* and *Zuikaku* were still refitting and would have to be left behind. But the Japanese admiral felt that the political situation required immediate action and subordinated all else to this requirement. The Midway expedition sailed from Hashira on 21 May.

Yamamoto's Plan
Yamamoto had prepared a complicated plan for this battle. Division of force was always part of strategy for the Japanese, who liked diversionary tactics to confuse and pull the enemy off balance. The standard Japanese pattern for a decisive battle was to lure the enemy into an unfavorable tactical situation, cut off his retreat, drive in his flanks and then concentrate their own force for the kill. Hannibal at Cannae and Ludendorff at Tannenberg were the examples used in Japanese staff colleges for Yamamoto's strategy at Midway. Specifically, his plan called for a strike on Dutch Harbor in the Aleutians on 3 June to destroy the American base there and to cover an occupation of the Western Aleutians but especially to deceive Nimitz into thinking that the Aleutians were the main objective. In response Nimitz would rush north with his fleet while the Japanese bombed Midway on 4 June and occupied it on the following day. When the American fleet returned from its wild goose chase to the Aleutians not later than 7 June, it would be bombed intensively by Japanese carrier and Midway-based planes, after which any remaining ships would be sunk by the gunfire of Japanese cruisers and battleships. Yamamoto knew that the Americans had no fast battleships and probably only two carriers, as both the *Lexington* and *Yorktown* were believed to have been sunk at the Coral Sea. Fully counting on the element of surprise, Yamamoto expected no challenge from the enemy until after Midway had been secured.

If Nimitz did not fall for the Aleutian gambit, his forces still could not get to Midway before 7 June at the earliest. Even if he did not contest the occupation of Midway, the resulting pressure on Pearl Harbor would quickly force him to counter-attack and Yamamoto would be waiting.

To carry out this plan, the Japanese force was divided into five sections. An Advance Force of sixteen submarines was to harass the American fleet as it came toward Midway either from the Aleutians or Pearl Harbor. The Main Striking Force under Admiral Nagumo, consisting of the big carriers *Akagi*, *Kaga*, *Hiryu* and *Soryu* and their screen, was to soften up Midway with air strikes so that the Midway Occupation Force under Admiral Kondo could make its assault. Kondo had 5000 men in twelve transports supported by two battleships, six heavy cruisers and numerous destroyers. Three hundred miles behind these forces was the Main Body under the immediate command of Yamamoto, composed of seven battleships and two light carriers screened by cruisers and destroyers. Yamamoto flew his flag in the awesome *Yamato* which, with its nine eighteen-inch guns, was the most powerful warship in the world. The Northern Area Force under Vice Admiral Hosogaya was built around the light carriers *Ryujo* and *Junyo* with two heavy cruisers, a destroyer screen and four transports carrying troops for the accupation of Adak, Attu and Kiska in the Aleutians. The Japanese Fleet totalled 162 warships and auxiliaries, including

Opposite top: The flight deck of the US carrier *Enterprise*. A destroyer, *Sabine*, and the carrier *Hornet* follow behind. The cockpits of the dive bombers are covered to protect them against the glare of the Pacific sun.
Opposite bottom: The Japanese carrier *Akagi*, sunk at Midway. **Below:** Admiral Nobutake Kondo, who came north with the Midway Occupation Force to support the Main Striking Force.

four heavy and four light carriers, eleven battleships, 22 cruisers, 65 destroyers and 21 submarines, almost the entire fighting force of the Japanese navy.

Yamamoto was indeed aiming a powerful and lethal blow at the United States. To parry this thrust, the United States had only the carriers *Enterprise*, *Hornet* and *Yorktown*, who had limped up to Pearl Harbor after the Battle of the Coral Sea in such poor condition that the enemy believed she had sunk. Working around the clock, the repair yard at Pearl Harbor made the *Yorktown* operational again in only three days, whereas in normal circumstances such repairs would have required not less than 90. There were no battleships, as the battle line of the Pacific Fleet now rested at the bottom of Pearl

Harbor. A force of old battleships on the American west coast was not included in any defense calculations because of its low speed. In addition to the three carriers there were eight cruisers and fifteen destroyers, more than Yamamoto thought the Americans could assemble at that specific moment.

The object of all this concern was a piece of coral only six miles in diameter lying 1136 miles west-northwest of Pearl Harbor. Since 1938 the United States had spent considerable sums fortifying Midway as an outpost of Pearl Harbor since, as Admiral Nagumo later wrote, 'Midway acts as a sentry for Hawaii'. The island served as base for 54 Marine Corps planes, 32 Navy Catalinas, 23 Air Force planes including seventeen B-17's, and six new Navy Avenger torpedo

bombers; an 'unsinkable aircraft carrier' as the Pacific Command thought of it. Midway also had two good search radars and in addition to its planes, the island was heavily defended by well dug in army and marine units.

The man responsible for countering the Japanese thrust was a 57-year-old Texan who was regular navy all the way. Chester W. Nimitz was a graduate of the US Naval Academy and had served in a variety of commands including submarine service in World War I. In 1938 he had been appointed to rear-admiral, followed by promotion to full admiral in 1941. Following the debacle at Pearl Harbor, he had been appointed Commander-in-Chief of the Pacific Fleet to salvage the situation. When he assumed command in the Pacific on 31 December, morale was at rock bottom, but Nimitz's calm demeanor and refusal to bring in new staff rebuilt confidence. Even though he was ordered to be on the 'strategic defensive' with his meager forces, he still was able to organize raids on Japanese bases in the Marshalls, New Guinea and New Britain in the spring of 1942. For over thirty years the American navy had been expecting war with Japan, thinking that when war came they would engage the Japanese Navy in the western Pacific in a series of epic Jutland-style battles. At Pearl Harbor, however, Yamamoto had destroyed the impressive facade of 'battleship row' and demonstrated that the bomb and air-borne torpedo rather than the big gun were the real striking power of the modern fleet while the fighter plane was its primary defense. By sinking its battleships, he had forced the American Navy completely into the age of carrier warfare. But Nimitz and his subordinates were already proving themselves apt students and developing a style of their own.

While Nimitz was the overall commander in the Pacific, the veteran of the Coral Sea, Rear-Admiral Frank Fletcher, was in tactical command of the forces mustered to defend Midway. In temporary command of Task Force 16 – the *Enterprise* and the *Hornet* – was Rear-Admiral Raymond Spruance; Rear-Admiral William Halsey (erroneously nicknamed 'Bull' by a confused journalist) had been hospitalized the month before. Since Fletcher had no air staff and Spruance had Halsey's, the latter exercised a virtually independent command. Neither did Fletcher control the Midway-based forces, the submarines operating in the area, or the force detached to defend the Aleutians.

With both the South and Central Pacific to defend, Nimitz would truly have been faced with a difficult decision as to how to dispose his modest forces had not American intelligence again come to his aid. By 10 May intelligence had confirmed what Nimitz already suspected, that the next objective was Midway. By decoding Japanese fleet messages, intelligence officers had also worked out the principal details of Yamamoto's plan with the approximate schedule and routes. While some of his officers thought that this was all an elaborate Japanese deception to cover a second raid on Pearl Harbor or even on the American West Coast, Nimitz predicted a full attack on Midway with the destruction of the American carriers as a primary goal and with enemy submarines penetrating to within 200 miles of Pearl Harbor. By 17 May Nimitz had decided not to abandon the Western Aleutians

Below: Douglas Dauntless dive bombers attack the Japanese Fleet at Midway. One ship is burning in the center.

to the enemy and formed the North Pacific Force under Rear-Admiral Robert 'Fuzzy' Theobald, comprised of two heavy cruisers, three light cruisers, a destroyer division, a nine destroyer strike group, six S-class submarines and many smaller craft. After concentrating his forces for the defense of Midway, Nimitz gave Fletcher and Spruance their orders: '. . . inflict maximum damage on the enemy by employing strong attrition attacks'. In the naval parlance of the time, that meant heavy air strikes. 'In carrying out the task assigned . . . you will be governed by the principle of calculated risk . . . the avoidance of exposure of your force to attack by superior enemy forces without good prospect of inflicting . . . greater damage on the enemy' added a further letter of instruction.

In the last few days of May, Japanese submarines were taking up stations east of Midway to intercept any American force that might be sent out to relieve the island but Nimitz had already stationed his carriers northeast of Midway beyond the range of the search planes of the approaching Japanese. From 30 May onwards, 22 Navy Catalinas from Midway were flying daily sweeps 700 miles out. A daily search-attack mission by the Midway B-17's to a point where the enemy was expected was also sent out. Nimitz was taking every precaution so that the Japanese could not sneak within plane launching range and achieve a Pearl Harbor type surprise at Midway. By 2 June Fletcher and Spruance were 375 miles northeast of Midway and conducting their own air searches.

Nagumo and the Japanese carrier force left Japanese home waters on 26 May, followed by Yamamoto's Main Body two days later. Nagumo's orders were to 'execute an aerial attack on Midway . . . destroying all enemy air forces stationed there' on 4 June to soften it up for the attack of the Occupation Force the following day. But the Japanese admiral was concerned, as his carriers had had hardly a month for maintenance and refresher training. 'We participated in the battle', he later wrote, 'with meager training and without knowledge of the enemy'. Even Yamamoto was in low spirits and suffering from stomach trouble from tension but morale in the fleet was high. Approaching Midway from the west, Nagumo's ships were covered by the many storms and fogs which occur there in May and June. Often the Japanese could hear American search planes above the clouds on their seemingly endless and fruitless missions.

The Aleutian Diversion
The Aleutian diversion began on 3 June according to schedule. Theobald had not actually reached Kodiak to take command until 27 May while the main body of his force did not finish assembling until after the first attacks on Dutch Harbor. On 28 May intelligence had informed Theobald of the enemy intentions but the admiral feared that this might be a maneuver to get behind him and seize Dutch Harbor in the Eastern Aleutians. He therefore deployed his force 400 miles south of Kodiak instead of trying to break up Hosogaya's force. On 3–4 June the Japanese light carriers easily got past the Ameri-

can force and heavily bombed Dutch Harbor unmolested. By the seventh, undefended Attu and Kiska had been occupied, but Army P-40's based on Unmak persuaded Hosogaya that occupying Adak would be too costly.

The third of June was also the day that a Midway-based Catalina first sighted a Japanese force precisely where intelligence had said it should be. This was probably Kondo's Midway Occupation Force. On the basis of the report, nine B-17's were sent out to attack from Midway but made no hits. The attack was subsequently renewed by four Catalinas which succeeded in torpedoing an oiler but without inflicting serious damage. At this time Fletcher's force was 300 miles east-northeast of Midway and 400 miles east of Nagumo. Based on the information then available, Fletcher decided that Nagumo would launch an air strike on Midway the following day, approaching from the northwest. Assuming that his presence was unknown to the enemy and would remain so until the Midway strike had been launched, Fletcher changed course in the evening to arrive at a point 200 miles north of Midway in the morning. From this position he could attack Nagumo the following day when the latter's position was certain. Thus on the night of 3–4 June, the two carrier forces were steaming toward each other on converging courses.

At 0430 on the morning of 4 June a hundred-mile search by ten planes was launched by the *Yorktown* as a routine precaution against the possibility of surprise by undetected enemy carriers. 215 miles to the west, Nagumo was launching his first strike on Midway. Although still sheltered by heavy cloud cover, the Japanese carriers were sighted by planes from Midway. At 0534 the report reached Fletcher, followed at 0545 by a further report of a heavy strike approaching Midway. A third sighting report at 0603 placed two Japanese carriers 200 miles west-southwest of

Fletcher. Although only two carriers had been reported, forty miles from their actual position, Fletcher now knew the approximate location of the enemy. Wishing to recover his search planes and wait for further information, he signaled Spruance to take the *Enterprise* and *Hornet* and 'Proceed southwest and attack enemy carriers when definitely located. I will follow as soon as planes recovered'. Even as this signal was being made, however, 108 Japanese planes were over Midway. At 0553 the radar on Midway had picked up the 36 Vals, 36 Kates and 36 Zekes 93 miles out. All planes capable of intercepting were immediately scrambled while the remainder were flown off to safer climes. The bulk of the interceptors were Marine Corps Buffaloes – old, slow and weak – which were easily swept aside by the efficient new Zekes. In twenty minutes of bombing a fair amount of damage was inflicted on the ground installations, but the runways were still usable. The anti-aircraft fire was good, and by way of compensation for the loss of 17 Buffaloes, about one third of the Japanese bomber force was shot down. Nimitz immediately ordered the Midway-based bombing planes to counterattack, so hard on the heels of the recent attackers were six navy Avengers and four army B-26's armed with torpedoes but with no fighter cover. One Avenger and two B-26's survived their attack which produced no hits.

Since according to Yamamoto's plan, no American forces and especially no carriers should have been in the vicinity of Midway for several more days, Nagumo's dawn air search had been routine and restricted. As a precaution, however, he had held back 93 planes and armed these with bombs and torpedoes in case any enemy surface forces were spotted. The returning planes of the Midway strike then radioed that the island was well defended and needed more softening up. The ten American planes from Midway arrived soon

Above left: Japanese aircraft goes down after being hit by anti-aircraft fire at Midway. **Above:** Heavy flak greets Japanese planes, which were shot down like clay pigeons over Midway. The smoke in the background comes from planes already shot down, as a cruiser moves into position on the left.

after, and emphasized this point with their attack. The Admiral then ordered the 93 planes to be rearmed with incendiary and fragmentation bombs for a second strike on Midway, a task which would take at least an hour, and the decks to be cleared for the recovery of the planes of the first strike. Only fifteen minutes after this order at 0728, Nagumo was amazed to receive a report from a reconnaissance plane catapulted from a Japanese cruiser: 'What appears to be ten enemy surface ships . . .' had been sighted to the northeast where no American ships were supposed to be. This was the first indication he had received of the presence of enemy ships but the report was vague and made no mention of carriers. After mulling the matter over for fifteen more minutes, he asked the reconnaissance plane for more information and ordered his planes to be rearmed once again for operations against ships. He did not wish to repeat Hara's great mistake at the Coral Sea by sending a major strike against a minor target but he was worried that the American actors might not be following Yamamoto's script for the drama. At 0809 the search plane reported five cruisers and five destroyers; at 0820 came the report 'The enemy is accompanied by what appears to be a carrier'. With his fears now realized, Nagumo felt he had been correct to order the second rearming of his planes but they could not take off once the rearming was completed because clear decks were needed for the recovery of the Midway strike planes.

While Nagumo was making these decisions, Yamamoto was becoming rattled as more attacks from shore-based planes were made on his ships. At 0755 sixteen Marine Corps dive bombers appeared, followed at 0810 by fifteen B-17's and at 0820 by eleven Marine Corps Vindicator bombers, but none of these strikes scored a hit of any kind. During this same period, the submarine *Nautilus* appeared, having intercepted the early reports of the Japanese position, and made her way to the scene posthaste. Under heavy depth charge attack from the Japanese destroyer screen, the *Nautilus* was only able to get off one inaccurate torpedo before she had to make her escape from the area. Once the various attacks had ended Nagumo could see that he was in a good situation. His own fleet was intact while over half the aircraft on Midway had been destroyed in the interception and in these ineffectual attacks. One more bombing would leave Midway ready for the assault of the Occupation Force and there was apparently only one American carrier to be dealt with. By this time, however, Spruance had determined his own strategy and American attack groups were already airborne.

Spruance had originally planned to launch a strike at 0900 at a distance of a hundred miles from the enemy, but on hearing of the attack on Midway his Chief of Staff, a brilliant if temperamental captain named Miles Browning, shrewdly deduced that Nagumo would order a second strike on the island and continue on his southeasterly course toward the target. The best opportunity for an American attack was while the Japanese planes were being refueled and rearmed for this second strike. Spraunce agreed with this strategy and began launching every operational plane he

had, except 32 Wildcats which were retained for Combat Air Patrol, in an all-out attack. More than an hour was required for the 67 dive bombers, 29 torpedo bombers and 20 Wildcats to be launched, but before this process was completed Spruance knew he had been sighted by a Japanese reconnaissance plane. Although he realized he had lost any element of surprise, he could not cancel the strike. Browning calculated that Nagumo could not completely recover his Midway strike planes before 0900 and must continue his course toward Midway until that time. Fletcher in the *Yorktown* had retrieved his search mission and was now on the same course as Spruance, but he held back his own attack force of twelve torpedo bombers, seventeen dive bombers and six Wildcats to see if any other carriers were in the vicinity. As no additional sighting reports came in, his planes were in the air at 0906. Like Nagumo, Fletcher had no wish to repeat the mistakes of the Coral Sea and held another deckload of planes in readiness.

The day was cool and clear with a 50-mile visibility at 19,000 feet. The four Japanese carriers were in a box formation in the center of a screen of two battleships, three cruisers and eleven destroyers. Recovery operations had begun at 0837 but Nagumo was understandably apprehensive as every few minutes reconnaissance planes reported the approach of a large force of carrier planes. Even before his recovery was complete, he turned east-northeast and signaled his ships 'We plan to contact and destroy the enemy task force'. Fueling and arming was hastily being done, exactly what Spruance and Browning had hoped for. Fortunately for Nagumo, his change of course caused 35 dive bombers from the *Hornet* to miss making a sighting. The strike had been launched at the limit of their fuel endurance and many of the planes had to continue on to Midway while a few ditched. Fifteen torpedo bombers from the *Hornet* located the Japanese ships by their smoke and attacked at 0925. They had lost their air cover and, pressing their attack in the face of heavy anti-aircraft fire and a flock of Zekes, were all shot down with only one pilot surviving the slaughter. At 0930 the torpedo bombers from the *Enterprise* came in, also without fighter cover. Ten of fourteen were shot down. At 1000 the torpedo bombers from the *Yorktown* arrived, shepherded by six Wildcats which were quickly overwhelmed by the Zeke's. Only five of the twelve torpedo bombers survived this attack, and three of the accompanying Wildcats went down as well. In all, only six of 47 planes returned after these attacks, which had registered no hits on the Japanese.

The massacre of the torpedo bombers had, however, prepared the way for the dive bombers of the *Yorktown* and *Enterprise* which arrived on the scene two minutes later. The violent evasive maneuvers forced on the Japanese carriers by the torpedo attacks had prevented them from launching more defensive fighters while those already airborne were at a low altitude after meeting the torpedo bomber attack and could not climb in time to meet the new threat. Thirty-seven dive bombers from the *Enterprise* had been searching for the Japanese ships and had only learned their position when the fighter group which had become

separated from the torpedo bombers informed Spruance that its planes were low on fuel, reporting the Japanese location as an afterthought. This was the first that Spruance and Browning had heard of their strike and the leader of the dive bombers could hear the latter screaming 'Attack! Attack!' over the radio, to which the leader replied 'Wilco, as soon as I find the bastards'. The dive bombers made their sighting and, diving from 14,000 feet swarmed over the *Akagi* and *Kaga* just as the carriers' evasive action from the last torpedo attack was ending. With 40 planes refueling on deck, the *Akagi* was hit three times within two minutes. One bomb exploded in the hangar detonating stored torpedoes. 'There was a terrific fire aboard ship which was just like hell' said a Japanese officer who survived. Another bomb exploded among the fueling planes on the flight deck. The carrier was burning fiercely and at 1047 an unwilling Nagumo was persuaded to transfer his flag to the light cruiser *Nagara*. By 1915 the situation aboard the burning ship was deemed hopeless and she was abandoned to drift northwards and be sunk by the torpedoes of a Japanese destroyer early the next morning.

The *Kaga* fared no better, taking four hits, one of which killed everyone on the bridge including the captain. The other bombs started fires in the gasoline and bomb storages. Soon the ship was a mass of flames from stem to stern and had to be abandoned. At 1925 the *Kaga* sank after severe internal explosions.

At the same time as the *Akagi* and *Kaga* were meeting their fates, seventeen dive bombers from the *Yorktown* were attacking the *Soryu*. Although they had started almost an hour and a half later than the other attack groups, by smart navigating they had managed to arrive simultaneously with the dive bombers of the *Hornet* and *Enterprise*. Attacking in three waves at one minute intervals,

they planted three 1000-pound bombs on the flight deck of the *Soryu* as she was turning into the wind to launch an attack group. The ship burst into flames and had to be abandoned within twenty minutes. Her captain was last seen standing on the bridge shouting 'Banzai!' By 1145, however, her fires had subsided and damage control parties were at work. By then the submarine *Nautilus* had caught up with the action and put three torpedoes into the *Soryu* which again set her blazing fiercely. At 1610 the gasoline storage exploded, breaking the ship in half and sending her down for good.

After the attacks most of the dive bombers barely made it back to their carriers and a few had to ditch because Spruance's staff had miscalculated Point 'Option', a point which moves in advance of the carrier and is calculated on the basis of course and speed as a guide for returning planes. Spruance was off schedule and his planes arrived at the Point 'Option' which they had been given only to discover that the carriers were 60 miles away. Some planes made it back literally on their last gallon of gasoline. The *Enterprise* had lost fourteen of 37 dive bombers, ten of fourteen torpedo bombers and one Wildcat. The *Yorktown* had lost seven of twelve torpedo bombers, two dive bombers and three Wildcats while the *Hornet* had lost all her torpedo bombers and twelve Wildcats, her dive bombers having failed to locate the enemy and landed on Midway. The returning fighter planes of the *Yorktown* gave Fletcher the first visual evidence that three Japanese carriers had been left burning. Aware now that there was a fourth enemy carrier, Fletcher launched a search mission to find the *Hiryu* which had been missed by the dive bombers.

Although three of his carriers were sinking, Nagumo still had the *Hiryu* untouched and with a full air group. He reasoned that the Americans had one or maybe two carriers which had probably already expended most of their planes. Deciding to continue the battle with the *Hiryu*, Nagumo radioed Yamamoto 'Sighted enemy composed of one carrier, five cruisers and six destroyers at position bearing ten degrees 240 miles from Midway. We are heading for it'. The first attack

group of eighteen Vals and six Zekes was launched at 1100, followed by a second attack group of ten Kates and six Zekes at 1331. The two reconnaissance planes which had located the American ships were ordered to guide the attack groups. Admiral Kondo had intercepted Nagumo's message to Yamamoto and signalled that he was coming north at 28 knots with the battle portion of the Midway Occupation Force to support the Main Striking Force. At the same time, Yamamoto ordered the light carriers *Ryujo* and *Junyo* south from the Aleutians to join the *Hiryu*.

At noon the *Yorktown* was refueling its fighters, with twelve Wildcats airborne as Combat Air Patrol and the last of its dive bombers on the circuit waiting to land, when radar showed between thirty and forty planes coming in only forty miles away. Evasive action began as the Combat Air Patrol went out to intercept. Both the Combat Air Patrol and the anti-aircraft fire of the cruiser and destroyer screen were highly effective. The interceptors knocked down ten Vals while anti-aircraft fire accounted for two more. But the remaining eight dive bombers hit the *Yorktown* three times. The first bomb damaged the boilers, bringing the carrier to a halt twenty minutes later. The second started a fire which was put out by flooding, while the third exploded on the flight deck causing many casualties and starting yet another fire. As the radar and communications had been knocked out, Fletcher transferred his flag to the cruiser *Astoria*. Damage control and repair parties worked quickly, however, and by 1340 the *Yorktown* could manage eighteen knots again. About 1630 the *Yorktown* was beginning to refuel its fighters when the radar of the attendant cruisers picked up the second attack group forty miles out. Low on fuel, the twelve Wildcats on Combat Air Patrol were no match for the fast Zekes and Kates. Coming in low from four different angles, four Kates were able to release their torpedoes at the short range of 500 yards, scoring two hits which ruptured most of the fuel tanks on the port side, jammed the rudder, cut all power and caused a seventeen degree list. Without power the list could not be corrected by counter-flooding. As her watertight integrity had been only half restored by the hasty repairs at Pearl Harbor, her captain was afraid that the *Yorktown* would capsize and gave the order to abandon ship at 1500.

The *Yorktown* continued to float for another 24 hours, having apparently reached equilibrium when her list became 25 degrees. The destroyer *Hughes* was detached to guard the carrier with orders to sink her if enemy surface ships appeared. At dawn the following day the commander of the *Hughes* informed Nimitz that the carrier could probably be saved. A small salvage party from the *Hughes* then boarded the vessel while other auxiliary ships including a fleet tug hurried to the scene. The salvage parties spent the day jettison-ing anchors and other loose gear while the mine-sweeper *Vireo* tried to take the carrier in tow. On 6 June Fletcher sent a proper salvage party of 171 on the destroyer *Hammann* to attempt to get the *Yorktown* back to port. After transferring the salvage party, the *Hammann* lay along side the carrier to provide power for the work. But in the interim the *Yorktown* had been sighted by a Japanese reconnaissance plane which reported her position. Having been ordered by Yamamoto to finish the job, submarine I-68 penetrated the destroyer screen and put two torpedoes into the *Yorktown* and one into the *Hammann* which sank within four minutes. The *Yorktown* finally sank at dawn the following day.

Before the *Yorktown* was attacked Fletcher had sent out a search mission of ten planes to locate the *Hiryu*. After a fruitless three-hour search, one plane on its way home sighted the *Hiryu*, two battleships, three cruisers and four destroyers steering north about 110 miles west by north of the *Yorktown*. At 1530 the *Enterprise* turned into the wind to launch 24 dive bombers, including ten refugees from the *Yorktown*. The mission was with-out fighter cover since all operational Wildcats were now in a defensive role. At 1700 the attack group swept in on the *Hiryu* and scored four solid hits. One took out all facilities on the 'island' while the others caused uncontrollable fires. Three dive bombers were lost in this attack which was re-newed an hour later by B-17's from Midway and Molokai. The land-based planes had their usual bad luck and scored no hits. At 1900 another

strike of five Vindicators and six dive bombers – all the operational aircraft left – took off from Midway but failed to locate the target. The *Hiryu* continued to burn until at 0315 the next morning she was abandoned by all hands except the captain. She finally sank at 0900.

Yamamoto on the *Yamato*

During the carrier battle of the fourth of June, Yamamoto and the Main Body had been several hundred miles west of the Main Striking Force. With his flag aboard the *Yamato*, the admiral was receiving reports of the battle 'with the utmost consternation'. Three of his beloved carriers had been lost but the successful attack on the *Yorktown* meant that there was still a chance for victory since if, as Nagumo claimed, there had been only one American carrier, it was now non-operational at the least. With his overwhelming superiority in gun power, he could still annihilate his weaker enemy in a traditional naval engagement. Break-ing radio silence at 0020, he ordered the Midway Occupation Force to retire to the northwest; its escort of battleships and cruisers under Kondo joined him the following day at noon along with the Aleutian force which had also been ordered south. It was not long, however, before the return-ing pilots of the *Hiryu* reported having seen three American carriers, information which was cor-roborated under duress by a captured American pilot. For the first time, Yamamoto was in posses-sion of an accurate picture of American strength. A few hours later he learned that the *Hiryu* had been rendered non-operational by an American attack. 'The game is up, thought everybody on the *Yamato's* bridge', recalled one witness. Al-though personally shattered by the collapse of his plans, Yamamoto still hurried toward the remains of Nagumo's force, radioing Nagumo and Kondo that he intended to engage the enemy. Nagumo demurred and was peremptorily relieved in favor of Kondo, who was ordered to prepare for a night engagement. But as further reports revealed that all four Japanese carriers were either sunk or abandoned and that two American carriers were still operational, Yamamoto accepted the fact that he could more likely expect a dawn air attack than a night gun battle with the enemy. Around

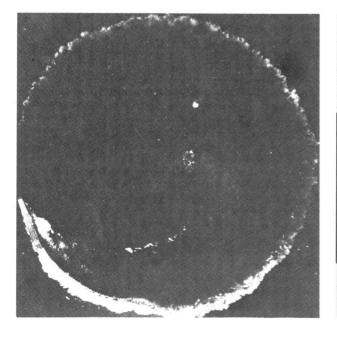

Far left: The Japanese carrier *Kaga* circles under the attack. *Kaga* as well as Yamamoto's other three carriers were all sunk at Midway. **Left:** Vice-Admiral Fletcher after Midway. His errors at the Coral Sea were not repeated at Midway, even though he finally lost *Yorktown*.

Below: Scene aboard the *Yorktown* after she was first hit. A bomb burst on the ship's funnel, which knocked out her boilers. **Right:** Japanese planes batter the *Yorktown*. **Center:** *Yorktown* listing badly just before she went under. **Bottom left:** Members of the crew and airmen of *Yorktown* examine the damage shortly before she sank. **Bottom right:** Survivors of *Yorktown* on a cruiser.

0300 on 5 June he accepted defeat and ordered all of his forces to turn west. Gloom lay like a pall over the retreating ships. 'We are retreating . . . It is utterly discouraging . . . The Marines, who were showing off, have not even courage to drink beer', wrote a Japanese officer in his diary.

At the end of the battle on 4 June, Spruance took stock of his situation. The *Yorktown* had been abandoned, the air groups of his two remaining carriers were decimated and there was no prospect of support from other American forces in sight. There were, however, other large units of the Japanese fleet which had not yet been located and these were known to include carriers. He also suspected that a fifth Japanese carrier might be in the vicinity. 'I did not feel justified in risking a night encounter with possibly superior enemy forces but on the other hand I did not want to be too far away from Midway the following morning. I wished to have a position from which either to follow up retreating enemy forces or to break up a landing attack on Midway', the admiral wrote in his report of the battle. He therefore headed east out of the battle area until midnight. Although Spruance was subsequently heavily criticized for withdrawing and allowing the defeated enemy to escape, he had made the correct decision. When Kondo heard of the first attacks on Nagumo's carriers, he headed north at high speed with two battleships, four heavy cruisers, a light carrier and his destroyer screen. Not far behind was Rear-Admiral Tanaka with ten more destroyers. By midnight this force was 125 miles from Nagumo. Had Spruance continued west he would have collided with this powerful fleet sometime close to 0100. The Japanese ships were well trained for night fighting while the American carriers had no night flying radar equipped planes. Even if Spruance had been able to hold his own against Kondo, Yamamoto and the Main Body were rapidly approaching from the northwest. Such a turn of events undoubtedly would have retrieved the victory for Yamamoto.

For all intents and purposes the Battle of Midway was over after the attack on the *Hiryu*. Before 0100 on 5 June, Yamamoto had cancelled a scheduled bombardment of Midway by four heavy cruisers under Rear-Admiral Kurita. These

Left: Rear-Admiral Raizo Tanaka, who followed Nagumo's carriers with a destroyer squadron. **Right:** The last known photograph of the carrier *Hiryu*, taken from a Japanese aircraft.

Right: USS *Hornet*, one of three carriers at Midway. Displacement: 19,800 tons. Length: 809 feet. Beam: 83 feet. Draught: 22 feet. Speed: 32 knots. Aircraft: between 85 (if Devestators or Avengers) to 100 (if Wildcats). Crew: 306 officers and 2613 enlisted men (in wartime). Armament: eight 5-inch, sixteen 1.1-inch and 23 20-mm cannon.

cruisers and two destroyers were retiring 90 miles west of Midway when they were sighted by the submarine *Tambor* which was spotted by the ships at the same time. In making an emergency turn during evasive action, the cruiser *Mogami* collided with the *Mikuma*, smashing her own bow, catching fire and reducing speed to sixteen knots while the *Mikuma* began to leak oil. Kurita continued to withdraw at full speed with his other two cruisers, leaving the two destroyers as a screen for the cripples. Unable to get into a position to fire its torpedoes, the *Tambor* continued to track the enemy ships.

Interpreting the *Tambor*'s contact with Kurita's force as an indication that the enemy might still be considering a landing on Midway, Spruance quickly headed his carriers toward the island to give air support. He then received reports of the two damaged cruisers and later of Kondo's force 200 miles to the northwest. Confused air reports concerning the burning *Hiryu* led to speculation that two Japanese carriers might still be afloat. Spruance decided to ensure that no carriers escaped, and turned northwest about 1100 on 5 June. Two search-attack groups of dive bombers were sent out at 1500 but they found no major target and then failed to sink a nimble Japanese destroyer they chanced upon as they returned home. Later that evening Spruance gave up his efforts to find the carriers or Kondo and turned west to deal with the *Mogami* and *Mikuma*. Early the following morning reconnaissance planes located the cruisers which were soon subjected to attacks by 83 dive bombers and three torpedo bombers. The *Mogami* took five bomb hits,

The Battle of Midway, 4-5 June 1942

Attu

Agattu

Aleutian diversion began on 3 June according to schedule. Theobald had deployed his force 400 miles south of Kodiak. On 3–4 June the Japanese light carriers got past the American force and heavily bombed Dutch Harbor. By the 7th, undefended Attu and Kiska had been occupied.

Kiska

Amchitka

Tanaga

Kanaga

ALEUTIAN ISLANDS

Unimak

Dutch Harbor

Adak

Atka

Amlia

Unmak

Unalaska

At 1331 on the fourth Yamamoto ordered the light carriers 'Ryujo' and 'Junyo' south from the Aleutians to join the 'Hiryu' since their presence was no longer necessary in the Aleutians.

NORTHERN AREA FORCE
Hosogaya
Light carriers Ryujo and Junyo, two heavy cruisers, a destroyer screen and four transporters

MAIN STRIKING FORCE
Nagumo
Carriers Akagi, Kaga, Hiryu and Soryu, with cruiser and destroyer screen

MIDWAY OCCUPATION FORCE
Kondo
Two battleships, six heavy cruisers plus destroyers and twelve transports with 5000 men

When Kondo heard of the first attacks on Nagumo's carriers, he headed north at high speed with two battleships, four heavy cruisers, a light carrier and his destroyer screen. Not far behind was Tanaka with ten more destroyers.

Although personally shattered by the collapse of his plans, Yamamoto still hurried towards the remains of Nagumo's force, radioing Nagumo and Kondo that he intended to engage the enemy.

But as further reports revealed that all four Japanese carriers were either sunk or abandoned and that two American carriers were still operational, he accepted defeat and ordered all his forces to turn west.

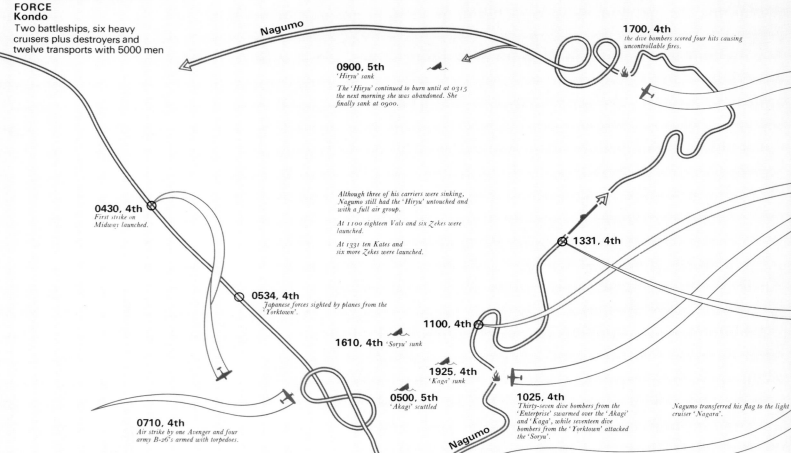

Nagumo

1700, 4th
the dive bombers scored four hits causing uncontrollable fires.

0900, 5th
'Hiryu' sank

The 'Hiryu' continued to burn until at 0315 the next morning she was abandoned. She finally sank at 0900.

0430, 4th
First strike on Midway launched.

Although three of his carriers were sinking, Nagumo still had the 'Hiryu' untouched and with a full air group.

At 1100 eighteen Vals and six Zekes were launched.

At 1331 ten Kates and six more Zekes were launched.

1331, 4th

0534, 4th
Japanese forces sighted by planes from the 'Yorktown'.

1100, 4th

1610, 4th *'Soryu' sunk*

1925, 4th
'Kaga' sunk

0500, 5th
'Akagi' scuttled

1025, 4th
Thirty-seven dive bombers from the 'Enterprise' swarmed over the 'Akagi' and 'Kaga', while seventeen dive bombers from the 'Yorktown' attacked the 'Soryu'.

Nagumo transferred his flag to the light cruiser 'Nagara'.

0710, 4th
Air strike by one Avenger and four army B-26's armed with torpedoes.

Nagumo

0755, 4th
sixteen Marine Corps dive bombers.

0810, 4th
fifteen B-17's

0820, 4th
eleven Marine Corps bombers

0837, 4th
Recovering Midway strike Force.

0925, 4th
fifteen torpedo bombers from 'Hornet' attack

0918, 4th
Nagumo turns east-north-east to intercept the American task force.

0930, 4th
fourteen torpedo bombers from 'Enterprise' attack.

1000, 4th
twelve torpedo bombers and six Wildcats from the 'Yorktown' attack.

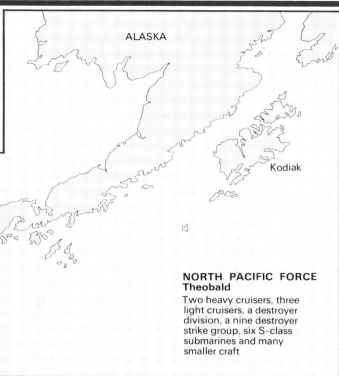

NORTH PACIFIC FORCE
Theobald
Two heavy cruisers, three light cruisers, a destroyer division, a nine destroyer strike group, six S-class submarines and many smaller craft

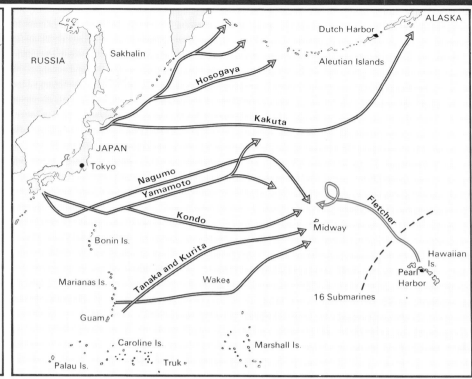

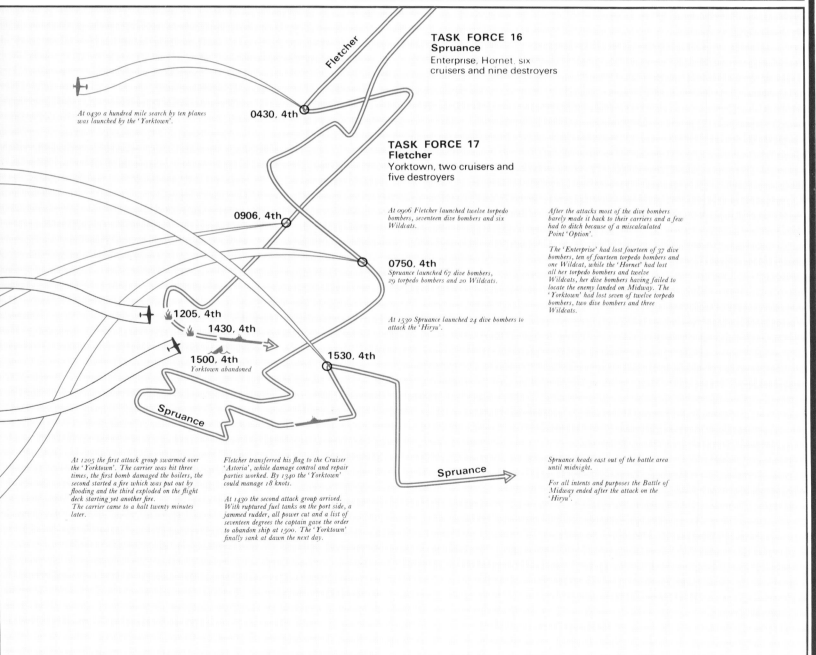

At 0430 a hundred mile search by ten planes was launched by the 'Yorktown'.

0430, 4th

TASK FORCE 16
Spruance
Enterprise, Hornet, six cruisers and nine destroyers

TASK FORCE 17
Fletcher
Yorktown, two cruisers and five destroyers

0906, 4th

At 0906 Fletcher launched twelve torpedo bombers, seventeen dive bombers and six Wildcats.

After the attacks most of the dive bombers barely made it back to their carriers and a few had to ditch because of a miscalculated Point 'Option'.

0750, 4th
Spruance launched 67 dive bombers, 29 torpedo bombers and 20 Wildcats.

The 'Enterprise' had lost fourteen of 37 dive bombers, ten of fourteen torpedo bombers and one Wildcat, while the 'Hornet' had lost all her torpedo bombers and twelve Wildcats, her dive bombers having failed to locate the enemy landed on Midway. The 'Yorktown' had lost seven of twelve torpedo bombers, two dive bombers and three Wildcats.

1205, 4th
1430, 4th
1500, 4th
Yorktown abandoned

1530, 4th

At 1530 Spruance launched 24 dive bombers to attack the 'Hiryu'.

Spruance

At 1205 the first attack group swarmed over the 'Yorktown'. The carrier was hit three times, the first bomb damaged the boilers, the second started a fire which was put out by flooding and the third exploded on the flight deck starting yet another fire.
The carrier came to a halt twenty minutes later.

Fletcher transferred his flag to the Cruiser 'Astoria', while damage control and repair parties worked. By 1340 the 'Yorktown' could manage 18 knots.

At 1430 the second attack group arrived. With ruptured fuel tanks on the port side, a jammed rudder, all power cut and a list of seventeen degrees the captain gave the order to abandon ship at 1500. The 'Yorktown' finally sank at dawn the next day.

Spruance

Spruance heads east out of the battle area until midnight.

For all intents and purposes the Battle of Midway ended after the attack on the 'Hiryu'.

causing heavy casualties and fires, but survived to get to Truk. A bomb on the *Mikuma* detonated her torpedoes, forcing her crew to abandon ship after the second attack, and she sank during the night. The destroyer screen picked up survivors and then made its own escape. Reassessing his position after these attacks, Spruance decided to turn east as only four destroyers were left to screen his two carriers and six cruisers and all were low on fuel. Also, three days of hard action had exhausted his pilots. His ships were 400 miles west of Midway and could come within range of Japanese bombers on Wake or on a concentration of enemy submarines.

Yamamoto made one last try. Learning that the American carriers were east of the *Mogami* and *Mikuma*, he formed a task force of six heavy cruisers and ten destroyers, and at noon on 6 June ordered this force to attack Spruance and relieve the damaged cruisers. He also hoped that Spruance would get within the 600-mile range of the Wake based bombers and ordered air reinforcements to Wake from the Marshall Islands.

Later that day, he gathered the remainder of his force – the Main Body, Kondo's group, the Aleutian force and the remnants of Nagumo's force – to steam toward the *Mogami* and *Mikuma* and the Americans beyond. He continued in this direction until the morning of 7 June when he turned west to fuel. On the following day he continued a westerly course toward his home bases, having lost any hope of renewed engagement with the Americans. Even so, two heavy cruisers and a destroyer division were left east of Wake to send out heavy radio traffic in a vain attempt to lure the American carriers within bombing range.

The long run of Japanese victories in the war came to an abrupt end at Midway, the first defeat ever suffered by the Japanese navy. Before Midway the *Shoho* at the Coral Sea was the most serious loss suffered by the Japanese but at Midway they lost four heavy carriers, a heavy cruiser, 322 planes and 3500 men against one American carrier, 150 planes and 307 men. It was some time before the Americans even realized how

Yamamoto blamed the debacle on the failure of his advance screen of submarines to harass the Americans, but in fact responsibility rests with him. He had deployed his submarines to attack the Americans where his calculations said they should be rather than where they were. The battle was really lost when Yamamoto first divided his mammoth fleet and then devised a highly complicated plan of attack based on what he assumed the Americans would do. The plan was rigid and so was the Japanese response to a battle which did not follow their script. The Japanese commanders did not display the professionalism and knack of rapid adaptation necessary to cope with this kind of action. Even so, the crucial factor in the battle had to be the prompt and wise use of intelligence reports by the Americans. Without them Nimitz would not have known how to dispose his forces and the Japanese plan might well have succeeded. 'Had we lacked early information of the Japanese movements, and had we been caught with carrier forces dispersed . . . the Battle of Midway would have ended differently' wrote Nimitz. Another element was the leadership of Spruance, made Nimitz' Chief of Staff after the battle, who by destroying the Japanese carrier force left the rest of their fleet vulnerable to air attack and thereby forced it to withdraw. Even more than the Coral Sea, Midway demonstrated the central role of the carrier plane in naval warfare. Despite possession of infinitely superior gun power and a fleet which was largely intact, without air cover Yamamoto had to abandon the fight without firing a shot.

Midway was the debut of the Zeke, or Zero 3. The original Zero fighter was superior to its American adversaries, being more maneuverable and having a rate of climb three times more rapid than any American plane. The Zeke was an improvement on the Zero and by far the best plane on either side in the battle. But however superior the Zeke may have been, the Japanese pilots at Midway proved themselves to be definitely inferior, one more indication of the decline of the Japanese naval air force as the war progressed. The Americans were so disturbed by the non-performance of their torpedo bomber, the misnamed Devastator, that it was taken off the list of naval combat planes and replaced by the as yet untried Avenger. The Dauntless dive bomber, on the other hand, had more than proved its worth and was to become the most successful American carrier plane of the war.

The Battle of Midway had been a near miss but the meaning of their defeat was clear to the Japanese. They had lost the ability to strike when and where they chose and thus to govern the course of the war. The Japanese side of the war would now become a holding operation as the Allies seized the offensive. Forced into an unaccustomed defensive role, the conquest of Port Moresby, Fiji, New Caledonia and Samoa had to be abandoned by the Japanese. Imperial General Headquarters reverted to its original plan to consolidate its gains, leaving the initiative to the enemy. As Yamamoto had predicted, this meant Japan would be overwhelmed by the United States as soon as American economic mobilization was complete.

complete their victory had been, for they thought that two Japanese carriers had survived and returned to Japan. Defeated by a much inferior American force, the Japanese Navy emerged from Midway with great loss of prestige and with its air striking power badly crippled. News of the defeat was completely suppressed in Japan. 'Our forces suffered a reverse so decisive and so grave that details of it were kept as a secret from all but a limited circle, even within the Japanese Navy. Even after the war, few among high ranking officers were familiar with the details of the Midway operation' said a Japanese admiral after the war. Returning sailors were held incommunicado while the wounded were brought ashore at night. 'It was like being a prisoner of war among your own people' said one. At Japan's capitulation in 1945, all papers concerning the disaster, hitherto classified as top secret, were destroyed. The Japanese public only learned of the events that took place at Midway when survivors began to publish accounts in the 1950's.

Leyte Gulf

1944

The Coral Sea was the first check received by the Japanese navy while Midway was its first defeat. The Battle of Leyte Gulf was its last encounter as an independent fighting force. The biggest naval battle in history, Leyte Gulf saw every weapon except the mine employed on both sides. As a measure of their desperation, the Japanese introduced new and deadly air tactics for which the Americans had no effective counter. Leyte Gulf is significant because it was not only the last big naval clash of World War II but the last big fleet action in history. Since late October of 1944, there have been no major naval engagements. While the Korean, Vietnamese and the various Middle Eastern wars have seen some monumental land battles, navies have played a distinctly auxiliary role. Leyte Gulf was the last epic sea battle fought to date.

After Midway it was clear that the Allies were to have two major commanders in the Pacific. Admiral Nimitz and General MacArthur were the two personalities who dominated the direction of the Pacific theater. Early in the war Roosevelt and Churchill had agreed that the Pacific area including Australia should be under the direction of the American Joint Chiefs of Staff while the Middle East and India were under British control and the European-Atlantic area had joint Anglo-American command. The command in the Pacific was divided between MacArthur's Southwest Pacific Command comprising Australia, New Guinea, the Philippines and most of the Netherlands East Indies, and the Central Pacific Command under Nimitz. The navy had long anticipated a war with Japan in the Pacific and knew that such a conflict must be essentially naval in character; its chiefs did not want any competition from the army – Europe was the army's war – and in particular did not want navy forces under army command. Nimitz and Admiral Ernest King, Naval Chief of Staff, wanted to launch a purely naval campaign west from Hawaii via the Gilbert, Marshall, Caroline and Mariana Islands to Japan; MacArthur was expected to stay on the defensive in the Southwest Pacific. MacArthur refused to accept this role, however, and planned to launch his own campaign to Japan north from Australia via New Guinea and the Philippines. In fact, MacArthur wanted the entire Pacific fleet placed under his command to cover his advance along what he called the 'New Guinea-Mindanao Axis'. King and Nimitz were determined not to turn their war over to the army and were adamant concerning their amphibious cam-

paign across the central Pacific, cogently arguing that as long as the Micronesian 'spider webs' which the Japanese had spread across the Pacific remained, every point on the New Guinea-Mindanao Axis was vulnerable to air attack. A shorter route to Japan must be opened up by sweeping up the spider webs.

The navy had a sound strategic argument but MacArthur was taking other factors into consideration. He knew that the Western colonial powers had lost great prestige in Asian eyes by their poor showing against Japan. The only way in which this prestige could be recovered was to reconquer the colonies by force of arms. If the United States wished to re-establish its interests in the Philippines, the islands would have to be wrested from the enemy forcibly. Although an advocate of Filipino independence, MacArthur was concerned that the United States regain its economic position in its colony. Also, having promised the people of the Philippines that he would return, MacArthur intended to do so. Thus MacArthur and Nimitz were competing against each other to see who could defeat Japan first. Fond of this sort of confrontation, Roosevelt had approved the divided command in the hope of

using the natural rivalry between the army and the navy to produce faster results. The navy openly hated MacArthur and welcomed the confrontation so much that Secretary of War Henry Stimson wrote 'the Navy's bitterness against MacArthur seemed childish'. 'Of all the faulty decisions of the war, perhaps the most inexpressible one was the failure to unify the command in the Pacific...' was MacArthur's subsequent view. The divided command was to have an important effect on the battle of Leyte Gulf.

Their smashing defeat at Midway again shifted Japanese attention to the Southwest Pacific. In an effort to retrieve some of their lost initiative, the Japanese high command formed a new Eighth Fleet under Admiral Mikawa to spearhead a fresh advance from Rabaul. New airfields were built at Rabaul and plans were laid for an infantry attack on Port Moresby over the Owen Stanley Mountains. Guadalcanal was to be occupied so that Japanese bombers would be able to menace the entire Allied position in the South Pacific. In July 1942, to counter this renewed threat and to get an Allied offensive underway, the Joint Chiefs of Staff finally formulated a strategy for the Southwest Pacific: to capture the New Guinea-New Britain-New Ireland area. In effect, this meant that MacArthur's American and Australian troops were to take the Solomon Islands and the northeast coast of New Guinea, along with Rabaul and adjacent positions in and around New Guinea and New Ireland. This was the origin of Mac-Arthur's 'island hopping' program, the object of which was to break through the barrier of the Bismarck Archipelago and open the way to the Philippines.

The Allies opened their own offensive in the Southwest Pacific with MacArthur's troops fighting a long hard jungle campaign in New Guinea from July 1942 to January 1943 when the last Japanese were finally evicted. At the same time, navy and marine forces under Nimitz's command fought an equally difficult campaign for the recovery of Guadalcanal and Tulagi from August 1942 to February 1943, a campaign which involved seven major naval encounters and at least ten pitched land battles. With the victories in Papua and Guadalcanal, the initiative in the Southwest Pacific decisively passed to the Allies. MacArthur's campaign had been considerably strengthened in October 1942 by the appointment of Admiral William Halsey as commander of the naval forces in the Southwest Pacific. Like Mac-Arthur, Halsey had a well deserved reputation for leadership, confidence and aggressiveness. Although 'island hopping' was proving successful, it was also proving too slow, and a new strategy called 'leap frogging' was devised. This meant by-passing the stronger Japanese positions sealing them off by sea and air and 'leaving them to die on the vine' or, as a baseball-minded member of MacArthur's staff put it, 'hitting 'em where they ain't'. This proved to be a wise course as it enabled the Southwest Pacific Command to by-pass the 100,000-man Japanese garrison at Rabaul and the 50,000-strong garrison at Wewak. By leap frogging MacArthur was able to gain control of New Guinea by 30 July, 1944 and could look across the Celebes Sea toward his next objective, Mindanao.

In the Central Pacific Nimitz was advancing atoll by atoll through the Marshalls and Gilberts, winning his victories by frontal assaults of overwhelming power. In June 1944 his forces began to attack Saipan, the key Japanese fortress in the Marianas. Saipan lay only 1350 miles from Tokyo and would be a valuable base for attacks on the Japanese home islands by long range B-24 bombers and the new B-29 super bomber. Loss of Saipan would also cut the lines of communications with Japanese forces to the south. Thus Imperial General Headquarters met the Allied attack on Saipan with the full force of the Japanese fleet. In the greatest air battle of the war, fifteen American carriers with 900 planes met five heavy and four light Japanese carriers with 370 planes. In what American pilots called the 'Great Marianas Turkey Shoot', the Japanese lost 315 planes in one day alone as well as a carrier, and several battleships and cruisers. The losses in planes and especially in pilots were irreplaceable at that stage of the war and Japan was never again able to launch an effective carrier force. The fall of Saipan was such an unmistakable sign of impending defeat that it brought down the war government of General Hideki Tojo.

With MacArthur now poised to cross the Celebes Sea to Mindanao and Nimitz occupying Saipan, Tinian and Guam on Japan's doorstep, the question of overall strategy was still unresolved despite fierce argument. Admirals King and Nimitz wanted to by-pass the Philippines, invade Formosa and then set up a base either on the Chinese mainland or in the Ryukyu Islands for the final assault on the home islands. MacArthur continued to insist on the liberation of the Philippines and on the use of Luzon as the base for the final assault on Japan. While Formosa had a hostile population, it was heavily defended and easily reinforceable from the Chinese mainland, Luzon was friendly and could easily be sealed off by Allied air and sea power. At a conference at Pearl Harbor in July 1944, MacArthur was finally able to convince Roosevelt and a dubious Nimitz of the merits of his 'Leyte then Luzon' concept. At the Octagon Conference at Quebec in September, the Allied Chiefs of Staff agreed that MacArthur and Nimitz should converge on Leyte and invade in concert in December. But within a week of this decision, Halsey's Third Fleet, spearheaded by the new Essex class fast carriers, found Japanese air opposition negligible while softening up Morotai, Yap and the Palau Islands. With no opposition from shore-based Japanese planes, MacArthur's forces could perform the ultimate in leap frogging, one long hop from New Guinea to Leyte, by-passing Mindanao and supported entirely by Nimitz's carrier-borne air power. In a remarkable example of strategic flexibility, the Octagon Conference advanced the date of the invasion of Leyte by two months to 20 October.

A Grim Struggle

For the Japanese, after their defeat in Guadalcanal and Papua, the war became a grim struggle to sell their short-lived conquests as dearly as possible. With control of 80% of the world's rubber, large quantities of tin, tungsten, man-

ganese, iron ore and the oil fields of the Nether-lands East Indies, Japan should have been able to face a prolonged war. But Imperial General Headquarters was several generations out of date in its concept of war, concerning itself largely with battles, tactics and territory. The Japanese could and did design better warships and air-planes than the Americans but did not give top priority to producing large numbers of these weapons on which their defense rested. Although a pioneer of naval air power, Japan built only three aircraft carriers in 1943 (against 22 for the United States) and failed utterly to mobilize the man-power needed even for its restricted air forces. To exploit the resources she now controlled, Japan needed a large merchant fleet but made no effort to enlarge its merchant navy. By 1943 so much tonnage had been lost to bombing, mines and submarines that it was difficult to hold the over-seas territories together. Yet the Japanese Navy made no adequate attempt to protect its merchant shipping through a convoy system, radar or asdic. For example, by 1943 Japan was already facing an oil shortage, a shortage which was severe enough to hamper production on the home front and curtail operations of the navy, because it no longer had the tanker capacity to move enough of this vital commodity from the Netherlands East Indies. This unimaginative planning and lack of coordination with the civilian sector of the economy meant that the essential weakness of the Japanese defense structure was economic. The Japanese were never able to exploit their huge resources to prolong the war.

The inability of the Japanese naval air force to seriously contest Nimitz' advance across the Central Pacific illustrates Japan's basic weakness by 1944. In two years of fighting 8000 navy planes had been lost and experienced pilots were in short supply. This huge loss of men and equipment had neither been foreseen nor prepared for and they could not be replaced. This was especially true of pilots, and the hasty training of replace-ments led to such a low level of fighting skill that

casualties mushroomed. One Japanese naval instructor wrote in his memoirs that 'The Navy was desperate for pilots, and the school was expanded almost every month, with corres-pondingly lower entrance requirements . . . We were told to rush the men through, to forget the finer points, just teach them how to fly and shoot . . . It was a hopeless task'. To make matters worse, the plane in which Yamamoto was making an inspection tour was ambushed by American fighters after American intelligence had decoded his route and schedule. No other Japanese admiral understood the use of air power so well. After his death the lessons taught by Yamamoto were forgotten and the navy fell back on its first love, the battleship.

By mid-1944 it was clear that Japan must fall back on an inner defense line extending from the Kuriles and the home islands through the Ryukyus, Formosa and the Philippines to the Netherlands East Indies. If this line could be maintained, Japan could still draw on the re-sources of her southern conquests and protect her lines of communication through the Formosa Straits and the South China Sea. Failure would mean that only the resources of China were left. As early as March 1944 Japanese strategists could see where the two prongs of the Allied offensive would meet, and the invasion of the Philippines was obvious to the Japanese long before the Allies had managed to agree on it among themselves. The main uncertainty was which island would be the first target. Although prepared to offer a 'general decisive battle' wherever the Allies struck, Japan's main interest was to hold Luzon, which would enable her to maintain communications with Malaya and Indonesia. Since she could not discover where the Allies would strike, four separate *Sho* (victory) plans were drawn up between 24 July and 1 August. *Sho* 1 covered the Philippines while the others concerned Formosa-Ryukyus, Honshu-Kyushu, and Hokkaido-Kuriles respectively. Al-though the other possibilities were covered, the

Above left: Vice-Admiral Kurita commanded the Center Force at Leyte, composed of the battleships *Yamato* and *Musashi*.
Above: Admiral Toyoda (left), Japan's C-in C Combined Fleet, who devised the Japanese counterattack which led to the Battle of Leyte Gulf. On the right is Foreign Minister Shigenori Togo, Minister of Greater East Asia.

The Battle of Leyte Gulf, 22-26 October 1944

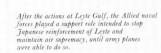

After the actions at Leyte Gulf, the Allied naval forces played a support role intended to stop Japanese reinforcement of Leyte and maintain air supremacy, until army planes were able to do so.

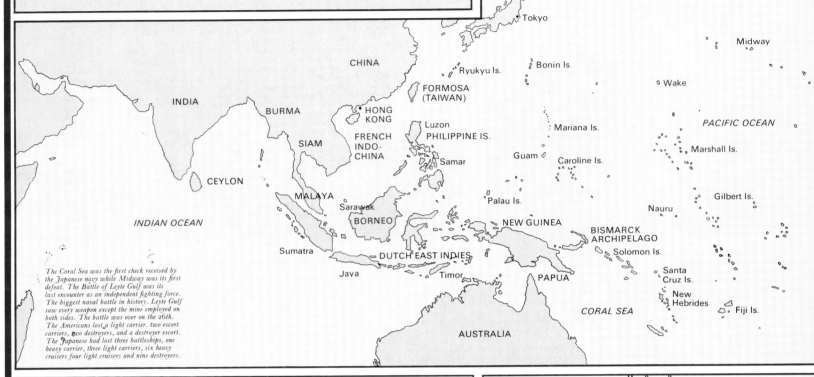

JAPAN
Tokyo

Midway

CHINA

Ryukyu Is.

Bonin Is.

Wake

FORMOSA (TAIWAN)

HONG KONG

Luzon

Mariana Is.

PACIFIC OCEAN

INDIA

BURMA

FRENCH INDO-CHINA

PHILIPPINE IS.

Marshall Is.

SIAM

Samar

Guam

Caroline Is.

CEYLON

MALAYA

Palau Is.

Gilbert Is.

Sarawak

BORNEO

Nauru

INDIAN OCEAN

Sumatra

DUTCH EAST INDIES

NEW GUINEA

BISMARCK ARCHIPELAGO

Solomon Is.

Santa Cruz Is.

Java

Timor

PAPUA

New Hebrides

Fiji Is.

CORAL SEA

AUSTRALIA

The Coral Sea was the first check received by the Japanese navy while Midway was its first defeat. The Battle of Leyte Gulf was its last encounter as an independent fighting force. The biggest naval battle in history. Leyte Gulf saw every weapon except the mine employed on both sides. The battle was over on the 26th. The Americans lost a light carrier, two escort carriers, two destroyers, and a destroyer escort. The Japanese had lost three battleships, one heavy carrier, three light carriers, six heavy cruisers four light cruisers and nine destroyers.

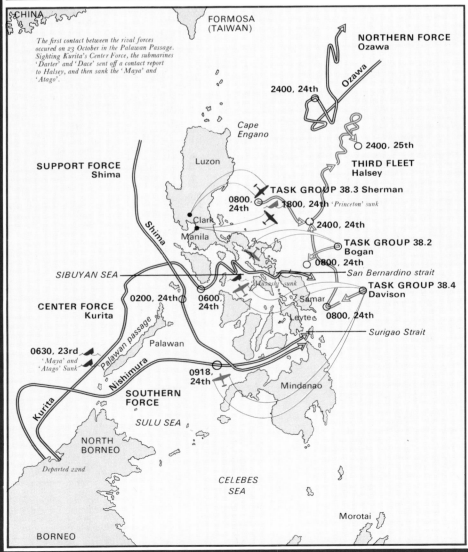

CHINA

FORMOSA (TAIWAN)

The first contact between the rival forces occured on 23 October in the Palawan Passage. Sighting Kurita's Center Force, the submarines 'Darter' and 'Dace' sent off a contact report to Halsey, and then sank the 'Maya' and 'Atago'.

NORTHERN FORCE Ozawa

Ozawa

2400, 24th

2400, 25th

Cape Engano

THIRD FLEET Halsey

SUPPORT FORCE Shima

Luzon

TASK GROUP 38.3 Sherman

0800, 24th

1800, 24th 'Princeton' sunk

Clark

2400, 24th

Manila

Shima

TASK GROUP 38.2 Bogan

0800, 24th

SIBUYAN SEA

San Bernardino strait

Musashi sunk

TASK GROUP 38.4 Davison

0200, 24th

0600, 24th

Samar

CENTER FORCE Kurita

Leyte

0800, 24th

Surigao Strait

0630, 23rd 'Maya' and 'Atago' Sunk

Palawan

Nishimura

0918, 24th

Mindanao

SOUTHERN FORCE

SULU SEA

NORTH BORNEO

Kurita

Departed 22nd

CELEBES SEA

Morotai

BORNEO

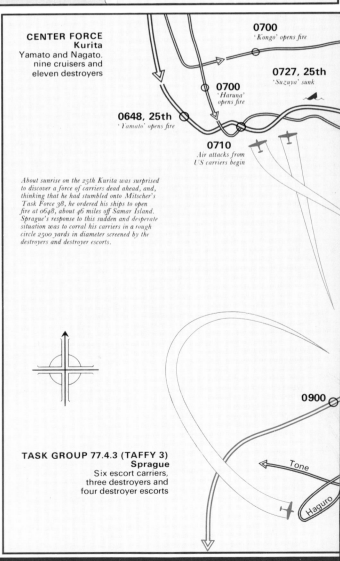

CENTER FORCE Kurita
Yamato and Nagato. nine cruisers and eleven destroyers

0700 'Kongo' opens fire

0727, 25th 'Suzuya' sunk

0700 'Haruna' opens fire

0648, 25th 'Yamato' opens fire

0710 Air attacks from US carriers begin

About sunrise on the 25th Kurita was surprised to discover a force of carriers dead ahead, and, thinking that he had stumbled onto Mitscher's Task Force 38, he ordered his ships to open fire at 0648, about 46 miles off Samar Island. Sprague's response to this sudden and desperate situation was to corral his carriers in a rough circle 2500 yards in diameter screened by the destroyers and destroyer escorts.

TASK GROUP 77.4.3 (TAFFY 3) Sprague
Six escort carriers, three destroyers and four destroyer escorts

0900

Tone

Haguro

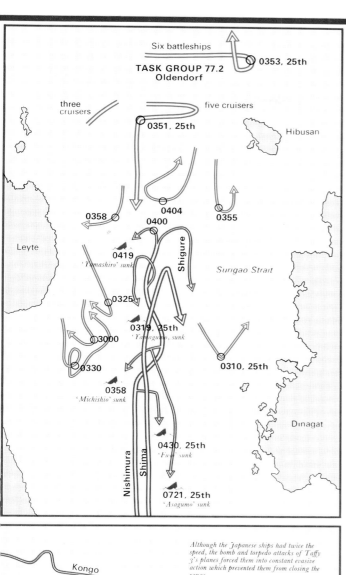

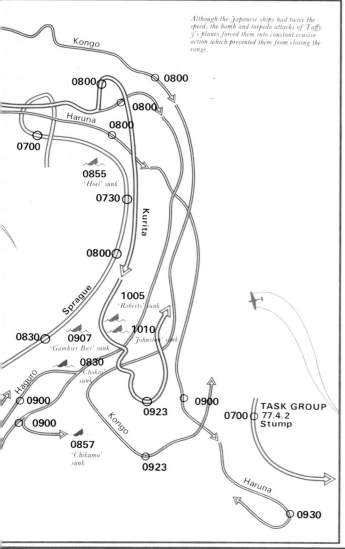

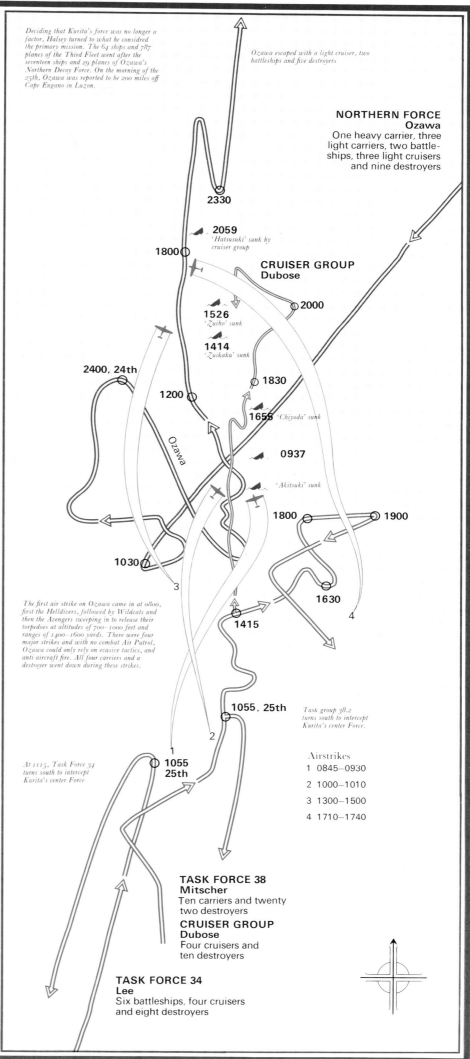

Japanese high command was certain that the Allies would attack the Philippines.

The basic elements of *Sho* 1 were that the Northern Force of Admiral Ozawa, built around the carriers *Zuikaku*, *Zuiho*, *Chitose* and *Chiyoda*, would decoy Halsey's Third Fleet to the north, thus removing the main American battle force from the vicinity of the real objective. Then Admiral Kurita's Center Force – the super battleships *Yamato* and *Musashi*, nine cruisers and supporting destroyers – would come through the San Bernardino Strait at the same time as the Southern Force of Admiral Nishimura came through the Surigao Strait to converge on Leyte Gulf. After destroying the gulf full of unprotected shipping and smashing the Allied beachhead, it is not clear what *Sho* 1 envisaged for Halsey's powerful Third Fleet when it returned from chasing Ozawa. Thus *Sho* 1 was a standard Japanese plan which employed division of force, diversions, unexpected attacks and a highly elaborate schedule.

Japan chose to regard the invasion of the Philippines as a crisis of the war. Although the naval air force had already been virtually eliminated, the fleet was still strong in surface ships. Ozawa's carriers had but 116 planes among them while land based air groups in the Ryukyus, Formosa and Manila could muster less than 200 planes. The carriers were therefore to be expended on the decoy mission while the battle would be decided by the gun power of the Japanese Navy.

If this plan succeeded, Japan would have achieved the equivalent of a second Pearl Harbor, destroying the American army as the navy had been smashed three years earlier. It would have been a year before the United States could replace the men and equipment lost at Leyte, and this was time which Japan desperately needed.

The Commander-in-Chief of the Combined Fleet was now Admiral Soyemu Toyoda, who directed operations from Tokyo. Toyoda was gambling on his forces making unimpeded contact with the enemy, free from air attack, and destroying them with overwhelming gun power. He accepted the probability that the Combined Fleet would be destroyed, but if the Philippines were lost, cutting Japan off from her only source of oil, the fleet would be immobilized from lack of fuel anyway. It was better, he thought, to go down fighting. *Sho* 1 was thus a huge *kamikaze* operation, a last desperate roll of the dice. Although Japanese intelligence had predicted that the invasion would come in the last ten days of October and that the target would be Leyte, it could be certain of neither time nor target. Due to the oil shortage, Toyoda could not activate *Sho* 1 until Allied ships were actually seen entering Leyte Gulf; if his forces were activated too soon, they would be short of fuel for the real engagement. Since the engagement off Saipan in June, now known as the Battle of the Philippine Sea, all the battleships and heavy cruisers had been stationed at Lingga Roads near Singapore in order to be near the sources of oil, while the carriers and their attendant ships had been in home waters waiting to embark new air groups as they emerged from the training schools. Thus the oil shortage meant that Toyoda could not activate *Sho* 1 early enough to catch the Leyte landings in their 'naked' stage as troops and equipment were being disembarked.

Allied preparations for the Leyte operation began immediately after the schedule was advanced by the Octagon Conference in September. Morotai was seized as a staging base against the Philippines for short range fighters and light and medium bombers. Peleliu was taken because an assault force had already been underway and Nimitz had not wanted to recall it. This was a

Top left: Kinkaid receives the Distinguished Service Medal from Admiral Nimitz for his action in the Coral Sea. Both were responsible for the American victory at Leyte Gulf two years later. **Above:** Toyoda sent his finest ships and all that remained of his Navy and Air Force against the Americans at Leyte in a desperate attempt to prevent the collapse of Japanese power in the Pacific. **Left:** Kinkaid in the Aleutians. He was transferred from that obscure posting to a position of vital importance at the head of the Seventh Fleet in 1944.

Above: Vice-Admiral Mitscher, Commander of Task Force 38, part of Halsey's Third Fleet. He made the big raids on Formosa in October 1944. **Above center:** MacArthur 'returning' to the Philippines at Morotai. His forces fought for months against General Yamashita throughout the balance of the war in the jungles of the Philippines. **Above right:** MacArthur, walking through the water with his Chief of Staff, Sutherland, and President Osmeña (left) of the Philippines. Some critics said that MacArthur would have preferred to walk on the water.

mistake, as the defenders offered tough resistance for over two months. Early in October MacArthur's forces and Admiral Thomas Kinkaid's Seventh Fleet were gathering along the coast of New Guinea. When fully assembled, the invasion convoy totalled 738 ships, including 157 combat vessels, 420 amphibians, 84 patrol boats, minesweeping and hydrographic specialists, and 73 service ships. These were supported by Halsey's Third Fleet which comprised seventeen carriers, six battleships, seventeen cruisers and 64 destroyers. The invasion of the Philippines was being undertaken by the most powerful naval force ever assembled (though an even mightier force would gather for the invasion of Okinawa the following April). On 10 October the mammoth convoy began to move away from the shores of New Guinea with the minesweepers in the van.

The invasion of Leyte was being undertaken in one giant hop from New Guinea because it was believed that carrier planes could provide adequate air cover for the convoy and landings in view of the demonstrated air weakness of the Japanese. It was still necessary, however, to destroy Japan's remaining land-based air power before the landings took place. A major air assault was launched against Formosa to neutralize its air groups and deny it to the enemy as a staging base against the Philippines. Task Force 38 under Admiral Marc Mitscher was detached from the Third Fleet for this operation. In excellent flying weather between 12–14 October, planes from nine American carriers swarmed over the island, doing heavy damage to ground facilities. Under the command of Admiral Fukudome, 230 Japanese fighters rose to intercept but over a third were lost on 12 October alone. 'Our fighters were nothing but so many eggs thrown against the wall of the indomitable enemy formation' lamented the admiral. In the end Task Force 38 destroyed over 500 Japanese planes and 40 transports and smaller craft. These operations were supplemented by a series of B-29 raids from the American base at Chengtu in China.

In the week before the assault date of 20 October, army and navy planes attacked Japanese air bases in Luzon, Mindanao and the Netherlands East Indies while a naval sweep was sent against the Kurile Islands. They met little resistance as the Japanese were hoarding their planes in anticipation of the 'general decisive

battle'. Allied knowledge of Japanese intentions and movements was both slight and wildly inaccurate. Halsey at least considered the possibility that the enemy would contest the landings but MacArthur's staff thought that a fleet action was not likely. 'The objective is relatively undefended – the Japanese will not offer strong resistance to the operation' was the estimate of General George Kenney, commander of the army air forces in the Southwest Pacific. On 20 October MacArthur's headquarters issued a statement that it would be impractical for the Japanese navy to use the San Bernardino or Surigao Straits due to navigational hazards and lack of space to maneuver. On 23 October Kinkaid and Halsey were still sceptical that the Japanese intended to use their fleet.

In fact, at 0750 on 17 October, Toyoda activated *Sho* 1 after receiving a message that American ships were approaching Leyte Gulf. The main battle force of Kurita sortied from Lingga Roads the following day. On the 20th, after topping up its fuel tanks at Brunei Bay in North Borneo, the force split. With most of the heavy cruisers, Kurita's five battleships set course for the Sibuyan Sea and the San Bernardino Strait. With its nucleus of two battleships, Nishimura's Southern Force headed for the Surigao Strait. Almost as an afterthought, two heavy cruisers, a light cruiser and seven destroyers under Admiral Shima were ordered from the Inland Sea to 'support and cooperate' with Nishimura. Undetected by the American submarines which had been sent to intercept any sortie, Ozawa's Northern Carrier Force slipped out of the Inland Sea on 20 October on its decoy mission.

Mine sweeping operations to clear the entrances of Leyte Gulf had begun on 17 October. By noon the following day rangers had secured the four islands at the mouth of the gulf. Rear-Admiral Jesse Oldendorf then moved his gunfire support ships from the Seventh Fleet into the gulf to bombard the beaches to cover the work of underwater demolition teams clearing obstructions from the landing areas. The assault day dawned with perfect weather and no surf. Only some light mortar fire opposed the landings. After the first wave was ashore, MacArthur and Sergio Osmena, who had become President of the Philippines after the death of Manuel Quezon, followed in a moment of high drama. Standing on the beach,

MacArthur made the broadcast for which he had been waiting two and a half years: 'People of the Philippines, I have returned. By the grace of Almighty God, our forces stand again on Philippine soil – soil consecrated by the blood of our two peoples'. The speech had a tremendous impact on the Philippines and there on the beach MacArthur scribbled a note to Roosevelt urging him to grant the Philippines immediate independence. The following day, Dulag and Tacloban airfields and Tacloban town, which had the only docking facilities on Leyte, were in American hands. By midnight 132,000 men and 200,000 tons of supplies and equipment had been landed. General Walter Kreuger's Sixth Army then faced the difficult task of evicting 60,000 Japanese defenders from Leyte. By the 22nd, with the amphibious phase of the operation complete, most of the shipping in Leyte Gulf had departed. Only 28 Liberty ships and 25 Landing Ships Medium (LSM's) and Landing Ship Tanks (LST's) remained.

The first contact between the rival forces occurred on 23 October in the Palawan Passage between Palawan Island and the reefs bordering the South China Sea. Sighting Kurita's Center Force, the submarines *Darter* and *Dace* sent off a contact report to Halsey, the first news he had had of Center Force since the report of its departure from Lingga Roads, and then sank three enemy heavy cruisers, one of which was Kurita's flagship. By noon of the following day, Halsey had deployed three of the fast carrier groups of Task Force 38 on a broad front. Rear-Admiral Sherman's group lay to the north, Rear-Admiral Bogan's off the San Bernadino Strait, and Rear-Admiral Dawson's 60 miles off Samar. But before these groups could launch strikes against Kurita's ships, now in the Sibuyan Sea, Japanese planes from Luzon attacked Sherman's group which was in the position to do the most damage to Kurita. Three separate waves of 50 to 60 planes each swept in with bombs and torpedoes. Many were shot down by anti-aircraft fire and Combat Air Patrol planes but one dive bomber broke through to drop a 550-pound bomb which penetrated through the flight deck of the light carrier *Princeton*.

The torpedo storage of the vessel was detonated and she had to be abandoned to sink later that day. The other two carrier groups did launch attack groups which gave Center Force, who lacked a Combat Air Patrol since most available Japanese planes were attacking Sherman, a heavy working over. The super battleship *Musashi* took 19 torpedo and 17 bomb hits and sank with most of her crew. Other ships were hit as well but all except the cruiser *Myoko* were able to proceed. Although weakened, Center Force was still formidable with four battleships, six heavy cruisers, two light cruisers and ten destroyers. Kurita had made repeated requests to Admiral Fukudome, commanding the air forces in the Philippines and Formosa, for air cover but Fukudome had decided that attacking the carrier groups was the best way of relieving Kurita. By 1400 hours American reconnaissance planes reported that the Japanese ships were turning west as if withdrawing but in fact they were only regrouping and assessing their damage. To avoid further air attack, Kurita asked permission to retire and run the San Bernadino Strait that night but Toyoda ordered him ahead. The air attacks in the Sibuyan Sea had lasted most of the day, putting Center Force seven hours behind schedule. There was now no way that it could keep its dawn rendezvous with Southern Force in Leyte Gulf.

While Center Force was being slowed down by the Battle of the Sibuyan Sea, Southern Force was approaching Leyte Gulf by its own route. Shima's supporting force was several hours behind Nishimura's squadron, the battleships *Fuso* and *Yamashiro*, the heavy cruiser *Mogami* and four destroyers. Before noon of the 24th, however, air reconnaissance had spotted Nishimura, leading Admiral Kinkaid of the Seventh Fleet to believe that the Japanese admiral intended to run the Surigao Strait that night. By 1830 of that same day Nishimura had been informed that Kurita could not keep to the time table, but when Toyoda signaled 'All forces will dash to the attack', Nishimura pushed on without even waiting for Shima to catch up. Since he had no air cover, the commander of the Southern Force believed that his only chance was to get to Leyte Gulf under cover of darkness. Kinkaid and Oldendorf in the meantime had laid a neat ambush for any enemy forces which tried to penetrate the gulf that night. A fifteen-mile battle line was formed between Leyte and Hibuson Island where the Surigao Strait enters Leyte Gulf. Six battleships, four heavy cruisers and four light cruisers were deployed to bar the way. Five of the battleships were now to

Left: The battleship *Musashi* blows up at Leyte Gulf. **Right:** Anti-aircraft fire from the USS *Sangamon* drives off Japanese dive bombers. **Below:** USS *Birmingham* hoses down the USS *Princeton*, which was sunk at Leyte on 23 October, 1944 during the the first phase of the battle.

have their revenge; they had already been sunk once at Pearl Harbor and had been refloated. Two destroyer divisions were deployed down the strait for torpedo attacks while a third was ordered to follow up the efforts of the first two and a fourth attended the battle line. As Kinkaid had no night-flying radar-equipped patrol planes, he had the strait patrolled by 39 torpedo boats with orders to report all enemy contact and then attack independently.

Contact was first reported at 2230, followed by more reports along the 50-mile length of the strait. Repeated PT boat attacks failed to score a hit, however, and by 0300 on the 25th the destroyer divisions were beginning their attacks. Nishimura was sailing in line ahead with the destroyers *Michishio, Asagumo, Shigure* and *Yamagumo* followed by the *Yamashiro, Fuso* and *Mogami*. Launching their torpedoes at ranges of 8200–9300 yards, the destroyers hit the *Fuso* which sheered out of line and began to burn and explode. The *Yamashiro* was also hit, and two of her magazines had to be flooded. The first Japanese destroyer was sunk while the second had her bow blown off and dropped out of line. When the follow up division of American destroyers made its attack ten minutes later, the *Yamashiro* received another hit and another destroyer was sunk, leaving only the *Shigure*. All of the American destroyers escaped without damage. During these attacks Nishimura ordered no evasive action nor took any notice of his damaged ships, even though the *Fuso* had gone down within 30 minutes of being torpedoed. Reduced to the *Yamashiro*, the *Mogami* and the *Shigure*, he maintained his course for his objective with single-minded concentration.

Oldendorf's formidable line had a left flank of three heavy and two light cruisers, a right flank of one heavy and two light cruisers, and a center of six battleships supported by a destroyer division.

Although the line was stationary, with Nishimura steaming toward it in single line ahead, the effect was the same as crossing the Japanese 'T'. At 0351 the American line opened fire, with the *West Virginia, Tennessee* and *California* doing most of the work as they were equipped with the new Mark 8 fire control radar. Fitted with the old Mark 3 radar, the other battleships had trouble finding targets, and the *Pennsylvania* never fired at all. Coming up at twelve knots, the *Yamashiro* could return the American fire only at visible targets since it had no fire control radar. It was supported feebly by the *Mogami* astern and the *Shigure* to starboard. By taking radical evasive action the *Shigure* escaped with only one hit but when the *Yamashiro* and *Mogami* began to retire at 0400 both had been heavily battered. A few minutes later the *Yamashiro* was burning brightly against the night; the *Mogami* stopped dead when its bridge was struck by shells, which killed most of the officers including the captain. Increasing their fire in rate and accuracy, the American battleships began to move up on the crippled enemy. The *Yamashiro* was retiring south at fifteen knots when she was struck by two torpedoes from the destroyer *Newcomb* lurking in the darkness. Immediately developing a 45-degree list, she quickly went down with Nishimura and most of her crew.

The *Shigure* was escorting the limping *Mogami* back down the strait as Shima was coming up past the burning hulks of some of Nishimura's ships. Having seen the flash of gunfire, Shima thought he was coming to the support of the van already engaged in wreaking havoc on a gulf full of unprotected shipping. The American PT boats were still patrolling the channel and knocked the light cruiser *Abakuma* out of formation with a torpedo. Two ships appeared on Shima's radar. He ordered his own destroyers to the attack, but when this failed he turned his ships to retire, joined by the *Mogami* and *Shigure*. As dawn appeared, Oldendorf began a general pursuit down the strait. The *Mogami*, which had fallen behind Shima's force, was discovered by three cruisers and received several more shell hits. Although 'burning like a city block', she was able to get up high speed and drive off some PT attacks, only to be sunk by planes some three hours later. The destroyer *Asagumo* with her smashed bow was sunk by two other cruisers. The *Abakuma* was dispatched the following day by New Guinea-based army bombers. The remaining two heavy cruisers and two destroyers of Shima made good their escape when Oldendorf decided to break off the pursuit and retire. With Kurita's Center Force still unaccounted for, the Seventh Fleet's main responsibility was the protection of the Leyte beachhead.

While his colleague Nishimura was being annihilated in the Battle of the Surigao Strait, Kurita was making his way 150 miles down the San Bernardino Strait unopposed. Halsey had accepted the inflated reports from his pilots of many sinkings in the Sibuyan Sea and had come to the conclusion that the Center Force 'could no longer be considered a serious menace to the Seventh Fleet'. Accepting air reconnaissance reports that Kurita was turning west in the afternoon to retire, and disregarding contradictory night sighting reports, he had not even alerted Kinkaid to the possibility that Center Force was a threat. He had then taken the entire Third Fleet north to chase Ozawa's decoy force, leaving not so much as a picket destroyer to watch the San Bernardino Strait. Due to an unclear message, both Kinkaid and Nimitz were under the impression that Halsey

had left a force of heavy ships to block any enemy penetration of the strait.

About sunrise on the 25th, Kurita was surprised to discover a force of carriers dead ahead and, thinking that he had stumbled onto Mitscher's powerful Task Force 38, he ordered his ships to open fire at 0648, about 40 miles off Paninihian Point of Samar Island. The crews of the ships, an escort carrier group with the code name 'Taffy 3', were equally surprised when shells began to splash around them as they were having breakfast on what was supposed to have been a day of routine operations. Often called jeep or Woolworth carriers, escort carriers were used to provide air support for landing operations until airfields ashore were usable. An escort carrier normally had a complement of 18 Wildcats and twelve Avengers. Taffy 3 consisted of six escort carriers, three destroyers and four destroyer escorts under the command of Rear-Admiral Clifton Sprague. Nearby were Taffys 1 and 2, similar escort carrier groups. The total complement of planes for the three groups was 235 Hellcats and Wildcats and 143 Avengers, but at 0648 that day few of these planes were available. A strike had been sent after Shima's ships as they escaped the massacre in the Suriago Strait while many others were engaged in patrol and other routine chores such as delivering fresh water to the troops on Leyte.

The 48-year-old Sprague, a former carrier commander at the Battle of the Philippine Sea, immediately turned his ships east into the wind and launched what planes he had. Ordering his group to the maximum escort carrier speed of $17\frac{1}{2}$ knots, he then began to broadcast urgent calls for assist-

Right: Two US carriers are pummeled by Japanese dive bombers. The plane which did the damage was shot down minutes later.

Above left: *Kamikaze*
attack on the USS *Columbia*.
These suicide missions,
however frightening they
were at first, only succeeded
in destroying what was left
of Japan's air power.
Above: A crew member of
an escort carrier watches a
Japanese bomb explode.
The carrier set up a smoke
screen to obscure the
kamikaze pilots' vision.

ance. The first response came from Taffys 1 and 2, over 130 miles away, who launched their planes in support. Before Sprague's unexpected SOS, Kinkaid had believed that a task force from the Third Fleet was covering the San Bernardino Strait and therefore had ordered only a modest night reconnaissance. When Sprague's cry for help came in, the ships of the Seventh Fleet were in Leyte Gulf refilling their ammunition lockers after their night battle with the Southern Force in the Surigao Strait and could not yet face another major engagement. The Third Fleet had let itself be taken out of the picture and could not send aid in time either. Halsey did order the air groups of Admiral McCain's task force to assist but McCain's ships were hundreds of miles to the east, and it would be hours before his planes could join the battle. Taffy 3 just had to fend for itself.

From the beginning Kurita bungled his golden opportunity. His staff officers reported the escort carriers as carriers, the destroyers as cruisers and the destroyer escorts as destroyers. When Taffy 3 was sighted the Japanese ships were sailing in anti-aircraft formation. On contact with the enemy a battle line of the heavy ships should have been formed and the destroyers sent in for torpedo attacks. But Kurita inexplicably ordered General Attack – every ship for itself – which threw his force into considerable confusion. Thus the Japanese squadron was not under proper tactical control as it came to the attack.

Sprague's response to this sudden and desperate situation was to corral his carriers in a rough circle 2500 yards in diameter screened by the destroyers and destroyer escorts. 'The enemy was closing with disconcerting rapidity and the volume and accuracy of fire was increasing', he later wrote. Faced with 'the ultimate in desperate circumstances', he ordered his destroyers and destroyer escorts to make a torpedo attack to divert the enemy, at the same time turning south-southwest to get nearer Leyte and his best hope of succor. This course offered the inside track to Kurita but the Japanese admiral preferred to keep the weather gauge and soon found himself due north of his quarry. Although the Japanese ships had twice the speed, the bomb and torpedo attacks of Taffy 3's planes forced them into constant evasive action which prevented them from closing in on the enemy.

The destroyers *Hoel*, *Heermann* and *Johnston* launched their torpedo counterattack. The *John-ston* got a hit on the cruiser *Kumano* which forced her, along with the bomb-damaged *Suzuya*, out of the battle. But on continuing her attack, the *Johnston* was hit at 0730 by three fourteen-inch and three six-inch shells. 'It was like a puppy dog being smacked by a truck', said one of her officers.

With all power gone and her engine room out, she still helped to break up an attack by Japanese destroyers by firing her guns manually. Then, said one survivor, 'We were in a position where all the gallantry and guts in the world could not save us' as three cruisers came up and blasted the hapless destroyer until she had to be abandoned. Trying to divert the enemy's major caliber fire from the carriers, the *Hoel* and the *Heermann* continued the unequal fight until the *Hoel*, hit 40 times, sank. The captain later noted that his crew 'performed their duties coolly and efficiently until their ship was shot out from under them'.

In spite of the efforts of the destroyers and the planes, which were making dry runs when out of ammunition to divert enemy fire from the carriers, the latter were taking a pounding. The *Kalinin Bay* had received thirteen eight-inch hits but managed to maintain her place in the formation. Center Force was somewhat scattered as four Japanese cruisers closed the range and sank the *Gambier Bay* at 0907. American planes then sank two of the cruisers, causing Kurita to break off the action. His communications were so poor that he apparently did not know what havoc his cruisers were beginning to work among the carriers. He intended to reassemble his scattered force and reorganize it for an attempt to get to Leyte Gulf. But when he was informed of the fate of the Southern Force, having already been attacked by submarines and planes in the Sibuyan Sea and with three more cruisers lost here, he decided to retire. At 1230 70 Wildcats and Avengers from Taffys 2 and 3 arrived to confirm him in this decision. As the Japanese ships turned away, a signalman on the bridge of Sprague's flagship yelled 'Goddammit, boys, they're getting away!'

Kurita's decision to retire was indeed prudent, for Oldendorf's battleships lay in wait at the mouth of Leyte Gulf and massive air attacks by land-based and Task Force 38 planes were being readied. Had it continued on, Center Force would undoubtedly have shared the same fate as Southern Force. As it was, Kurita's mistakes coupled with Sprague's determined resistance had enabled a weak and relatively defenseless

Overleaf: Crew members
of a rescue ship search for
further *kamikaze* attacks as
they help an LST already
struck by a suicide pilot.

squadron to turn back the most powerful gunfire force Japan had put to sea since Midway. It was yet another demonstration of the helplessness of capital ships without air cover.

The travail of the Taffys did not end with Kurita's withdrawal for 25 October marked the first appearance of the *kamikaze*. Organized by Rear-Admiral Arima in 1944, the *kamikaze* were a special air corps designed to meet Japan's desperate need for air power. The Japanese naval air groups had been essentially eliminated, and land based planes were in short supply. American fighter pilots had become very competent at interception, while the invention of the proximity armed fuse for anti-aircraft shells made it nearly impossible for a bomber to get near enough to a ship to score a hit. Arima's *kamikaze* pilots were to crash their planes into the enemy ship, to detonate the bombs carried by the planes and start gasoline fires from the fuel. An added advantage was that obsolete planes and untrained pilots could be used. Such sacrifice for the Emperor appealed to the thousands of young Japanese who volunteered. Taffy 1 had the dubious distinction of being the first American force to endure a *kamikaze* attack; later that same day Taffy 3 underwent eight attacks, one of which sank the *St. Lo*. Between them, Kurita and the *kamikazes* had succeeded in sinking two escort carriers, two destroyers and one destroyer escort and badly damaging several ships on the 25th.

Kinkaid's Seventh Fleet was under Mac-Arthur's command for the Leyte landings with the specific mission of protecting the beachhead and providing fire support. Since MacArthur would have no cover from his own land-based planes, he had been guaranteed naval air support from Nimitz's command. Nimitz had assigned this task to the powerful Third Fleet under Halsey. Halsey's orders were to 'cover and support' the army in pursuit of the Allied objectives in the central Philippines and to 'destroy enemy naval and air forces in or threatening the Philippines'. But the orders went on to say 'In case opportunity for destruction of a major portion of the enemy fleet is offered or can be created, such destruction becomes the primary task'. Although the primary duty of a covering force in an amphibious operation is always the protection of the landing force, Halsey interpreted his orders to mean that his primary objective was to destroy the Japanese fleet if the opportunity appeared. Indeed, Halsey had a hand in drafting these orders with this very thought in mind. Not being under MacArthur's orders, he was not required to seek approval or even inform the army command of any action the Third Fleet might see fit to take. And *Sho 1* was designed to offer the aggressive admiral the apparent opportunity to attain his primary objective.

All day on the 24th, Third Fleet search planes had been seeking a Japanese carrier force reported to have left the Inland Sea. Ozawa's Northern Force, equally anxious to be sighted, comprised one heavy carrier and three light carriers with a total of 116 planes between them. To make the force more attractive to Halsey two 'hermaphro-

Below: The wardroom of the USS *Sewanee* is used as a temporary sickbay during the Battle of Leyte Gulf.

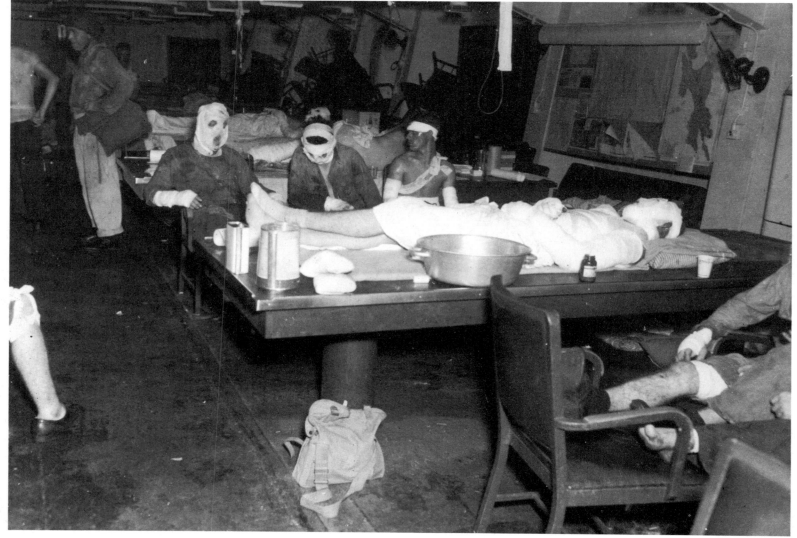

dite' carriers – battleships with cut down super-structures to make room for a short flight deck but carrying no planes – were included, along with the screen of three light cruisers and nine destroyers. In the morning Japanese search planes discovered a part of Task Force 38 and Ozawa sent a 76-plane strike against it. Only 29 planes returned to Northern Force; the remainder were shot down, ditched, or landed on Luzon airfields. American search planes finally located Ozawa at 1540 but their report did not reach Halsey until 1700. The sighting of Japanese carriers was a red flag to 'Bull' Halsey, causing him to make a crucial error in judgement for which he received great criticism. Deciding that Kurita's force was no longer a factor, the admiral turned to what he considered his primary mission, the destruction of the Japanese carrier force, Around 2000 the 64 ships and 787 planes of the Third Fleet went after the 17 ships and 29 planes of the Northern Force. At 0220 on the morning of the 25th, the Northern Force was reported to be 200 miles off Cape Engano in Luzon. At 0430 the carriers prepared full deckloads and launched at daylight. The first strike on Ozawa came in at 0800, first the Helldivers, followed by strafing Wildcats and then the Avengers sweeping in to release their torpedoes at altitudes of 700–1000 feet and ranges of 1400–1600 yards. There were five major strikes, and no Combat Air Patrol, Ozawa could only rely on evasive tactics and anti-aircraft fire. All four carriers and a destroyer went down during these strikes despite the fact that the Japanese anti-aircraft fire was possibly the most deadly on either side during the war.

By 0820 Halsey was beginning to get urgent plain language appeals for help from Kinkaid but, anticipating a gun battle with Ozawa, he made no move to relieve Taffy 3 other than to direct McCain's distant task force to send air strikes when possible. As a result of a vague message from Halsey both Kinkaid and Nimitz assumed that he had left a force to watch the San Bernardino Strait. By 1000 even Nimitz was making inquiries as to where this force was and what Halsey was doing. In fact, Halsey had wanted to keep his battle force with him to clean up the enemy 'cripples' after the air strikes and to catch up with the two hermaphrodite carriers which had not succumbed to the air attacks. Largely because he now knew that Nimitz was concerned for the safety of the Seventh Fleet, he sent one carrier group and most of the battle line south at 1055. Even at top speed, however, this force could not have reached the strait before 0100 on the 26th. If this force had been detached immediately on Kinkaid's first appeal, it might have caught Kurita in the strait but as it was, the Japanese admiral escaped without further loss.

Halsey's remaining cruisers and destroyers were ordered in pursuit of Ozawa and finished off a crippled light cruiser and a large destroyer. Ozawa, who was considered the ablest Japanese admiral after Yamamoto, escaped with a light cruiser, the two hermaphrodite carriers and five destroyers. Although he later said 'We expected

Below: US sailors watch as the *Princeton* (background) is hit by Japanese dive bombers.

complete destruction in this mission', he had saved Center Force and his own from annihilation. Forced to use his carriers on what amounted to a suicide mission, the battle was a 'bitter experience' for him, coming as it did only five months after his defeat in the Battle of the Philippine Sea. Halsey, on the other side, had followed one error with another. The first was rising to the bait. The second was his failure to leave a strong part of his battle force behind to block the strait or even to inform Kinkaid that the strait was unguarded, while the third was his failure then to retain the battleships to complete the annihilation of Ozawa's force.

The End of the Battle

The battle was over on the 26th. The Allies had lost a light carrier, two escort carriers, two destroyers and a destroyer escort. The Japanese had lost three battleships, one heavy carrier, three light carriers, six heavy cruisers, four light cruisers and nine destroyers.

On the American side, it can be said that the air power of both the Third and Seventh Fleets was fully exploited but that the battle line of the former, with more gun power than the whole Japanese navy, never got into action through bad handling. The battle line of the Seventh Fleet engaged a Japanese force one-fifth of its strength and already decimated by destroyer attacks for a few minutes. With half of the surviving gun power of the Imperial Navy, the Center Force was allowed to sail undetected within gun range and take units of the Seventh Fleet by surprise. Only the fast reaction of air power prevented a major disaster. The Center Force then made its escape almost unmolested. The greatest weakness of the American side, however, was its divided command at the top. Had one commander, whether Mac-

Arthur or Nimitz, been in overall control at Leyte, Halsey could not have acted as he did. Before removing the Third Fleet from its station in the San Bernardino Strait for whatever reason, he would have had to ask permission of his superior.

For the Japanese side, it should have been obvious that *Sho* 1 was too complicated to succeed. There was bad coordination between the commanders, who showed an inability to avert disaster with new tactics and dispositions. Although brave and reasonably competent, the commanders were not up to maneuvering a modern fleet in battle and had no common doctrine of strategy or tactics to unite them. The best (or worst) example is Kurita who should have sunk all of Taffy 3 but failed because he lost tactical control of his force. The expenditure of Nishimura's Southern Force was pointless and again indicative of the Japanese inability to adapt a predetermined strategy to a new situation. In terms of command performance, the high points of the battle were Oldendorf's disposition and handling of the Seventh Fleet in the night battle of the Surigao Strait and Ozawa's execution of his decoy mission.

The great lesson of Leyte Gulf was the helplessness of a modern fleet without air cover. Taffy 3 was able to block a powerful force of battleships and cruisers for precisely this reason. Key events were, therefore, the Battle of the Philippine Sea in June and the October air strikes on Formosa. This earlier decimation of Japanese naval air power predetermined the Battle of Leyte Gulf. Had the invasion come in December as originally planned, new Japanese air groups would have been trained and the Imperial Navy could have put up a better fight.

After the actions at Leyte Gulf, the Allied naval forces played a support role intended to stop

Japanese reinforcement of Leyte and maintain air supremacy until army planes were able to do so. Although the initial landings had met with little resistance, Leyte ultimately proved a tough nut to crack, forcing MacArthur to commit a quarter of a million troops to the task. By the end of the year, however, only mopping up operations remained and preparations for the Luzon landings were well underway. After its desperate gamble at Leyte Gulf, the Japanese Navy ceased to be an independent fighting force and was relegated to an auxiliary role for the remainder of the war. Leyte Gulf was the death of the Japanese Navy, a death which meant that final defeat was imminent for Japan. As the Chief of Naval Staff, Admiral Yonai, said after the war, 'Our defeat at Leyte was tantamount to the loss of the Philippines. When you took the Philippines, that was the end of our resources'.

Conclusion

There have been no main fleet actions since Leyte Gulf nor are there likely to be any in the future, since the character of naval warfare has been completely revolutionized. From Trafalgar to Jutland the battleship constituted the striking power of a fleet, and as a result tactics were largely determined by the essential characteristic of the battleship – its reliance on gun power. During the nineteenth century the nature of naval warfare did not change radically because the development of the gun was more than matched by the corresponding development of armor. It was only after 1900 that the development of the mine, the torpedo and the submarine began to alter naval combat noticeably, but even though its position was now more vulnerable, the battleship still reigned supreme. Coronel and the Falklands were the last battles to be decided solely by gunfire

while it has already been seen how deeply the strategy, tactics and course of the action were affected by these factors at Jutland. In 1916 as in 1805, however, the essence of the sea battle was still two lines of battleships pounding each other with their guns.

While technical developments and innovations were influencing some facets of traditional naval warfare after 1900, in 1903 an event occurred which was a harbinger of a total revolution in naval warfare. In that year Wilbur and Orville Wright successfully flew the first airplane. The airplane developed rapidly as did its adoption for naval uses. In 1910 the first aircraft landing was made on the USS *Birmingham*, a light cruiser with a short flight deck. Throughout the First World War the Royal Navy experimented with airplanes and ships until by 1918, several modest aircraft carriers were in operational use in the North Sea. Japan acquired its first carrier in 1921, while the United States converted a collier into the USS *Langley* in 1922. During the time of the Washington Naval Limitation Treaty, a number of battle cruisers were converted to carriers, including the *Lexington* and *Saratoga* for the United States and the *Kaga* and *Akagi* for Japan. With the development of the 'Kate' torpedo bomber and the 'Zero' fighter, Japan achieved a definite superiority in carrier aircraft, a superiority which came as a rude awakening to Britain and the United States in 1941.

Between 1939 and 1945 the carrier came to dominate naval warfare. Already at Matapan in 1941, it was a carrier which struck the key blows and gave victory to the British. It was at Midway a year later, however, that the death knell of the battleship truly sounded. Although the Japanese had eleven battleships and the Americans none, the Japanese ships never got into action, the battle being wholly fought by carriers hundreds of miles away from each other. The role of the battleship was changing, a fact which Admiral Yamamoto for all his brilliance failed to grasp adequately. He committed the error of separating his carriers and battleships at a time when the carriers needed the anti-aircraft fire support of the battleships. It was a costly lesson, but one which the Americans learned well. For the remainder of the war, battleships were always assigned to provide support for American carriers. The role of the battleship thus came to be to provide anti-aircraft support and fire support for amphibious landings, while the carrier definitely became the predominant capital ship. This fact is reflected in the postwar period when the major navies ceased building battleships but continued the construction of carriers, culminating in the 75,000-ton nuclear-powered American carrier *Enterprise*.

At the present time, yet another technological revolution is threatening the supremacy of the carrier. The emergence of the atomic submarine and ultra-sophisticated missilry may well mean the relegation of the carrier to an auxiliary role alongside the battleship. Whatever the case, however, one fact stands out. Naval battles as Nelson, Jellicoe and even Nimitz knew them will never be repeated. The era of epic sea battles ended appropriately with the largest naval engagement in history at Leyte Gulf.

Index

Acknowledgments

The editor and author would like to thank Antony Preston for his most patient and valuable assistance in the preparation of this book. The editor would also like to thank Judith Holmes for her editorial assistance.
The publishers would like to thank John Batchelor for the armament illustrations, Chensie Chen for the design of the maps and the following individuals and organizations for their kind permission to reproduce the pictures which appear on the following pages:

Franklin Roosevelt Library 92/93.

Giraudon 76/77; 80/81; 147 top left.

Imperial War Museum 144/145; 145 left; 147 Top left; 148-149; 150/151; 154 top and bottom; 155-157; 158· top; 160-163; 166 bottom; 167; 169 bottom; 170-171; 174/175 top; 179 top; 181; 183; 184 top right; 184/185; 184 bottom; 185 top; 185 bottom; 186; 188-197; 214 bottom; 235 bottom; 238.

Library of Congress 84-85; 86 top; 87; 90 top right; 102; 104-105.

Musee de la Marine 23 bottom; 25; 28-29; 32; 52-53; 66.

National Maritime Museum 2-22; 23 top; 30-31; 33-35; 39-41; 42/43; 44-51; 56-65; 67-75; 78/79; 81 top; 83; 93 top; 98-99; 144 top; 154 centre; 158/159; 172 top; 173 inset.

Paul Popper 147 bottom left.

Robert Hunt Library 36/37; 42 top; 91 top; 94 top left; 94/95; 97; 103; 106 top; 106/107; 108/109 top; 109 left & right; 112 top; 114 top; 140 top & centre;

141-143; 145 right; 147 top right; 147 bottom right; 150 top; 166 top; 168/169; 169 top & centre; 172/173; 174/175 bottom; 175 top; 176; 179 bottom; 180; 182; 184 top left; 187; 200-201; 205 bottom; 206; 213 bottom.

Roger Viollet 38.

Sonia Halliday 79 inset.

State of Vermont 116.

Transworld Features Syndicate 205 top.

United States Airforce 212/213; 220.

United States National Archives 86 bottom; 90/91; 100 top; 101 top; 204; 208/209; 239-241.

United States Navy 90 top left; 92 top; 94 top right; 100/101; 107 top; 108 left & right; 108/109 bottom; 112 bottom; 114/115; 118; 126/127; 130/131; 140 bottom; 198/199; 207; 210/211; 214 top; 215-219; 221-233; 235 top; 238; 242-253.

Victoria & Albert Museum 120; 124/125; 125 top; 128/129.

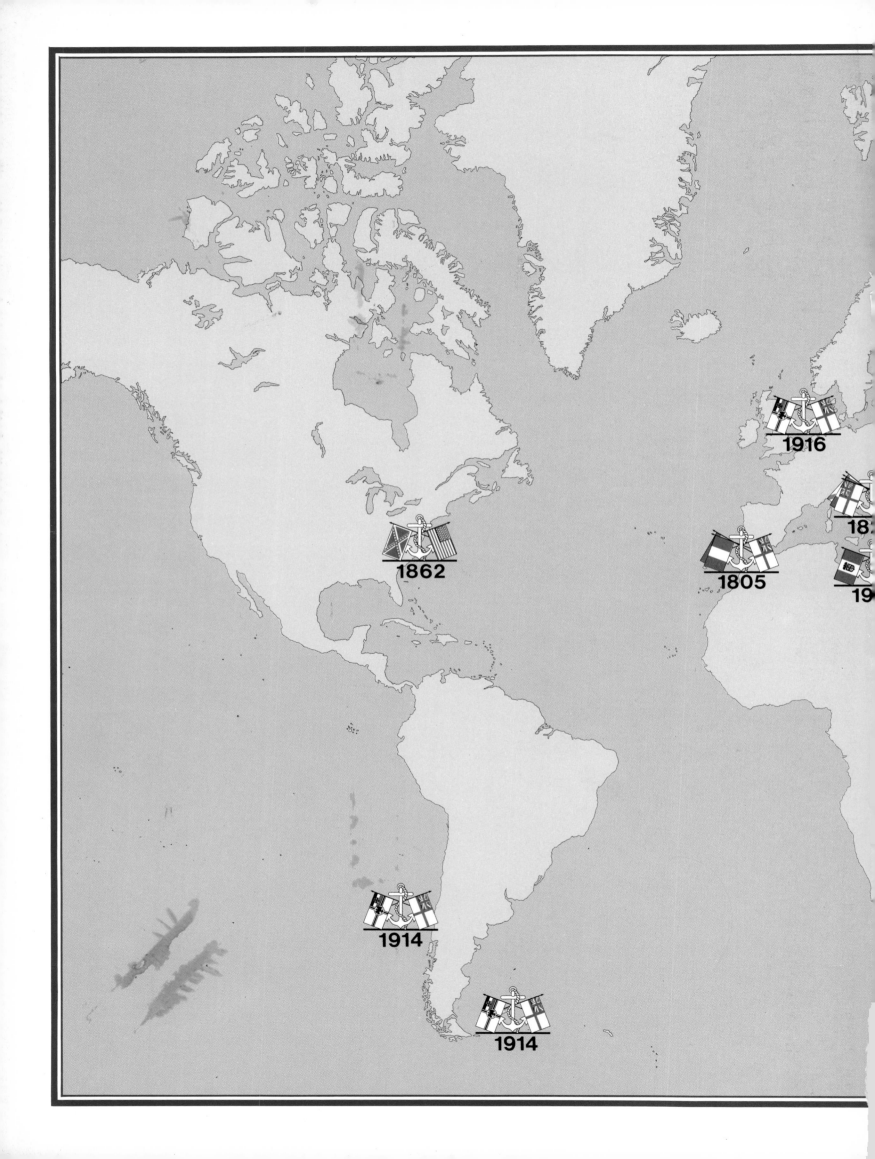

1916

1862

1805

18

19

1914

1914